The Practical Researcher
A Student Guide to Conducting Psychological Research

Dana S. Dunn

Moravian College

McGraw-Hill College

Boston   Burr Ridge, IL   Dubuque, IA   Madison, WI   New York   San Francisco   St. Louis
Bangkok   Bogotá   Caracas   Lisbon   London   Madrid
Mexico City   Milan   New Delhi   Seoul   Singapore   Sydney   Taipei   Toronto

McGraw-Hill College

A Division of The **McGraw·Hill** *Companies*

ISBN 0–07–018323–6

Editorial director: *Jane E. Vaicunas*
Senior sponsoring editor: *Joseph Terry*
Developmental editor: *Susan Kunchandy*
Marketing manager: *James Rozsa*
Senior project manager: *Peggy J. Selle*
Production supervisor: *Laura Fuller*
Freelance design coordinator: *Mary L. Christianson*
Supplement coordinator: *Tammy Juran*
Compositor: *Shepherd, Inc.*
Typeface: *10/12 Palatino*
Printer: *Quebecor Printing Book Group/Fairfield, PA*

Freelance cover designer: *Sheilah Barrett*
Cover image: © *Christie's Images/SuperStock*

Library of Congress Cataloging-in Publication Data

Dunn, Dana S.
    The practical researcher: a student guide to conducting
psychological research / Dana S. Dunn. — 1st ed.
    Includes index.
    ISBN 0–07–018323–6
    1. Psychology—Research—Methodology. 2. Psychology,
Experimental. I. Title.
BF76.5.D864 1999   98–26089
150'.7'2—dc21   CIP

For Sarah, Jacob, and Hannah
meine Liebe und meine Arbeit

ABOUT THE AUTHOR

Dana S. Dunn is currently Associate Professor and Chair of the Department of Psychology at Moravian College, a liberal arts and sciences college in Bethlehem, Pennsylvania. Dunn received his PhD in experimental social psychology from the University of Virginia in 1987, having previously graduated with a BA in psychology from Carnegie Mellon University in 1982. He has taught research methods in psychology for over 10 years. Dunn has published numerous articles and chapters in the areas of social cognition, rehabilitation psychology, the teaching of psychology, and liberal education. He lives in Bethlehem with his wife and two children.

CONTENTS

PREFACE

Knowledge is learned contextually, but meant to be applied broadly, in general ways; with experience, students should come to know this truth. I teach at a liberal arts college where it is the norm to have the same students in several different classes across their four undergraduate years. Like many teachers, I notice that my students sometimes fail to apply knowledge acquired in one class to related issues in subsequent classes. I notice an acute breakdown between knowledge and application in the case of research methods, an especially troubling occurrence because research methods is arguably the most important course for undergraduate psychology students. Yet I know that my students *know* their methodology: They just are not sure what to do with it or how to go about using it outside the familiar context of a research methods class.

Ideally, students will use *The Practical Researcher* in a traditional first research methods course where some exposure to research occurs. In combining basic theory with a step-by-step guide to developing a research project, this text will also serve as an excellent practical guide for independent studies or honors students embarking on a semester-long or yearlong project.

The Practical Researcher addresses the gap between knowing and using the discipline's research methodology. It is written in an intentionally accessible style so students will not wrestle with overly technical prose while learning about the technical processes of research methods. A "practical researcher" is someone who knows how to translate the theoretical side of research methodology into practice. Theory is critically important to the teaching of research methods, but it does little good if students cannot use it effectively in actual research

Experiential

x

projects. Generally speaking, most undergraduate research methods books describe essential concepts about what constitutes good psychological research, but rarely provide concrete guidance about how to actually go about *doing* good research. Unlike most books, this text acknowledges that research methodology was created to be used, not merely studied.

Practical

Thus, *The Practical Researcher addresses the "how-to" side of doing psychological research by teaching students to organize a research project from start to finish.* It contains the material that is traditionally presented in solid research methods texts (e.g., the logic of random assignment, measuring and manipulating psychological variables), but supplements it with exercises designed to help students practice research skills (e.g., How do you randomly assign a subject to one of three conditions in your study? How does one keep a record of independent and dependent variables?). I believe that teaching students practical techniques will enable them to more easily conduct psychological research. Additionally, establishing pedagogical links between knowledge and its application, emphasizing theory as well as practice, will help students retain what they learn, thereby preparing them for graduate school or careers where problem solving and familiarity with research methodologies are desirable.

ORGANIZATION

Research Oriented

The text chapters are arranged sequentially, following the basic order of a research project. Because the book is a guide to the practical side of the research process, however, chapters can be read either sequentially or in an order determined by the instructor. As a textbook, *The Practical Researcher* is a hands-on guide that helps students develop research skills, conduct research, and learn to be researchers. Most chapters include one or more practical research exercises. These exercises, which *are designed to enhance writing, interpretive, organizational,* and *time management skills,* appear after a brief conceptual introduction of relevant topics. Students can model these examples for their own work, modify them, or in several cases, "fill in" the blanks or checklists provided in the exercises. Those who engage in collaborative research, for example, will be encouraged to write and sign a research contract with their peers so that an effective division of labor is possible (chapter 1). Chapter 5, which is devoted to ethical issues, provides instruction on developing and writing Informed Consent Forms, debriefing scripts, Human Subject Pool sign-up sheets, and research participation credit slips. In chapter 8, students learn to interpret basic statistical results by putting into words the relationships that common inferential tests examine, a required skill invariably neglected by many existing methodology texts. Chapters close with brief summaries and lists of key terms with page numbers where explanation or examples can be found in the text. Recommended readings with short annotations conclude each chapter, building upon themes discussed therein.

Each chapter contains one or more boxed features called "Research Digressions." The Research Digressions are meant to provide the reader with contextual information that supplements the main text. The boxes variously answer questions provoked in the reader, present practical applications of the material, indicate advanced topics for further study, or clarify discussions in the main text by exploring detailed examples.

The importance of writing well and often is stressed throughout the book, and I have taken a decidedly different approach than most methods texts where writing is concerned. Unlike most informal research methods textbooks that give short shrift to writing, I devote an entire, early chapter to writing in psychology (chapter 3). This text does far more than place its discussion in a final or "throwaway" chapter, or focusing exclusively on American Psychological Association (APA) writing style issues (though the latter are discussed in great detail). I also avoid the worst sin of all, which is to consign matters of writing to oblivion—or simply an appendix.

Writing Oriented

What do I do about writing? I make the case that writing is—or should be—the first and last consideration of all teachers, researchers, and students of psychology. Beyond learning to present research results in prose form, I discuss how to generate research ideas through writing, how to outline papers, and how to give and receive effective peer feedback on written material. As will be evident to many readers, I am indebted to pedagogical strides made by writing instructors over the last decade or so (and it is my fond hope that psychologists will embrace, even extend, this good work done by their colleagues in the humanities). Writing is germane to the majority of the book's aforementioned exercises, and a necessary skill for developing research ideas, searching the psychological literature, laying the ground work for the eventual research project, and presenting results to peers in formal or informal settings.

Studying the methodology of psychology matters a great deal, but learning to use these methods to explore research questions matters still more. I hope this book will help students to gain disciplinary knowledge as well as practice, to use the particular to interpret the general.

SUPPLEMENTS

The Practical Researcher is accompanied by an Instructor's Manual/Test Bank (ISBN 0-07-018324-4). I wrote the Instructor's Manual/Test Bank, which provides the instructor with additional course tools that will expand on the course material presented in the text. It contains complete and detailed outlines for each chapter, lecture suggestions, chapter exercises, additional class activities (including debate topics, guest speakers, field trips to campus sites, discussion suggestions), suggested readings, and class discussion/essay questions. Each chapter is followed by approximately 30 multiple-choice questions, which are classified as factual, conceptual or applied. These test questions are also available in both Windows (0-07-025184-3) and Mac (0-07-025200-9) versions of a computerized test bank. Please contact your local McGraw-Hill representative for details concerning policies, prices, and availability, as some restrictions may apply.

ACKNOWLEDGMENTS

Writing often involves listeners before readers, and in any case, it is never a solitary pursuit. I am grateful to the many individuals who assisted me with this project. Editor Sarah Dunn was, at turns, compassionate or appropriately ruthless about my prose. Stacey Zaremba good naturedly heard my complaints, offering insights and references in return. The usual suspects—Steve Gordy, Robert Stinson, and Peter von Allmen—offered advice, quips, and sometimes solace. As she has done on so many prior occasions and projects, Mrs. Jacqueline Giaquinto helped in ways great and small with manuscript preparation, organization, and details too numerous to track. The Moravian College Faculty Development and Research Committee provided a summer grant enabling me to finish the work. Bob Brill, Reeves Library's crack Reference and Interlibrary Loan Departments, and my students, Carolyn Vicchiullo, Brett Stoudt, Barbara Loecher, and those enrolled in my statistics and research methods classes, provided comments or materials for particular sections of the manuscript. Dah K. Dunn merits special thanks for her perpetual enthusiasm for the book.

The peer reviewers who read and critiqued various and sundry chapter drafts offered me wisdom, occasional wit, and pedagogical advice. I am grateful for the exceptionally helpful editorial comments made by Carolyn Gosling, Marion Harrell, and Demarie Jackson of the American Psychological Association. The manuscript was much improved by the thoughtful and substantive comments of Bernard Beins (Ithaca College), David B. Conner (Truman State University), Susan Dutch (Westfield State College), Kathleen Hart (Xavier University), Rosemary Hornak (Meredith College), John C. Jahnke (Miami University), Brenda Kirby (Le Moyne College), Donna J. LaVoie (Saint Louis University), Leslie MacGregor (Berry College), Dennis Musselman (Humboldt State University), Mark A. Pitt (Ohio State University), Kirk Richardson (Georgia State University), Jerome Siegel (The City College of New York), Christopher Silva (Dickinson College), Benjamin Wallace (Cleveland State University), and several anonymous reviewers. I relied upon many of the ideas, suggestions, and insights given by these teacher-scholars, though by no means all; remaining errors are mine alone.

Any author should have the good fortune to work with dedicated professionals like those inhabiting the McGraw-Hill College Division. Craig Brooks initiated contact about this project, and then Jane Vaicunas, Brian McKean, Susan Elia, with their collective editorial prowess, moved it forward. Meera Dash, Joe Terry, and Susan Kunchandy helped to refine the book's scope in its later stages, and drew the writing and editorial process to a successful close. Sarah Greer Bush copyedited the manuscript with aplomb. The support and interest of all of these professionals in the book was unstinting, and therefore, most gratifying.

Naturally, I am keenly interested in faculty and student reaction to the book. Comments concerning what you liked, disliked, missed, or wanted more of are most welcome. A short questionnaire appears at the end of the book. I urge you to complete it and mail it to the publisher, who will share it with me. You may also contact me directly at the Department of Psychology, Moravian College, 1200 Main Street, Bethlehem, PA 18018-6650; via e-mail: dunn@moravian.edu.

In the end, I am especially grateful to my family—Sarah, Jacob, and Hannah—for their love, tolerance, and understanding throughout the project.

Dana S. Dunn

The Why and How of Psychological Research

A practical researcher is one who knows how to cleverly transform the theory behind psychology's research methodology into practice. Most research methods text books describe essential, though often abstract, concepts about what constitutes good psychological research, but they rarely provide concrete guidance about how to actually *do* good research. Theory is obviously very important—even crucial—to research methods, but so is being able to effectively implement key ideas and techniques in actual research projects. This book will combine these two perspectives in order to teach you to be a practical researcher. Indeed, by the time you have finished reading it, you will be able to conduct a theory-based research project in psychology from start to finish.

Chapter 1 is an overview of the issues presented in the remainder of the book. The first half of this chapter will introduce the theoretical orientation of the field of psychology. Practical issues to consider when beginning psychological research will be the focus of the second half of the chapter.

WHY DO RESEARCH?

An obvious question relevant to any book on research methods in psychology is the following: Why study human behavior? In a sense, we need to think about why research is important or worth doing before we launch into an entire book devoted to the mechanics and intricacies of actually doing it. In what ways does research allow us to move from armchair musings to the active exploration of a topic? Here are some of the things that research allows you to accomplish:

- To move beyond idle curiosity into formulating questions.
- To reduce error and bias in the process of answering these questions, thereby improving both the answer and your own reasoning skills.
- To test competing interpretations of events against one another so that a best account of some phenomena can be isolated.
- To use quantitative and qualitative skills to solve problems.
- To gain perspective on questions, to obtain a broader view, to go beyond the given information.
- To add to collective knowledge, as well as your own personal store.
- To create connections among otherwise disparate sources of information.
- To apply results to the benefit of humanity.
- To effectively communicate your ideas, written or spoken, to other people.

This list is by no means exhaustive. Some of the points are lofty goals, whereas others are more concrete. Some may be accomplished in an initial research effort, whereas others may only be achieved after much experience. Collectively, however, these points all suggest that research allows us to make claims about the world—and events that occur within it—that are supported by other sources besides mere opinion, conjecture, and belief. In essence, we conduct research to provide an objective rather than a subjective description of the world. We will now consider the issue of objective versus subjective descriptions in more detail by discussing reason, a precursor to the scientific method.

Reasoning Before Research

There are two general types of reasoning—inductive and deductive—that scientists use in order to begin to think about research questions, and each satisfies a different sort of research problem depending upon what information is currently available. *Inductive reasoning* is the process of generalizing from one or more observations in order to develop a more general idea about a phenomenon. Such reasoning occurs when psychologists begin to think about a relatively novel topic (e.g., daycare and its effects on children) and they do not know what to expect (e.g., Does daycare promote or hinder child development? Does daycare's effect depend on particular circumstances?). They may collect various sorts of observations on children in daycare settings, examine them, and then formulate some preliminary ideas about the possible psychological consequences of the experience.

Induction is very useful when it comes to formulating preliminary hypotheses and, eventually, an integrated theory to explain some set of events. The downside to inductive reasoning is that it may miss unobserved factors that could be responsible for the effects we encounter. Knowing that an especially aggressive child has been in daycare since one year of age might lead to the conclusion that nonparental care leads to behavior problems. This sort of inductive reasoning is not valid because it ignores a host of other situational or individual factors besides daycare that could cause childhood aggression (e.g., parenting styles, temperament).

Inductive reasoning is said to be the hallmark of a younger science, one that lacks a unified theory and methodology. By this standard, psychology is an inductive science because currently there is no single, dominant theory of behavior. Indeed, your prior exposure to the field probably revealed a host of competing theories, some of which were no doubt inconsistent with one another. Similarly, there is no single, agreed upon psychological method, but a variety of different and still emerging techniques.

In contrast to psychology, older, more established sciences, notably physics, rely more heavily on *deductive reasoning*. Deductive reasoning involves the use of an existing theory to create specific *deductions*, or conclusions, regarding how an as-yet-unexamined phenomenon operates. Thus, a general idea about relations among some collection of variables in the world is examined in terms of its specific consequences for related variables. Deductions lead to specific, logical predictions that can be proposed in an "If-Then" analysis ("If event A occurs, then event B should follow") and eventually tested in some investigation, experimental or otherwise.

Not all psychology is inductive, of course; deductive reasoning is employed as well. An intriguing case of deductive reasoning in developmental psychology, for example, concerns the origins of inhibited or socially restrained temperaments in some children. Is temperament environmental or dispositional in origin? If inhibition is genetically inherited, then a greater degree of inhibition should be observed between identical twins than between members of the general population (e.g., Kagan, 1994). Support for the prediction—a greater percentage of inhibited temperaments is found among twins than strangers—implies that there is a genetic link. The absence of support would also be useful because it challenges the researcher to re-evaluate the assumed link between temperament and genetics. Deductive reasoning, then, allows researchers to make inferences about what variables did or did not lead to some outcome.

Figure 1.1 illustrates the difference between inductive and deductive reasoning by highlighting the direction of the inference process. When observations lead a researcher to create a theory, a "bottom-up" process, the reasoning process is inductive. When the reverse occurs and an existing theory is used to predict particular observations—reasoning begins in a "top-down" fashion—the process is deductive. Psychology is a largely inductive enterprise, but both types of reasoning are essential to the field and, more generally, to the scientific method.

The Scientific Method

Across time, both natural and social scientists have focused reasoning and formalized procedures of inquiry into what has come to be called the

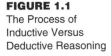

FIGURE 1.1
The Process of
Inductive Versus
Deductive Reasoning

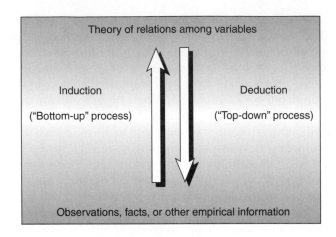

scientific method. Although there is no completely agreed upon definition, the scientific method is an organized way of both asking and answering questions about how the world works. The eventual goal of the scientific method is to determine cause and effect relationships in the world: that is, what particular event or series of events can definitively be said to lead to—to *cause*—some subsequent state of nature.

The logic behind the emphasis on *causality* is very straightforward: If a change in one event predictably leads to a change in another event, then we can argue that the first event caused the change in the second. The link between the two events allows us to draw a tentative conclusion about the world. This conclusion is a basis for systematically changing other events, observing their effects on still others, and ruling out alternative explanations so that both knowledge about the events and our confidence in our conclusions grow.

With its emphasis on establishing causality among observable events, the scientific method relies very heavily on *empiricism.* Empiricism is a philosophy relying on direct experience to draw conclusions about the world and events in it. For example, if I see a cue ball strike another billiard ball, sending the latter flying across the pool table into a corner pocket, then I can say that the first ball caused the second one to fall into the pocket. Not only am I identifying cause and effect, but I do so by relying on my visual sense.

The scientific method, however, requires that we verify our empirical knowledge of the world in particular ways that reduce the possibility of error or bias; after all, my eyesight may not be 20:20. We will discuss four generally accepted criteria that comprise the scientific method.

First, the scientific method requires that researchers make careful observations about the world so that general conclusions—or facts—can be drawn. A *fact* is a statement that is known to be true. For example, one fact is that the average body temperature of a human being is 98.6 degrees Fahrenheit. Facts are useful because they allow scientists to assume that if certain states of nature are true, then other ideas may logically follow from them. Scientific knowledge is expanded by using existing facts as a base from which to derive and to test out new ideas. Of course, this search for facts also implies the identification of falsehoods—ideas that do not conform to established knowledge.

The field of psychology is still in its infancy, so there are not many facts per se that define the field. Indeed, psychology's formal origin can be traced to the year 1879 when the first psychological laboratory was founded by Wilhelm Wundt. Historically speaking, one-hundred years or so is not much time to assemble an array of scientific facts to account for the depth and breadth of human behavior. For a particularly daunting contrast, consider that physics, said to be the queen of the natural sciences, has been churning out facts about the nature of the world since ancient times. Nonetheless, some facts are emerging in each subarea of the field of psychology. In the clinical area, for example, we now know that schizophrenia has a genetic component (e.g., Gottesman & Wolfgram, 1991) and that chronic denial of emotion leads to health problems (e.g., Traue & Pennebaker, 1993).

Second, the scientific method uses collections of such facts to build theories. A *theory* is a set of coherent ideas that are formulated by inductive reasoning from the known facts in order to explain something. Theories are used in science to guide and direct research. They tell scientists what questions to ask, where to look for information, what they can reasonably expect to find, and importantly, how to test specific predictions.

Psychology is becoming increasingly reliant on theory, and one noted social psychologist, Kurt Lewin, is credited with using the oft-quoted credo, "There is nothing so practical as a good theory" (Lewin, 1943; Marrow, 1969). What Lewin meant is that good psychological theories foster explanation, organize facts, predict observations, and guide new exploration of a topic. As more facts are gathered, a theory is either confirmed or modified accordingly.

Third, the scientific method advocates the use of controlled experimentation to pull fact and theory together. An experiment is a controlled test to determine how something works, to find out what happens when conditions are varied, or to illustrate some known fact. Experiments are used to make valid inferences about the relationship of one variable to another (e.g., Does heat promote aggression?). Arguably, experimentation is the most important part of the scientific method precisely because it allows for competing interpretations of the world to be tested against one another (e.g., Are more aggressive acts apt to occur in warmer conditions?; e.g., Griffitt, 1970). Only the most accurate interpretations are retained so that facts may be culled, theories built, and further experiments planned.

Fourth, the scientific method requires that any observation can be independently verified by other researchers. For instance, you can take your own temperature or have someone else do it for you. In both cases, unless there is some problem with the thermometer that is used or you are ill, both parties should find a reading of 98.6 degrees Fahrenheit. Such independent verification is an attempt to rule out error and bias in

> **BOX FEATURE 1.A**

A Research Digression: Is Psychology A Science?

What makes a science a science? Is it methodology? Subject matter?

Is psychology a science? To some psychologists, these are "fighting words," but not to others. Historically, the belief that psychology is or ought to be a science has been around for some time. As Thomas Leahey (1997, p. 25), a historian of psychology, put it:

> For at least a hundred years, psychology has claimed to be a science. There are three main reasons for this claim. First, human beings are a part of the natural world, so it seems logical that natural science should encompass them. Second, by the nineteenth century, when scientific psychology was founded, it seemed no discipline could be respectable were it not a science. Finally, especially in the United States, scientific status was important to psychology's pretensions to social control . . .

The first reason is certainly compelling, but the other two raise questions, if not eyebrows. What do you think?

Since psychology parted ways with philosophy toward the end of the last century, the academic community sometimes groups psychology with the social sciences, other times with the natural sciences. Many psychologists prefer to be in company with the latter—physics, biology, and chemistry—because these disciplines are scientific by virtue of their subject matter, knowledge, and systematic methods of inquiry. The research methods and logic of the psychologist may be *scientific* but does the knowledge gained or its subject matter—mind, brain, and behavior—constitute *science?*

The debate continues. Currently, the field and its teachers, researchers, and students generally assume its status as a science is more or less assured. Research emanating from evolutionary biology (e.g., Rosenberg, 1980; Hull, 1984) challenges this view by arguing that human psychology cannot be a natural science. Some philosophers have gone so far as to suggest that not only is psychology *not* a science but that eventually it will be replaced by neurophysiology (P. M. Churchland, 1985; P. S. Churchland, 1986)!

What is the basis for such arguments? The belief that psychology can be—will be—subsumed by other sciences (Putnam, 1982). These arguments represent one form of *reductionism,* the idea that complex phenomena can be explained by reducing them to simpler, underlying elements. In this case, a hierarchy of the sciences runs from high to low; each science—including psychology, biology, and chemistry—is reducible to a more basic one until we reach physics, the base of all the sciences.

Will the breadth and depth of human psychological experience be reduced to neurophysiology and physics? Fighting words, indeed, but what should we do? We should continue the debate by choosing a side, and then reading, thinking, writing, and doing research to support that view. In doing so, we can remind ourselves that one of the decided strengths of psychology is the search for meaning in human experience and that productive disagreement is what makes the search interesting and, in the end, successful.

A History of Psychology, 4e, by Leahey, T., © 1997. Reprinted by permission of Prentice-Hall, Inc. Upper Saddle River, NJ.

research. If other scientists find the same results using the same or similar methodology, then particular information is deemed to be trustworthy, even "scientific."

Given psychology's youth and the varied theories that are used within the field, independent verification is a crucial component. It is not sufficient for one psychologist to describe a particular psychological

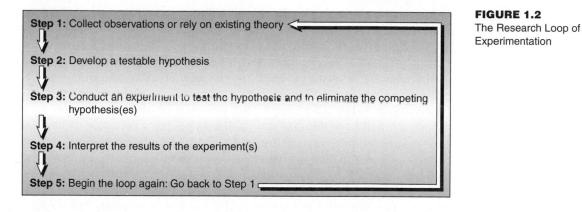

FIGURE 1.2
The Research Loop of
Experimentation

finding and then to assume that the entire community of psychological researchers will accept it. In practice, this rarely happens because psychologists, like any scientists, are a cautious lot. It is very likely the case that any published finding has been carefully scrutinized not only by the researcher who wrote it up but also by a group of independent peer reviewers who anonymously commented on the strengths and weaknesses of the work. More to the point, however, is that no matter how interesting or convincing it may be, one study of one effect is not accepted as definitive proof. To verify a result, it is not at all unusual for a psychologist to conduct the same study or a variation of it several times over. Independent confirmation of an effect by another researcher is still the best evidence because it means that, using a similar methodology, another person has been able to find the same result at another time and in another place using different research participants.

THE RESEARCH LOOP OF EXPERIMENTATION

Most science that is conducted using the scientific method follows what we can call the *research loop of experimentation*, which is in part based on Platt's (1964) views of scientific inference. As shown in figure 1.2, a series of discrete steps are followed in a specified order before looping back to the first one. Let's go through the figure step-by-step. In step 1, a researcher makes observations or collects facts and then puts them together to form a theory. Alternatively, the researcher may decide to pursue an existing theory but by taking it in some new, heretofore untested direction (recall our discussion of inductive and deductive reasoning).

Step 2 involves the creation of a research *hypothesis*. A hypothesis is a statement or expectation based on the theory devised in step 1. It explicitly concerns the outcome of a proposed experiment based on the identification of *variables* and how they affect one another. A variable is anything that can be measured or can take on a different value, such as height, weight, a rating on a scale, the air temperature on a summer day, an IQ score, and so on. Hypotheses are largely educated guesses or predictions based on observations or a theory about how one thinks the world might work with respect to a particular set of variables.

Psychology is largely an empirically based science because it is focused on identifying which personal or situational variables cause a given behavior to occur. Psychologists usually want to examine some hypothesized connection between two or more variables. In laboratory-based experiments, for example, the presence or absence of some variable is studied to determine how it affects people's behavior. When we treat a variable this way we are said to be manipulating the *independent variable* in order to examine its effects on some measure of outcome, the *dependent variable*.

An independent variable must have a minimum of two levels, typically an experimental treatment and a control treatment. The experimental treatment or condition represents our hypothesis, whereas the control treatment represents its antithesis, the absence of any intervention. Quite literally, the control condition represents the state of nature where no change or intervention is introduced, so that we can compare it against the result of the experimental treatment. We compare the effects of both levels of the independent variable on the dependent variable in order to assess a difference that can then be attributed to the experimental treatment.

The third step of the research loop gives life to both the theory and the hypothesis by conducting an actual experiment. An experiment is said to test a hypothesis by the manipulation of an independent variable and by the measurement of a dependent variable. Usually, step 3 tests one prediction, although some experiments can test several competing or alternative hypotheses simultaneously.

In step 4, the results of the experiment are interpreted. By this we mean that the experiment's findings are analyzed and critically evaluated to determine if they make sense, to see if they are consistent with the hypothesis and, in turn, the theory. If they pass scrutiny—usually anonymous peer review—then the results are typically published in a scientific article or presented at a professional meeting. Such sharing of information within the scientific community advances knowledge and allows other investigators, as well as interested readers, to benefit.

Finally, step 5 signals that although this one piece of research is over, the process must loop back and begin anew. An important lesson from this stage in the research loop is that science, manifested in the research process and the acquisition of scientific knowledge, never ends. It is a continuous cycle of observation, theory development, hypothesis testing, and interpretation (and many times reinterpretation!).

In practice, of course, the research loop of experimentation is much more detailed than this description because many smaller steps intervene between the five noted here. What we have just reviewed is a basic framework that is accessible to individuals who are outside the process. People who are inside the process know that there are a variety of unspoken activities that researchers just do without thinking about them very much, let alone writing them down. You will learn about many of these activities as you begin to conduct your own research.

Variations of the research loop of experimentation are possible and it should not be regarded as a "lock step" sort of enterprise. Indeed, a researcher can begin at any step in the loop, say, by employing an existing theory, by making use of someone else's hypothesis or observation, or even by offering alternative interpretations of heretofore established results. For the time being, then, think of the research loop of experimentation as a guide or starting point that we will flesh out with many necessary details, techniques, and perspectives as we proceed through the remainder of this book.

Using the Research Loop

Let's consider the research loop by using a straightforward example related to education. Imagine that you are teaching two sections of a course on research methodology, and you want to find out if active learning exercises enhance the students' academic performance in the class. *Active learning* refers to the use of in-class activities, exercises, and discussion topics that provide students with "hands on" experience with a topic. In contrast, more passive or traditional styles of teaching rely on a lecture format with a modest question-and-answer component.

You develop the hypothesis that because active learning exercises promote meaningful connections among disparate pieces of information, their use in the classroom will result in higher student grades at the end of the semester. How can you test this hypothesis? First, you designate the teaching/learning method as the independent variable, and you identify the two levels of the variable as active and passive. Active learning is the experimental treatment and passive learning will be the control condition. Second, you decide that the dependent measure will be student grades in each of the two classes. Your intention is to compare the average final grade for each class, and you predict that the active learning class will have a higher average than that of the passive learning class.

How will you decide which students are exposed to which teaching/learning method? Researchers typically rely on a method of *randomization*, where a given subject or group is assigned to receive a particular treatment solely based on chance. In this instance, the use of randomization means that each student has the same chance of being assigned to one class or the other (assume the institution's Registrar is helping with the project). We will discuss randomization at length in chapter 6.

Because you have two classes, you need to choose which one will receive the experimental treatment and which will experience the control level of the independent variable. You decide that you will flip a coin so that "heads" means your first class receives the active learning material, and "tails" means the second section does (note that prior to the coin flip, each group has a fifty-fifty chance of being taught by active learning).

"Tails" it is, and you dutifully spend the semester using active learning methods when teaching the second course section. The first section is treated identically to the second—the same books, lectures, notes, quizzes, paper assignments, tests, class length, and so on—except that no active learning exercises are employed. When teaching both sections, you do not draw the students' attention to this single difference.

After the semester ends and the final grades for each of the two sections are determined, you calculate the average grade for both sections of the course. You find that the section exposed to the active learning exercises earned an average grade of B+ (87 out of 100 possible points in the course) while the control group had a B- as an average grade (81 out of 100). Is the hypothesis supported; that is, did the independent variable have an effect on the dependent variable? The two means do demonstrate the hypothesized relationship to one another—the experimental group did get a relatively higher grade when compared to the grade of the control group—but it is still necessary to conduct a statistical test to establish that a difference really exists. You will learn about the appropriate test later in the book, but for now let's assume that there is what statistician's call a significant difference between the two class averages. In other words, the active learning group's average of 87 was measurably greater than the control group's average of 81. Is this support for the hypothesis definitive?

Well, the results do seem to confirm your ideas, but two issues must be addressed in response to the observed difference between the two classes: sufficiency of the evidence and philosophy of science. Regarding the first issue, ask this question: Does one simple experiment constitute sufficient evidence that active learning causes higher grades? How can we be sure that the higher average in the class that received the active learning exercises was really caused by those exercises? The results of this experiment are suggestive, appealing, and interesting, but they are by no means conclusive. You no doubt will agree that more evidence is needed (remember the role of independent verification of results in the scientific method). We should, of course, argue in favor of these results because they are consistent with the hypothesis. At the same time we are treating them as if they are correct, however, we must be thinking of the next experiment that can even better establish the case for active learning as the causal factor (and we should be hoping to inspire other researchers to join the effort, as well).

As we begin to contemplate the next experiment in a program of research, we are back to the research loop of experimentation. A good experiment should suggest another, and so a more detailed hypothesis should be developed. Regarding the hypothetical active learning experiment we just reviewed, the course instructor might wonder whether it is all the active learning exercises that increased the grades or if it is only certain ones, say, the writing exercises, that did so? The process begins anew.

Now that we have discussed sufficiency of evidence, what about the promised discussion of philosophy of science? Although the averages seem to corroborate your expectations, even in the guise of a carefully controlled experiment the scientific method never proves that your hypothesis is true; rather, it only proves that some alternative hypothesis is false. In other words, the process of doing science involves systematically disproving or falsifying hypotheses. This particular approach to the philosophy of science is called *falsificationism,* and it is based on the ideas of Sir Karl Popper (1959).

Popper argues that scientists can never prove that a theory is correct, only that it is incorrect. Thus, when scientists conduct research they must use hypotheses that are empirically falsifiable. They must test predictions that can be demonstrated to be false. By this standard, you must be able to ask—and test—any hypothesis for it to be evaluated as scientific. For example, the hypothesis that "organic compost will improve crop yield" can be readily tested in agricultural experiments or even in a home garden. Compare it with the hypothesis that "there is life after death," which is not falsifiable because it is not testable—there is no evidence for or against it—hence, it is not scientific.

The process of falsificationism closely follows the pattern of the research loop of experimentation. A hypothesis based on observation or theory is created, a test of the hypothesis is developed, and then actually tested. If the hypothesis is proven to be false, then a new hypothesis replaces it. If the hypothesis survives the test—it is not yet falsified—then the original hypothesis will continue to compete with the available, plausible alternatives until it is falsified. This looping process, too, means that the major task of the scientific enterprise is the falsification of incorrect theories.

Many people find falsificationism to be a somewhat disquieting view of how knowledge progresses because, in effect, scientists are always working against themselves—and it almost seems as if they never really prove anything. Indeed, good science only demonstrates that a given hypothesis has not proved to be false *yet.* Its time may well come. By continually discarding false hypotheses, science may not be establishing the truth per se, but the scientific process moves us closer to it.

As it turns out, however, falsificationism is not the only unusual perspective to emerge from the philosophy of science being done in the 20th century. Beyond never really proving anything, it also turns out that science is not the orderly, even mechanical, process that is commonly supposed. Instead, it is an inherently human process that is marked by moments of chaos, creativity, and sometimes disarray.

Another noteworthy philosopher of science, Thomas Kuhn (1970), persuasively argues that science does not progress in a neat, incremental way. The accumulation of knowledge, it seems, is anything but incremental. The process of conducting science is cyclical (Leahey, 1992) and marked by periods of unification and disarray. Unification occurs when scientists go about the business of doing what Kuhn calls *normal science*, or the puzzle-solving activity of research done within a framework of community and shared norms. In other words, scientists understand one another because they agree on certain basic issues and goals for the research done within their disciplines.

During a period of normal science, puzzles are solved within a discipline's *paradigm*. A paradigm is essentially a model or example of how scientific activity should be done. Good, accepted research within a discipline follows a paradigm, and scholarship that is rejected may fail to conform to this set pattern. Kuhn suggests that a paradigm flourishes with a period of normal science until an *anomaly*, or insoluble problem, occurs. By insoluble problem, Kuhn means some phenomenon that cannot be explained by the existing theories and methods of the current paradigm.

Two responses result from the presence of an anomaly. In the first, the anomaly is solved (perhaps inadequately) within the paradigm by making adjustments to it, or else the problem is put aside for later consideration. The second response is more dramatic in that the anomaly creates a *crisis* in the scientific community. Why a crisis? Because the anomaly cannot be reconciled with and interpreted by the existing paradigm. At such a decisive moment, scientists are literally not certain what to think.

A scientific crisis, in turn, elicits a variety of reactions, including a sense of insecurity among the scientists affected by it. In fact, as a means to try to understand the anomaly, the scientific community often loosens the strict rules of the paradigm so that new theories may be aired. In some cases, the crisis passes so that the discipline falls back on the reactions of the previous stage. That is, the anomalous result is put aside for later consideration or it is assimilated into the dominant paradigm. Sometimes, however, there is different reaction to a crisis—a new paradigm begins to emerge.

What is the new paradigm said to be like? It is, in Kuhn's words, a *scientific revolution* in that the new paradigm confronts the older heretofore established paradigm, and rebel scientists confront traditionalists with new interpretations not only of the anomaly but of disciplinary issues generally. In the short run, these now different groups of scientists do not agree, but in the long run, the new paradigm becomes increasingly attractive to younger generations of scientists who now begin to solve problems using it. Some scientists who were trained in the older tradition also convert to it, but many do not and, like the old paradigm, lose influence and are forgotten.

With the rise of the triumphant new paradigm, science and the work within the discipline of concern are transformed. Gradually, the excitement dies down and a new period of normal science begins where novel puzzles are identified and solved. This state of affairs will continue until another anomaly occurs, and the cycle, like the research loop of experimentation, repeats itself.

How does Kuhn's (1970) notion of normal science, paradigms, and scientific revolutions affect psychological research? More to the point, is this cycle representative of the work done within psychology? Probably not, or at least not yet. Kuhn (1970) suggests that less mature sciences—including social sciences like psychology—must first pass through a phase known as the *preparadigm* period. Preparadigm periods are prescientific in that there is no general agreement concerning boundaries, questions, methods, and so on, within the immature discipline. Rival camps offer competing interpretations of the field and phenomena of study, and different schools of thought compete with one another as they more or less randomly gather facts. While it may sound like an intellectually charged atmosphere, no science in the Kuhn-ian sense is getting done because there is no agreed upon paradigm. Contemporary psychology more or less fits this preparadigm description, which should not be surprising given the field's short life.

Is Kuhn right where psychology is concerned? While we are awaiting the birth of a psychological Newton (Leahey, 1990), is anything scientifically useful going on or are psychologists spinning their proverbial wheels? Important things *are* going on, of course, and it is not even clear that a Kuhn-ian account of psychology is appropriate. Robert Watson (1967), an eminent historian of psychology, offers systematic *prescriptions* as an alternative to Kuhn's paradigm. A prescription is a recommended orientation or customary approach toward the selection and formulation of a problem within psychology, and how research regarding the problem is carried out. Prescriptions are theme-oriented and usually of historical note, as their popularity waxes and wanes across time. Finally, prescriptions have a memorable quality that enables them to convey a great deal of meaning without the need of supporting detail.

Watson (1967) identified 18 contrasting pairs of prescriptions, and there is no need to review each here. One example, however, will illustrate Watson's point while at the same time demonstrating a framework that psychologists use in lieu of an agreed upon paradigm. Conscious mentalism-unconscious mentalism is a prescription that orients psychologists to study mental structures as either readily accessible or as outside of human awareness. Cognitive psychologists, for example, assume that many cognitive structures, such as working and long-term memory, can be easily studied in laboratory paradigms. Psychoanalytically inclined psychologists, in contrast, believe that unconscious mental states, such as the id, ego, and superego, can only be indirectly examined through dream interpretation or free association in the context of therapy. Both groups will say they are studying the human mind, but they do so in very different ways with opposing techniques for reasons of theory and philosophy. The groups' attitude toward one another is generally indifferent and occasionally acrimonious—yet adherents in both groups call themselves psychologists.

As you continue to study psychology, you will probably be drawn to adopt one if not several research prescriptions to inform your thinking about human behavior. Some other prescriptions, however, will elicit skeptical reactions. We will now turn to a broader consideration of skepticism as a healthy perspective for practical researchers and consumers of psychological data.

Becoming a Healthy Skeptic

Skepticism is a useful, even healthy, response to psychological research because it promotes a critical mindset. A healthy skeptic is one who carefully and thoroughly evaluates the claims made by any piece of psychological research. Before accepting the conclusions being advanced, healthy skeptics turn their attention to the quality of the link between a study's hypothesis and its method for exploring it: Was the hypothesis specific enough? Are there any potentially influential variables that were overlooked? Were the study's participants a representative sample of some larger population and were they randomly assigned to a condition? Did the independent variable really cause the observed difference in the dependent variable? Such doubt and friendly suspicion regarding methodological precision and obtained results are common reactions. Healthy skeptics ask tough questions of their own research and that conducted by others because they believe that constructive criticism advances knowledge and promotes clarity in reason.

Healthy skeptics are *not* overly negative about their own work or that done by other researchers, however, nor do they doubt or question every psychological theory or effect they encounter. The brand of skepticism you foster should not be counterproductive to the goal of advancing scientific knowledge about human behavior. As the Enlightenment philosopher David Hume (1777/1962, p. 158) put it, " . . . no durable good can ever result from [excessive skepticism] while it remains in its full force and vigor." Like Hume, however, we must acknowledge that psychology is an empirically based enterprise dependent upon the sensory world, with all its inherent shortcomings, for fodder for theories and experiments. To do otherwise is to retreat from activity in the laboratory or the field to armchair musings about cause and effect in the world. Thus, a moderate degree of healthy skepticism should guide us as we think about and conduct research.

How can healthy skepticism be fostered? You can begin by being aware of two of the most common pitfalls in psychological research: confusing correlation with causation and missing the influence of confounding variables. Each of these pitfalls will be defined so that, hereafter, you can keep each one in mind when you read the psychological literature and work on your own projects.

Do not confuse correlation with causation   A *correlation* is an association between two variables, and a common pitfall is to assume that one of these variables caused the other. Consider a simple example of what is called a *negative correlation:* Are the number of hours of TV watching per week associated with the academic success of elementary school children? On the face of it, the answer would seem to be a resounding "yes": Children who watch less television probably have higher grades relative to those who watch more. This is called a negative correlation because as the value of one variable increases (hours of TV watching), the other variable decreases (grades). Note that the reverse relationship—higher grades are associated with less TV watching—also makes sense and is implied by a negative correlation, as well.

A *positive correlation* occurs between two variables when as the value of one variable either increases or decreases, the other behaves similarly. Thus, perhaps childhood obesity is also correlated with TV watching. It makes sense to argue that overweight children probably watch more television than slimmer children. Greater physical activity in the latter group might, for instance, preclude inordinate amounts of TV watching.

Do these two correlations—the association between TV and grades and that between TV and weight—allow us to make causal statements similar to those resulting from controlled experimentation? In a word, no. A fundamental principle of behavioral science is that *correlation does not imply causation.* Reflect back on the above negative and positive correlational relationships for a moment. Is it the case that TV watching actually *causes* lower grades? Perhaps, instead, it is the case that poor performance in school leads students to watch more TV, or maybe it is not poor performance but a lack of intellectual motivation that promotes too much television watching and poor performance in school, and so on. There are any number of compelling explanations that might account for this negative correlation. Consider the purported link between TV and obesity—what other variables might lead to the positive correlational relationship described above?

By now, you undoubtedly recognize the problem. When we examine a correlation between any two variables, the relationship can be portrayed in a bi-directional manner: Variable X can lead to a change in variable Y just as Y can lead to a change in X. To complicate matters further, a third but unknown variable Z may actually be driving the relationship between X and Y. We do not know the actual causal chain of events unless we experimentally manipulate and measure the relevant variables in order to test a particular hypothesis.

Does this mean that correlational relationships are not helpful to psychological research? No, not at all. Correlations must be understood, however, as suggestive associations pointing to possible causal factors that must be explored experimentally. The main point here is the necessity of avoiding confusing correlated variables with causal variables when evaluating, planning, or conducting research.

Be on the look out for confounded variables The second pitfall to avoid when evaluating research is the *confounding* of variables. Confounding occurs when the effect of the independent variable becomes mixed up with the effect of another variable, one that is not under the researcher's control. For example, a confound could be introduced into an allergy medication experiment if one group began taking a drug at a time of year when few allergens are present (winter), and another group began the drug regimen when pollen counts are high (spring). Gender, too, can be a confound in any study if more women, say, than men participate, or if a preponderance of males end up in one experimental group.

Confounds can systematically bias a study's results, and it is virtually impossible to control every variable that could potentially have an influence on either the outcome or interpretation of an experiment. Nonetheless, a good researcher tries to anticipate confounds in the planning stages of a project by carefully assessing what variables could affect the independent and dependent variables being used. Many times, more than one experiment must be undertaken to either eliminate or rule out the influence of a confound, but such tenacity increases interpretive clarity and establishes the reliability of results.

A potential confound could exist in the hypothetical results of the education study that we discussed previously (see pp. 9–10). Although the group of students who received the active learning treatment did earn a higher class average than that of the control group, at least one influential variable—the time of day each class was taught—was not controlled in the study. Perhaps the students in the control group received a lower average because their class met early in the morning (8 A.M.), whereas the active learning group met in the early afternoon (1 P.M.). If so, early morning fatigue could be a confounded factor that affected the control group's performance so that the active learning group only *appeared* to score higher. Thus, it is possible that fatigue, not teaching style, led to the results.

THE HOW OF RESEARCH: PRACTICAL ISSUES WHEN BEGINNING A PROJECT

Organizing A Project: An Overview

To begin a research project, you must organize it in a series of stages proceeding from the start to the finish. Subsequent chapters in this book will help you to think about and execute the various activities necessary to conduct research in psychology. Before you learn the variety of skills related to the research process, however, you need to conceptually break your project down into stages and understand the activities that take place within each one. There is a heuristic value in doing so, particularly because contemplating a research project as a whole can be a little overwhelming. This book identifies five stages, the Idea Stage, the Implementation Stage, the Analysis and Interpretation Stage, the Writing Stage, and the Presentation Stage. We will review each stage in turn, highlighting the main activities involved as well as the future chapters that present relevant strategies and activities.

The first stage is the *Idea Stage*. Initially, you must choose a particular subfield of psychology to study, and within it, you must select a particular question or problem to examine. Table 1.1 shows a list of the current divisions within the American Psychological Association (APA), one of the primary organizations for psychologists in the United States. As you

TABLE 1.1

LIST OF CURRENT DIVISIONS IN THE AMERICAN PSYCHOLOGICAL ASSOCIATION

Division 1: General Psychology
Division 2: Society for the Teaching of Psychology
Division 3: **Experimental Psychology**
Division 5: Evaluation, Measurement & Statistics
Division 6: **Behavioral Neuroscience & Comparative Psychology**
Division 7: **Developmental Psychology**
Division 8: **Society of Personality and Social Psychology**
Division 9: Society for the Psychological Study of Social Issues—SPSSI
Division 10: Psychology and the Arts
Division 12: **Clinical Psychology**
Division 13: Consulting Psychology
Division 14: Society for Industrial & Organizational Psychology
Division 15: Educational Psychology
Division 16: School Psychology
Division 17: Counseling Psychology
Division 18: Psychologists in the Public Service
Division 19: Military Psychology
Division 20: Adult Development and Aging
Division 21: Applied Experimental & Engineering Psychology
Division 22: Rehabilitation Psychology
Division 23: Society for Consumer Psychology
Division 24: Theoretical & Philosophical Psychology
Division 25: Experimental Analysis of Behavior
Division 26: History of Psychology
Division 27: Society for Community Research & Action
Division 28: Psychopharmacology & Substance Abuse
Division 29: Psychotherapy
Division 30: Psychological Hypnosis
Division 31: State Psychological Association Affairs
Division 32: Humanistic Psychology
Division 33: Mental Retardation & Developmental Disabilities
Division 34: Population & Environmental Psychology
Division 35: Psychology of Women
Division 36: Psychology of Religion
Division 37: Child, Youth, & Family Service
Division 38: Health Psychology
Division 39: Psychoanalysis
Division 40: Clinical Neuropsychology
Division 41: American Psychology-Law Society
Division 42: Psychologists in Independent Practice
Division 43: Family Psychology
Division 44: Society for the Psychological Study of Lesbian, Gay & Bisexual Issues
Division 45: Society for the Study of Ethnic Minority Issues
Division 46: Media Issues
Division 47: Exercise & Sport Psychology
Division 48: Peace Psychology
Division 49: Group Psychology and Group Psychotherapy
Division 50: Addictions
Division 51: Society for the Psychological Study of Men & Masculinity
Division 52: International Psychology

Source: Division Services Office of the American Psychological Association, Washington, DC, 1997.

can see, there are currently more than 50 divisions that constitute special interest groups, and each has member psychologists who are interested in questions and issues pertaining to the divisional interest. Although it may seem lengthy, this list is by no means an exhaustive one where psychological topics are concerned. The list is included here to demonstrate the current breadth and depth of topical research areas in the field.

Having so many different subfields available can seem a bit overwhelming. Chances are, however, that you will choose to conduct or be assigned a research project relevant to one of the core subfields of psychology: developmental psychology, experimental psychology, social psychology, personality psychology, clinical psychology, or psychobiology. "Core" refers to basic topical and methodological themes that are central to the entire field of psychology. For example, human change and adaptation are organizing themes in developmental and clinical psychology, respectively, but these themes transcend the boundaries of these subfields and are useful to virtually every division in table 1.1. Each of the six core areas is either a freestanding subfield or under a slightly different heading in table 1.1 (see the boldface entries). Descriptions of the core areas and sample topics appear in table 1.2.

If you were interested in social psychology, for example, then you might decide to research helping behavior. This topic might have been covered in class, for instance, or it might be of interest to you due to personal experience (remember the inductive and deductive origins of research questions). Within the study of helping, you might settle on the question, "In public settings, what situational factors promote rather than hinder helping behavior?" At this point you may be thinking, "Wait a minute—how did you come up with that question?" We will discuss specific strategies you can use to develop and refine research questions in chapter 2. Alternatively, of course, you may be assigned a particular question to research by your course instructor, and all students in the class will be examining it or some variation in their projects.

Whether you are given a research question or if you develop your own, you will need a research approach to use in your project. By research approach, I am referring to making a choice among conducting an *experiment*, performing an *applied or field study*, or employing a *descriptive methodology*. As discussed in the earlier section of this chapter, an experiment tests a particularly focused question by comparing one or more experimental groups to a control group. In contrast, applied or field studies often use *quasi-experiments*, which suggest rather than specify cause and effect relations, and do not necessarily use control groups. Instead, quasi-experiments are very useful for examining relationships among several variables and for generating hypotheses for subsequent research. Descriptive methodologies, in turn, use observation, case study, or archival techniques, among others. We will discuss these and other approaches in detail in subsequent chapters of this book.

Once you have a research question, you can complete the activities comprising the second half of the Idea Stage—searching the psychological

TABLE 1.2

CORE AREAS OF PSYCHOLOGY

Clinical Psychology

Orientation: Studies, assesses, and treats mental, emotional, and behavioral disorders.
Sample topics: Abnormal behavior; schizophrenia; depression; drugs and behavior; short- and long-term therapeutic interventions.

Developmental Psychology

Orientation: The study of psychological development, its emergence and change, throughout life.
Sample topics: Cognitive, social, and emotional development in childhood; gender and sex-role development; moral reasoning in childhood and adolescence; effects of heredity on intellectual functioning; aging and memory.

Experimental Psychology

Orientation: Uses experimentation to study selection, perception, interpretation, storage, and retrieval of information, as well as response processes and problem solving.
Sample topics: Working- and long-term memory processes; perception and psychophysics; application of learning theory to animals and humans; cognition; inferential reasoning.

Personality

Orientation: Study of private, internal, enduring characteristics of individuals that make them different from others.
Sample topics: Consistency and stability of traits or styles; temperament; heritability of traits; construction of personality tests and measures; conscious versus unconscious influences; psychopathology and personality.

Psychobiology

Orientation: Direct or indirect study of physiological systems that underlie human and animal behavior.
Sample topics: Mechanism of learning and memory; structure and function of sensory systems; development, structure, and function of the brain and the nervous system; hormones and behavior; effects of stress on behavior and physiology.

Social Psychology

Orientation: Psychological study of how individuals think about, influence, and interact with one another.
Sample topics: Attitudes and attitude-behavior consistency; social cognition; prejudice and stereotyping; conformity; aggression; helping behavior; interpersonal attraction; group influence.

literature for work related to your project. Anyone who conducts research needs to know how to locate existing material to support or, in some cases, even contradict, the question of interest. The psychological literature is quite vast, even forbidding, and many people feel intimidated when they first attempt to wade through it in search of materiafor their projects. Fortunately, this literature is also extremely well-organized and cross-referenced, and much of it is easily accessed through various computer data bases. Chapter 4 will provide you with the skills needed to begin searching for references—chiefly books, chapters, and journal articles—to expand your knowledge of and tighten your thinking about your research question. In the course of doing so, you will learn how to seek out and to critically read a journal article, as well as to take careful notes on what you find.

The second stage of the project, the *Implementation Stage*, follows. Once you have studied the literature related to your research question, you must formulate a hypothesis. If you are creating an original hypothesis from scratch, then you will want to make effective use of the knowledge gained from your literature search to be certain that your idea is a new one. You could also rely on a research design from previous work by altering it somewhat. This approach is often called a *conceptual replication* in that a basic, prior result is being verified in a slightly different way. On the other hand, you might simply conduct a replication study, which means that you are conducting the same study in the same way as prior researchers in order to obtain the expected results. If you are assigned a research hypothesis by your instructor, there is a good chance that you are out to replicate a prior finding.

Once the research design is identified, you will need to *operationally define* the variables you intend to manipulate and measure. Operational definitions change the conceptual elements from a research hypothesis into concrete, testable terms that can be observed, understood, agreed upon, and even used by other researchers. Operational definitions, then, are designed to diminish subjective interpretations of research concepts. An operational definition of public helping, for example, is how much time passes after a staged pratfall—you drop a stack of books in the library—before bystanders stop and offer to help you pick them up. By being both clear and procedural, operational definitions move beyond the descriptive nature of conceptual definitions. Suggestions for writing operational definitions for hypotheses as well as selecting independent and dependent variables appear in chapter 6.

After the operational elements are determined, several other practical aspects of the implementation stage must be addressed. An experimental script, which can include dialog and staging instructions, and separate record sheets for the experimental conditions and dependent measures need to be written. A variety of methods for avoiding bias during the experiment must be carefully reviewed with your study's design in mind. You must also decide how many subjects you need to "fill" your research design and, if necessary, how each one will be assigned to an appropriate treatment condition. Each topic, most with a supporting exercise, is discussed in chapter 6.

If you elect to conduct an applied or field study, you will need to consider keeping track of situational variables and, if possible, biographical variables from participants that may support or even broaden your hypothesis. Working outside the confines of a controlled setting means that you will have the opportunity to capitalize on *external validity*, the ability to generalize from research findings. On the other hand, you will also have to pay particular attention to the various threats to *internal validity*—

the identification of cause and effect among variables—that can occur when you depart from the inferential safety of controlled settings. These and related topics pertaining to applied and field research are covered in chapter 7.

The third stage of the research process is the *Data Collection Stage*, and it is here that the action of the research process really takes place. In the laboratory, the researcher creates a controlled setting where some information is systematically presented to or withheld from research participants, while other information is collected and duly recorded. Outside the lab in applied or field settings, real life is studied in a less systematic fashion, but a lack of rigorous control does not preclude collecting useful information on what people do, say, or think. Chapters 6 and 7 offer advice on how to assign subjects to experimental conditions, to maintain records of those conditions as well as subjects' responses, and to keep track of other variables that can increase our understanding of psychological effects.

The ethical treatment of research participants, whether human or animal, is also a crucial component of the data collection stage of a project. A variety of binding guidelines exist to guide the researcher as he or she interacts with and obtains information from research participants. But there is much more to conducting ethical research that must occur before the first participant arrives. Chapter 5 will show you how to properly gain institutional permission to conduct a study, if need be, as well as how to recruit research participants, to obtain their informed consent once the study is underway, and to administer credit for their participation. Finally, the writing of a debriefing script and its presentation to participants will be discussed.

After the data are collected, they must be analyzed, usually by statistical formulas, and then interpreted: In light of the hypothesis, what do the results mean? Are they meaningful or due to chance? In short, what did you find out? The *Analysis and Interpretation Stage* is critically important because it is here that you learn if your hypothesis is supported. Similar to most of the social and natural sciences, psychology is heavily reliant on the statistical analysis of data. Chapter 8 provides a review of basic descriptive and inferential statistics, illustrates ways to select the appropriate test statistics for your research questions, and most important of all, perhaps, shows you how to put statistical findings into words. Suggestions about organizing and properly displaying results in tables, diagrams, and figures are also reviewed.

The *Writing Stage* builds directly upon the analysis and interpretation stage by effectively communicating the substance of your results to others in written form. When conducting a research project in psychology, nothing is more important than good writing. In fact, I hesitate to even identify a writing stage as such because writing should occur during *every* stage of the research process, not just the one where the results are summarized in a standard form. The APA, for example, proscribes a standard scientific writing style for reporting the results of psychological studies (American Psychological Association, 1994). If you have ever read a journal article for a psychology class, you may already be familiar with it. Learning to properly use, if not master, APA style should be one of your priorities as you study research methodology in psychology.

Chapter 3 goes beyond this point, however, by arguing that writing should be the first and last consideration when putting a project together. To this end, you will be exposed to a variety of writing strategies to help you generate research ideas, as well as advice on effectively outlining, drafting, and revising papers. You will also find that your writing can be greatly improved by receiving peer feedback on it, just as you can learn a great deal about the writing process by commenting on the work of others. Techniques for these two related activities will also be presented in chapter 3.

Some texts about research methodology would stop with four stages, but I prefer to add a fifth, the *Presentation Stage*. Though common in the college classroom, I do not believe that it is sufficient to share your ideas on psychological topics with others in written form only. It is equally important to expound your ideas in public settings. When psychologists conduct empirical research, many of them not only publish articles or other written summaries containing their findings but also attend professional conferences where they give a presentation, often called a "talk," summarizing the results of their work and putting it into a larger psychological context. Such presentations allow for an intellectual give-and-take with an audience, something that is precluded (at least directly) by a written manuscript or class term paper. Chapter 9 includes advice on how to give an oral presentation in a classroom setting or at an undergraduate or professional conference, as well as suggestions about answering a "Call for Papers," the traditional invitation to submit scholarly work.

How long should these five stages take? That depends on several factors, including the scope of your project, the amount of time available to conduct it, whether you are working alone or with others, and most importantly on your own workhabits, organizational abilities, and commitment to the project. Before you begin your project, however, it is a good idea to get a rough but reasonable idea as to how much time you have available to conduct it (see figure 1.3). The following exercise will enable you to begin to plan your project so that it will fit into the time you have available. You can refer to it as you begin to build your research project so that if it becomes too grand and too little time remains, then you can scale back as needed. If you find that you have ample time to complete your project, then you may want to consider expanding it so that additional independent variables or dependent measures can be included.

Exercise 1.A: Creating A Realistic Project Time Line
This time line exercise (see table 1.3) is meant to serve two purposes. First, the time line is a guide to identify necessary research activities. It

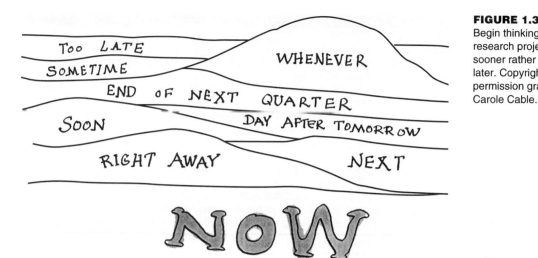

FIGURE 1.3
Begin thinking about a research project sooner rather than later. Copyright permission granted by Carole Cable.

will encourage you to think about what activities need to be done for a project and to estimate how long they will take to complete. At this point, you may not feel ready to begin actually answering questions in the exercise or to offer any specific time estimates. Not to worry. As you read subsequent chapters in this book, you will be able to complete the time line, which leads to its second purpose. The time line is also meant to serve as a convenient reference point that you can come back to as you progress through the book.

The bulk of this exercise involves identifying the number of actual working days available and then determining how well that number matches up with the time estimates for specific project activities. Please note that some of the activities in the Project Activities list can, even should, be done simultaneously (e.g., literature search, the brainstorming and study design) so that they may share start and finish dates. You will want to keep track of activity start and finish dates so that you can assess how good you are at meeting self- or group-imposed deadlines. As you gain experience conducting research, your time estimates should become more accurate as you do more projects. In any case, if you do begin to fall behind, the time line will remind you to review the remaining project activities so that adjustments can be made. If you find that you are ahead in the project, then you will have the luxury of taking more time with some activities or even finishing ahead of schedule!

Record Keeping

Beyond getting started by organizing your project and creating a realistic time line for completing it, you must also consider how you are going to organize your *data*. Data refer to the observations you collect in the course of your project. Data can be almost any type of information—a

TABLE 1.3

Project Time Line

Set aside 30 to 45 minutes to complete this worksheet. You will need a calendar and a good idea of what your work load in this and other courses will be like during the period when the project will be conducted. Before you begin to answer the questions that follow, carefully read through the entire sheet at least one time. If you are collaborating on a project with others, then everyone should be present when the time line is created.

Important Note: This time line is meant to be a helpful guide for realistically planning the activities needed for your project, but its contents are not cast in stone. As you work on the project, you may discover some activities take longer than others or vice versa. The time line should be adjusted accordingly and as many times as necessary.

1. Project title _____
2. Today's date _____ Project due date _____
    Number of available working days between today and due date _____
3. Note that each of the following activities can be broken down into a series of activities:

Project Activities	Time Estimates
a. Literature search	_____ day(s)
b. Brainstorming and study design	_____ day(s)
c. Gather or create project materials (e.g., scripts, questionnaires, stimuli, etc.)	_____ day(s)
d. Subject recruitment and data collection	_____ day(s)
e. Data analysis and interpretation	_____ day(s)
f. Writing Paper (drafting to final revision)	_____ day(s)
g. Other necessary activities unique to this project?	_____ day(s)
Estimated total working days	_____ days*

*If the number of estimated total working days is greater than the number of working days calculated earlier in 2, you will need to redistribute the time allotted to the project activities until the estimate is equal to or less than the time available.

4. Once you have answered these two questions, you will know which activity should be started as soon as possible and which one may be delayed a bit:
    What is the *most* time consuming activity in the project?_____

    _____
    What is the *least* time consuming activity in the project? _____

    _____
5. A time line is only useful if it is actually used. It is recommended that you consult and update this time line frequently—indeed, once a week would be ideal. No fewer than *three* times during the course of the project, however—at the project's start, its middle (during data collection), and toward its end (analysis, interpretation, and writing) is recommended. If an activity is completed prior to a timeline review, then it should not be included in the estimated total working days. Note the date of each review of the following time line.
    Review 1 _____ Review 2 _____ Review 3 _____

rating of liking on an attitude scale, a person's height or weight, an IQ score, the amount of time it takes to retrieve a fact from memory, the acidity of a soil sample, and so on.

In psychological research, data tend to be quantitative rather than qualitative; that is, they are often numerical (a score of 87 on a 100-point test) rather than descriptive (the color of the water was azure). In fact, qualitative variables are frequently converted to numbers for ease of

BOX FEATURE 1.B

A Research Digression: The Data on "Data"

I would like to mention one important fact about the word *data:* It is plural. When people use the word in everyday speech, there is a pronounced tendency to treat it as a singular word, as in "where is the data?"; however, it should be "where are the data?" The singular form of data is the word *datum,* which refers to one observation from a sample of data. If you were trying to modify your study habits by keeping track of the numbers of hours per day that you did course work for a month, then the 30 or so observations would constitute your data. The number of hours you studied on any given day, say, 3 hours on a Thursday, would be a datum. As an observational exercise, listen carefully in your classes and see how often people (including psychologists who should know better) misuse these two words—then vow never to misuse them again yourself!

analysis and reporting purposes (scales of measurement are reviewed in detail in chapter 8). If an evaluation reveals that a person's performance in a class was rated as "good," we are using a qualitative description. The label "good" can be converted to a numerical equivalent by assigning numbers to each of the possible ratings one could receive. Thus, if there are five possible ratings—"poor," "fair," "average," "good," and "excellent"—then poor could be assigned the value of "1," fair a "2," and so on, so that "good" would receive a rating of "4." Note that no information is lost by relying on these numerical equivalents; the rating is simply being presented in a different form.

Before you even collect the data, you must recognize that they are a precious resource; in effect, knowledge is power. Thus, you must plan how to keep track of the data so that they are not misplaced or lost. At a minimum, you should keep your data record in a notebook or a file. If you have only a few bits of data from each participant in your research project, then a written record like a notebook should be sufficient until it is time to analyze the data. On the other hand, if you have a large amount of information from each subject, then you might want to consider using a computer to store the data in a data file. In either case, it is extremely important for you to have an accurate and interpretable record of the information collected by your project.

Small Is Beautiful

The economist E. F. Schumacher (1973) once wrote a provocative book titled *Small Is Beautiful.* Although this is not an economics text book and Professor Schumacher's arguments have not been widely embraced by the economic community, his message of scale is nonetheless a good one, particularly when it is applied to the generation of knowledge. When I teach research methods and when I conduct my own research, I like to keep the small-is-beautiful message in mind. I do so as a reminder that, generally speaking, smaller scale projects in psychology that are well done expand our knowledge by examining a relatively small number of variables in order to offer a few choice insights.

Projects that are too comprehensive risk being incomprehensible. When doing any research project, let alone your first one, there is often a strong tendency to want to do it all. Many undergraduate students (and graduate students and even seasoned faculty members) feel that if they undertake a project, then they must discover something earth-shattering or revolutionary about human behavior. Still others believe that they have to address each and every possible question pertaining to their chosen topic. Such enthusiasm should be applauded but it has to be tempered with a bit of realism: No study, no matter how thoughtful, creative, or detailed, can address every interesting question.

Nor should it. If you begin a research project by thinking that it must make a major contribution by demonstrating something new, then you are very likely setting yourself up for considerable frustration, if not failure. There are very few new ideas under the empirical sun, as it were, but there is ample room for endless variation and extension of important themes relevant to mind and behavior. Attempting to address even a handful of good questions can be a daunting enterprise unless you plan ahead. If you try to tackle too much in a project, it inevitably becomes a frustrating enterprise—what initially excited you becomes bogged down with too much cumbersome detail. Many first time student researchers make the mistake of collecting so much information that they do not know where to begin when it comes time to make sense of it. Thus, you should select a research topic or problem that not only genuinely interests you but also is reasonable in its scope.

Good research is based on a question of scale, and I advocate the view that, in general, smaller scale projects are better than larger ones. Why? First, smaller scale projects can be readily conceptualized for yourself and interested others, including the person who is grading you. To that end, you should be able to summarize your study's main idea (the *hypothesis*) in a sentence or two. In the course of doing so, you should highlight what you are manipulating (the *independent variable*), what you are measuring (the *dependent variable*), and what results you anticipate finding. If you cannot give a brief summary containing these few elements, then chances are that you do not fully understand the project you are conducting or that you have taken on too much. To borrow from Henry David Thoreau (1983, p. 136), "Simplify, simplify."

Second, a smaller project is usually easier to execute within a reasonable amount of time. Most student projects are carried out within one semester and very often in a period of a few weeks at most. A richly nuanced set of hypotheses coupled with a detailed methodology may be impressive on paper, but it will do you little good if you cannot carry it out in the allotted time. You must be able to collect whatever information you need, analyze and interpret it, then write it up into a report, and, very possibly, present it to your peers in some public forum within several weeks or a month. An appropriately scaled project can be completed in that period with time to spare, and it will look like what it is—a well-conceived and executed piece of work. In contrast, a wide-ranging, overly ambitious project will be accepted for what it is—a potentially good idea that did not reach its full potential.

Third, smaller projects are often *parsimonious*. That is, they provide a simple and direct description of the phenomenon of interest rather than an elaborate, overly complex account. Why does *parsimony* matter? A parsimonious account separates the empirical wheat from the chaff; that is, it eliminates detail that is superfluous and therefore unnecessary to demonstrate the effect of interest. This cutting away of excess detail has been applied to depictions of psychological events since at least the 14th century. It is often called *Ockham's razor* after William of Ockham, a Franciscan thinker who advocated the study and use of simplified accounts when interpreting human psychology (Leahey, 1992).

Note that parsimony does *not* mean we should conclude that human nature is simple and thus our experiments must always be simple. On the contrary, people and their behavior are often incredibly complex, and many studies involve multiple variables and complicated predictions. In the context of the theories we create and the hypotheses we test in our experiments, however, parsimony serves as a useful guide. If judiciously used, it will allow us to conduct research that addresses those questions we most want to answer in a manageable fashion.

Please note that the small-is-beautiful approach to conducting psychological research does not advocate that you throw away grand ideas or abandon what is often called "the big picture" of human behavior. If you continue to pursue your education in psychology, there will be time enough for broader questions and bigger projects. In the mean time, the planned, doable scale of a reasonably sized but well-developed project will teach you practical skills in preparation for future work. Through the benefit of practical experience, it will also teach you an invaluable lesson about scholarship: It is better to know a lot about a little than a little about a lot.

TO COLLABORATE OR NOT TO COLLABORATE?

The Lone Researcher

There is a popular image of the natural scientist as a loner who, sporting the obligatory white lab coat, is forever hard at work in the isolation of the laboratory. The counterpart of this image in the humanities is that of the learned scholar ensconced in a cluttered library amidst dusty books and papers, resplendent in tweed and pipe smoke. In both cases, we are left with the impression that true scientists and scholars make their discoveries alone. But these images—stereotypes, really—do not do justice to the actual activities of the researcher or to the many people who conduct various types of research.

No researcher, for example, truly works in isolation. Even the most reclusive researcher depends upon the scholarship of others in order to inform his or her own thinking and writing. Researchers regularly study the work of others, and it may be done by their contemporaries or based on scholarship from long ago. Sir Isaac Newton's (1675/1676) remark that "If I have seen further it is by standing on ye shoulders of Giants" is apt here. The lone scholar is always adding to knowledge by building upon what is already known, and this is true even when that scholar challenges a presumed fact. Dispute generates knowledge, as well.

Though not necessarily in the formal sense of the lab researcher or the scholar poring over dusty tomes, students like yourself who do course work during college, as well as library or lab work, are conducting research as well. Like the scientist, scholar, or teacher, you are actively creating new connections among existing ideas in order to develop knowledge that is new, if only to you. If you are fulfilling your role as a student, you should also be actively questioning—and sometimes even doubting—what you learn during your college career (recall the aforementioned benefits of healthy skepticism). What you learn as a student is ultimately up to you, as you spend much of your time alone in thought.

Why do many researchers choose to work alone? How should you decide whether to pursue a solitary or a group research project? One main reason that some people elect to work alone is the independence the experience provides. If you work alone on a project, the project is entirely your own—you are responsible for its success or its failure, and neither of these outcomes can be shared. Many people find such responsibility exhilarating, and they enjoy being intellectually "rugged individualists" who navigate their own way through the research process.

A second compelling reason that some people choose to work alone is the control one has over the whole project. When you work alone, for example, you need never worry how various parts of the project are shaping up because you *know* how the project as a whole is progressing. There is, of course, much to be said for learning to cooperate with others, and chances are that your future career will require you to work closely with others. If you know that you do not work well with others, however, and your instructor will allow you to conduct a solo project, then this option may appeal to you.

Third, there is the issue of scheduling. If you have a demanding schedule outside this course, so much so that you cannot commit to the scheduling needs of other students, then it may be very appropriate for you to consider working alone. An unreasonable schedule will only create undue friction or tension among the members of a research team. You will be doing yourself, other members of your class, and your course instructor a favor if you acknowledge this difficulty at the outset. Some instructors may insist that you participate in a group project. If so, having raised the issue of scheduling difficulties will still be helpful, as both you and the members of your research team will know that this issue must be dealt with at the outset of any project.

Did you ever consider working on a research project with others? You may have assumed that you would have to work alone, that cooperative arrangements would not be acceptable for college level work. If you believed this, then you have been misled and you should give some consideration to the virtues of working with others on a research project. With this in mind, we will turn to the issue of research teams in psychology.

Research Teams

In contrast to the tradition of working alone on a piece of research, teams of researchers pursuing a question collaboratively have become common, particularly in health-oriented research (e.g., Grady & Strudler Wallston, 1988). A research team can be defined as more than one person cooperatively pursuing a piece of research. Research teams come in many sizes, but for an undergraduate research project of the sort described in this book, the optimal number of team members ranges from two to six.

Many important research questions are pursued collaboratively for a variety of reasons. In the first place, research teams allow for division of labor so that the necessary legwork in a project can be accomplished quickly and efficiently by more than one person. Second, many questions are interdisciplinary in nature and they require that scientists from disparate fields of study combine their intellectual expertise in order to search for answers. For example, it is becoming routine for psychologists, physicians, sociologists, and statisticians to cooperate with one another in the study of how stress affects health and psychological well-being. Third, participating on a team allows individuals to gravitate toward roles that they are comfortable filling, and that match interests with abilities (Grady & Strudler Wallston, 1988). Some people prefer activities that involve writing or library research, whereas others are drawn to those that require "people" skills, such as interviewing or putting the participants through their paces in an experiment.

Research teams composed of students appear to be becoming more commonplace as an educational tool as well (Dunn, 1996; Dunn & Toedter, 1991; McKenna, 1995) and not just in psychology (e.g., Elbow & Belanoff, 1995). Considerable research and plain commonsense suggest that students learn as much, if not more, from peers in cooperative arrangements than they do as solo learners (e.g., Goldstein, 1993; Levine, 1990; see also, Elbow & Belanoff, 1989). Working with another person provides you not just with partnership but with a peer reviewer. That is, the person or people you work with can supply you with helpful, informal comments on your ideas for a project. Having the opportunity to air your views with sympathetic, motivated listeners—after all, a shared grade is likely to be at stake—and, in turn, to comment on their point of view will improve the work. Debate sometimes occurs, but if it is constructive in content and tone, then the project will be better because of it. In a collaborative effort, you and a peer will often develop questions

BOX FEATURE 1.C

A Research Digression: Authorship Credit, Author Responsibility

Authorship—defined here as conducting research, as well as presenting or writing about it—entails responsibilities that should not be taken lightly by a solo investigator or a research team. The "Ethical Principles of Psychologists and Code of Conduct" (American Psychological Association, 1992) is succinct on the issue of publication credit:

> Psychologists take responsibility and credit, including authorship credit, only for work they have actually performed or to which they have contributed.

Read the sentence again, but this time substitute the word "students" in place of "psychologists." Now you know your professional obligation as an author.

What research activities are entailed in this obligation? Critical activities, such as conceiving the hypothesis, designing the experiment, selecting the statistical analyses and then performing them, interpreting any results, and writing the research summary. Lesser activities—photocopying materials, giving advice, entering data, recruiting participants—are necessary, but they serve a supporting role in the research enterprise. If you work alone, you will do both types of activities; however, if you collaborate with others, you are ethically bound to contribute the same amount of effort toward critical activities as the rest of the members of the research team (see Fine & Kurdek, 1993, for discussion of related issues on authorship; see also, Box Feature 9.C).

together or see potential relationships among variables that neither of you would have noticed working alone.

Beyond commentary on ideas and carrying out the project, though, peer collaborators can also positively affect the reporting of a project's findings. Fellow students can provide useful feedback on your writing style, as well as on the written summary the research team will produce (see chapter 3). Hearing or reading remarks on your written work mimics the professional activities of psychologists, who often share and critique drafts of papers and articles before submitting them for publication (Dunn, 1996; Dunn & Toedter, 1991). These remarks are invaluable, as they inevitably improve the writing before it is submitted to an instructor for a grade.

Collaborating with others on a project also provides important social and emotional support for what some students find to be an unfamiliar, even stressful situation. A peer can be there to offer understanding and support when parts of the project are not running on schedule or as planned. Of course, a peer can also keep you in line and motivated or confront you if you are not pulling your weight in the project. When things are going well with your research project, you have someone who can share the success with you. But you must remember that if you work with others, they are going to depend on your efforts and good will, and you will come to expect the same in return (see Box Features 1.C and 9.C). This aspect of collaboration leads us to the issue of responsibility.

Individual Versus Group Responsibility and the Division of Labor

Good scientists and scholars take responsibility for their ideas and their work. If you work alone on a research project, you owe it to yourself and the course instructor to take this responsibility seriously. You will have the satisfaction of working independently, but you will still need to develop a plan of attack for conducting your own research project. It will be very important for you to use the available time wisely, so you should be certain to complete the project time line exercise (see table 1.3) at your earliest opportunity. (Please also note that you will not be working entirely alone, as many exercises in this book are designed to be shared with peers in your class.)

On the other hand, if you are working with others on a research project, then you have a responsibility not only to yourself and the course instructor, but also to your project partners. It is therefore very important for you to establish a working relationship with your peers early on. You must all agree on what tasks need to be done for the project and how they are to be assigned to each group member. Deadlines will need to be established for these tasks, so it is important that everyone in the group has a hand in developing the project time line. Moreover, one member of the group should be assigned the responsibility of tracking how well everyone is following the time line.

Inevitably, most groups rely on a term from the field of economics, the *division of labor*. A division of labor entails identifying all the activities that need to be accomplished and dividing them equitably among the individuals available to carry them out. The benefit of the division of labor is that it generally makes efficient use of the available time and staff so that quite literally "many hands make light the work." Of course, this plan of action assumes that all participants will do their fair share. We are back, then, to the issue of responsibility.

How can you ensure that once the work is divided among the members of the research team that it will be done correctly and in time? One invaluable way to proceed is to draw up a *peer research contract* wherein everyone commits to the project, has a hand in choosing and accepting the required responsibilities, and carrying out the activities that are necessary for the success of the project. The benefit of a peer contract is that all who sign it are publicly acknowledging their willingness to fulfill their obligation to the other members of the group and to the project. Usually, the course instructor also reads and signs the contract, acknowledging his or her awareness of how a group has decided to proceed with a project.

If the group members carry out their responsibilities to the project, then they have fulfilled the peer research contract. Whether the grade is high or low, each member of the group should share equally in the results of the evaluation of the project. If any member or members of the group fails to fulfill any or all obligations to the project, then the peer research contract serves as a reminder of the original commitment. Depending upon the course requirements and the inclination of the instructor, failing to meet one's original commitment to the project may result in a lower grade than other group members receive. The point here, though, is not to be punitive but to create a situation where every person understands what he or she has to do to ensure a good and successful research project in psychology. Similar to the timeline exercise, the peer research contract is meant to motivate—not threaten—group members.

Some readers may assume that a peer contract is not really necessary to encourage their own or their peer's compliance with the goals of a research project. Indeed, many students who choose to do group research often choose to work with close friends or acquaintances who are enrolled in the same class. Their logic is simple: I want to work with people I know because I can trust them to do a good job. No contract seems to be necessary. Sadly, experience teaches otherwise. In fact, it is precisely in this sort of situation, one with friends, where a contract is most needed.

Why? Consider this: Who is more likely to be forgiving if someone reneges on a small agreement, a friend or a relative stranger? In most cases, friends will be more understanding and they may, in fact, pick up the slack for us. After all, if a friend fell behind, you'd do more than your share, wouldn't you? Perhaps and perhaps not. The point is that group work requires a shared and equal commitment from all parties. Though extra effort on someone's behalf may appear to be a generous act of friendship, it is not an equitable or acceptable state of affairs for a group project. Moreover, in an educational context it is intellectually suspect, if not dishonest.

Acquaintances—groups members whom we do not know well outside the classroom—are going to assume a reciprocal relationship. That is, because there are no prior relationships among the group members, they will anticipate that everyone involved in the project will pull an equal share in the division of labor. A word to the wise: If you are going to conduct a group project, then let everyone do his or her part by developing a peer research contract.

Exercise 1.B: Developing A Peer Research Contract

The peer research contract is meant to give everyone a sense of ownership over and commitment to the project. It is also a piece of physical evidence that at least at one point in time, everyone involved in a project agreed that it should proceed in a particular manner. With these two points in mind, it is probably a very good idea to make enough copies of the completed peer research contract so that all group members and perhaps the course instructor can each have one.

Please note that it is essential for a project time line to have been created before the peer research contract can be signed and sealed. In other words, before people can commit themselves to various project activities, those activities need to be identified. Thus, point 3 in table 1.4 explicitly requires that group members agree to a time line before proceeding. Please note that time is not limited to the time line, however. Point 4 in table 1.4 requires that group members agree to attend

TABLE 1.4

PEER RESEARCH CONTRACT

1. Project Title _____ Date _____
2. Names of Group Members (6 or fewer)

   _____ _____
   _____ _____
   _____ _____

3. Has a project time line been developed? If yes, go on to section 4, which follows. If no, then complete Exercise 1.A *before proceeding.*
4. How often will the group meet? Write specific date(s) and time(s) in the space provided:

   Record the name of each group member and his or her responsibilities here.
5. Group Member: Responsibilities:
   a. _____
   b. _____
   c. _____
   d. _____
   e. _____
   f. _____
6. We each agree to complete our individual responsibilities as part of the group project (each group member must sign here):

   _____ _____
   _____ _____

   Instructor's signature _____

meetings to report on and to discuss the project's progress. How many meetings and the times for them will depend on various factors, including the number of group members, the time to complete the project, the amount of work involved in doing the research, and so on. These meeting times and their frequency must be determined by the group *here at the outset of the project,* though they may, of course, be changed as often as necessary.

Under point 5, each group member's name is recorded and his or her responsibilities are specified. These responsibilities are based on a division of labor where each group member puts forth effort that is relatively equal to the effort of each peer. In essence, simple logic and decency should prevail here: Desirable and less desirable tasks should be evenly divided among group members so that everyone has at least one of each. Based on the project activities identified in the timeline exercise and subsequent discussions about the project, group members should feel free to note their preferred activities as responsibilities are assigned in the peer research contract. Whenever possible, then, there should be a conscious effort to match a person's interest or ability to an appropriate activity; however, this goal is balanced by awareness that all team members should participate in each phase of the project (see Box Feature 1.C).

Once all responsibilities have been divided up and each group member has reviewed the assignments, then the contract can be signed. After the student signatures are affixed, then the instructor should also review and sign off on it. Copies of the signed peer research contract should then be made and distributed to all signatories.

Similar to the project time line, the peer research contract is meant to serve as a flexible guide and a reference. Any changes to the group or the project responsibilities must be noted in the contract. Again, the goal here is not to engage in mock legal activities but to keep all group members informed about the status of the project and their role in it. Sharing information in this way will enhance group commitment to the project and ensure that everything proceeds smoothly.

Some readers might feel that we are getting ahead of ourselves by already focusing on time lines and whether to collaborate or conduct a solo study. Not so. It is never too early to start thinking about the larger scheme of a project and, as noted earlier, the issues and exercises in this chapter are reference tools for your research as well as the rest of this book. Now that you have a broad perspective on planning a project, it will soon be time to narrow the focus by selecting a research approach, the goal of the next chapter.

SUMMARY

Chapter 1 introduced the philosophy behind this book: Practical researchers know how to effectively translate the theoretical side of methodology into practice. The first half of the chapter introduced motives for conducting research, the role of inductive and deductive reasoning before beginning research, and presented an overview of the scientific method. The looping process inherent in experimental research, and the relevance of philosophy of science to it, were then examined. Moderate skepticism was portrayed as a healthy stance to adopt when reading or planning research. The second half of the chapter reviewed practical issues that must be carried out when starting research, including the five stages of a project, an exercise on creating a realistic time line, the importance of record keeping, and a rationale for doing smaller scale projects. The remainder of the chapter offered reasons for conducting research either alone or with a team, and included discussions of responsibility and dividing project tasks among a group. The chapter ended with an exercise on developing a peer research contract.

KEY TERMS

anomaly (p. 12)
causality (p. 4)
confounding (p. 15)
conceptual replication (p20)
correlation (p. 14)
data (p. 23)
datum (p. 25)
deductive reasoning (p. 3)
dependent variable (p. 8)
empiricism (p. 4)
external validity (p. 20)
fact (p. 4)
falsificationism (p. 11)

hypothesis (p. 7)
independent variable (p. 8)
inductive reasoning (p. 2)
internal validity (p. 20)
negative correlation (p. 14)
normal science (p. 12)
operational definition (p. 20)
paradigm (p. 12)
parsimony (p. 27)
peer research contract (p. 31)
positive correlation (p. 15)
prescriptions (p. 13)
project time line (p. 22)

quasi-experiment (p. 18)
randomization (p. 9)
reductionism (p. 6)
research loop of
    experimentation (p. 7)
scientific method (p. 4)
scientific revolution (p. 12)
theory (p. 5)
variables (p. 7)

SUGGESTED READINGS

Aron, A., & Aron, E. (1989). *The heart of social psychology: A backstage view of a passionate science.* Lexington, MA: Lexington Books. A personal, behind-the-scenes account of research and researchers in the discipline of social psychology. More broadly, however, the book can be read as an enthusiastic portrayal of what is involved in doing psychological research.

Kuhn, T. (1970). *The structure of scientific revolutions* (2nd ed.). Chicago: University of Chicago. An intellectual classic concluding that scientific research and advances do not proceed in an orderly manner, nor are scientists themselves a dispassionate, objective group. Not easy, but a worthwhile read.

Medawar, P. B. (1979). *Advice to a young scientist.* New York: Basic Books. The author, a Nobel Laureate, describes a life devoted to scientific inquiry in an accessible and winning fashion. His advice is helpful and witty, and his passion for understanding nature is contagious.

CHAPTER 2

Research Approaches and Generating Ideas

To the average person, the process of discovery in science is shrouded in mystery. How do researchers think of topics, let alone the methodologies to study them? How do psychologists become interested in particular questions? How can one question lead to myriad related issues? Simply, it's through effort, planning, and a bit of luck. More to the point, though, is that practical researchers are aware of the diversity of research approaches available, how to appropriately choose from among them, and then how to develop good research questions. We will explore these practical matters of research approach and idea generation in this chapter.

The first half of chapter 2 introduces some select approaches to conducting psychological research. In our review, we will progress from more passive approaches (e.g., observation) to more active ones (e.g., experimentation), and particular examples will be used to illustrate each approach. The remainder of the chapter will deal with an important issue, often more of a concern for students—how to think of a good research topic. Several sources of ideas will be presented, as well as a few exercises for generating and developing fledgling topics and then sharing them with peers. Techniques for giving and receiving constructive peer feedback are suggested, as is advice about learning to trust your own opinion when evaluating psychological research.

SOME APPROACHES TO RESEARCH

Distinguishing Between Qualitative and Quantitative Research

Generally speaking, there are two broad categories of research: *qualitative research* and *quantitative research.* Qualitative research approaches are distinguished by a reliance on verbal reports, descriptions, and interpretations of events. Qualitative data are not numerical nor are they usually subjected to traditional (i.e., statistical) methods of analysis. Instead, they are examined in their raw form. For example, a developmental psychologist interested in the affective tone of communications between parents and children could listen to and then categorize the emotional content of conversations between fathers and toddlers. Utterances classified as either positive or negative could then be linked to nonverbal behaviors, such as body orientation, interpersonal distance during speech, frequency of eye contact, and so on. Do parents' words and actions match up, or are parents sometimes sending mixed messages to their children?

The real benefit of most qualitative approaches is that they disclose the richness of human experience (e.g., Lincoln & Guba, 1985). Thus, qualitative research uses an *open systems* view in that any information gathered is of no fixed variety. Studying the idiosyncratic responses of many people to a given stimulus, say, a natural disaster, can be fascinating, thought provoking, and enlightening because there is no "correct" way to understand it. The openness of many qualitative approaches proves to be very useful when it comes to generating hypotheses in the early stages of investigating a topic. On the other hand, the downside to such qualitative detail must be acknowledged as well. Qualitative approaches cannot be quickly, easily, or efficiently summarized, nor is it often possible to generalize from one set of qualitative observations to other situations.

Quantitative research approaches, on the other hand, are numerically oriented. No matter what their original form, the data used in quantitative research are always converted into numbers for ease of interpretation and statistical analysis. Using a numerical scoring system, for example, a neuropsychologist could administer psychological tests to rate the severity of brain injury. Alternatively, participants in an impression formation study could rank their level of liking for six target persons after reading descriptions and personal histories of each one.

The chief advantage of the quantitative approach is that numbers are easy to work with—data are readily collected, coded, summarized, and analyzed. A decided strength of quantification is that dependent measures within the context of an experiment usually allow the researcher to use one set of data to infer the characteristics of other, similar populations. The disadvantage of quantitative research is that researchers know much about the collective or average experience of research participants, but not their individual experiences. Quantitative approaches, then, often represent a *closed systems* view because the categories and responses of interest are decided upon in advance. This is not to say that novel information is discarded, but it may not receive as much credence as it would in a qualitative design.

Social science disciplines such as anthropology, sociology, education, and social work have relied on qualitative methodologies for some time. In contrast, psychology is a relative newcomer when it comes to conducting qualitative research. The experimental tradition in psychology is decidedly quantitative, but qualitative research is becoming increasingly common and accepted in the psychological literature (e.g., Creswell, 1994; Highlen & Finley, 1996; Hill, 1994).

Without a doubt, it is best to view these two categories of research as complementary to, not opposite of, one another. Both the categories and their respective methods have strengths as well as limitations, and really the best that any researcher can do is to select the approach that best demonstrates some desired psychological result. In fact, shrewd but practical researchers use qualitative and quantitative measures in concert within the same study. This combined approach is called *triangulation* (Campbell & Fiske, 1959), and its strategic use can enhance the scope and reliability of most research projects.

Try to think of qualitative and quantitative methods as anchoring points on either end of the research continuum. Beginning at the far left of this continuum, we will consider various approaches to observational research that are strongly qualitative, including naturalistic observation in its various guises, ethology, participant observation, ethnography, and unobtrusive measures. We then focus on case studies, qualitative accounts that rely on interviews as well as observational data. As we move to the center of the continuum, we will consider archival research methods and questionnaire studies, approaches that bridge the gap between the continuum's two extremes by using descriptive and numerical information in combination. The heavily quantitative domains of experimentation and applied and field research, including so-called quasi-experiments, are introduced only briefly because each area has its own chapter later in the text (see chapters 6 and 7, respectively).

Observational Research

When most people think of observational research, they are probably thinking of *naturalistic observation,* a technique pioneered by *ethologists* in the early 20th century. *Ethology* is a branch of biology that studies the behavior of individual animals or animal groups under natural conditions. Naturalistic observation involves systematically observing, describing, and somehow recording information about behavior. In general, researchers using this method do very little or no intervention into the settings they observe. Naturalistic observation has two main strengths: identification of naturally occurring behaviors (which is often linked with hypothesis generation) and verifying relationships among variables that have been studied in controlled environments, such as the laboratory.

The settings for naturalistic observation are natural and familiar so that research participants—human or animal—are relaxed and unaware their actions are being assessed. Observational research involving humans, for example, often occurs in public or field settings. Patterns of play in young children can be observed on playgrounds, just as the social networks of male retirees can be examined by watching conversations in the seating areas of indoor shopping malls. Animal behavior, however, is literally observed out in the field, though some structured observation can occur in semicontrolled environments, such as zoos.

A prominent observational method that is frequently used to study naturally occurring animal behavior is the *ethogram*. An ethogram is an accumulation of systematically collected observational data that describe the characteristic behavior pattern of some species (Zaremba & Toedter, 1991). Pairs of trained observers usually take detailed notes on a species, describing its physical characteristics, its environment, and the weather conditions when the observation took place. The observers identify some target activities performed by the animal (e.g., grooming, eating, climbing, running, vocalizing), define them in behavioral terms, and then record how frequently the activities occur within specified blocks of time (e.g., 1-minute intervals). Target behaviors are assessed either globally (e.g., eating, grooming) or in a more molecular fashion (e.g., eating behaviors include searching for food, sniffing food, sampling food, chewing food). One group of researchers, for example, developed a classification system for 200 behaviors that could be performed by a group of primates of the Genus *Papio* (Coelho & Bramblett, 1981). Ethograms are often the first step in establishing research questions that can be investigated systematically in future studies.

Participant observation is a second method of naturalistic observation (e.g., Spradley, 1980). This phrase or its variant, "participant observer," may seem ironic: How can a "participant" (active role) be an "observer" (passive role)? Participant observation involves watching some behavioral phenomenon unfold while reporting on it in the style of the investigative journalist (Rosnow & Rosenthal, 1996). Like a journalist, the researcher is *in* the situation, meticulously watching and listening, but not *of* the situation; that is, professionals in both fields must remain appropriately detached from, not embroiled in, their subjects. Some differences do exist, however. Researchers are not under the time constraints of reporters, nor are they trying to get a "story" (Rosnow & Rosenthal, 1996). Instead, participant observers patiently observe behavior as nature takes its course.

What do participant observers do? Using a variety of record keeping strategies, they look for consistent themes or behavioral patterns in the subjects they observe. Tape recorders and notebooks are common tools in the field, though many researchers write up their observations from memory. Participant observers usually have some theory and an accompanying hypothesis to guide their thinking and record keeping. On the other hand, a decided advantage of observational research is the ability to take advantage of the moment. Researchers may capture some fleeting phenomenon that happens only rarely or could never be recreated in an experimental investigation (Weick, 1968).

Unique human social phenomena, such as doomsday groups, require disguised participant observation. In a classic work on cognitive dissonance, for example, Festinger, Riecken, and Schachter (1956) give a participant observer's account of a group of Midwesterners who believed a massive flood would destroy much of the earth. The flood was prophesied by beings from another planet who contacted the group's leader, a suburban housewife, through automatic writing. Festinger and his colleagues knew that in order to truly study the group that they would have to join and be accepted by it. The researchers were particularly interested in the group's reaction when the world did not end as predicted, and if they had not been participant observers, they could not have tracked the behavior or conversations occurring before and after the nonevent.

A third observational method, one closely aligned with participant observation, is *ethnography*. Ethnography involves undisguised, objective documentation of the customs, habits, and behaviors of some group of people, usually a culture. Typically, ethnographers attempt to understand how the members of a culture or group "make sense" out of their experiences. As a variation of observational research, ethnography is used more frequently in sociology or social and cultural anthropology than in psychology. Methodologically, ethnographers take naturalistic observation to a different level, as they frequently interview their research participants about particulars of the culture. As additional data sources, such interviews extend the observational records previously described.

One ethnographer studied a group close to his own experience— students inhabiting various dormitories at his institution, Rutgers University (Moffatt, 1989). To understand undergraduate culture, he lived on and off "among the natives" in Rutgers dorms between 1977 and 1987. As Moffatt (1989, p. xv) put it, "Participant observation with the undergraduates . . . amounts to hanging around with one's subjects for a long enough time to start hearing them in their more natural adolescent tones . . . and to start sensing their own priorities as they understand them." In lieu of using questionnaires or interviews, the professor listened, watched, and took notes on the lifestyle of students at this major state university.

Moffatt (1989) added an interesting collaborative element to his ethnographic work, however. During a 2-year period after he completed the dormitory phase of his work, he taught preliminary findings to students in his anthropology classes. The students then wrote reaction papers on his conclusions, offering their own interpretations, refinements, and suggestions, ultimately adding insightful comments about their own college experiences. As a result, Moffatt's research is peppered with descriptive quotations and anecdotes portraying student culture in the 1980s. This rich piece of work is an ideal example of how researchers can take advantage of an often overlooked resource—the immediate environment, a topic we will return to later in this chapter.

The various approaches to observation that we have discussed so far—ethology, participant observation, and ethnography—can be classified as potentially highly *reactive* in nature. That is, the act of observing research participants can affect whatever behavior is being systematically observed. Animals, for example, often adjust their actions when humans are nearby (e.g., Chamove, Hosey, & Schaetzel, 1988). When some of the Rutgers University students described in Moffatt's (1989) book discovered he was an anthropologist, they began to speak to him differently than they did with peers (e.g., they used fewer swear words in his presence). When doing any form of reactive observation, then, the researcher must be aware of this potential pitfall or risk, which we might constructively label *social contamination*. If such contamination occurs or is suspected, a researcher must try to document its possible influence on the study's results.

In contrast, *nonreactive observation* avoids this pitfall because neither the researcher's presence nor the method of data collection alter any of the behavior being observed. *Unobtrusive observation* is a form of nonreactive observation because it involves the study of participants who are not aware that they are being observed for research purposes. Indeed, most of the measures used in unobtrusive observation are either concealed or are nonobvious to the people who encounter them. Examples of concealed measures include hidden tape recorders or video cameras, as well as the counting devices in turnstiles found at the entrances to museums, subways, and other public venues. One-way mirrors are often used in child development research, for example, so that psychologists can observe children's behavior in laboratory or daycare settings without fear of disrupting or changing it. Animals with radio collars can be studied from a distance and their migration over large areas can be efficiently tracked without unnecessary provocation by or encounters with humans.

Unobtrusive measures come in different forms, but some of the most common ones are physical traces, the material evidence or remnants of people and their actions (Webb, Campbell, Schwartz, Sechrest, & Grove, 1981). Measures of physical traces come in two basic varieties: erosion and accretion. *Erosion measures* show some wear and tear that is usually selective. A museum curator might learn that a collection of impressionist paintings is popular as a result of having to frequently repaint the smudged walls and replace the worn flooring tiles in the gallery. Similarly, she might observe that the pop art is less well received by the public if its display space rarely needs to be refurbished.

Accretion measures, on the other hand, usually involve the examination of evidence that has been left behind or somehow deposited (Webb et al., 1981). Sechrest (1971) suggested that college women were more likely to lock their car doors than were men, demonstrating this result by checking cars parked next to men's and women's dormitories. Perhaps movies favored by children have more debris (e.g., popcorn, candy wrappers, soda cups) left behind on the floor of the theater than do films enjoyed by adults. If you wanted to learn if vanity license plates (e.g., "LVIS 4EVR," "BIO PHD," "LUV 4 U") were associated with socioeconomic status, you could spend time in parking lots recording what model of cars have or do not have personalized plates. Perhaps expensive cars are more likely to have vanity plates than are cheaper vehicles, suggesting some drivers' penchants for ostentation and display of wealth.

Beyond the virtue of being nonreactive, unobtrusive measures are also creative, even elegant, research demonstrations. They highlight the cleverness of many researchers by allowing them to capitalize on people's public and private selves as they go about the business of daily living. These measures do have at least one problematic quality, however: They offer mute testimony regarding the interpretation of human behavior. Many times, researchers are left to infer the psychological import of accretion or erosion measures. To do so adequately, researchers must always try to make interpretable comparisons between the unobtrusive measure and the psychological reality of the event being studied. A large part of this comparative process must be the identification of plausible rival hypotheses and their systematic elimination (Webb et al., 1981).

Webb et al. (1981) bemoan the fact that unobtrusive measures are rarely used in psychology or the other social sciences. Why? Largely because researchers become overly dependent on one class of measures or methods to examine their phenomena of interest. In one sense, the experimental method's triumph in contemporary psychology carries an unfortunate side effect—alternative methodologies are rarely considered. Unobtrusive measures are no better or worse than any other social science measures, but they do offer a means—in combination with other similar and not so similar approaches—to approximate the true state of things. In other words, establishing a result with different, complementary measures is a more convincing way to support an argument than relying on any single approach, no matter how good it might be (Campbell & Fiske, 1959; Webb et al., 1981).

I hope the lesson here is clear: If possible, feasible, and useful to your purpose, consider employing more than one type of measure in your research projects. To give you an opportunity to think more about unobtrusive measures, table 2.1 displays a variety of physical trace measures and the variables they are meant to approximate. The list shown in table 2.1 is by no means an exhaustive one; other examples can be found in Webb et al (1981) and, with a bit of ingenuity on your part, in your current situation. As you can see, some space is left in the table for you to write in your own physical trace examples and the variables with which they are conceptually linked.

Case Studies

Case studies are intensive, detailed histories of people's lives or descriptive accounts of important aspects therein. In the minds of many people

TABLE 2.1

SAMPLE VARIABLES AND EXAMPLES OF PHYSICAL TRACE MEASURES THAT APPROXIMATE THEM

Variables	Physical Traces
Erosion	
popularity of library books	wear of covers, pages
popularity of museum exhibit	wear of flooring (e.g., tile)
children's activity levels	rate that shoes wear out
food intake	weight of food before and after meal
safety habits	wear of seat and shoulder belts
other _____	_____
other _____	_____
Accretion	
affluence	length of discarded cigarette butts
social, political, sexual attitudes	graffiti in restrooms
wastefulness or frugality	contents of garbage
alcohol consumption	contents of garbage or recycling
popularity of a museum exhibit	finger/nose-prints on display cases
musical tastes/listener preferences	radio dial settings in vehicles
other _____	_____
other _____	_____

Source: Adapted from Webb et al., 1981.

who are not in the field, the case study personifies (or should personify) research in psychology. Why? Because the image of Sigmund Freud and subsequent generations of clinical psychologists of various orientations doing therapy with individual clients is a powerful one. As you know, however, the contemporary reality of academic psychology is very different from this image. Relatively few research psychologists work in the case study tradition because most are concerned with the commonalties, not idiosyncracies, of human experience. Nonetheless, the case study tradition continues to be a rich source of ideas in clinical psychology, personality, medicine, and even biological psychology (e.g., the study of brain and behavior relationships).

Similar to other qualitative approaches, case studies (sometimes referred to as *case histories*) are often dependent on interview data, though observational and archival (see following discussions) materials are sometimes used as well. A case study is often the only research option available when you are trying to understand the experience of one person, particularly if the individual in question exhibits some rare or unusual characteristic.

Ericsson, Chase, and Faloon (1980), for example, described the case of "S. F.," an undergraduate participant in an extended memory experiment. In 3 to 5 hourly sessions each week over 1½ years, S. F. was read sequences of random digits (e.g., 4-6-2-1) at the rate of 1 per second. His task was to recall correct sequences of numbers, and, when he succeeded, he heard another list that was 1 digit longer than the previous list. Across 230 hours of hearing and repeating digit sequences, S. F.'s memory span for digits increased from a typical 7 to an unheard of 79 digits! S. F., a skilled long-distance runner, converted the number strings into running times, a mnemonic feat enabling him to organize and store the digits into meaningful units in memory—but his memory span per se did not change (see Ericsson, Chase, & Faloon for a discussion of the implications of this work for understanding the capacity of short-term memory and the effects of practice). Such mnemonic skill is extremely rare and worthy of study as a unique case (for a related example, see Luria, 1968).

Case studies are also a rich source of ideas when little is known about an area of inquiry. The ascendance of psychoanalysis in the late 19th and early 20th centuries, for example, can be traced back to the rigorous use of case histories to unravel, understand, and deal with psychological dysfunction. Historically, the first recorded use of the "talking cure" (later termed "free association") of psychoanalysis is in the famous case history of Anna O. (Gay, 1989). Although the case was Josef Breuer's, Freud, not his colleague, was responsible for drawing clinical insight from Anna O.'s hysteria. Other famous cases followed, including the "Rat Man" and the "Wolf Man," as well as the host of specimen dreams in *The Interpretation of Dreams* (Freud, 1900/1965) and in other of Freud's publications (see Gay, 1989).

To Freud, his cases, the patients' comments and their dreams, were scientific data and the analytic hour comprised both a laboratory of sorts and a reliable method of investigation (Leahey, 1997; Malcolm, 1982). A variety of debates and developments in psychology have cast doubt on such views, and the status of psychoanalysis as a science—Freud's most ardent desire—is questionable (Leahey, 1997; Masson, 1985). Nonetheless, clinical case studies remain an important source of new knowledge, touchstones for established techniques, and guides for future direction in much of the therapeutic work done in psychiatry and in clinical and counseling psychology.

Not all case studies are used to portray clinical pathology, however. At least one large scale study—The Grant Study of Adult Development—was designed to counter the focus on maladaptive behavior. The Grant Study followed a select group of healthy, bright undergraduate men longitudinally. For over 40 years, 268 recruits from Harvard University's classes of 1939 to 1942 participated in interviews and answered surveys about their lives, loves, work, and general adaptation to stress. The sheer amount and diversity of the information collected across this length of time qualifies the Grant Study as a unique psychological archive (see subsequent discussion of archival research) of almost 300 cases.

George Vaillant, the psychiatrist most recently in charge of the Grant Study data, examined how the men used a variety of adaptive mechanisms and psychological defenses to cope with the ups and downs of everyday life (Vaillant, 1995a; 1995b). These individual differences in coping were examined through representative cases from the Grant Study (e.g., How does a once optimistic eighteen-year-old fare when his marriage collapses 30 years later? Why do some individuals fail to use their innate talents, whereas others exceed their natural abilities?). The importance of Vaillant's approach is that his case studies are not time-bound snapshots; rather, this longitudinal perspective—where the same people are studied over time—shows how some defenses can be helpful at one time and problematic at another. The biographies of the Grant Study's protagonists provide an important context for illustrating coping mechanisms, while reminding readers and researchers alike that case studies make theoretical concepts come alive in ways that standard experimental research cannot.

More recently, one variant of case study research has taken on an even more autobiographical flavor. Dan McAdams (e.g., 1985; 1993), a personality researcher, advances a narrative approach emphasizing autobiography, as well as social roles, culture, and self-perspectives on identity development. McAdams argues that people derive meaning and order in their lives by essentially telling stories *about* themselves to others and *to themselves.* We all use these personal myths to navigate through the experience of living. McAdams and his colleagues examined both individual and shared aspects of personal myths through the judicious use of both open-ended and structured interviewing techniques. McAdams's autobiographical narratives are untraditional case studies that extend this research approach into new areas that meld personal truth with fiction (see also, Dunn, 1997).

Case studies are also used to portray particular clinical disorders, medical knowledge, and, occasionally, the experience of daily living. The neurologist, Oliver Sacks, wrote a series of "clinical tales" on neurological disorders that comprise a famous book called *The Man Who Mistook His Wife For A Hat* (Sacks, 1985). A distinguished surgeon has recently written about the most common ways that people die by using illustrative patient cases showing the strength and limits of modern medicine (Nuland, 1993). Finally, some intrepid psychologists have conducted case studies illuminating common events in uncommon ways, such as recording every event in life of one child for one day (Barker & Wright, 1951) or positing personality traits through letters written by one person over many years (Allport, 1965).

Archival Research

Archival research involves the use of preexisting data that were probably collected for another purpose. An *archive* is any place where records or documents are maintained, and the term can refer to a formal place that stores information (e.g., The National Archives in Washington, D.C.) or an informal repository (e.g., the professor teaching your class might keep grade books from years past). Archival research involves the systematic examination and interpretation of existing records or documents in order to answer some question. Psychologists and other social scientists use a variety of archival resources in their research, including newspapers, census data, court records, telephone logs, medical records, videotapes of television programming, clinical case files, hospital or medical records, accident reports, crime statistics, college or university graduation records, phone books—anything that can provide information that can be subjected to some interpretive framework. Researchers hope that archival information is both objective and unbiased; however, they must be vigilant against bias in the form of missing data, erroneous entries, or the subjective perceptions of record keepers.

A very interesting set of archival studies was done by Craig Anderson and his colleagues (Anderson, 1989; Anderson & Anderson, 1984; Carlsmith & Anderson, 1979), who examined the purported link between heat and aggression through newspaper accounts and weather reports. Comparing records of outdoor temperature and riot incidents, for example, Carlsmith and Anderson (1979) found that between the years 1967 and 1971, the likelihood that a riot occurred on a given day increased in the presence of higher temperatures. Similarly, Anderson and Anderson (1984) found that when it is hot in Houston, the number of murders and rapes tends to accelerate rapidly.

Can archival records lead us to conclude that heat leads to aggression? First, archival records are silent on the issue of cause and effect. It is up to the investigator to critically evaluate the available information and develop a plausible account of its implications. Second, similar to correlational results, archival data frequently point to but do not directly identify causal culprits—as was noted in chapter 1, correlation does not imply causation. In the case of hot weather and aggression, it is true that hotter days have more violent crimes, as do hotter seasons and warmer summers (see Anderson, 1989), but it is also true that more people tend to be outdoors in such weather. If more people are outdoors, then various group influences may come into play so that the heat-aggression link is by no means definitively shown by archival results. The appropriate recourse is to head to the laboratory, where any link between heat and aggression can be experimentally demonstrated (e.g., Griffitt & Veitch, 1971).

Occasionally, archival research can be used in tandem with other research approaches. Peterson, Seligman, and Vaillant (1988) used a variation of *content analysis,* a method of categorizing the content and frequency of communications, on a sample of participants from the aforementioned Grant Study of Adult Development. These researchers were interested in showing that pessimistic explanatory style (Peterson & Seligman, 1984), the habitual way people explain bad events, could be coded from open-ended questionnaires completed between 1942 and 1944. Peterson, Seligman, and Vaillant found that sample members who believed that bad events were caused by stable, global, and internal factors were more likely to have poor health at ages 45 through 60 than those with more positive outlooks.

The application of content analysis to other archival sources has proven to be quite revealing, allowing history, records, and personality to constructively meet. Zullow and Seligman (1990), for example, found that presidential candidates who were pessimistic ruminators (i.e., apt to dwell on negative thoughts) in their party's nomination acceptance speeches lost 9 out of 10 times between 1948 and 1984, and that the margin of electoral victory was proportional to the difference between candidates in pessimistic rumination. A primary mechanism underlying a candidate's loss may be passivity. Using other archival data, Zullow and Seligman found that pessimistic ruminators made fewer "whistle stops" per day on the campaign trail as the election drew near.

Even Freud has not escaped archival scrutiny. Peterson (see Peterson & Bossio, 1991) examined Freud's voluminous personal correspondence, finding that an increasingly pessimistic style emerged in his letters across time. Indeed, his letters reveal that he increasingly attributed bad events to his mounting age. This pattern dovetails with his later scholarly works, which are known to be dark, even fatalistic, in their tone, for example, *Civilization and Its Discontents* (Freud, 1930/1961). As Freud grew older, his fame and influence grew but he was beset by a series of personal tragedies, including cancer of the mouth, the death of two sons in World War I, and the public burning of his books by the Nazis (Gay, 1988). Ironically, Freud the scientist may have fallen prey to an all too human foible—he confused changes wrought by age with external events (Peterson & Bossio, 1991).

Clearly, archival research provides psychologists with an opportunity to mine riches from resources that may otherwise lie dormant or untouched. Both public and private records can be examined in new ways. The onus of responsibility is upon the researcher, however, to conceive of an interesting question, support it with both archival and nonarchival evidence, and then convince the scientific community that the obtained results are sound.

Questionnaire Research

Research using questionnaires or surveys is based on a fundamental, if self-evident, premise: If you want to know what people think, do, or believe to be true, why not simply ask them? Across our lives, we have all answered questionnaires in a variety of settings. Your applications to college were probably in a questionnaire format, as were any accompanying financial aid forms. When you buy a new product, whether it is a toaster or a car, there is typically a warranty form that contains questions about your income and lifestyle. Both colleges and manufacturers want to know something about you, though for somewhat different reasons, and yet both choose the questionnaire format as the easiest way to obtain the information that they need.

Questionnaires are comprised of a series of questions that usually pertain to the same issue or set of issues. These questions can be read and subsequently answered (usually in writing) by respondents. Alternatively, the questions can be asked in an interview format, which allows a respondent to speak while the interviewer somehow records his or her answers.

Beyond the goal of finding out people's reactions to some person, place, or thing, questionnaire studies are usually conducted to determine the beliefs of a *population*, or all members of a particular group. Of course, it is rarely practical to survey every member of a population—imagine trying to ask every dorm resident a question pertaining to college life, let alone polling all taxpayers in a state the size of Oregon about proposed changes in the tax code.

How can the opinion of a population be approximated with a reasonable degree of confidence? By using one of several possible sampling procedures. A *sample* is a group of observations drawn from a larger population. Such observations are not necessarily representative of—that is, reflect the characteristics of—that larger population. In social science research, the most common method is random sampling, a technique introduced in chapter 1. A *random sample* is an attempt to ensure that every member of a population has the same likelihood of being chosen as every other member (techniques for randomization are presented in chapter 6). This powerful methodological tool reduces the likelihood that potential biases are present in a sample, thereby increasing confidence in any results.

What sorts of potential biases create concern? Any nonrandom or systematic influence that affects the composition of a sample and the subsequent inferences a researcher makes about it and its parent population. For example, if you were studying the attitudes of health professionals toward recent changes in health care costs and delivery, a sample would be potentially biased if *only* the opinions of doctors were solicited. What about other health professionals, including nurses, nurses aids, medical students and residents, medical researchers, hospital administrators, and insurance industry representatives? Surely, a more representative profile of opinion regarding current health care would include people from these—and no doubt other—groups in the population from which a random sample was drawn. The main point is this: When an adequate random sample is obtained, the results can be used to infer general characteristics (e.g., majority opinions, experiences, beliefs) of the larger population.

A second method is *stratified sampling*, where particular subpopulations (or "strata") within a population are identified. For example, if you wanted to know students' opinions on alcohol use at your college or university, you might treat the first-year, sophomore, junior, and senior classes as discrete strata. Why would stratification matter here? Keep in mind that most undergraduate schools experience attrition across each class; thus, an entering class of 400 first-year students is somewhat smaller, say 330, at graduation four years later. Using lists of the current first-year through seniors classes, you could randomly sample an appropriate number of observations (e.g., 10 percent) from each one. Of course, within each of these classes, you might also want to take into account gender, race, ethnicity, and whatever other co-occurring strata seem to be relevant to the questions you are addressing or to the population you are studying.

In practice, much psychological questionnaire research conducted in college settings relies upon what is called *haphazard* or *convenience* sampling. Researchers literally hand out questionnaires to whoever happens by or is conveniently available to fill one out. The advantage of convenience sampling is clear the researcher quickly gets some data to work with. The disadvantage is equally clear in that the lack of randomization means the researcher has reduced confidence in the representativeness or generalizability of the questionnaire's results: You know some student opinions, but not whether they accurately reflect the opinion of the entire student population.

Drawing accurate inferences about the beliefs of a population, then, is somewhat problematic if randomization is not used. On the other hand, the practical benefits of gaining experience doing a questionnaire study should not be overlooked. Indeed, many students choose to conduct a questionnaire study as their first research project in psychology. If you cannot obtain a random sample but you choose to proceed with the research anyway, be sure to acknowledge this shortcoming in the study's execution, and discuss its impact on the interpretation and reliability of the results. We will revisit questionnaire and survey research in more detail later in chapter 7.

Experimental Research and Applied Research in Brief

Experimental research, which was introduced in chapter 1, relies on experimental methodology and control to generate new knowledge about psychological topics. You may recall that experimental research emphasizes the search for cause and effect relations. In general, research participants are assigned to one of two or more groups and then exposed to a treatment condition (i.e., a level of a manipulated independent variable). Subsequent to this treatment, the participants react to some dependent measure so that any resulting between-group differences can be statistically analyzed and interpreted.

Applied research grew out of the experimental approach in that the latter's methodology was adapted to deal with the lack of control over causal events found in real world settings. Some applied research is experimental. Much of it, however, relies on quasi-experimental designs because researchers do not have the ability to randomly assign participants to groups or to eliminate the effects of influential variables that may be present. Immediate social problems, chronic societal concerns, and any issue that does not lend itself to manipulation and measurement—that is, where cause and effect cannot be easily identified—fall under the heading of applied research (Hedrick, Bickman, & Rog, 1993). When studying the effects of unemployment on marital satisfaction, for example, a researcher cannot assign individuals to an unemployed group or to an employed comparison group. Other applied research

BOX FEATURE 2.A

A Research Digression: *Caveat Emptor:* Method Can Drive Results

The phrase *caveat emptor* is Latin for "let the buyer beware," and these are words of wise counsel for research consumers. Consider this: I recently came across a new book touting the availability of free time in contemporary American culture. In *Time for Life* (Robinson & Godbey, 1997), two time management experts argue that in addition to the typical 40-hour work week, Americans are also enjoying an average of almost 40 additional hours of leisure time a week! On the average, moreover, leisure time has actually *increased* almost 5 extra hours since 1965. How can this be? Well, consider their observation that the average American watches 15 hours of television a week and another 4.4 hours talking on the phone—perhaps bits of time here and there do add up (Raphael, 1997).

Yet, these findings are controversial because they challenge the subjective experience of many Americans, particularly women, who will readily tell you that they feel overworked, stressed, and always on the go. *Time for Life* also challenges the assertions made by two well-known and authoritative studies dealing with time, work, leisure, and family issues. Previously, sociologist Arlie Hochschild (1990; see also, 1997) concluded that American women essentially begin a second shift of work *after* work; that is, household demands and childcare pick up where career pressures leave off each day. Similarly, careful scrutiny of labor statistics led economist Juliet Schor (1991) to suggest that Americans are overworked, that we have collectively experienced unexpected declines in leisure during the same period where Robinson and Godbey see an increase (for a related discussion of work issues, see Wolfe, 1997). Again, how can this be?

One clue may be the research approach used by these respective researchers. John Robinson and Geoffrey Godbey (1997) relied on detailed hour-by-hour activity diaries kept by their research participants. In contrast, Schor (1991) used a variety of governmental labor statistics and demographic data. Hochschild (1990, 1997), in turn, employed a mix of questionnaires and intense naturalistic observations to draw her conclusions. Each of these research methods has distinct advantages and disadvantages; "right" or "wrong" depends on the issue as well as the point of view. No doubt these and other researchers are now trying to understand the discrepancies among these three studies. As a consumer of—and potential contributor to—the research enterprise, you must always evaluate a research approach on its own merits, especially its potential to answer the main question of interest.

takes basic, fundamental relations identified in controlled experimental contexts and extends them by studying their effects in less controlled settings (e.g., knowledge about the characteristics of attention deficit disorders is used to create educational interventions).

We will consider both experimental and applied approaches, as well as field research, in detail later in this book, but for the present one other issue remains: Should we draw a distinction between "basic" and "applied" research? This distinction is often played out as "knowledge for knowledge's sake" versus "knowledge for purpose" (please note that this distinction is *not* the same as that between experimental and quasi-experimental research). More than that, however, the distinction

TABLE 2.2

COMPARING BASIC AND APPLIED RESEARCH

Basic	Applied
Develop universal knowledge	Understand/address problems
Answer single questions	Answer multiple questions
Discover statistically significant relationships or effects	Discover practically significant relationships or effects

Source: Adapted from Bickman, 1981, and Hedrick, Bickman, and Rog, 1993.

often seems to be an artificial one, although some researchers have compared the purposes of these two types of research (e.g., Bickman, 1981). Table 2.2 outlines the major differences between basic and applied approaches, which will be discussed in detail in chapters 6 and 7, respectively. The best advice regarding this distinction is given by Salkind (1997), however, who suggests that we avoid evaluating research by worrying about its basic or applied nature. Instead, we should examine each piece of research closely and judge it on its own merits.

Figure 2.1 summarizes the research approaches we have just reviewed. You will notice that the approaches are arranged on a continuum highlighting qualitative and quantitative distinctions, open versus closed systems, the presence or absence of control over the research, and whether causal conclusions can be reached. Keep in mind that this collection of research approaches is selective and that many other useful, interesting ways to study behavior exist. Nonetheless, these approaches represent a good starting point as you begin to generate research ideas.

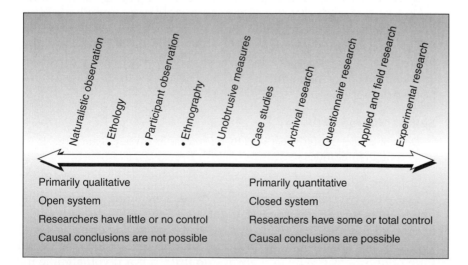

FIGURE 2.1
A Continuum of Research Approaches and Their Qualities.

GENERATING RESEARCH IDEAS

In my teaching experience, students are usually not afraid of *doing* a research project but they are often fearful that they will be unable to come up with a good topic. In fact, each time I teach research methods, about one third of the students come to me to express concern about whether their project ideas are worth doing. Many of these students abandon their ideas before we meet and subsequently plead with me to assign them a topic instead. I always courteously decline to do so.

Why? For the simple reason that setting your own course in research is crucial. After all, what interests one person may not interest another, so, where possible, the first project you do from beginning to end should deal with questions that appeal to you. Exercising simple choice provides a profound sense of control (Dunn & Wilson, 1990; Langer, 1975), so you should avoid embarking on a research project unless you have a hand in shaping it from the start (if you join a project that is already underway, perhaps you can make a contribution in its later stages). Your heart as well as your mind must be behind any project you work on. Indeed, you must be committed to a project and act responsibly whether you work alone or with a research team (recall the discussion concerning collaboration in chapter 1).

If you already have an interesting topic for a psychological research project, then you are fortunate indeed. Nonetheless, I hope that the following discussion will still help tighten up your reasoning or allow you to consider other points of view as you undertake your research. On the other hand, if you are undecided and still searching for a topic or considering an array of possibilities, then the following strategies will suggest places to look for inspiration or to help you generate ideas. We will examine four readily available sources of research ideas—you, your situation, paradoxes, and existing knowledge—by focusing on illustrative, not exhaustive, examples (for a discussion on creative hypothesis generation in psychology, see McGuire, 1997). After these sources are reviewed, three exercises promoting idea generation—two for individuals and one for research teams—will be introduced. Following these exercises, recommendations for obtaining useful peer feedback through research critiques are presented.

Self As Source of Ideas

> Do I contradict myself? Very well then I contradict myself. (I am large, I
>   contain multitudes.)
>
> —Walt Whitman (1891/1921) *Song of Myself*

Every day, you spend a great deal of time engaging in introspection, that is, reflecting on your own thoughts and feelings. Like Whitman, you contain multitudes, and your private reactions to the ebb and flow of everyday life are actually quite rich. Many of your reflections take the form of questions ("Why do I always do *that?*"), but if you are like most people, you probably don't bother to articulate them, write them down, or discuss them with anyone. You may not realize it, but your thoughts, hopes, fears, dreams, and experiences are excellent sources of research ideas. You need to frame them the way psychologists do, of course, and in the process polish them until they are appropriate research topics.

Naturally, I cannot tell you which of your experiences or thoughts, once refined, will make a good project topic. The choice, and what you do with it, is up to you. I can, however, provide some examples and hope that they serve as useful guides to spur you to identify others and to think creatively about your work. Let's begin.

If you could change something about yourself, what would it be? You may have a bad habit you would like to break (e.g., procrastination) or a good habit you would like to increase (e.g., regular exercise). Either of these habits is a fine springboard to a project on individual behavior modification (see, for example, Martin & Pear, 1996). Alternatively, consider how shared habits influence the behavior of your peers (How many continually procrastinate on their school work, why, and with what effect? Why do most people have a difficult time maintaining an exercise or diet regimen for even a short period of time?).

In a somewhat related vein, you could generate a project idea by using a technique called "bug listing." Bug listing was originally developed as a way for inventors to think of promising problems to solve (Adams, 1974; see also, Hayes, 1981). The premise is simple: You make a list of everyday things that bother you (e.g., remembering to mail letters, taking out trash, fastening seatbelts, turning off lights, saving energy, keeping track of money, etc.). If the items on the list bug you, there is a good chance that they bug other people as well—so, if you were an inveterate inventor, you could invent a contraption to solve a problem and simultaneously find a market niche with relative ease.

Modifying the bug listing task with research possibilities in mind is a snap. Think about the common bugs that you (and others) experience in everyday life, write them down (because they are so common, bugs can easily be forgotten), and then see if any could be modified into an interesting psychology project. For example, if you identified "keeping track of time" as a bug, you might consider doing a project examining why many people are chronically late despite the fact that clocks, watches, and other timepieces are ubiquitous in our experience. Why are so many people poor at being on time, maintaining schedules, and so on?

Interpersonal relations are also a good source of research ideas. Reflect on your relationships with your friends or roommates over the last week or two. Were there any conflicts? If so, were these predictable disagreements, possibly erupting over minor, even laughable circumstances (e.g., neglected promises, a noisy stereo, minor but unpaid debts)? They may seem so in retrospect but not in the heat of the moment when passion and reason sometimes collide. Look to social groups for ideas, as well. Do you belong to a club, social organization (e.g., fraternity, sorority, athletic team), or even a tightly knit group of friends that occasionally requires a certain level of public allegiance with which you privately disagree? Perhaps you are tired of attending obligatory but endless meetings or drunken revels. What keeps you (and others) from speaking out or staying home? Is it conformity, respect, or something else that motivates you and others to cooperate with attitudes or actions you might not otherwise condone?

Still another possibility is to examine the ways that you present yourself to other people. In other words, take a look at the various methods you use to manage the impressions that you convey to other people. Self-presentation is a term that covers a wide range of behaviors designed to create positive impressions of ourselves in the mind of others (Schlenker & Weigold, 1992). We all project images of ourselves to others, assess their reactions, and then adjust our subsequent actions accordingly. You might examine why you—and indeed, most people—worry about what others think (e.g., self-esteem needs) or you could examine a particular way individuals manage impressions (e.g., facial expression, eye contact, speech).

Happenstance

What thought provoking events or materials have you chanced upon lately? Instead of looking to your ongoing thoughts for topic possibilities, look to your immediate situation for ideas. What are some of the current hot topics on your college or university campus? Current controversies or public disagreements are often a very good source for budding research projects. Take a few minutes and scan the student newspaper for breaking stories or keep your ear to the ground for the latest gossip. Perhaps your institution is raising tuition, changing admissions standards, or revamping its alcohol or drug policy by stiffening its penalties. Any one of these campus issues is ripe for a survey of student, faculty, and administration attitudes.

Male and female relationships always provide material for more than idle speculation. Think about gender relations among the students on your campus. Do males and females expect and receive equal treatment in some campus settings but not in others? How have dating rituals changed? Are blatant examples of sexism tolerated or challenged? Many campuses are more successful than others at recognizing gender inequality and rectifying it. If your campus is lagging behind in this regard, then consider studying the problem and creating some intervention to heighten awareness, if not to promote change.

On the other hand, why does popular opinion often contradict campus history or even factual evidence? Some groups on your campus may feel that too much has been done to advance the interest of women (and possibly other minority groups) both in and outside of the classroom. Why do some individuals believe that these historically underprivileged groups have already "arrived" and therefore deserve no special consideration? A very interesting study might be conducted to assess the origins and implications of such perceptions at your school.

Cast an even wider net for ideas by reading current articles in newspapers or magazines. A variety of political, ethical, and moral issues should not invite only heated commentary, but the much needed clarity that a scientific approach can provide. We have all had the experience of being bombarded with information, arguments, or attitudes we find questionable, if not objectionable, but we lack the tools necessary to refute them. Knowledge is power, and several content areas are entirely appropriate for psychological inquiry. Topics easily gleaned from any newspaper or periodical include affirmative action, prejudice and stereotyping, discrimination, racism, and sexual preference.

As I write this chapter, a study done by the Population Reference Bureau, an independent nonprofit research organization, appeared in the local newspaper (Keil, 1996). The article debunks several popular but erroneous myths about Americans on welfare. In brief, the study found that most welfare recipients are white, live in rural and suburban areas, and that a third of them pull themselves out of poverty within 12 months. Contrast these pallid facts with the widely shared belief that most welfare recipients are minorities living in cities who receive public aid for many years—in short, people who are "taking advantage of the system." Will this undeniable but favorable evidence change people's beliefs? Probably not, but you could use this sort of newspaper story to construct an interesting piece of research on stereotyping, belief perseverance, and related phenomena (see, for example, Hamill, Wilson, & Nisbett, 1980; Nisbett & Ross, 1980).

Finally, take a walk around campus or your neighborhood and observe what you see. Martin (1996) advocates that one way to come up with research ideas is to go outside, take a good look around, and start to speculate. In the course of a ten-minute or so walk, for example, he identified nine potential project ideas. These projects range from the influence of the weather ("Do people work more or less when the weather is nice?") to bicycling ("Are mountain bikes easier to ride than road bikes?") (Martin, 1996)! Granted, not everything you see will lend itself to a good piece of psychological research, but getting out and about will get you started.

Paradoxical Events

People love paradoxes. A paradox is any situation that appears to contradict established beliefs or expectations. Paradoxes are attractive to us because they are puzzles that are often accompanied by a jolt of self-recognition. Many times, paradoxes conflict with common sense, although upon closer examination they may actually contain a kernel of truth. Indeed, it is often the case that two contradictory ideas each describe a true state of affairs but within particular boundaries.

Consider folk wisdom. Superficially, for example, the two popular proverbs "absence makes the heart grow fonder" and "out of sight, out of mind" are at odds with one another. Yet both experience and reason tell us that sometimes one is right, sometimes the other—it all depends. I am not suggesting that you run out and examine what people think about proverbial wisdom, though it has been done (Murphy, 1990), but you could look at situations where standard cultural beliefs are invoked. What would it mean for a psychology of folk wisdom if expectation rarely or only selectively meets reality?

Behavioral expectations that are paradoxical can also be studied in the context of attitude and behavior consistency, a classic topic from social psychology. An attitude is the tendency to evaluate some entity—a person, place, thing, concept—either favorably or unfavorably (e.g., Eagly & Chaiken, 1993). It follows that the strength of an attitude should predict a behavioral response; if you like someone, then you should spend more time with that person than with another whom you dislike, and so on. Experience teaches a different and paradoxical lesson about some attitudes, however. We rarely report spending enough quality time with close friends or family, but seem to spend all too much time with acquaintances, co-workers, and the relative strangers who populate our busy lives.

Cultural examples of the attitude-behavior breakdown in everyday life are equally illustrative, as a classic review by Wicker (1969) reveals. Belief in God and religion, for instance, was only modestly linked with participation in worship services. In other words, favorable attitudes were not highly predictive of church attendance on any given Sunday, or "the spirit is willing but the flesh is weak." Even more sobering, attitudes that students held toward cheating had little influence over whether they actually did cheat when the opportunity presented itself.

What about a well-defined situation like deciding whom to vote for? Many members of the American electorate believe that they carefully evaluate all relevant information about political issues, yet voting decisions are only infrequently based on such analyses. Instead, most voters rely on their own party affiliation—as Republicans or Democrats—when they find themselves alone in the voting booth (Campbell, Converse, Miller, & Stokes, 1964; but see Nie, Verba, & Petrocik, 1979). It is only when voters have considerable information about their choices that they are apt to defect from their own party and vote for a candidate from the other party (e.g., Burns, Peltason, Cronin, & Magleby, 1994). Thus, attitudes that people of voting age often maintain, such as "issues matter to me a great deal," are not necessarily the driving force behind their actions.

With minimal effort, then, we can identify a variety of situations where desire and motivation do not meet, and a paradoxical state of affairs results. There is no doubt that you, too, can meaningfully add to the list of attitudinal paradoxes by looking to important issues that affect college students on your own and other campuses. Concern about sexually transmitted diseases, notably HIV and AIDS, is unfortunately laden with paradoxical overtones. As a group, students are aware of the risk of HIV infection if they do not practice safe sex and yet many routinely engage in unprotected intercourse. A possible explanation is that a global sense of invulnerability is so ubiquitous in college populations that sexual knowledge and behavior do not predict one another. To explore this possibility, you could design a project to study the paradox among a group of students and then subsequently "inoculate" some of them by educating them about the potentially dire consequences of harboring beliefs about one's own invulnerability.

Beyond folk wisdom and attitude-behavior consistency, there are other paradoxes in everyday life. Consider the relatively liberal social beliefs espoused by most college students where issues of race, religion, or ethnicity are concerned. Many college students are against, even justly outraged by, blatant acts of racism or other forms of bigotry. Yet many of these same students are willing to both tell and laugh about off-color jokes about these same topics in private. Are the people who tell such jokes racists or bigots? If not, how do we explain an individual's apparent willingness to perpetuate negative stereotypes about others by repeating such jokes? Moreover, why do so many listeners laugh at these unfortunate jokes instead of becoming upset by them? Such paradoxes pose a series of interesting questions worthy of exploration in a psychology project.

Building Upon Previous Research

By building upon previous research, I mean selecting a topic from the psychological literature that has generated a good deal of scholarly interest. In other words, many investigators have seen fit to research, write, and publish on the same topic because it possesses either a timeless quality (e.g., the nature of human consciousness) (Freud, 1900/1965; James, 1890/1950; Cohen & Schooler, 1997; Searle, 1990; Wundt, 1873/1904) or advances a relatively novel line of inquiry (e.g., suppressing unwanted thoughts) (Wegner, 1989). The formal use of the psychological literature is discussed in detail in chapter 4, but a brief mention of strategies for topic selection besides a literature search is appropriate here. In keeping with the theme of this section of the chapter, these strategies involve being practical by taking a quick look around for ideas.

First, read your psychology texts carefully and thoughtfully. Any good psychology text you encounter, whether it is introductory or intermediate, will outline the current issues of interest to the field. If a topic from introductory psychology interested you once upon a time, here is an opportunity to explore it further. If there is a subject area within one of the core areas of psychology that has always excited you, then by all means skim a relevant text or two with an eye to extending what is known. Alternatively, ask your friends or classmates if they have any textbooks from any intermediate psychology courses and, if so, borrow them and go on an intellectual scavenger hunt for ideas.

Second, listen carefully to your professors. During lectures or discussion, many of them will explicitly mention research topics that have received very little or even no research attention. When I teach, for example, I try to point out areas where little is known or where confusion reigns. Your professors are a rich resource of topical ideas, so you should ask questions about the extent of what is known about a topic in class or during their office hours. Doing a project that pushes the boundaries of knowledge further out is an exciting proposition. Similarly, introducing even a small degree of conceptual clarity to a challenging topical area is a real contribution.

Finally, if you have ever conducted a replication of a classic psychology experiment as either a demonstration or a laboratory exercise in another course, consider redoing it once more but by introducing some changes into the experimental procedure. The classic experiments I am referring to include Craik and Lockhart's (1972) levels of processing and memory research, the Sperling (1960) task on sensory storage, the Stroop (1935) effect on lexical interference, Asch's (1946) personality impression formation study, Shepard and Metzler's (1971) work on the mental rotation of three-dimensional objects, Miller's (1956) "magic number seven" paper on processing limitations in working memory, Darley and Latane's (1968) bystander intervention studies, Skinner's (1948) study of superstitious behavior in the pigeon, and Sternberg's (1967) serial versus parallel processing in memory experiment, among many, many other possibilities. Changes could include introducing new independent or dependent variables, altering the stimuli, or changing the experimental context from the laboratory to a field setting (or vice versa). If you elect to conduct this type of conceptual replication, you must develop a compelling rationale for introducing any changes to an existing paradigm and be enthusiastic about conducting the study. In other words, do not choose this option because it is the path of least resistance—pursue a research topic because you really care about it!

We now turn to three exercises that are useful for generating research topic ideas. Each exercise complements the others in some way, so you could try all three, or do one singly or in combination with another.

Exercise 2.A: *Keeping a Notebook of Research Ideas*

Now that we have discussed the process of discovery in science and reviewed four sources of potential projects, you need to begin to search for a topic in earnest. One easy way to begin to identify possible topics is by writing down ideas as they come to you. When I was an undergraduate and later a graduate student, I invariably came up with research or paper topics when I least expected to do so. Frequently, I would be sitting in class when an idea struck, so I developed the habit of writing these fledgling ideas down in the margins of my notebooks for later use. The following steps make my old approach less haphazard and better suited to developing good research topics from the outset.

Step One—Recording your ideas.   To record your thoughts about potential topics, obtain a small notebook or memo pad and begin to carry it with you wherever you go. Take it to class as well as meals, and by all means keep it by your bedside so that you can jot down stray thoughts in the middle of the night or when you wake up. Do *not* assume that if a good idea comes to you while you are without pen and paper that you will remember it later. You will not remember it—you will reconstruct it—and there is a good chance that what you recreate will be a pale shadow of the original. (Think about how many times you have vowed to write down important ideas and then forgotten to do so.)

You need not be overly conspicuous with your notebook, nor should you write down every fleeting thought. On the other hand, avoid engaging in too much self-censorship before you record ideas or you may find that you are not writing anything down. Keep the four sources of potential project topics—yourself, happenstance, paradoxes, and existing knowledge—in mind over the next few days. As ideas come to you, write down a few sentences or a short paragraph description for each one. After you have five or so ideas, go on to step two.

Step Two—Narrowing your scope.   This step involves ranking and refining the ideas you have collected, and then narrowing their scope. Review each of your ideas from the notebook and revise any, as needed, for clarity. Now, rank order your topic ideas from the one that most interests you to the one you want to know the least about. Starting with the topic that received the highest rank, evaluate its breadth. If the topic is too broad, then you will need to narrow its scope. How do you know if a topic is too broad? When a topic can be summarized in a handful of words rather than a relatively detailed sentence or two, it is probably too broad as a project topic.

To narrow a broad topic, you can add modifying words and phrases that change or extend the topic's meaning (Booth, Colomb, & Williams, 1995). Perhaps you are interested in personality and, in particular, which traits consistently seem to differentiate people from one another. Consider the trait labeled extroversion (e.g., Eysenck, 1976)—being lively, active, sociable, even impulsive—and a broad question emanating from it: How do extroverts differ from introverts, their shy counterparts? There are any number of meaningful ways to address this topic because no context is provided. One way to provide context is to relate the topic to your immediate experience, college life, and its emphasis on scholastic achievement. You could narrow your scope on extroversion by examining whether extroverts respond differently to achievement settings than do introverts.

Once you sufficiently narrow the first ranked topic idea, go on to the second one, narrow it down, and repeat the process with the remaining ideas from your notebook. When you are finished, look over the narrowed topics, pick the one you find most interesting, and go on to step three.

Step Three—Generating questions. After a topic is sufficiently narrow, back away from it for a moment and think about what questions are relevant to it. If you were going to study the reactions of extroverts and introverts to an achievement situation as part of an experiment, questions to consider could include the following:

- Are extroverts better or worse at achievement tasks than are introverts?
- How is extroversion measured in achievement settings?
- How should this personality trait affect performance on an achievement task?
- Do extroverts respond differently to some achievement tasks than do introverts? If so, which ones?

And so on. The goal here is to generate as many questions as possible, but *not* to answer them just yet. Answering questions comes later, when you do a literature review and plan an experiment. Before committing to these two forms of answering, you will first want to look at your topic from as many perspectives as possible, and developing focused questions is a good way to begin this process. Writing down obvious and less obvious questions about a now narrow topic allows you to explore it, as well as to identify what you do not yet know but feel that you must find out by doing research (Booth et al., 1995).

Coming up with questions will also help you to determine whether there is enough material here to keep you interested in the topic. If your interest remains high, then you have found a reasonable project topic. If not, then you should go back up to the next highest ranked idea (from step 2) and repeat the step 3 process of question generation. The step-by-step process of generating and narrowing down project ideas from a notebook is outlined in figure 2.2. It is important to repeat these steps as many times as necessary until a good topic and a satisfactory set of questions are identified.

Exercise 2.B: *Freewriting to Generate and Refine Ideas*

Writing teachers have developed some tried and true techniques that help to jump start the idea process. One of the most versatile and popular techniques is *freewriting*, a private, continuous form of writing where a writer puts down on paper whatever comes to mind (Elbow & Belanoff, 1995; see also, Williams & Brydon-Miller, 1997). Although freewriting was originally used in expository writing classes, it has proven to be an effective tool for writing in psychology courses as well (Dunn, 1994).

The directions for freewriting are easy to follow: Simply write for 10 minutes or so without lifting your pen from the paper. During this time, put down whatever thoughts come to mind regarding possible research topics (you can either start from scratch or freewrite about ideas from the notebook exercise). Don't worry if your initial ideas are bizarre or disjointed. The point is to be free with your writing and not to worry about grammar, punctuation, and spelling. Similarly, the

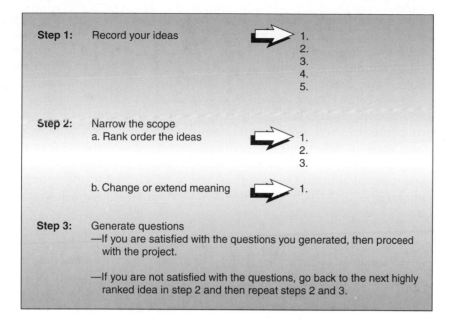

FIGURE 2.2
Generating and Narrowing Down Project Ideas from a Notebook.

usual concerns about style, neatness, paragraph structure, and so on, do not apply to freewriting—your only concern is to generate ideas.

I recommend that at this point you take a 10-minute break from reading this chapter and try out freewriting. Once again, take out a sheet or two of paper and a pen or a pencil. Alternatively, if you have a word processor, you can achieve the same ends by turning off the screen and typing in what ever comes to mind. If you have an alarm clock or some sort of timer handy, set it for 10 minutes. Now, sit at your desk or table and start writing (or typing) *without stopping until the time is up.* Do not censor your thoughts—anything, no matter how absurd or seemingly irrelevant, can and should be recorded. You may find yourself having nothing to say about potential topic ideas; if so, write about why you are lost for words, why you cannot think of a topic, and so on. Remember, this writing is for you and you alone to read, and there is no right or wrong way to do it. All you are trying to do is to develop an idea or two that can be used to create a research topic. When the time is up, continue reading the chapter.

Is the time up? How was your first shot at freewriting? It might have been a bit awkward at first, but if you are like most people it probably became easier to do after a few minutes. Now, take some time and read over what you wrote. Much of the prose may seem disjointed, but my guess is that you will find a passage or two in your writing that will be very clear. You may even be surprised to see how well you wrote about an idea. This is not to say that what you have come up with as an idea is anywhere near fully developed—quite the contrary. No doubt, your initial ideas—indeed, any ideas or writing begun through freewriting—will need to be explored more fully through additional trials of freewriting and by discussion with peers (see Critiquing Research Ideas, pp. 65–67). As you begin to formulate your ideas more specifically, it will also be necessary to rewrite them with grammar, spelling, and punctuation in mind, and to flesh them out in more detail.

If you cannot locate any ideas in your first try at freewriting that fit this description, take heart. With more practice, freewriting will become easier and you will become more comfortable with it, thereby allowing your ideas to flow more freely. In fact, because it does not take much time, I suggest that you practice freewriting once or twice a day until you have identified a satisfactory project topic. The use of and logic behind freewriting will be expanded in chapter 3, where we will discuss how it and related techniques can be used to write a project paper.

Exercise 2.C: *Brainstorming to Generate Project Ideas with Peers*
As fellow collaborators, peers can be an integral part of a research project when they collect data, run participants, write paper drafts, and so on (see chapter 1). They can also provide very useful feedback on your writing, and you can return the favor (chapter 3). All of these activities, however, presume that a project idea exists. If you and your research team have no topic yet, then you should consider using the following group activity to find one.

The process known as *brainstorming* can be a particularly effective way for a group of peers to generate ideas. Early on in the research process, brainstorming can "jump start" the search for a topic by pooling the ideas of a research team. Once a project is underway, *focused brainstorming* is a useful way to refine some aspect of an already selected research design, to identify related variables (called *covariates*) that covary or "change together" with those under study, or to pick out potentially confounded variables or rival hypotheses related to a topic.

As both term and technique, brainstorming was first used by an advertising executive named Alex Osborn (1948), who believed it was an effective way to increase the flow of bright ideas in small groups (Hayes, 1981). The real benefit of brainstorming is that members of a project group experience a positive form of social contagion (Osborn, 1948) where one individual's suggestion inspires another member to come forward with an even better idea, one that would not have occurred otherwise. As a result, brainstorming sessions can be riotous, creative settings where ideas fly fast and furiously.

How is brainstorming different than traditional forms of idea sharing in groups? Even in the most egalitarian groups, discussion is usually based on (1) airing a novel proposal and then (2) receiving criticism on it (Hayes, 1981). Although most of us are used to this approach—it is ubiquitous in family, social, educational, and work life—it is by no means ideal for coming up with new ideas or seeing established modes differently. In contrast, brainstorming offers an alternative to the usual way ideas are created or envisioned.

In the directions that follow (adapted from Hayes, 1981), I will assume that you are the member of a research team comprised of 2 to 6 people. If you are working alone, you may wish to consult the individual brainstorming section that follows this one. Alternatively, you could brainstorm with a group of peers who have no intentions of collaborating with one another. After all, if everyone is without project ideas, why not get together to develop a list of potential project topics that can be informally shared among you?

Step One: Brainstorming sessions have two phases—*idea generation* and *idea evaluation.* It is crucial for the research team to first generate a large number of potential ideas before beginning the process of winnowing them down to a more manageable (and reasonable) number. Thus, during the idea generation phase any and all criticism must be held back so that every group member feels free to offer ideas and to respond to those of others. Team members must learn to squelch comments like "Oh, come on, how are we ever going to be able to do that . . ." or "That's not only ridiculous, it's entirely too time consuming . . ."

Ideally, the topic of a brainstorming session should have some focus. Thus, it may not be particularly productive for some teams to sit down without some already determined topic. In other words, beginning a session by stating "So, what should we research?" is probably not an effective start. Instead, deciding upon either a general topical area (e.g., personality psychology) or a specific issue (e.g., factors that predict leadership ability) in advance is more helpful. A good idea might be to begin by reviewing each team member's research idea notebook (see Exercise 2.A) either before or after an individual's entries are narrowed. Similarly, if you are doing focused brainstorming after a topic is decided, say, to refine methods or explore alternative hypotheses, the team must be kept focused on the task.

For the idea generation phase to be particularly effective, two roles in a brainstorming group must be assigned: a *leader* and a *recorder.* The leader's role is simply to enforce the basic rules of brainstorming, which should be quickly reviewed out loud before each session. These rules are summarized in table 2.3, which can be used as a reference guide during a session. As you can see, the leader's role is to create and maintain an environment where people can exchange ideas freely. If anyone begins to criticize or "nay say" any points offered, it is the leader's responsibility to gently remind that individual of step one's "no criticism" ground rules.

As you might guess, the recorder's role is to write down any and all comments or suggestions generated by members of the group. Whenever possible, group members' comments should be recorded verbatim by the recorder, as shorthand summaries can unintentionally change meanings, shift emphasis, or otherwise alter a contributor's point of view. Similar to the leader, then, the recorder's role is one of idea facilitation, not interpretation.

TABLE 2.3

RULES FOR TEAM PROJECT BRAINSTORMING SESSIONS

1. No idea is criticized until the evaluation phase (step 2).
2. Wild, silly, even implausible, ideas are encouraged.
3. Generate as many ideas as possible (if idea generation slows, revisit those already proposed).
4. Encourage team members to combine, extend, and improve on any ideas already on the table (but keep rule 1 in mind).
5. The team acts as a whole, not as individuals or smaller groups.
6. *Optional:* Use turn taking, a helpful way to ensure that everyone contributes.

Source: Adapted from Hayes, 1981.

As idea generation slows down—the team yields fewer and fewer new ideas—two options are available. First, the group can try to restart the process by reviewing and then reacting to the recorder's notes, which often refocuses energies considerably. The remaining option is to move directly to the second step, idea evaluation.

Step Two: After the idea generation phase is complete and suggestions are exhausted, idea evaluation can begin. Idea evaluation involves the systematic review of all the comments taken by the recorder. The recorder could read the entries out loud, write them on a black board, or pass out copies in list form. The point is that the entire team has the opportunity to see and respond to the entire list of ideas.

Although criticism was held in check during the first step, it is now actively encouraged, albeit in friendly, constructive tones. In the first pass at evaluation, many ideas can be discarded from further consideration if they do not offer practical, doable approaches to a team project. If the majority of team members do not find a given idea to be either interesting or viable, then it, too, should be eliminated. The evaluation process is inherently similar to that described as the narrowing down process in Exercise 2.A. When a project idea is finally agreed upon by a majority (preferably a unanimous one!) of the research team members, then discussion should turn to formulating a hypothesis, identifying independent and dependent variables, selecting a method and research design, the writing of a research contract, and so on (see chapter 1 and the project check list in chapter 10).

Some final advice on team brainstorming. Does it matter how team members go about providing ideas during step one in the brainstorming process? Put another way, is simply having individuals spontaneously voice ideas any better or worse than having team members take turns? Some research on this question indicates that in any group, some members will be more dominant during idea exchanges than others. Therefore, some group members will be more willing to offer up suggestions, others less so. To examine the pro or con influence of such dominance, Bouchard (1972) added a turn-taking rule to some brainstorming groups but not to others. The results indicated that reducing dominance by taking turns actually increased the number of ideas generated in any given session. You may want to keep this subtle dominance dynamic in mind as you proceed (the turn-taking rule is noted as an option in table 2.3).

Variation of Exercise 2.C: *Individual Brainstorming*

Brainstorming need not be done in a team or group setting. If you are working as a lone researcher, doing *individual brainstorming* is a good way to pick a topic or to refine your current thinking about it. Additionally, individual brainstorming can readily be used in combination with the research notebook exercise (Exercise 2.A) and freewriting (Exercise 2.B). That is, rough ideas could be found through the notebook exercise, expanded upon or revised through individual brainstorming, and then explored further through freewriting.

An individual's brainstorming session is really not that different than a group session, except that you must act as both leader and recorder (Hayes, 1981). To do so, use the rules shown in table 2.3 in order to carefully record your uncensored thoughts, improving and adding to them as you go along. It can be much more difficult to control your inclination to edit and criticize your own work, but you must if this solo brainstorming is to work.

When you run out of ideas, review what points you have generated, adding to them as necessary in order to jog other ideas. When you can come up with no more new points or variations, begin the evaluation phase. Review each idea with an eye to selecting those that seem most promising, practical, interesting, and so forth. Again, you may want to rely on some of the suggestions made in Exercise 2.A so that you can narrow the scope of the brainstorming results.

CRITIQUING RESEARCH IDEAS

At the start of this chapter, I noted that many students worry that they have not selected the "right" project or paper topic, and that such uncertainty can be unsettling. You have no doubt had a similar feeling at some point in your academic career. If you have used any of the idea generation techniques presented in this chapter, then you probably have a project topic by now—but you may still be wondering, like students past, present, and future, if you have found that *right* one.

There are two ways to proceed from this point. The first, the subject of chapter 4, is to search the psychological literature for previous studies, articles, and books. This option is a fine one and, in any case, it is an essential part of any research enterprise. If you want to proceed in this fashion, turn to chapter 4 and begin your search.

The second option is also a good one and, as you've probably guessed, it is the one I am going to advocate that you do now. This option involves critiquing the project idea you are currently thinking about pursuing. My goal in having you do a critique—literally judging the merits of the project idea—is so that you will firm up your commitment to the project or select another, more compelling topic. A critique can be a short written evaluation or simply listening to reactions from others whose opinions you respect. In the social sciences, for example, critiques are usually written as evaluative reactions to published sources (e.g., book reviews) or unpublished works (e.g., anonymous peer reviews of submissions). Studio critiques in the arts are usually oral; an instructor walks around a studio commenting on each student's work while the others listen.

Although they are inherently subjective (Hult, 1996), critiques are meant to offer guidance, direction, and validation. Many psychologists routinely share ideas with their peers before beginning a program of research. The book you are now reading was reviewed by a large number of peers before it was published. Why? The reason is simple: Colleagues often see important issues or aspects of an idea that were missed until now. Critiques, then, are little more than thoughtful opinions, but really what you want before you undertake a research project in earnest is just that—a thoughtful opinion on your work. If you are conducting a solo project, I recommend that you seek a thoughtful opinion before you begin by asking a peer to critique your project idea. Members of research teams, however, should continue to rely on group meetings as a means to critique a developing project. Suggestions for accomplishing either form of critique follow.

Seek Peer Opinion

Ask someone whose opinion you trust to discuss your project idea with you, such as a research methods classmate or a student who is majoring in one of the social sciences. Take a few minutes and describe your project idea to your peer (remember, as chapter 1 suggests, your description should be concise, thorough, and to the point). Be sure to explain why you believe the topic is psychologically interesting; define your terms, including any relevant independent and dependent variables; summarize the predicted relationships among these variables; and, if you have a study design in mind, outline the hypothesis, method, and anticipated results.

After you have finished your short summary, there are two ways to proceed with the critique. First, you could ask your peer reviewer to read and respond to each of the questions shown in table 2.4. These questions are meant to serve as a way to prompt discussion and raise issues about the project that you may have overlooked during the idea generation and refinement stages. As your peer answers the questions, listen carefully to his or her comments—when another person talks about your idea, does it still make sense or ring true? Has your peer reviewer found some interesting aspects of the idea that you missed? Do your peer's comments make you feel more certain about your idea? Thank your peer for the critique, write down a short summary of the peer commentary, and then use any feedback that you feel will improve your project.

TABLE 2.4

QUESTIONS TO GUIDE RESEARCH TOPIC CRITIQUES

1. Do you see the significant points made by the research idea? What are they? How well are the points made?
2. What are the assumptions about thought, behavior, people, organizations, and so on, underlying the arguments?
3. Have any points been overlooked? Is there any evidence or an alternative point of view that should be considered?
4. Can the research idea be improved? If so, how?
5. Can you identify any particular implications of the predicted results? What are they?
6. Can you identify any particular applications of the predicted results? What are they?

Source: Adapted from Hult, 1996.

A second method for soliciting a peer review relies on a technique from expository writing known as *sayback* (Elbow & Belanoff, 1989). Sayback is a form of active listening where an author reads a paper draft to a listener who "says back" what was heard, a helpful way to think about what points have not yet been made or even thought of. The technique is readily modified for use as a peer critique. Describe your project as outlined previously and then ask your peer to "Say back to me in your own words what you hear me getting at in my project. But say it back more as a question than an answer—to help me to figure out better how I want to approach this project" (cf. Elbow & Belanoff, 1989, p. 64). Hearing another person describe your ideas back to you early in the research process can raise important questions or issues that help you to focus on exactly how the project should proceed.

Use a Research Team's Collective Wisdom

Take advantage of one of the early meetings scheduled in your research contract (see chapter 1) or call another. Begin by having a team member briefly summarize the proposed project and then, as a group, review the questions listed in table 2.4. Assign each team member a question (or two), take a few minutes for reflection, and then use the answers to each question to guide a critical discussion of the project. Alternatively, the questions from table 2.4 could be used by the team in a brainstorming session (see previous discussion). In either case, allow the team to decide on any changes or additions to the project's scope, and be sure to get a sense of whether any uncertainties have been rectified.

TRUST AND CONDUCTING RESEARCH

As you delve more into psychological research, you will be exposed to a variety of opinions regarding what is or is not important in the field. Sometimes it is difficult to avoid feeling overwhelmed by different and often conflicting points of view. If you are like most students, you may doubt that you will ever be able to constructively contribute an opinion of your own. Perhaps you feel that your beliefs are already well-represented by others or that there is really nothing left to say about a topic, even when it interests you a great deal. Alternatively, your view might conflict with published research, causing you to assume that it does not merit further exploration or even that you are just plain wrong.

Although these reactions are normal, try to avoid them as much as possible. Instead, start trusting your own opinions as long as you can support them with reasonable arguments and appropriate evidence. Trusting yourself is an important part of learning to conduct research and to develop research ideas. Some opinions—especially your own—are better than others when they are based on a thoughtful consideration of what is known and what can be discovered through the research process. Keep this advice in mind as you read the remaining chapters in this book and when you begin to conduct your own research.

SUMMARY

Practical researchers are aware of the variety of research approaches available in the field of psychology as well as means to generate research ideas. The distinction between qualitative and quantitative research was discussed at the chapter's outset, and several examples representing both open and closed approaches were presented. Four sources of ideas—yourself, your situation, paradoxes, and existing knowledge—were reviewed, as were two related exercises, one on keeping a research notebook and the other using freewriting for topic development. The third exercise involved brainstorming to produce ideas, and variations for a group and individuals were presented. The chapter closed with advice on how to seek peer feedback on research ideas and learning to trust one's own opinions on psychological research.

KEY TERMS

accretion measures (p. 41)
archives (p. 45)
brainstorming (p.62)
case study (p. 42)
closed systems (p. 37)
content analysis (p. 46)
erosion measures (p. 41)
ethnography (p. 40)
ethogram (p. 39)
ethology (p. 38)

freewriting (p. 61)
individual brainstorming (p. 65)
naturalistic observation (p. 38)
nonreactive observation (p. 41)
open systems (p. 37)
participant observation (p. 39)

qualitative research (p. 37)
quantitative research (p. 37)
random sample (p. 48)
reactive (p. 41)
sayback (p. 67)
social contamination (p. 41)
triangulation (p. 38)
unobtrusive observation (p. 41)

SUGGESTED READINGS

Campbell, D. T., & Stanley, J. C. (1963). *Experimental and quasi-experimental designs for research.* Chicago: Rand McNally. A short but detailed exposition of basic research designs. It remains an ideal reference tool for the strengths and weaknesses of various designs.

Coffey, A., & Atkinson, P. (1996). *Making sense of qualitative data: Complementary research designs.* Thousand Oaks, CA: Sage. An illustrative data set is analyzed by a small number of complementary but powerful qualitative techniques.

Leong, F. T. L., & Pfaltzgraff, R. E. (1996). Finding a research topic. In F. T. L. Leong & J. T. Austin (Eds.), *The psychology research handbook: A guide for graduate students and research assistants* (pp. 3–16). Thousand Oaks, CA: Sage. This chapter contains a concise and helpful discussion of strategies for identifying research topics.

Lincoln, Y. S., & Guba, E. G. (1985). *Naturalistic inquiry.* Newbury Park, CA: Sage. An iconoclastic book, one that challenges the positivistic assumptions of established social science research. A "naturalistic" paradigm is offered to replace the historic, dominant "rationalistic" approach to doing research.

Spradley, J. P. (1980). *Participant observation.* New York: Holt, Rinehart and Winston. A book that shows beginning students how to go about the business of research by being a participant observer. It is a very good introduction to a creative form of field work.

Webb, E. J., Campbell, D. T., Schwartz, R. D., Sechrest, L., & Grove, J. B. (1981). *Nonreactive measures in the social sciences.* (2nd ed.). Boston, MA: Houghton Mifflin. A rich and creative guide of physical traces, archives, observational techniques, and other unobtrusive means used to acquire knowledge about private and public behavior. It is clever and full of keen insights into underutilized methods of psychological research.

CHAPTER 3

Writing: A First and Last Consideration

As a practical researcher, you should make writing your first and last consideration when doing any piece of research. Writing is an activity that is necessary to all phases of a research project—from conception, to library research, to execution of an experiment, to the dissemination of any findings. When it comes to writing, then, practical researchers prefer to treat it as an ongoing activity that can always be improved, not as the end of a project.

Nonetheless, a major portion of the writing associated with a research project occurs once the results are known. These results should be shared with the scientific community of psychologists, students of psychology, and any interested others. One important and established mode of communication in psychology and the natural and social sciences is the journal article. Journal articles provide writers and readers with a formal way to pose, defend, and understand arguments; to review, question, and affirm existing knowledge; and, most importantly, to expand scientific knowledge. The scientific literature in psychology is a storehouse for knowledge that any reasonably educated person should be able to access (recall our discussion in chapter 2), but such access is predicated upon written communication.

The ability to write well is an essential tool for the practical researcher, and this chapter covers two topics to underscore its importance: learning to use APA style, and practical issues for improving writing. Learning to use APA style involves understanding the structure, content, and writing style of journal article manuscripts. In the first half of this chapter, I review ways to master APA style, the writing style used by the American Psychological Association, including a model for conceptualizing the APA style paper, and presentation of its sections and their format.

The focus on practical issues to improve writing in the second half of the chapter addresses the all important business of putting your ideas on paper. In other words, you may understand APA style and what it entails, but still be wary about how to actually put pen to paper (or more likely finger to keyboard). Although I cannot teach you expository writing, I can offer advice about generating initial ideas and outlines, recommend a series of steps leading to a first draft, introduce the revision process, and offer suggestions about giving and receiving helpful criticism on papers. To do so, I rely on recent innovations in the teaching of writing, including freewriting and peer feedback (e.g., Elbow & Belanoff, 1995; Williams & Brydon-Miller, 1997).

Before we begin, it is necessary for you to understand the goals of good scientific writing, of which psychology is a part. One writer put it thus:

> The primary criteria for good scientific writing are accuracy and clarity. If your article is interesting and written with style, fine. But these are subsidiary virtues. First strive for accuracy and clarity. (Bem, 1987, p. 173)

Words to write, repeat, and live by. Keep them in mind as you read this chapter and begin to put your thoughts on paper.

MASTERING APA STYLE

Many students find APA style to be daunting because it seems to have so many rules and regulations associated with it. At first glance, it can appear to be a rather restrictive, even foreign, writing style, so much so that many students and even some academic psychologists despair that they will ever master it.

APA style can be mastered, but it takes practice. Similar to many of the other topics presented in this book, APA style is something you simply need repeated exposure to and experience using. As you gain experience writing up project results, the style requirements will become easier for you to follow. Having APA style become second nature to you is probably a bit too much to hope for in one research methodology course, but you can certainly begin to retain the fundamentals for use in future psychology courses. To achieve this end, I will offer a few suggestions that should make your initial acquaintance with the use of APA style a less frustrating one. At the same time, these suggestions are meant to improve your writing more generally because not all of the writing you will do in psychology will follow APA style. Good writing transcends disciplinary boundaries.

Write in the active voice. This invocation is by far the most frequent one given to student writers in every discipline. It is also the invocation most often ignored by social science writers and researchers. The term *active voice* refers to situations where the subject of a sentence does an action, as in "The experimenter delivered the instructions." In the *passive voice*, the subject of the sentence receives the action: "The instructions were delivered by the experimenter." Note the difference. Both voices are grammatically correct; however, the active voice is preferred because it is typically simple, direct, and not wordy (Hacker, 1991). When revising a paper, check to see if some sentences can be transformed from the passive to the active voice; that is, make the actor the sentence's subject.

Write with a general but educated audience in mind. In a literal sense, you are actually writing for an instructor who is grading you, but that is not the audience you are seeking to reach through your writing. Instead, you should be writing for people—real or imagined readers—who are interested in learning about the study of human behavior. What you must do is convey enthusiasm for and expertise about a psychological topic through writing about it. It is a truism that if you are not interested in writing about a topic, then no one will be very interested in reading what you have written.

Many first time writers of APA style papers make the mistake of writing over the heads of their readers by overuse of esoteric jargon (e.g., "The stimuli were a JND over the baseline measure") without defining it ("JND refers to a 'just noticeable difference,' a psychophysical term referring to . . .") and explaining its use in context ("A JND measure was used in this study to . . ."). Other first time writers err in the opposite direction by writing in a manner that is too basic (e.g., "What is psychology? Psychology is the scientific study of human behavior. In this study, behavior was defined as . . ."). Strive to be in the middle of these two extremes so that your writing is neither too little nor too much of a challenge for a general reader.

Of course, you must still satisfy the mechanics of an assignment (e.g., page length, required number of references, etc.) for your instructor, but you should write a paper that persuades the reader to see your point of view about the psychological topic you studied. Why this topic and not others? What makes it so interesting? What can you tell readers that they might not already know or have not thought about in quite the way you have?

Use correct spelling, grammar, and punctuation. You are no doubt tired of the emphasis placed on correct spelling, grammar, and punctuation in higher education. After all, worrying about spelling can seem to be a trivial activity, and you probably feel that you know all you ever will (or care to) about grammar. In turn, punctuation seems to be such a picky, if not debatable, affair. Yet spelling, grammar, and punctuation each lend clarity and credibility to writing. If your readers encounter too many misspelled words, poorly crafted sentences, or sentences that lack cadence, then they will not understand what you are trying to say. A lack of understanding will quickly lead to lower confidence in your ideas.

Improving spelling, grammar, and punctuation is not a difficult task. Careful editing and proofreading of what you write will catch many errors. You should also use whatever spell-checking and grammar-checking software that is available to you. Finally, as recommended later

TABLE 3.1

COMMON GRAMMATICAL AND USAGE ERRORS IN STUDENT WRITING

*Do not confuse *affect* with *effect:*

Affect is often used as a verb and it means "to exert an influence," as in "As predicted, the independent variable affected the dependent variable." Be aware, however, that psychologists sometimes use *affect* as a synonym for "mood" or "emotion," as in "The study of affect and cognition has been an important topic in recent social psychological research."

Effect is often used as a noun that means "result," as in "A significant main effect was found in Study 2."

*Do not confuse *since* with *because:*

Since is temporal, and it means "after that time," as in "Since the experiment's conclusion, several participants requested additional information."

Because is not temporal, and it means "for the reason that," as in "Because the experiment was over, the participants were debriefed."

*Do not confuse *while* with *although, but,* or *whereas:*

While is temporal, and it means "at the same point in time."

Although is not temporal, and it means "in spite of."

But is not temporal, and it means "however" or "on the other hand."

Whereas is not temporal, and it means "it is the fact that" or "in contrast."

*Do not confuse *that* with *which:*

Used in restrictive clauses, *that* provides essential meaning to a sentence, as in "The stopwatch that was used recorded milliseconds."

Used in unrestrictive clauses, *which* adds more information to a sentence. Unrestrictive clauses using *which* are offset by commas, as in "Reaction time, which was measured by a stopwatch, was also recorded."

*Do not mix singular referents with plural pronouns, or vice versa:

Incorrect: "A *person* may rely on stereotypes to simplify their social experience."

Correct: "*People* may rely on stereotypes to simplify *their* social experience" or "A person may rely on stereotypes to simplify *his or her* social experience."

---

*For additional guidance with grammar, I recommend this outstanding, witty book:
O'Conner, P. T. (1996). *Woe is I: The grammarphobe's guide to better English in plain English.* New York: Grosset/Putnam.

---

in this chapter, relying on feedback from peer reviewers is another way to correct misspelled words, as well as errors in punctuation and grammar.

Table 3.1 illustrates some of the most common grammatical and usage errors that occur in student writing. I suggest that you review it now to refresh your memory of grammar and usage. Later, when your paper is written, refer to it again as a checklist for final proofreading.

Avoid using gender-biased or sexist language. When psychologists write about human behavior, they must write inclusively. There is a history in psychology, as well as in most every other academic discipline, of undue emphasis on men over women. Indeed, a no longer accepted historical convention was to use masculine pronouns (he, him) when writing about both men and women, or to use "man" and "mankind" to refer to humanity.

Unless there is a specific and compelling reason to use a masculine or a feminine pronoun in a sentence, an alternative should be found. One alternative is to rephrase a sentence using plural nouns and pronouns so that both genders are implied (e.g., change "Although a participant could review the stimulus materials again, he was not likely to do so" to "Although participants could review the stimulus materials again, they were not likely to do so"). A second alternative is to eliminate the use of a pronoun in a sentence (e.g., change "A therapist should counsel his client about the average time treatment requires" to "A therapist should counsel a client about the average time treatment requires" or better still "Therapists should counsel clients about the average time treatment requires").

Some writers substitute a singular pronoun, usually *he*, with *he or she*. If used at all, this sort of substitution must be done sparingly because it quickly becomes tedious to read over and over again. Other combinations such as *he/she* or *(s)he* not only fail to conform to APA style, but they are also very awkward to write as well as read. Although it is sometimes acceptable, writing that alternates between the use of *he* and *she* can quickly become distracting, as the reader learns that an example using *she* will inevitably be followed by one using *he*, and so on.

Eschew quotations. Quotations should be used rarely, if at all, in student writing, and yet many students persist in using them. Some student writers quote other authors in order to fill up space; that is, they use lengthy quotes from published works in their papers so that they have less to write (faculty members are well aware of this tactic and tend to grade accordingly). Other student writers rely on extensive quotes in the mistaken belief that published authors necessarily "say it better" than they do or can. Finally, some students rely on quotations as a crutch because they are afraid that they have little or nothing to say about a topic. As a result, some papers appear to be little more than strings of quotations linked together by a few transitional sentences, an unfortunate practice known as "quilting." (We will revisit excessive reliance on quotation and the prevention of plagiarism in chapter 4.)

Beyond avoiding these tactical reasons for the use of excessive quotes, there is a more compelling guide: Quotes are boring to read. If a reader ends up reading two or three pages of quotes in a 15-page manuscript, why not simply read the original sources instead of bits and pieces?

My advice is to learn to put others' ideas into your own words instead of relying on quotes. This chapter contains a few writing techniques designed to help you do so, as well as to put together an APA style paper that uses the psychological literature without literally (and liberally) quoting from it. If you absolutely feel that you must quote, then limit yourself to a *one sentence quote per paper*—and make it a gem.

Write so that each section of a paper stands alone. As you will see shortly, papers written in APA style have a minimum of five sections and sometimes as many as ten, and each section serves a discrete function. The Abstract section, for example, summarizes the purpose, hypothesis, method, and results of a study in a few sentences. The introduction to an APA style paper contains a detailed literature review that presents research related to the current topic, and so on. A well-written APA style paper is written so that any section of it can be read *independently* of the others; that is, readers should receive a general idea of what the paper is about whether they choose to read one or more of its sections. Readers should even be able to skim the last section of a paper, the Discussion, rather than the introduction, in order to discern the rationale of the research.

Why should each section of a paper be able to stand alone? Two reasons, really; one practical, the other pedagogical. The structure is practical because readers can scan an article for particular pieces of information about the study. One reader of the psychological literature may be interested in a particular research design (e.g., a randomized block design), and so she might read the Method section of a paper to determine if and how the desired design was employed. Another reader might want to know how the data were analyzed, and so he would turn to the Results section first. The "stand alone" structure also allows readers to decide very quickly if an article is not useful for their current work, so that they can move on to the next one in a literature search.

As for pedagogy, having each section of an APA style paper be a cohesive unit serves a helpful educational function: You do not necessarily need to re-read prior sections in order to recall the general purpose of a study. A study's hypothesis, for example, is not only carefully described in a paper's introduction, it is also reviewed in the Results and the Discussion sections. This review of important ideas provides each section with contextual information, so that a study's meaning and purpose are always firmly in the reader's mind.

Neither of these points is meant to suggest that reading only one section of an APA style paper is acceptable when doing scholarship; to the contrary, a good scholar familiarizes him or herself with the contents of every section. Yet the opportunity to quickly refresh one's memory on some point or to scan for a detail makes APA style writing very useful for practical researchers.

Prepare the reader for what is to come. Use transitional phrases, sentences, and paragraphs that link ideas together in a smooth way. The goal is to help the reader to anticipate what is to follow and why it is deemed important to the arguments being made in the paper. A writer can help readers to anticipate the contents of a paper by introducing a topic and research focus within the first few paragraphs of the introduction (the infamous, though often neglected, topical sentence plays a role here). Similarly, the opening paragraphs of the Results and Discussion sections should remind the reader about a study's hypothesis and how it was tested. The former emphasizes what was found and the latter interprets what particular findings mean to the theory being examined.

Preparing readers for what is to come also means that they should not be abruptly surprised by how and when information is presented in an APA style article ("Once the data analyses were underway, we decided to test a second hypothesis that has not been mentioned previously"). Surprises are best used in mystery, not scientific, writing. An important issue, such as how an independent variable was manipulated or citing a heretofore unmentioned but apparently key reference, should not be held until the Discussion section, where it will seem out of place. Independent variables should be defined in the introduction and Method sections, respectively. If a very important reference that sheds light on your argument is found *after* the paper is written, then you must go back and revise the introduction, and so on, in lieu of simply noting it as an afterthought in the Discussion. Avoiding surprising the reader by using good transitional sentences or paragraphs may sound like common sense, but in the course of writing a paper, details are very often stuck into the text when they come to mind.

Use examples to illustrate your points. There is an analogy between the good teacher and the good writer here: A good teacher uses many examples to illustrate important points, and so does a good writer. Too often, however, less experienced writers often assume that good writing is exemplified by the use of abstract ideas, and the more abstract they are, the better. Actually, a hallmark of good writing is the frequent use of concrete examples to support and demonstrate ideas. When you introduce and define a concept, an example should accompany it:

> *Cognitive dissonance* is a state of psychological tension that arises when one is aware of two or more inconsistent cognitions (Festinger, 1957). People who smoke cigarettes, for example, are usually all too aware that smoking is a cause of cancer. To reduce the tension created by these two dissonant thoughts, many smokers justify their actions by suggesting that the medical evidence is questionable or by pointing out that they smoke few cigarettes on a daily basis. By appealing to these or other reasons, the smokers are engaging in a form of dissonance reduction . . .

The appropriate use of examples within a piece of writing educates readers and also allows you to see if you fully understand the concepts you are writing about. If you cannot provide examples to illustrate your points, then you do not have a good working knowledge of the topic.

Use headings and subheadings. Headings and subheadings play a crucial role in a well-written paper. As the reader proceeds through the paper, he or she knows what is to come based on the framework provided by headings and subheadings. If you question their worth, think about this: Outside of novels, how much do you enjoy reading pages and pages of unbroken text? Scientific writing is usually very technical, and psychological prose is no exception to this rule. The judicious use of headings and subheadings throughout a paper maintains a reader's understanding of a topic as well as his or her interest.

There are two levels of headings that student writers tend to use in APA style papers—main headings and subheadings. Main headings appear centered on the page (double spaced above and below) and they contain both upper- and lowercase letters. Subheadings are flush with the left margin (again, double spaced above and below), underlined, and also contain upper- and lowercase letters.

Here is an example of a main heading and a subheading:

Method

Participants

The easiest way to create good main headings and subheadings is take key words or phrases directly from an article's outline (see discussion that follows) or from the text itself. In fact, a reader should be able to write down a list of all the headings and subheadings used in a paper in order to re-create the outline of an article (detailed tables of contents in textbooks often serve the same purpose). As an exercise, the next time you read a good article from a psychology journal, go back through it and write down the section headings and subheadings in order so that you can observe the flow of the author's argument.

Revise and rewrite. The fundamental message here, and really for this chapter, is this: revise, revise, revise. Revision is the process of reexamining, altering, and correcting written text. Revision can include everything from starting a paper over, adding or deleting whole sections of prose, changing the order of topic presentations, or checking for transitional phrases between sections of a paper.

Few writers can write a perfect first draft that requires only minimal revision. In practice, most psychologists probably write a first draft for themselves; that is, as creators of the experiments they are summarizing, they write initial drafts from the perspectives of insiders. Some points, definitions, and so on, are purposely left unsaid—that is, unwritten—because the author is intimate with them. Here, a writer writes to get preliminary thoughts down on paper so that a draft can begin to take shape (see, for example, Peterson, 1996).

Subsequent drafts of an article are written for outsiders, that is, for others for whom an author cannot assume intimate knowledge of an experiment. In these later drafts, such assumed knowledge must be identified, clarified, and explained so that readers can follow the line of argument being advanced. Authors must try to get inside the heads of their readers in order to anticipate what sorts of questions they will have, what points they will see as easier or harder to understand, and so forth. Continually revising a paper with the needs of other readers in mind, hypothetical or real, will greatly improve the clarity of the final product.

Put your draft away. Review your draft after a day or so of being away from it. I know that many student readers are balking at this point: Who finishes a paper earlier than the night before it is due?! If I have not revealed my bias on work habits where writing is concerned, I will do so now. I understand but am opposed to the common practice of waiting until the last minute to write a paper and the implicit message that pressure leads to creativity in writing. In my teaching experience, such 11th-hour pressure rarely results in better writing—it usually results in rushed or haphazard writing and, in the end, lower grades.

BOX FEATURE 3.A

A Research Digression: *Nota Bene*—
Save and Back Up Your Work

Nota bene is Latin for "observe what follows" or "note well," and it is often used to draw attention to wisdom that can easily be overlooked. The wisdom I have in mind concerns your wordprocessing habits where saving and maintaining backup copies of files are concerned. When writing with a wordprocessor, be certain to frequently save your work to a file on a diskette and on the hard drive. Why save frequently? If there is a power failure, you will lose everything. Why save to two places? Hard drives do crash and diskettes, too, can be lost, damaged, or contain manufacturer errors. One writer (Smyth, 1996, p. 37) offers some eminently practical advice on this matter: "Preferably keep two copies in separate locations (e.g., one at home and one at university). If your home (or the university) burns down, or either is flooded, you will still have at least one copy. It has been known to happen!"

Smyth, T. R. (1996). *Writing in Psychology: A Student Guide.* New York, NY, John Wiley & Sons.

With practice and planning, you can finish a paper (or most of it) two or more days before it is due. By "putting it away" I mean taking a break from a paper to work on something else for a while so you can return to writing refreshed. Why? After a break, you are likely to see parts of the text that can be improved by editing or rewriting, as well as parts that are fine as written (Peterson, 1996). You can also catch the final few spelling, punctuation, or stylistic errors usually found in the penultimate draft of a paper. Finally, "sitting on" a paper for a while allows good but unwritten ideas to gestate in your head, so that in your final writing session, some may find their way into your paper.

THE FORMAT OF AN APA STYLE PAPER

The issues discussed in this section of the chapter are drawn from the fourth edition of the *Publication Manual of the American Psychological Association* (1994). In fact, I will frequently cite specific sections of the *Publication Manual* where more detailed advice on the parts of APA style manuscripts can be found. The *Publication Manual* is *the* style book used by writers, researchers, teachers, and students in the field of psychology. This guide to style is also used by professionals who work in the other social and behavioral sciences, as well as nursing, criminology, and personnel studies.

It is impossible to convey all aspects of APA style or the contents of the *Publication Manual* here, nor is that my purpose. There is no ideal substitute for learning the subtleties of this writing style; you must learn to read and consult the manual when questions arise. If you have not already done so, you should obtain a copy of the *Publication Manual* in the not too distant future if you intend to continue in psychology. It is an invaluable and relatively inexpensive reference tool that will pay for itself many times over.

My goal is to familiarize you with the basics of APA style and the formatting of papers based on that style. You will be able to produce an APA style paper based on the directions that follow, but I must warn you that I cannot provide answers here to every question about style and formatting that may occur as you write a paper. This fact should not create problems for you because learning to put psychological concepts into words is more important at this stage of your education than undue worry over style or how a paper looks.

One of the best ways to improve your familiarity with APA style is easy to do. Go to your college or university library's periodical section and examine one or two APA journals. The point is not to read every article in a given journal, but to take a few minutes to leaf through a few of the articles, taking note of how they are structured. You will find using a published journal article as a model for your paper to be helpful once you start to write. For your reference and convenience, table 3.2 lists all the journals currently published by the APA.

TABLE 3.2

JOURNALS CURRENTLY PUBLISHED BY THE AMERICAN PSYCHOLOGICAL ASSOCIATION (APA)

American Psychologist
Behavioral Neuroscience
Contemporary Psychology
Developmental Psychology
Experimental and Clinical Psychopharmacology
Health Psychology
Journal of Abnormal Psychology
Journal of Applied Psychology
Journal of Comparative Psychology
Journal of Consulting and Clinical Psychology
Journal of Counseling Psychology
Journal of Educational Psychology
Journal of Experimental Psychology: Animal Behavior Processes
Journal of Experimental Psychology: Applied
Journal of Experimental Psychology: General
Journal of Experimental Psychology: Human Perception and Performance
Journal of Experimental Psychology: Learning, Memory, and Cognition
Journal of Family Psychology
Journal of Personality and Social Psychology
Neuropsychology
Professional Psychology: Research and Practice
Psychological Assessment
Psychological Bulletin
Psychological Methods
Psychological Review
Psychology and Aging
Psychology, Public Policy, and Law

FIGURE 3.1

The Hourglass Model of Writing an APA Style Paper.

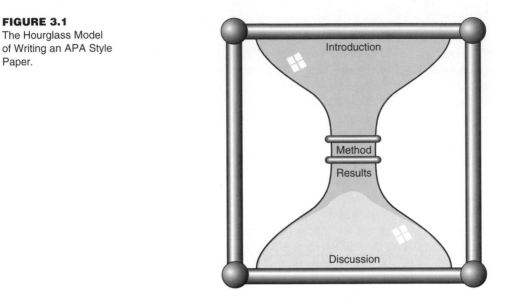

A Brief Overview of APA Style: The Hourglass Model

The social-personality psychologist and skilled writer Daryl Bem (1987) points out that APA style articles are written in the shape of an hourglass. Figure 3.1 shows the hourglass model for journal-style articles. Note that this model only involves the main sections of the article, of which there are four—the introduction, Method, Results, and Discussion sections. Starting at the top of the hourglass, you begin the introduction by making relatively broad statements about the psychological issues under study and then gradually present your specific arguments as you near the Method—the most narrow point, or "neck," of the hourglass. Your prose should be relatively specific when reporting what exactly happened in the Results, but it should broaden once again as you move toward the base of the hourglass, the Discussion section, where the study's implications are explored. This model is a simple but invaluable aid that will give the right focus, as well as metaphorical shape, to your papers. Keep it in mind as you read the rest of this chapter and when you begin to write a paper summarizing your research efforts.

Including the four main sections comprising the hourglass model, APA style papers can have as many as twelve parts, beginning in order with a Title page; an Abstract page; the main text or body of the paper, which usually includes an introduction, a Method section, a Results section, a Discussion section; References; Author Notes; Footnotes; Tables; Figures; and Appendixes. The style, format, and content of each section will be reviewed in turn, and then a recommended plan of attack—which section should be written first, which last—will be presented.

Title   The title page, page 1, is the first thing a reader sees (refer to section 1.06 in the *Publication Manual*). A good paper title summarizes the main point of the research in a simple, direct fashion. Ideally, a paper's title should be concise and, if possible, it should include some reference to the variables or theory being examined. Every word matters in a title and those that do not, such as "A Study of" or "An Experiment on" should be deleted.

If a paper is based on an experiment, it is quite common to use a title that explicitly mentions the independent and dependent variables that were used. Examples of such titles are "Effects of Locus of Control on Collegiate Study Habits" or "Infant Habituation and the Perception of Contour Information." If your paper is more of a literature review or an essay on a selected topic, then you can use a title that conveys an organizing theme, as in "Attachment Theory and Adolescent Rebellion: A Critical Review" or "Current Perspectives on the Controversial Weapons Effect."

Beneath the title is the author's name and below it appears an institutional affiliation. You should use your first name, middle initial, and last name, as well as the full name of your college or university. If you are working as a member of a research team, then more than one name will appear above the affiliation.

The third component of the title page is the running head. A running head is a shortened title ("Type A Behavior") that is printed at the top of every page of a printed article. It should be no more than 50 characters long, including all letters, punctuation marks, and spaces between words. In a manuscript, the running head appears close to the left margin a few spaces from the top of the title page, and it looks like this:

Running head: TYPE A BEHAVIOR

Note that the short title appears in all capital letters.

Abstract   The Abstract in an APA style paper is a short but detailed summary of a paper's contents (refer to section 1.07 in the *Publication Manual*). The Abstract's purpose is to help readers decide whether to read an entire article, and thus to save the time and energy of readers who search the psychological literature (see chapter 4 of this book).

An abstract for an experiment should be no more than 120 words long, and it must convey the topical area of the study, the hypothesis used, what variables were manipulated and measured, the methods used, a brief summary of the results, and perhaps some mention of conclusions, implications, or applications. It appears alone on page 2 of the paper. Abstracts written for review or theory papers are much shorter, between 75 and 100 words in length. The contents of a review or theoretical abstract include a topical sentence, the purpose of the article, a description of the sources used, and the conclusions drawn.

Writing a clear abstract takes practice and revision, and many authors feel that this is the most difficult piece of an APA style paper. Because it does summarize an entire project, it should probably be the last section written in the APA style paper.

Here is a sample abstract from an article by Lee, Hallahan, and Herzog (1996) that appeared in *Personality and Social Psychology Bulletin:*

> Several lines of experimental research have shown that attributional styles are affected by the attributor's culture, inferential goals, and level of cognitive processing. Can these findings be replicated in natural settings? This study compared the attributions made in two domains (sports and editorials) of newspapers published in two culturally distinct countries (Hong Kong and the United States). Consistent with the cross-cultural research, attributions were less dispositional in the East than in the West. This cultural difference was weaker in editorials than in sports articles. The authors argue that the higher level of complexity, accountability, and uncertainty in editorials increased the cognitive effort expended to make attributions, which, in turn, attenuated their extremity. Implications for the mixed model of social inference are discussed.

The abstract for a project in a research methods course does not need to be as long as the Lee et al. (1996) example, of course. Here is an abstract from a student research method project conducted by Carolyn Vicchiullo (1994):

> Students who sat proximate to the front of a classroom were hypothesized to have higher midterm grades and overall grade point averages (GPAs) than those closer to the back of the room. Proximity was operationalized as the self-assigned seating distance between student and instructor. Absences were expected to be inversely related to proximity. After seating choices were recorded, 30 college students answered self-report items about their interest in a class, participation, attentiveness, involvement, and confidence of receiving high grades. Students who sat in close proximity to the instructor had higher midterm grades and GPAs, but not lower absence rates. Confidence also predicted better academic performance. Recommendations for future research include the use of larger samples of participants.

Introduction   The opening section of the APA style paper, the introduction, is often referred to as "the literature review," but it is much more than that. Beyond examining the existing literature pertaining to some area of inquiry, the introduction provides a statement of purpose for the research and it explains the author's reasoning to readers. Please do not misunderstand this point: A review of the literature must be done and done well, but it will only be as good as the idea—and the supporting logic—driving the research.

The introduction begins on page 3 of the paper, which is listed in the upper right corner following a manuscript page header (refer to section 1.08 in the *Publication Manual*). The paper's title reappears centered and in upper- and lowercase letters at the top of the page (because its placement reveals its purpose, the introduction is not labeled like the other sections of the paper). The opening sentence of the introduction is then double-spaced and indented underneath the title.

The first few sentences of the introduction must present the specific problem being examined, as well as the research strategy that will be used to explore it. A very good way to begin is with some general statement about human behavior: "People attribute many favorable qualities to individuals who are physically attractive." Issues that a writer should address for readers here include the following: Why this study? How does the proposed hypothesis address the topic? Why is the experimental design appropriate?

When reviewing the literature, focus only on those studies that are of direct relevance to your project instead of providing a historical review of every available study. In the course of reviewing previously published research, briefly summarize the main points, conclusions, pertinent findings, or methodologies that inform your work. Avoid going over nonessential details, such as the number of participants in the earlier work, where the research was conducted, and so on.

When you describe the arguments made by previously published researchers, treat the material, not the authors, as the subject of your discussion. If you were reviewing selected articles from the literature on stress and coping, for example, then you would discuss major theoretical contributions (e.g., appraisal theory) that have been proposed rather than emphasizing who the authors were (e.g., Richard S. Lazarus). Many student writers make the mistake of making the contributor—and not the contribution—the focus of their writing. As you will see in the section devoted to References, proper citation is essential; just don't neglect the correct presentation of psychological ideas in pursuit of precise citations!

After the general topic and the literature review are completed, the remainder of the introduction should focus on the purpose and rationale behind your study. The last few paragraphs of the introduction should explicitly state your reasoning, identify any relevant variables that will be manipulated or measured, and provide a hypothesis that will be tested. Novice writers are often afraid to anticipate their results and, as a result, unintentionally leave the reader hanging. Don't be afraid to briefly introduce the method of the study and to specifically inform the reader about the anticipated results:

> . . . In the present study, participants were presented with a list of either abstract or concrete words and then told that they would later be asked to recall them. Due to their imagery-provoking properties, it was hypothesized that participants would remember relatively more concrete than abstract words during a subsequent free recall task.

To summarize, the introduction proceeds from the presentation of a general topic to the identification of a particular problem or question. Once the problem is noted, a review of prior but related research is undertaken. A brief rationale for the current project, including the identification of a hypothesis, follows. The introduction concludes with a few sentences or a paragraph linking a description of the study to come with the anticipated results, which are often presented in a reiteration of the hypothesis. Stylistically, then, the introduction begins with broad, conceptual statements and moves increasingly to specific descriptions of the author's own investigation.

Method   The Method section of the APA style paper is a concise description of exactly what took place in the course of the experiment (refer to section 1.09 of the *Publication Manua*l). In effect, it also serves as a complete set of plans that readers could use to replicate the experiment. The Method section is very similar to the script used to produce a play. It includes both the lines the actors speak (direct quotes the experimenter uses when giving directions to participants) as well as stage directions, everything from how stimuli were presented, variables measured or manipulated, and how participants were debriefed when their role was over.

There is a general rule of thumb for writing a Method section: Find the appropriate level of detail for the reader. Too much detail overwhelms readers, whereas too little detail leaves them with too many (unanswered) questions. Strive for a middle ground so readers understand what was done in the course of an experiment and why, thereby allowing them to replicate your work without difficulty.

Most Method sections are divided into appropriately labeled subsections, the most frequently used of which are *participants* or *subjects, materials* or *apparatus,* and *procedure.* Creating novel subsections is appropriate if the description of an experiment is especially long or detailed.

The *participants* or *subjects* section provides a description of the individuals who took part in the study (the term *subjects* is only properly used for nonhuman participants, and though some writers persist in using it to refer to humans, you should not; see Box Feature 5.1). It includes information such as the number of participants, their gender, age if relevant, and whether they were college students or a particular population. Usually, the Method section mentions if the participants were volunteers or if they completed the experiment for course credit or even a modest remuneration. An indication that the participants, whether human or animal, were treated in accordance with the Ethical Principles and the Code of Conduct (American Psychological Association, 1992) is becoming more commonplace here as well (a discussion of the importance of ethical issues in research can be found in chapter 5). Here is a relatively short participants section from Feather and Volkmer (1988):

> There were 80 student volunteers (32 men, 48 women) who participated in the study. These students were enrolled in an introductory psychology course at Flinders University in 1986. Their ages ranged from 17 to 45 years ($M = 25.10$, $SD = 8.11$).

As you can see, the authors provide basic information, including the specific number of participants, their gender, the fact that they were all drawn from the same volunteer population, and the information about their ages. This information is disclosed in a few succinct sentences. Any additional descriptive detail about the participants or how they were recruited could easily be added.

The *apparatus* or *materials* subsection of the Method section briefly and specifically describes any experimental apparatus or materials employed and their purpose within an experiment. Any common materials, such as stopwatches, a desktop computer, or the furnishings in a room do not need to be mentioned in any detail. If specialized equipment, such as an operant chamber, a device for measuring reaction time, or a particular computer program, were used, then the name and model number of the piece of equipment, the name of the supplier and its location must be noted. A custom-made apparatus or any complex piece of equipment can be illustrated in an APA style paper through a photograph or a drawing. If necessary, complex equipment can also be described in an appendix to the paper. Here is an excerpt from an apparatus section from an animal behavior study done by Whishaw and Mittleman (1986, p. 423):

> The water task pool was a circular black plastic water tank, 100 cm in diameter and 40 cm deep. The pool was located in the center of a large test room and surrounded by many cues external to the pool (e.g., windows, door, cupboard, sink, overhead lights, animal cage trolley, etc.), which were visible from within the pool and could be used by the rat for spatial localization. The pool was filled to a height of 30 cm with 18 C water made opaque by the addition of a film of small wood chips floating on the surface . . .

Many student researchers assume that they must include an apparatus section in an APA style paper even if they did not use any equipment. It is not necessary and should only be included if equipment or other materials were used.

The *procedure* subsection provides a step-by-step account of what the participants experienced in the course of the experiment. It typically includes the instructions that were given to the participants, a description of how experimental or control groups were formed, and the experimental manipulations, if any, that were used. A good way to write a procedure section is to mentally go back over exactly what happened to participants from the moment they arrived until they left the experimental setting. Similar to the *participants* or *subjects* section, the *procedure* can be more or less detailed, and it can even contain subsections devoted to descriptions of the *dependent measures* used. A recent study by Lassiter, Koenig, and Apple (1996) includes a straightforward procedure section:

Procedure

> On arrival, the subject [participant] was met by a male experimenter and was seated at a desk in front of a video monitor. The experimenter handed the subject [participant] a button (mounted on a small wooden box), briefly demonstrated how to operate it, and then delivered the following instructions taken from Lassiter and Stone (1984):

> What I would like you to do is firmly push the button whenever, in your judgment, a meaningful action occurs in the videotape you are about to see.

Let me explain what I mean by that. Consider, for example, the following behavior: I could get up, turn, walk over to a door, push the door closed, turn, walk back, and sit down. You could see each of these as discrete and meaningful actions. Or, you might see that same behavior as being composed of only three actions: getting up, pushing a door closed, and sitting down. Finally, you might see that behavior as only one action—that of closing the door.

What I would like you to do as you view this videotape is to segment the behavior into whatever actions seem meaningful to you. Simply press the button when, in your judgment, one meaningful action ends and another begins. As I said before, these should be meaningful to you. There are no right or wrong ways to do this. I am simply interested in how *you* do it. The subject [participant] then viewed and segmented a 12-min videotape of a woman performing a variety of activities, such as cleaning up a room and working on a block puzzle. (Pretesting indicated that the content of this behavior sequence is judged to be neutral: $M = 4.96$ on a 9-point scale of negativity/positivity.) The videotape was in black and white and had no sound. Immediately afterward, a questionnaire, which included the BDI (Beck Depression Inventory) as well as measures assessing both liking for the stimulus person and memory for her behavior, was given to the subject [participant] to complete. At this point, the experiment was concluded and the subject [participant] was debriefed.

Depending upon the variety of activities that take place during the course of an experiment, a procedure section might be longer or shorter than this example. Including a specific script of an experimenter's instructions to a participant, too, is not necessary unless it is essential to an unusual task (as it is here) or if it involves the presentation of a key stimulus or measurement of a variable.

In closing our discussion of the Method section, it is important to remind you that it is possible to be somewhat flexible in how you present an experiment's methodology. It is very common, for example, to combine the *participants* and *procedure* sections or the *apparatus* and *procedure* sections into one subsection. The respective subheadings would appear as follows:

<u>Participants and Procedure</u>
<u>Apparatus and Procedure</u>

Various other combinations are not only possible, but encouraged, when appropriate; that is, you have determined the most clear, concise, and direct way to convey information about how the study was conducted to readers.

Results The Results section summarizes the data collected and how they were statistically analyzed (refer to section 1.10 of the *Publication Manual*). At the start of the Results section, I believe that it is always helpful for readers to be reminded about the hypothesis that was tested, especially if the introduction and Method sections were long and detailed. Your reminder should be only an efficient restatement of the question the research addressed, such as "The experiment was designed to determine if males would respond more aggressively to a minor insult than would females." Then turn to the main results, and in doing so you may wish to remind the reader about what behavioral measure was used, and report what was found and whether it supports the hypothesis: "As can be seen in table 1, males retaliated to an insult by administering more shocks to the confederate than did females." Only after you have clearly stated the results do you report any statistical information: "On average, males gave almost twice as many shocks than did the females, F (1,48) = 5.43, $p < .01$."

When presenting statistical results, you must tell the reader what statistical test was used and what specific between or within group comparisons were made. Chapter 8 discusses the analysis, interpretation, and presentation of statistical results in detail, so such information will not be repeated here. There is one important point, however, I would like to emphasize: Though important, statistical results are secondary to prose explaining their meaning. Do not assume that all readers are familiar with whatever technique (e.g., the analysis of variance) you used in your study, nor does this admonition mean that you must explain the theory behind any statistical test. Rather, you must explain how two or more groups were compared against one another, how they behaved or thought differently, and so on.

After the main result is reported, move on to any additional results, and in doing so, be sure to use a smooth transition: "Although males were more aggressive following the insult, should we assume that fewer shocks from the females means they are less aggressive or that they did not view the insult as an attack? To explore these competing interpretations, participants' reactions to the postexperimental questionnaire were analyzed . . . ."

Remember that your goal in the Results section is to state the results clearly, not to discuss their implications or to interpret them, which is the purpose of the Discussion section. If the results are consistent with expectation, then say so; if they run counter to the hypothesis, then be up front about that as well. In either case, describe conceptually and behaviorally what the results indicate. To paraphrase Bem (1987) in this regard: Inferential statistics have their place, but descriptive statistics are the heart of the matter. In other words, although the reader needs to know what statistical test was used on the results, it is much more important to know what the participants actually did: "Not only did males administer twice as many shocks, the average duration of their shocks was 3 sec longer than those given by the females."

Tables and figures are often included in the Results section, and they are very helpful to both writer and reader because they provide an economical way to summarize what happened in a study (see following discussion and discussion in chapter 8). There is an important requirement for their use, however: Lead the reader carefully through any table or figure. Do not assume that it is sufficient to simply point to a graph in passing and then let the reader do all the work. The text of the Result section must forge a link to any display of data: "As shown in table 1, males pressed the shock button for a significantly longer period of time ($M = 7$ sec) than females ($M = 4$ sec)."

Students often feel compelled to report individual scores or raw data within their papers, and many wonder if it is necessary to include actual statistical calculations or computer printouts. Raw data and any analyses (including summary tables from the analysis of variance or regression) should only appear in a condensed, summary form unless you have conducted a single-subject design or case study, or if illustrative behavior or responses (both anonymous) are noted in the text (e.g., "One male participant administered shocks even when correct responses were provided"). Your instructor may want to see your data and calculations, of course, so they could be attached, but they should not be in the body of the paper. And by all means, hold onto raw data and all the analyses, as they may prove to be useful later (we will consider this issue in more detail in chapters 5 and 8).

Discussion   In contrast to the reporting style of the Results section, the Discussion section of the APA style paper interprets the results of the study for readers (refer to section 1.11 of the *Publication Manual*). How well do the results fit the hypothesis? What are their implications? In retrospect, were the methods used appropriate to the task? Could any changes or improvements be made? What questions, if any, do the results answer about the topic? What new questions do they raise for future studies?

A Discussion section can be written in several ways, but it will typically have three parts. First, the opening paragraphs of the Discussion remind the reader about the purpose of the study and report the main finding. The second part usually identifies problems or limitations about the obtained results. Perhaps the method that was used had a flaw that affected the participants' responses or the study's design contained an unforeseen confound. Few, if any, studies are perfect and a good researcher owes the reader the honest identification and evaluation of any problems that become apparent. The third part of the Discussion considers the implications of the research, relates the current findings to existing studies, and specifically addresses whether and how the results expand what we know about the topic in question.

Once the implications of the results are discussed, the paper is brought to a close. There are two schools of thought about how to conclude the APA style paper. One group of adherents suggests that an explicit concluding paragraph that (once again) summarizes the purpose and findings of the study is necessary. I disagree with this advice because the structure of the APA style paper already provides this service. The other school advocates that authors explicitly identify where research should go from here; that is, now that we know something about human behavior, how can we find out more next time? This sort of conclusion is acceptable only if it is interesting to read. To make it interesting to read requires that you think broadly about human behavior, that you be creative, and that under no circumstances you simply end the paper with some variation on the vague "future research on this topic is necessary."

References   The References section of the APA style paper is often treated as an afterthought, but it is extremely important. Why? Because it serves as a detailed record of the various articles and books that informed your ideas and, ultimately, your project. It is not just a reference for you, so that you can keep track of the sources you used during the course of conducting your project or writing it up. It is an important source of information for your readers who can use it to locate useful works to aid their own research (refer to sections 1.13, and 3.94–3.117 in the *Publication Manual*). Indeed, it is not too far off the mark to suggest that the References section is a repository promoting scholarly communication as much as the rest of the APA style paper (see chapter 4 for further discussion of this issue).

Students often become concerned about how many references should be cited, whether articles are better sources than chapters or books, and so on. Here are a few criteria that you can use to decide whether a work should be cited in your paper:

- Was any scientific fact, hypothesis, or definition from the reference used?
- Were *any* ideas from the reference used to shape your thinking about the theory used in your project?
- Did you borrow or adapt any methodology from a reference for your project?
- Did you use the same statistical tests or other analytic procedures discussed in the reference?

If you answered "yes" to any of these criteria, then the reference in question should be cited appropriately in the body of your text and within its References section.

There are two general issues about references that concern writers, citing a reference in the body of the text and in the References section itself. The proper way to cite a reference in the text of an article can be done in one of several ways. The most common way is the parenthetical citation, which appears at the end of a sentence (note that APA style generally avoids writing out first names):

> Recent research indicates that emotional development in toddlers is contingent on both age and the quality of their social experience (Smith, 1993).

The hypothetical author's last name appears in parentheses, followed by a comma, and the date the work was published. Alternatively, the author's name could be treated as the topic of the sentence, in which case he date appears inside parentheses immediately after the author's last name:

> Smith (1993) argues that emotional development in toddlers is contingent on both age and the quality of their social experience.

In APA reference style, the date of publication should accompany an author's name the first time a citation is made within a paragraph. The date does not appear, however, with subsequent citations of a work within the *same* paragraph.

What if a reference has more than one author? There are a few issues to contend with here, but none is insurmountable. If a two author citation is being used as a parenthetical citation, an ampersand (&), the sign for "and," appears between the authors' names:

> Until recently, the psychological study of optimism has been oversimplified and misunderstood (Peterson & Bossio, 1991).

When treating the authors as the subject of a sentence, however, the ampersand is replaced:

> Peterson and Bossio (1991) suggest that until recently the psychological study of optimism has been oversimplified and misunderstood.

A three or more author parenthetical citation, however, has an additional twist to it. For the *first* citation of a work in a paper, every author's name is cited. For every citation of the book or article thereafter, however, the Latin abbreviation *et al.* from *et alii*, which means "and other people," is used:

> Behavioral statistics is one of the most important courses in the psychology curriculum (Runyon, Haber, Pittenger, & Coleman, 1996). Although they may be unaware of the formal laws of probability, people actually behave statistically in everyday life (Runyon et al., 1996).

The aforementioned rule for having a multiple author citation serve as the subject of a sentence applies here as well; just remember to use *et al.* and the date in parentheses after that first citation.

Here is one final style note about parenthetical references in the body of the text. When using more than one source to support some point you are making in your paper, be sure to alphabetize the citations inside the parentheses and to separate each one by using a semicolon:

> Imagery continues to be a rich area of research in cognitive psychology, and comprehensive theories abound (Kosslyn, 1983; Pavio, 1971; Shepard & Cooper, 1983).

And remember, when you are in doubt about how to cite something, do not hesitate to consult the *Publication Manual.*

We now turn to the proper formatting of references appearing in the References section of the APA style paper. Before we start, I must tell you that there are over 75 different reference forms in APA style—everything from periodicals to abstracts on CD-ROM. Fortunately, they

TABLE 3.3

SAMPLE REFERENCES USING APA STYLE

Citing a journal article:

Anderson, J. R. (1982). Acquisition of a cognitive skill. *Psychological Review, 89,* 369–406.

Anderson, J. R. (1991). The adaptive nature of human categorization. *Psychological Review, 98,* 409–429.

Anderson, J. R., & Schooler, L. J. (1991). Reflections of the environment in memory. *Psychological Science, 2,* 396–408.

Bower, G. H., Montiero, K. P., & Gilligan, S. G. (1978). Emotional mood as a context for learning and recall. *Journal of Verbal Learning and Verbal Behavior, 17,* 573–587.

Citing a book:

Nisbett, R. E., & Ross, L. (1980). *Human inference: Strategies and shortcomings of social judgment.* Englewood Cliffs, NJ: Prentice Hall.

Vaillant, G. E. (1993). *The wisdom of the ego.* Cambridge, MA: Harvard University Press.

Citing an edited book and a chapter from that book:

Pennebaker, J. W. (Ed.). (1995). *Emotion, disclosure, and health.* Washington, DC: American Psychological Association.

Wegner, D. M., & Lane, J. D. (1995). From secrecy to psychopathology. In J. W. Pennebaker (Ed.), *Emotion, disclosure, and health* (pp. 25–46). Washington, DC: American Psychological Association.

Citing a chapter from an edited book in a series:

Langer, E. J. (1989). Minding matters: The consequences of mindlessness-mindfulness. In L. Berkowitz (Ed.), *Advances in experimental social psychology* (Vol. 22, pp. 137–173). New York: Academic Press.

all follow the same basic format, but if you find yourself using an eso-teric reference you can always consult the *Publication Manual.* You will probably find yourself relying primarily on articles from psychology journals, as well as some books, edited books, and book chapters. To that end, table 3.3 shows the format for each of these sorts of references.

Please note that APA references for articles submitted for publication are always double-spaced and indented five spaces from the left margin. As shown in table 3.3, the entries in a reference list appear in alphabetical order by the surname of the author. If an author has more than one entry, then you must also arrange them by year of publication so that the earliest publication comes first (see the Anderson example in table 3.3). For a reference with more than one author, the last names of all authors, as well as their first and middle initials, must appear in the order they appear on the publication.

The titles of journals and books are always underlined in a typed manuscript; in table 3.3, they are typeset in italics. In addition to this required underlining, you may initially be puzzled by the capitalization scheme that is used in the APA style reference list. The titles of journals (e.g., *Psychological Review, Journal of Verbal Learning and Verbal Behavior*) are always capitalized. Except for any proper nouns appearing in a book title, for example, *In the Freud Archives* (Malcolm, 1984), however, only first words in book titles, for example, *On dreams* (Freud, 1901/1952) or subtitles, for example, *Influence: Science and practice* (Cialdini, 1993) are capitalized. If you have occasion to cite the title of a book, book chapter, or article in the body of a paper, then you must capitalize all words in the title except for articles, such as *a, the, or,* and so on.

I would like to close this section by offering an important piece of advice about references: Keep track of them. Practical researchers keep a running reference list or, where copies of articles or chapters are concerned, a file or folder (see chapter 4). Both lists and files are constantly updated to reflect changes in your thinking and writing. Such detailed record keeping and repeated updating may sound overly compulsive, but both activities are real time savers in the long run. You will not want to be under pressure to submit a project paper and then, at the last minute, be unable to locate the references you used to write it!

Author Note   The Author Note page follows the last page of the References section (refer to section 1.15 of the *Publication Manual*). In practice, students rarely need to add this page to a paper for a course project. Nonetheless, anyone who learns to use APA style should understand all parts of a manuscript. The Author Note includes the institutional affiliation of each author, any source of financial support, allows authors to acknowledge the assistance of colleagues with the research, and identifies the corresponding author who may be contacted for further information concerning the manuscript. If the research was presented at a professional meeting, the sponsoring organization and the date should be mentioned here as well. If you include an Author Note page in any paper you write, I recommend that you use it to acknowledge peer commentary that you receive on drafts of your paper.

Tables and Figures   To begin, a *table* summarizes results or reports data, such as means, standard deviations, or more complex statistical analyses. In contrast, a *figure* can be a graph, a picture, or a drawing. Tables and figures simplify results for ease of comprehension so that readers should be able to glance at them and quickly understand their meaning independent of any reference to text (refer to sections 3.62–3.86 in the *Publication Manual*). Yet, as noted previously in the section on Results, accompanying text must still interpret any tables and figures for readers in a supplementary, not a repetitious, way. A guiding rule of thumb for creating tables and figures is the modified KISS rule ("Keep It Simple, Student"). Be economical in terms of space used, information conveyed, and style—report just what is necessary and no more.

It is impossible to review the myriad types of tables and figures that can be used in an APA style paper. As a result, I urge you to examine published journal articles, as well as the *Publication Manual*, for examples. Keep in mind that tables frequently contain summary information,

TABLE 3.4

CHECKLIST FOR FORMATTING APA STYLE PAPERS: SOME COMMON MISTAKES

— Is the paper typed or printed on white paper (section 4.01)?
___ Is the entire paper double-spaced (section 4.03)?
___ Are the paper's margins at least 1 inch (section 4.04)?
___ Do the Title page, Abstract, References section, Author Note, as well as any table, figure, or appendix appear on separate pages (section 4.05)?
___ Does page numbering begin with the Title page (section 4.05)?
___ Is the title 12 words or fewer (section 1.06)?
___ Is the Abstract the proper length (empirical articles are 120 words or fewer and review papers are 75 to 100 words; section 1.07)?
___ Do references in the text match those in the References section (section 3.104)?
___ Do text and References section citations match in terms of spelling and publication date (section 3.104)?
___ Are journal titles spelled out fully (section 3.114)?
___ Are references in parenthetical citations in the text and in the References section ordered alphabetically by authors' last names (sections 3.99 and 3.107)?
___ Are page numbers specified for all articles and book chapters in the References section (sections 3.114 and 3.116)?

Note: The section numbers indicated above can be found in the fourth edition of the *Publication Manual of the American Psychological Association* (1994). Copyright (1994) by the American Psychological Association. Adapted with permission.

such as descriptive statistics or main effects (i.e., mean differences among two or more groups). In contrast, figures, notably graphs, are often used to show statistical interactions that involve the observed change in some dependent measure due to the effects of two or more independent variables. We will return to a more detailed examination of how to display data in chapter 8.

Appendix An appendix is a useful place to display materials that are relevant to a piece of research, but not to the heart of the manuscript (i.e., the introduction, Method, Results, and Discussion). As noted previously in the review of the Method section, complex stimuli, raw data, or equipment descriptions are appropriate here, as are unpublished computer programs, psychological tests, mathematical proofs, and any other materials that can promote readers' understanding, evaluation, or replication of an experiment (refer to section 1.14 of the *Publication Manual*).

Final Advice on Paper Preparation When it comes to preparing a paper, first time writers using APA style are apt to make relatively predictable mistakes. Table 3.4, which was adapted from Appendix B of the *Publication Manual*, contains a checklist of some common oversights. Once you have a final draft of your paper, you should carefully review it using this checklist (relevant sections of the *Publication Manual* are noted in the parentheses at the end of each question). In addition, be sure to compare your paper's format with the sample APA style paper located in Appendix A of this book.

PRACTICAL ISSUES FOR WRITING

When writing, I assume that you are taking advantage of the available, ever evolving technology. In other words, I assume that you are using a computer or wordprocessor of some sort. Wordprocessing has revolutionized the writing, revising, and editing process. There is no excuse for not learning to use a wordprocessor. Besides your research work in psychology, wordprocessing will also enhance your writing and college work more generally. In addition to improving your performance in college, wordprocessing and computing experience is a virtual necessity for postgraduate life. Whether you enter the work force following college or attend a graduate or professional school, the ability to compose at a computer will serve you well.

So if you have been postponing the inevitable, use the experience of learning to conduct psychological research to also learn to use a wordprocessor. Quite simply, a wordprocessor is another very useful tool for the practical researcher. And in any case, in what follows, I will assume that you are using some sort of wordprocessor to write your APA style papers (if you are not, you are creating too much work for yourself, as well as setting yourself up for a frustrating experience).

Freewriting Revisited: Benefits and Focus

One of the most common laments of students who must write a paper is that they do not know how to get started. Being confronted with a blank piece of paper or a blank computer screen is anxiety provoking. Many wonder how they will ever think of anything to fill one page (screen), let alone an entire paper!

You will recall that freewriting—a technique involving continuous writing where anything that comes to mind is recorded—was introduced in chapter 2. Freewriting was presented to help generate research topics, as it provides writers with a wide latitude to see what ideas occur to them and a chance to explore where they lead. A prominent writing teacher suggests that freewriting provides an "evaluation free zone," a notably rare commodity where writing assignments are concerned (Elbow, 1993, p. 197). That is, you have the opportunity to write about whatever comes to mind and is of passing or sustained interest to you. It is not an assignment, but a starting point, a way to generate some ideas that can lead to others. (If you did not try the freewriting exercise that was introduced in chapter 2, I strongly urge you to read the brief directions on page 61 and to try some freewriting before proceeding with this chapter.)

What are the benefits of freewriting? There are several, and an obvious one has already been mentioned: Most people can do it easily after only a few trials. There is no set format to worry about, and because it is your private writing, freewriting is not graded. Freewriting is also a quick and easy way to create pages of material, some of which can be revised and then integrated into a developing paper. An added strength is that your writing is likely to become much more interesting to read because it is self-expressive rather than labored or formulaic. Relatedly, freewriting is

BOX FEATURE 3.B

A Research Digression: Overcoming Writer's Block

You may be surprised to learn that many academic psychologists often have trouble starting to write a professional publication. Many times this form of writer's block develops because they have unwittingly set themselves up to make writing an anxiety-producing experience. Every time they start to write they become anxious, and so they never really get their writing going.

Shelley Taylor and Joanne Martin, two prolific writers who happen to be psychologists, discuss this issue in a chapter they wrote for beginning professors. They note that

> . . . you can get yourself to tackle a tough paper by thinking that "It's just a rough draft that no one will ever see." A prominent psychologist reports that an assistant professor came up to him once to thank him profusely for teaching him how to write. "What did I do?" exclaimed the astonished psychologist. "I saw you writing on blue paper, and realized that by writing on blue paper you could think of your writing as preliminary. I had always been writing on white paper and feeling that the writing had to be fully polished. When I switched to blue paper, my productivity increased enormously." (Taylor & Martin, 1987, p. 42)

If you ever encounter writer's block, you should try to find the equivalent of the blue paper in this anecdote. By doing so, you may have to trick yourself into writing or set up a reward system—say, a break in the snack bar between section drafts. Whatever technique you use, however, you must write, and the sooner you get started overcoming any block, the more comfortable you will be with your writing.

a way to synthesize what you read with diverse course materials, not only to explore their meaning but also their relationship to your personal experience (Pennebaker, 1990a; 1990b). Finally, learning to use freewriting can be exhilarating because you will not feel as pressured as you might about a typical writing assignment, nor will you censor your thoughts by attempting to produce a perfect essay at the outset (Elbow, 1993).

Once you have the general idea of freewriting in hand, you can move onto *focused freewriting*, which is quite useful in moving toward our goal of writing a psychology paper. Focused freewriting involves writing nonstop for short periods of time on *one* particular topic. This form of freewriting is a relatively painless way for you to start an APA style paper. Once you have your topic in mind, you simply write about it using the freewriting technique, gradually producing pieces that can be fit together to form a paper.

There are two ways to use focused freewriting to produce material that can be used in a project paper. First, focused freewriting can be used to create ideas for the topical discussions within the paper. You may be familiar with the literature on some effect, say, the loss of information from human working memory, but you are looking for some way to give life to the effect and move beyond an empirical description. Focused freewriting is a good way to generate examples, such as maintenance rehearsal strategies in working memory, which give some weight and psychological character to the effect.

Alternatively, focused freewriting can be used to develop rough drafts of each section of an APA paper. Having begun to conduct your study, you may know its methodology, but you are unsure about where to begin when writing a Method section. Take 10 or 15 minutes to write down everything you can remember about what measures you used, for example, as well as the setting, the independent variables, or what your participants experienced. The resulting description may allow the Method section to begin to take a more concrete form both on paper and in your mind. Once you have something written, you can begin to edit it, adding or subtracting information as you go along as a detailed methodology begins to take shape.

To this point, you have learned that freewriting can spark the writing process by generating ideas for what to write about or by creating a starting point for your writing. When focused on a particular theme, say, a topic from psychology, freewriting can help you apply what you know or it can give both shape and substance to section drafts of a paper. No matter how rich or interesting it may be, however, writing a psychology paper is more than generating text through freewriting. You need a framework for what you already wrote and what you still need to write. In short, you need to develop an outline.

Exercise 3.A: Doing an Outline

An outline is essentially a framework, the "bones" if you will, for your paper. A good outline serves as a guide to where your writing is going; if you have the bones, you need only to flesh them out with the details of your research. Fortunately, the four main sections of the APA style paper already provide some of the bones for us, and the freewriting and focused freewriting you have finished should provide you with some text that can be inserted into an outline and, eventually, the developing paper. All that remains is to add some levels of detail to an outline before writing the paper in earnest.

Table 3.5 shows the outline of a typical APA style paper. As you can see, this outline only includes the four main sections that comprise the bulk of a paper; the other six sections do not need to be outlined. In this sample outline, the paper's sections and their function are shown in regular typeface. To illustrate the outline of an actual psychology experiment, the outline of a student paper is shown in italics.

Use table 3.5 as a model from which you can develop an outline for your paper. Similar to the paper itself, the outline must be flexible and subject to ongoing revision. Remember, it is a guide and not a contract. If parts of it are not working, then revise or discard them accordingly. A good outline will help you to begin the process of drafting and revising your paper.

TABLE 3.5

A SAMPLE OUTLINE FOR AN APA STYLE PAPER

I. Introduction
   a. General overview of the research area.
      Positive affect enhances problem solving.
   b. Specific problem examined.
      Humor may have more marked, favorable effects on problem solving than positive mood.
   c. Literature review.
      Review studies on mood, cognition, and problem solving; music and spatial reasoning. Establish links between literatures.
   d. Specific hypothesis and proposed methodology.
      Exposure to humor will enhance spatial reasoning relative to positive mood or a neutral condition.
      Three groups exposed to different stimuli (humor, positive mood, control) complete a spatial reasoning task.
II. Method
   a. Participants.
      Males and females from college and work place.
   b. Apparatus.
      Spatial reasoning task taken from a standardized intelligence test.
   c. Procedure.
      Pretesting of cartoons for humor group; random assignment of participants to treatment group.
      • independent variable *Treatment group: humor, mood, or control*
      • dependent variable *Score on 18 problems from spatial reasoning task*
      • participants were debriefed
III. Results
   a. Conceptual review of hypothesis.
      Did humor lead to better spatial reasoning? No, hypothesis wasn't supported.
   b. Report of main result.
      Analysis of variance (ANOVA): The means in the three groups did not differ from one another.
      Make a table.
   c. Report of secondary result.
      The manipulation check indicates that some cartoons were not seen as funny by the humor group.
IV. Discussion
   a. What does main result mean for theory?
   b. What does main result mean for human behavior more generally?
      No clear results. Discuss manipulation check: The study should be replicated with better stimulus materials.
   c. Implications of results for future research.
   d. Concluding comments: Where do we go from here?
      Replicate, and refine procedure and theory.

Note: The regular typeface identifies the function of an outline section. The italicized print represents the outline of the student paper found in Appendix A.

TABLE 3.6

A RECOMMENDED ORDER OF STEPS FOR WRITING AN APA STYLE PAPER

Step 1—Draft the Method Section
Step 2—Draft the Results Section
    —Revisit Step 1 for revising and editing
Step 3—Draft the introduction
    —Revisit Steps 1 and 2 for revising and editing
    —As references are used, add them to the References Section
Step 4—Draft the Discussion Section
    —Revisit Steps 1, 2, and 3 for revising and editing
Step 5—Draft the Abstract
    —Create the Title page
    —Write the Author Note (if any)
    —Create tables and figures
    —Verify references
    —Add appendix (if necessary)
    —Revisit Steps 1, 2, 3, and 4
Step 6—Obtain peer feedback on the complete draft
    —Revise the draft based on peer review
    —Repeat Steps 1–6 as needed
Step 7—Submit the final draft

Drafting: A Recommended Order of Steps for the APA Style Paper

Once you have done some freewriting and focused freewriting to get started, as well as developed an outline, you can begin to draft your paper. Where should you begin? Many student writers assume that, like Alice, it is best to begin at the beginning; that is, start with the title, write the Abstract, launch head-on into the introduction, and so on until the last table is finished. The experience of many practical researchers reveals otherwise, however. There is a proper order for writing a draft of an APA style paper, but it does *not* follow the linear layout of the typical article. Table 3.6 illustrates a recommended order of steps for creating a draft once a project's data are collected and analyzed.

Why start writing with the Method section (see table 3.6)? Chances are that the methodology you used is fresh in your mind, so putting it down on paper should pose little difficulty. Furthermore, many practical researchers write a draft of the Method section *while* they are still in the midst of collecting their data. No time is wasted and they get a head start on writing a summary of their work.

Please note that after the first step, each subsequent step in the writing process (except Step 7) requires that the writing accomplished in the earlier step(s) be revisited. "Revisited" in this context means that the writer should check that the writing done to that point is reviewed for accuracy and clarity, and that appropriate—and ongoing—editing and revising are performed.

As can be seen in table 3.6, once the Method section is drafted, a preliminary version of the Results section should be written. In order to write the Results, of course, all the data must be both coded and analyzed (see chapter 8). Assuming that these two tasks are completed, the Results section should be written because the study's findings truly inform the rest of the paper. How so? Well, before the introduction can be drafted (Step 3), a writer needs to have a firm grasp of the study's outcome in mind so that the problem description and the literature review is crisp and focused.

Only when Step 3 is completed—the introduction is drafted and the References section begins to take shape—does the writer turn to the Discussion section. Once the Discussion is drafted and all previous sections have been reviewed, the opening and closing sections of the paper are addressed. As noted previously, a good Abstract is never easy to write, so adequate time must be allotted, nor can it be written until the author has a complete sense of the entire project. Creating a Title page and any tables or figures, verifying references, and adding any appendices follow.

Before the last two steps, the entire paper draft is edited and revised again. Step 6 involves obtaining and using peer comments, issues we will discuss in detail shortly, and Step 7 is the submission of the final version of the paper for a grade, presentation, or publication.

Are the steps listed in table 3.6 the only way to draft an APA style paper? Certainly not. Some researchers prefer to write a proposal at the start of a project. A proposal has a Title page, Abstract, and introduction, as well as proposed Method, anticipated Results, and References sections, and it is written *before* any data are collected. Obviously, one would probably write the introduction, proposed Method, and anticipated Results section first, and then the remaining sections. In effect, a proposal serves as a first draft of the APA style paper that will take shape as the proposed Method is approved, and the data are collected, analyzed, and written up. Note that the Discussion section is usually the last section written using this alternative approach.

A complete APA style manuscript written by a student is included in Appendix A. Please use this sample manuscript as a model when you write a paper summarizing research you have conducted. Although this sample paper is relatively complete, keep in mind your project may require a slightly different format than the one shown here or you may have very specific questions about style issues that are not addressed here. If so, don't despair: Seek out your course instructor for advice or, better still, consult the *Publication Manual* for guidance.

Revising

The importance of ongoing revision of what you write is a prominent theme in this chapter, but a more detailed presentation of what revision entails seems appropriate after directions for drafting a paper. There are three main levels to the revision process (Elbow & Belanoff, 1995): rethinking, restructuring, and proofreading. Each level and its activities will be described.

BOX FEATURE 3.C

A Research Digression: Maladaptive Myths About Writers and Writing

You might be interested to learn that many faculty members share the same resistances about writing that students do. Boice (1990) discussed common but mythical beliefs about writers that members of both groups hold to their mutual detriment. The beliefs are that (from Boice, 1990, p. 15)

1. Good writers do not share their writing until it is finished and perfect.
2. Good writers do not begin writing until they are in the mood.
3. Good writers do not begin writing until they have a novel, creative concept.
4. Good writers delay writing until they have big blocks of undisrupted time available.
5. Good writers produce finished manuscripts in a single draft.
6. Good writers are born, not made.

Make no mistake: These beliefs are maladaptive. One particularly disruptive side effect is that they lead to "bingeing" where writing is concerned. Bingeing, a by-product of procrastination (Boice, in press; see also, Boice, 1996), involves waiting to the last minute to begin a writing assignment and then literally throwing it together in a spree of writing. The product of this flurry of writing is rarely any good, and its hurried nature no doubt maintains the larger myth that writing is an aversive activity.

How can you combat these myths effectively? Following the wisdom of experienced writers and writing teachers, Boice (1990) argues that would-be writers must change their thinking about motivation and intentions. Specifically, the belief that motivation (e.g., "I have to be in the right mood to write") and intention (e.g., "As soon as I finish all this other homework, I'll get down to that writing") comes before—rather than after—an established writing routine must be changed. Regular, short sessions of freewriting, writing in the same place and time avoiding distractions, and putting off preferred activities are good ways to begin, thereby increasing the chance that writing will, indeed, get done (see also Box Feature 3.B).

Rethinking involves changing what a paper says once a draft is written. Reading what you wrote can help you see parts of the text that do not make sense or to notice what important information has been left out. You may simply think of a better way to present something that is already written. Perhaps a peer reviewer offers an insightful suggestion that greatly improves a section of the paper.

Rethinking your paper can be done by making editorial comments on a draft copy or by typing in changes on a wordprocessor. Changes to a paper in the rethinking process may be major—discarding entire pages of the text—or minor—rewriting a few sentences, perhaps a paragraph. All writers rethink their writing to clarify what they want to say and to make the presentation an effective one.

Restructuring, the second level of revision, is the act of changing how a paper conveys information. In restructuring or reworking a paper you reconsider its organization or how it is put together. Obviously, you cannot change the standard format provided by APA style (Abstract, introduction, Method, etc.), but you can restructure the organization of the writing within any given section. A good way to proceed with restructuring a paper is to revisit your outline to check for consistency (keeping in mind that outlines, too, are fodder for revision). Another technique is to adopt the perspective of your future readers: Have you told them what they need to know clearly and accurately? Does the current structure help them to anticipate your arguments or are they left with too many questions?

To restructure a paper, obtain a hard copy of the text and spread the pages out on a large, flat surface—the floor, a table top. If you use a wordprocessor, you may be tempted to restructure the text right on the screen. Instead of reviewing a screen at a time, I advise you to go over a hard copy because you need to see the whole text at once. Read through the pages with the hourglass model of APA style argument in mind. Is the paper broad and conceptual where it should be, as well as concrete and specific in the right places? If not, then you may need to move sentences or paragraphs (scissors help here), even pages. Do not be afraid to mark up, cut up, or move around what you've already written.

Proofreading, also known as copyediting, is the third level of revision. Proofreading involves reviewing the entire paper with an eye to catching errors in grammar, punctuation, and spelling. Regarding spelling, use of a "spellcheck" computer program is *not* proofreading; though helpful, such devices routinely miss correctly spelled but out-of-place homophones (e.g., sun for son; knot for not). In the case of the APA Style research paper, the proofreading phase is also an opportunity to check for adherence to the prescribed format for scientific writing in psychology. Proofreading is the last revising that is done before the paper is given to peer reviewers or submitted for a grade.

SHARING PAPER DRAFTS

After drafting and revising a paper, you need to learn what others think of it. The process of peer review—giving or receiving constructive criticism on research—is integral to scientific writing. The goal is to teach you to share your writing with others in order to ask for and receive helpful feedback on it. You will also learn some suggestions about reading and commenting on papers written by your peers. Each of the exercises that follow will sharpen your writing and reading skills as a practical researcher. I am indebted to the work of Peter Elbow and Pat Belanoff (1995), whose ideas and techniques inform this section of the chapter (see also, Boice, 1990; Flower, 1993; Maimon, Nodine, & O'Connor, 1989).

There is a guiding premise behind each exercise, one that is prominent in workshop approaches to teaching writing (e.g., Dunn, 1994; 1996; Elbow & Belanoff, 1995): Summary evaluations are not enough. Being informed by a peer or a professor that your paper is "good" or "really well-written" is not very informative. You need to know *what* specifically makes it a good paper (the organization? the literature review?) and *what sections* of the paper are really well-written (the Discussion but not the Method?). In short, you need to ask readers questions about your work and, in turn, you need to give your peers directive feedback on their writing.

Exercise 3.B: Receiving Feedback on Writing

Who should read your rough draft? Another student from your class? Your roommate? Your grandmother? There are two schools of thought on this point. One view is that you should ask someone familiar with the topic to read your work. After all, who better to ask than an expert? There is some merit to this point, as a more expert reader can clarify the logic of your work as well as raise issues you have neglected. An expert can even recommend additional studies or references to support your argument.

The other view advocates obtaining feedback from someone who is unfamiliar with the topic of your paper. Why? Because a general reader will readily identify ideas in the paper that do not make sense or that are written solely for experts. Naive but interested readers can see the forest, as it were, without getting lost among the trees.

Which sort of reader should you get? I suggest a happy, as well as constructive, compromise: If possible, why not ask one or two from each group? When I finish a draft of an article that I intend to submit to a journal, I always have one or two psychologists read it. I also ask colleagues from different disciplines to read the draft, as well. Two of the latter reviewers are usually a labor economist and a theologian (incidentally, I frequently comment on their work, as well). They invariably make different sorts of suggestions and identify different things in my writing, but they always improve the work. Ask a peer from one of your psychology classes to read your paper and, of course, offer to return the favor. If your friends or roommates are from different academic majors, you should consider asking them to read your work, as well.

Setting the stage for feedback. Let's turn to the specifics of how to receive feedback on what you've written so far. I will assume that you have a relatively complete rough draft of an APA style paper. Ask your reader to take as much time as necessary to read through the paper and, while doing so, to jot down any questions or concerns he or she has in the paper's margins. Your reader is *not* a proofreader; that is, it is not the reader's job to correct your spelling or punctuation. Grammatical errors, however, fall under the heading of portions of the text that are not clear and should be pointed out, if possible, by readers.

Receiving feedback. One of the most difficult aspects about being a writer is avoiding being defensive about your writing—but you must try not to be defensive. There is a cardinal rule for receiving comments from a reader: No matter what, the reader is always right. If a reader finds a passage to be unclear, does not understand the point of the study, or cannot identify your hypothesis, do not start to quibble, qualify, or explain what you were trying to say. Remember: You are

TABLE 3.7

QUESTIONS FOR PEER REVIEWERS AFTER THEY READ YOUR PAPER

Summary: Ask the reader to summarize your paper—*"Using your own words, please summarize what you read. What were the main points of the study?"*

Reply: Ask the reader for thoughts or reactions to your paper—*"What do you think about my experiment? Now that you've read what I think about this topic, what do you think about it?"*

Reasoning: Ask the reader to describe the chain of reasoning laid out in your paper—*"Please tell me the reasoning you see in my paper. What is the hypothesis? Is there support for it? Do the study's data support its conclusions?"*

Criteria: Ask the reader to react to specific criteria you believe are important to your paper—*"Is there too much jargon in the paper?" "Is the text too wordy?" "Are the results clear and easy to understand?" "Is the introduction too short?" "Do I need to have more supporting references?"*

Source: Adapted from Elbow & Belanoff, 1995.

interested in what is clear or not clear in your writing, and how it is being interpreted by your reader. Your writing—not you—should speak for itself. If a reader does not understand what you are trying to say in your paper, then other readers, including your instructor, are not likely to understand your points either.

What to ask. After your peer has gone over any questions and concerns with you, it is your turn to ask for specific feedback that you believe will help you to improve the paper. First, thank the reader, and then explain that you would like to ask a few questions. Then, consider asking the sorts of questions listed in table 3.7. Please note that these questions are only guidelines; you must tailor them to fit your paper. For example, ask for a summary of the paper: It is always helpful to hear a quick summary of what you wrote so that you can determine if your main points stood out. Remember, this approach to writing and review is active, not passive. You must ask for what you need to tighten your prose.

Seeking other feedback. Beyond the sort of peer feedback advocated here, you can take advantage of other helpful resources that may be available in your class or elsewhere on your campus. Your professor may welcome the opportunity to read and comment on a rough draft of your work. If so, by all means, take him or her up on the offer, but follow these recommended guidelines. Be appreciative and understanding of your professor's time, as it may be several days before your draft is read and returned to you. In the meantime, continue to revise the paper anyway. To speed up the process, you might offer to come to your instructor's office and to wait while your draft is read. I prefer to read rough drafts this way so that I can discuss my points with the writer, but do not be alarmed if this offer is rebuffed—instructors all work differently.

If your instructor is unable to read drafts of your paper, you should find out if your college or university has a writing center available to students. A good place to start is with a call to the English Department to learn if your institution offers this resource. Many schools have writing centers that are staffed by faculty members, adjunct writing teachers, graduate students, and sometimes advanced undergraduates, all of whom are trained to help you to improve your written work. More often than not you must schedule an appointment at the writing center; if you make one, by all means keep it or cancel it well in advance. Bring a draft of your paper and a detailed description of the writing assignment, and be prepared to receive the sort of feedback we have discussed in this chapter. Be forewarned: Writing staff who are not in the social sciences will probably be unfamiliar with APA style, and they may try to dissuade you from using it. Be pleasant but firm, and tell them that you are required to write the paper using APA format.

Exercise 3.C: Giving Feedback on Writing

Giving feedback on a psychology paper can be just as helpful to your writing as receiving comments on one of your own papers. Why? Because carefully reading the work of others allows you to practice editing skills, to exercise what you know about grammar, spelling, and punctuation, and to learn how others craft an argument, review the literature, and so on. All of these activities can inform your own writing.

The recommendations given previously on receiving feedback now apply to you as a reader, so this section will be shorter than the last. Carefully read through a peer's paper, jotting any questions or concerns in the margins of the text. Try to evaluate both the argument and the content of the paper, as well as checking for adherence to APA style. After reviewing your comments with the writer, ask if more specific sorts of feedback are desired. Refer back to table 3.7 in order to give the writer a summary of the paper, a reply to issues raised in it, or a description of the paper's chain of reasoning.

A peer reviewer is wise to reconcile two seemingly contradictory pieces of advice. First, do not be timid in your peer review of another's work—silence will not improve a paper. At the same time, however, your job is not to do a "search and destroy" mission on the work of another. You are not judge and jury, but another writer whose goal is to expand psychological knowledge. The golden rule of "Do unto others as you would have them do unto you" certainly applies to the process of peer review.

WRITING ALL THE TIME

One final issue remains: When to write? As noted above, many student writers wait until the last minute to begin writing. Avoid doing this by establishing a writing routine for yourself. If possible, write every day, and do so at the same time and the same place. You could write at your desk every morning or in the library every afternoon. The place and time do not matter as long as you are comfortable and they are familiar.

Ritual matters. Make your coffee or tea, adjust the lights, and read what you wrote during your last session. If you write using pencil and paper, then have your pencils sharp and your tablet ready. If you compose on the computer, start with an empty screen or load the file you are working on from its diskette. The goal is to turn your ritual into a habit so that your ideas and words will flow smoothly from established activities.

After the ritual is complete and you begin to put words to paper or screen, you must write for a set period of time. How long is up to you, but I would suggest at least an hour to an hour-and-a-half per day. You can begin gradually, of course, with 15 minutes the first day, 30 the second, and so on until you reach your goal. B. F. Skinner, for example, wrote for a couple of hours early in the morning of each day, noting that interruptions from the phone or knocks on the door were least likely then (Skinner, 1981).

Focus on quantity first—that is, generate text—and quality will follow. In this vein, Skinner (1981) advocated taking advice from the Romans, *Nulla dies sine linea*—No day without a line. Heeding this advice will enhance the writing of any practical researcher.

SUMMARY

Practical researchers treat writing as a first and last consideration in all phases of a research project; however, much of the writing occurs after the results are known. To share the results subsequently with the psychological community, two topics were presented: learning to use psychology's journal article format, APA style, and practical issues for improving writing. The review of APA style involved the structure, content, and writing style of journal article manuscripts. The first half of the chapter reviewed ways to master this style, including the hourglass model and presentation of the sections, and their respective format, of the APA style paper. The chapter's second half addressed putting ideas into writing, including freewriting to get started, outlining, a sequence of steps for drafting an APA style paper, recommendations for revising writing, and receiving and giving peer criticism on papers. The chapter concluded by advocating that writing should become a routine.

KEY TERMS

Abstract (p. 81)
APA Style (p. 80)
Discussion (p. 88)
drafting (p. 98)

focused freewriting (p. 95)
freewriting (p. 94)
hourglass model (p. 80)
introduction (p. 82)
Method (p. 84)

outline (p. 96)
peer feedback (p.102)
References (p. 89)
Results (p. 86)
revision (p. 99)

SUGGESTED READINGS

American Psychological Association (1994). *Publication manual of the American Psychological Association* (4th ed.). Washington, DC: Author. Every psychologist's and practical researcher's Bible. Obtain a copy.

Bem, D. J. (1987). Writing the empirical journal article. In M. P. Zanna & J. M. Darley (Eds.), *The compleat academic: A Practical guide for the beginning social scientist* (pp. 171–201). New York: Random House. Although it was written for senior graduate students and new assistant professors, this chapter provides some advanced techniques for writing and polishing APA style papers.

Booth, W. C., Colomb, G. C., & Williams, J. M. (1995). *The craft of research.* Chicago: University of Chicago Press. An excellent book offering insightful, down-to-earth advice about how practicing researchers in any discipline can do their work. I heartily recommend it.

Hult, C. A. (1996). *Research and writing in the social sciences.* Boston, MA: Allyn & Bacon. A solid, interdisciplinary text focusing on how to conduct library research and to write research reports.

McCloskey, D. N. (1987). *The writing of economics.* New York: Allyn & Bacon. Do not be put off by the title, as this wonderful little book is about writing first and economics second. It contains some of the best advice on writing I have ever encountered.

Sternberg, R. J. (1993). *The psychologist's companion: A guide to scientific writing for students and researchers* (3rd ed.). New York: Cambridge University Press. A prolific and consummate practical researcher provides chapter by chapter advice on everything from starting papers to writing lectures. This book really does appeal to student as well as professional audiences.

Strunk, W., & White, E. B. (1972). *The elements of style* (2nd ed.). New York: Macmillan. A perennial and concise classic about writing, as well as an inexpensive investment.

CHAPTER 4

Searching and Reading the Psychological Literature

To contribute to psychological research, you need to know what questions have been asked and what ones await answers. You must immerse yourself in ideas and opinions of psychologists who, dedicated to their craft, have written and published on all aspects of behavior. Not surprisingly, there is a great deal to know about what we think and do, more than any one person or even an army of scholars could master in a number of lifetimes. Although you cannot learn everything there is to know, you can certainly master a small part of it while you research your project.

This chapter is designed to teach you how to search and use the psychological literature. The first half of the chapter provides practical advice about systematically using the library and other resources to search for references pertaining to your chosen topic. You will learn, for example, how to search various CD-ROM and on-line databases relevant to psychology. Once you locate a number of appropriate references, the second half of the chapter will provide advice on selecting the most useful ones for your project. Specific procedures for evaluating empirical articles, books, and book chapters are presented, as are suggestions about taking notes and avoiding plagiarizing references in the course of your research.

WHY ARE JOURNALS EMPHASIZED?

The first time students begin to examine the psychological literature closely, they are often surprised by the emphasis placed on using research published in journals rather than in books. Psychology, as well as the other social and natural sciences, is time centered. That is, researchers in the social and natural sciences are busy and need to be kept abreast of any new developments, theories, and techniques in areas relevant to their own specialties. Journals achieve this end because they are published much more frequently than books, thereby allowing members of the psychological community to keep up to date. They also come out more quickly, so the information in them is relatively current.

Time is not the sole consideration, however. There are several other reasons for the emphasis placed on journals, including the following:

Journal articles are subject to peer review. Before any article is published, it is evaluated by an editor who assigns it to a handful of experts who provide (usually) anonymous reviews. Based upon these reviews, the editor decides if the work will be accepted outright, revised, or rejected. The top ranking psychological journals reject over 80 percent of the submissions they receive each year. Generally, such high rejection rates indicate that the accepted articles appearing in print are of high caliber and quality.

Journal articles always have the same format. As discussed in chapter 3, most psychological journals follow the style of the American Psychological Association or a set of similar guidelines. Readers know what to expect and how to find the information they need quickly and efficiently.

Journals are specialized. Each journal appeals to a particular audience of researchers who share an interest in a topical area. Indeed, there is probably at least one journal publishing articles on almost any area of psychology you can name. There is a very good chance, then, that you can locate research appealing to whatever your particular interests happen to be.

Journals are numerous. There are thousands of academic journals in existence, and in psychology alone there are over 350 (American Psychological Association, 1993).

Journal articles address specific questions. Whether a question is empirical or theoretical, a journal article focuses on one substantive issue. This degree of specificity allows researchers to incorporate a piece of research into their own thinking, to verify or challenge a result, or to read about a detailed examination of one aspect of human behavior.

Please do not misinterpret the role of journals in psychology by assuming that books and book chapters have no place; psychologists do not live on periodicals alone. Books and chapters, too, are quite important to students, teachers, and scholars. Nonetheless, most of the publications you are apt to encounter in the course of your searches of the psychological literature will be from journals, the foundations of the field's scholarly research.

LOCATING THE LITERATURE

To locate the psychological literature, the first step for any researcher is a visit to the library. If you have already made use of your college or university library, then you are probably familiar with its layout. If you have yet to darken the door of the library, the time to do so has arrived. Once there, you must develop a strategy to search for and find what resources you need for your project.

Developing a Search Strategy

The psychological literature is vast, daunting, constantly growing, and ever changing. It is not too far from the mark to suggest that this literature is a rich form of chaos, full of diverse opinion, speculation, and insight. The first time a person tries to make sense out of it, however, the literature is apt to appear more than a bit unwieldy. The job of the psychological researcher, then, is to impose some order on this chaos. The best way to begin to create order is through a systematic search of the literature. What follows are two reasonable approaches to organizing a literature search, the bottom-up and the top-down search strategies.

When you are new to a research question, as most students are, the best approach to take is a *bottom-up search*. Conceptually, "bottom-up" refers to the importance of building one's knowledge from the ground up by gaining a broad view of a topic prior to targeting specific questions. Bottom-up searching entails learning the most basic information about your topic and then gradually refining a search to include more specific information about current issues, gaps in knowledge, and any ongoing controversies surrounding it. As a result, I strongly recommend that most readers of this book use this strategy for any literature search. There are 5 steps to a bottom-up search, as is shown in table 4.1, and we will review each one in detail (note that "bottom-up" and "top-down" are figurative, not literal, directions for the steps in a search).

Established researchers who are familiar with a topic—they know the key terms used in research as well as the names of important authors who contribute frequently to it—sometimes use a *top-down search*. A top-down search begins with Step 5 in table 4.1, as useful references and a concrete focus for a paper or project are already in the researcher's grasp. The researcher may not feel that these references are entirely sufficient, however, so some backtracking through Steps 3 and 4 occurs. Indeed, the term "top-down" means that you already have a very good conceptual grasp of a research area, and you just want to check it for new references or some older ones you may have neglected to examine. Let me caution you against using this search strategy because you are apt to miss or simply overlook a variety of relevant references. In fact, top-down searches are usually less systematic than bottom-up searches precisely because missed index terms mean missed references.

Let's assume that you will do a bottom-up search by following table 4.1 in a step-by-step fashion. Your college or university's reference library serves a critical role in this search. If you are not familiar with its purpose, location, and operation, rest assured that you will be by the end of your literature search.

TABLE 4.1

STEPS IN CONDUCTING A BOTTOM-UP LITERATURE SEARCH

Step 1—Look up your topic in a general reference, such as

Eysenck, H. J., Arnold, W., & Meili, R. (1979). *Encyclopedia of psychology.* New York: The Seabury Press.

Read the topic's entry, jot down any key terms, and examine the entry's bibliography. If the topic interests you, go to Step 2; otherwise, choose a new topic.

Step 2—Look up your topic in the *Thesaurus of Psychological Index Terms* and select relevant index terms for your literature search. If necessary, narrow your search by selecting specific terms within a category (e.g., *Illusions* as part of *Perception*).

Step 3—Use the index terms to do a

a. *Computerized Literature Search* using an on-line or CD-ROM database, such as PsycLIT.

b. *Manual Search of the Literature* using *Psychological Abstracts* (which includes published articles since 1927).

Repeat Step 3 as needed. If search results are limited, go back to Step 2. Otherwise, proceed to Step 4.

Step 4—Begin to search other sources on-line (your library's on-line catalog, the Internet), via CD-ROM (e.g., ERIC), or close at hand (e.g., text books); if necessary, look farther away (e.g., interlibrary loan). Proceed to Step 5.

Step 5—Obtain and evaluate the references, select from among them, and begin note taking.

Step 1 Researchers gain perspective on the development of thought and empirical inquiry by reading background material on a topic. Imagine that you were interested in doing a research project on some aspect of *perception,* or how people understand and experience objects and events in the external world (Gleitman, 1991). A very good place to begin your research is by reading background material from a general psychological reference. By using such a reference, you can familiarize yourself with the scope of a topic and learn its basic terminology. The one-volume *Encyclopedia of Psychology* (Eysenck, Arnold, & Meili, 1979), for example, is an excellent general reference often found in the Reference Department of academic libraries. The *Encyclopedia* contains short overview entries on numerous psychological topics, many of which were written by internationally prominent psychologists. (Other very good single and multivolume reference books, as well as some guides to reference materials and review sources, are shown in table 4.2. One or more of these references can provide you with some perspective on your chosen topic.)

The *Encyclopedia's* (Eysenck et al., 1979) entry on *perception* is approximately 1.5 pages in length, and it provides a working definition of perception, a concise history of perceptual research, brief discussion of major perceptual theories, and a bibliography of standard references in the field. In addition, related entries in the *Encyclopedia,* including *attention, auditory perception, neuroanatomy,* and *visual perception,* are listed at the end of the article. It is always a good idea to take a look at these related entries, as well as any entries located near those you decide to read.

TABLE 4.2

OTHER USEFUL BACKGROUND REFERENCES ON PSYCHOLOGICAL TOPICS

Single Volume Reference Works

Bruno, F. J. (1988). *Dictionary of key words in psychology.* London: Routledge & Kegan Paul.

Chaplin, J. P. (1985). *Dictionary of psychology* (2nd ed.). New York: Dell.

Eysenck, H. J., Arnold, W., & Meili, R. (Eds.) (1979). *Encyclopedia of psychology.* New York: The Seabury Press.

Harre, R., & Lamb, R. (Eds.) (1983). *Encyclopedic dictionary of psychology.* Oxford: Basil Blackwell.

Wolman, B. B. (Ed.) (1989). *Dictionary of behavioral science* (2nd ed.). New York: Van Nostrand Reinhold Company.

Multivolume Reference Works

Corsini, R. J. (Ed.) (1994). *Encyclopedia of psychology* (2nd ed.). New York: Wiley. (4 volumes)

Goldenson, R. M. (1970). *Encyclopedia of human behavior.* New York: Doubleday. (2 volumes)

Magill, F. N. (Ed.) (1993). *Survey of social science: Psychology series.* Pasadena, CA: Salem Press. (6 volumes)

Ramachandran, V. S. (Ed.) (1994). *Encyclopedia of human behavior.* San Diego, CA: Academic Press. (4 volumes)

Wolman, B. B. (Ed.) (1977). *International encyclopedia of psychiatry, psychology, psychoanalysis, and neurology.* New York: Van Nostrand Reinhold Company. (12 volumes)

Reference Guides to Reference Books

Balay, K., Carrington, V. F., & Martin, M. S. (Eds.) (1996). *Guide to reference books* (11th ed.). Chicago: American Library Association.

Reed, J. G., & Baxter, P. M. (1992). *Library use: A handbook for psychology* (2nd ed.). Washington, DC: American Psychological Association.

Reviews of the Psychological Literature

Psychological Bulletin (a bimonthly journal of literature reviews published by the American Psychological Association).

Annual Review of Psychology. New York: Academic Press. (a yearly volume of literature reviews that has been published since 1949)

Step 2 If the background information from a general reference sparks your interest in a topic, you will next need to select precise terms for your expanding search of the psychological literature. To do so, you must use the reference guide to such terms—the *Thesaurus of Psychological Index Terms* (Walker, 1997)—which should be in the reference section of your library. Organized by main terms and subject headings, the *Thesaurus* is nothing less than an extensive vocabulary of psychological terms that will allow you to locate the articles and books you need.

To begin, look up your area of interest in the *Thesaurus.* Table 4.3 is a reprint of the *Thesaurus* page containing the entry for *perception.* As you

---

TABLE 4.3

PAGE EXCERPT CONTAINING THE ENTRY FOR PERCEPTION FROM THE THESAURUS OF PSYCHOLOGICAL INDEX TERMS

Perception	67	
PN	3780	SC 37350
SN	Conceptually broad array term referring to the process of obtaining cognitive or sensory information about the environment. Use a more specific term if possible.	
UF	Sensation	
N	↓ Auditory Perception	67
	↓ Extrasensory Perception	67
	Form and Shape Perception	67
	↓ Illusions (Perception)	67
	↓ Intersensory Processes	78
	Numerosity Perception	67
	Object Recognition	97
	↓ Olfactory Perception	67
	Perceptual Closure	73
	↓ Perceptual Constancy	85
	↓ Perceptual Discrimination	73
	↓ Perceptual Distortion	82
	↓ Perceptual Localization	67
	↓ Perceptual Motor Learning	67
	↓ Perceptual Motor Processes	67
	↓ Perceptual Orientation	73
	Perceptual Style	73
	Risk Perception	97
	Role Perception	73
	Self Perception	67
	Sensory Gating	91
	↓ Social Perception	67
	↓ Somesthetic Perception	87
	↓ Spatial Perception	67
	Subliminal Perception	73
	Taste Perception	67
	↓ Time Perception	67
	↓ Visual Perception	67
R	Apperception	73
	↓ Attention	67
	Constructivism	94
	↓ Discrimination	67
	Mind	91
	↓ Perceptual Development	73
	↓ Perceptual Disturbances	73
	↓ Perceptual Measures	73
	↓ Perceptual Stimulation	73
	↓ Priming	88
	↓ Rhythm	91
	Sensory Neglect	94
	Signal Detection(Perception)	67
	Perceptiveness (Personality)	73
	PN 15	SC 37360

TABLE 4.4

ENTRY FOR ILLUSIONS (PERCEPTION) FROM THE THESAURUS OF PSYCHOLOGICAL INDEX TERMS

	Use Autokinetic Illusion		
	Illusions (Perception) 67		
	PN 2197		SC 24440
SC 24320	SN Misperception or alteration of reality in subjective perception.		
	UF	Optical Illusions	
	B	Perception 67	
	N	Mueller Lyer Illusion 88	
	↓	Perceptual Aftereffect 67	
		Spatial Distortion 73	
	R ↓	Perceptual Distortion 82	
	↓	Perceptual Disturbances 73	

can see, this entry lists a number of terms representing both more specific and related terms in the psychological literature. Any given *Thesaurus* entry typically includes a *scope note* (SN) or description of a term, terms that are sometimes *used for* the term (UF), *broader* terms (B), *narrower* terms (N), and *related* terms (R). As shown in table 4.3, the entry for *perception* includes all of these components except broader terms.

At this point, most researchers focus their search by identifying a narrow (N) term or terms before continuing (the small arrow next to terms in table 4.3 means that there are additional terms underneath that particular entry in the *Thesaurus*). I decided to focus on *Illusions (Perception)* (see table 4.3 and locate this N term under the *Perception* entry). I then looked up the term *Illusions (Perception)* in the *Thesaurus,* as well, and discovered a somewhat smaller set of entries (see table 4.4, where 7 terms are shown). I further narrowed my search by choosing 1 of the 7 terms under the heading *Illusions (Perception),* which identified a classic demonstration in perception, the *Mueller Lyer Illusion.* As can be seen in table 4.4, the heading for the *Mueller Lyer Illusion* is also an N term.

The Mueller Lyer illusion (e.g., Coren & Girgus, 1978) occurs when familiar perspective cues mislead us. As shown in figure 4.1, the center line in line drawing A appears to be relatively longer than the center line in line drawing B. It turns out, however, that the two lines are of equal length. Why does this occur? The perspective cues available—here, the arrows at the top and bottom of each drawing—cause our perceptual system to infer a 3-dimensional object from a 2-dimensional image, leading us to conclude that A is more distant than B. Try thinking of the two perspectives represented in figure 4.1 as the edges of buildings, for example, and the subtle distortion in our perception makes even more sense. If I were interested in seeing what research has been conducted on this intriguing illusion, then I would proceed to Step 3 in the literature search.

FIGURE 4.1
Graphic of the Mueller
Lyer Illusion

A   B

Step 3   Once a key term (or terms) from the *Thesaurus* is selected, the third step in a bottom-up search is to begin examining possible references. There are two ways to proceed from this point: a computerized search or a manual search of the psychological literature. Guidelines for doing each follow.

Computerized searches   The computer revolution has changed the face of education and research rather dramatically, and working with the psychological literature is no exception to this trend. The work of students, teachers, and scholars is quicker and more efficient with the increasing presence of computer access to CD-ROM indexes and on-line database searches. After all, what could be more practical than accessing the information you need in a matter of seconds?

   The best computerized access to psychological literature is PsycLIT (on CD-ROM) or PsycINFO (on-line), databases that are increasingly available at academic institutions. (For convenience and ease of reading, PsycLIT is used in the discussion that follows to refer to one or the other of these databases.) One of the first things you should find out from the reference desk in your institution's library is whether PsycLIT is available. The PsycLIT database contains citations and abstracts for journals, books, and book chapters. The database is quite broad. Besides psychology, for example, PsycLIT references related disciplines, including sociology, nursing, psychiatry, and education.

The instructions for PsycLIT are user friendly, although you may want to make an appointment with a reference librarian the first time you access the database. The entries in the database fall under the broad and narrow topical areas listed in table 4.5, and it is possible to search using key words or phrases, subject headings, and author names. Depending upon the topic you search, however, you may need to expand your search terms if you locate too few references, or limit your terms if you find too many references. As you gain experience using PsycLIT you will develop a sense of how and when to limit or broaden a search.

I performed a subject search using the index term *Mueller Lyer Illusion* from the *Thesaurus,* and in a matter of a few seconds located 43 relevant references published between January 1990 and September 1996 (the two discs in the current database contain publications from 1974 to 1990 and 1990 to the present). Not all of these citations are apt to be useful, of course, but the goal at this stage in the bottom-up process is to locate as much appropriate literature as possible (the process of winnowing it down is presented later in this chapter). As an added benefit, the computer that accesses the PsycLIT database is usually linked to a printer, which will allow you to print the references you believe are most helpful to your project. You may also be able to save references to a diskette to be printed out later through wordprocessing software.

A sample printout of a citation (Devane, 1993) dealing with a variation on the *Mueller Lyer Illusion* is shown in table 4.6. As you can see, a typical PsycLIT journal citation is a wealth of information and detail. Table 4.6 identifies the citation's media type (here, a journal article); the work's title; the author's name and institutional affiliation; the source (i.e., the journal's name, year and month of publication, as well as volume, issue, and page numbers); year of publication; the language in which the article appears (here, English); the indexing area that contains the key phrase and subject terms for searching; the classification area (here, Human Experimental Psychology; see table 4.5); and, most importantly, a complete abstract describing the research. Reading abstracts enables you to decide whether to read and eventually include references in your own work.

If you have any difficulty with the PsycLIT program, all that you need to do is ask a reference librarian for assistance. In fact, let me repeat that the practical approach to becoming familiar with the database is to make an appointment with a reference librarian in advance (when doing so, consider taking a few members of your research team with you so that everyone can contribute to the library research portion of your project). A few minutes in a private tutorial will help you learn to search PsycLIT with ease, efficiency, and confidence—and always remember that reference librarians are particularly skilled at refining or broadening the scope of any search.

Manual searches If you do not have access to PsycLIT, then you will need to use *Psychological Abstracts* in order to do a manual literature

TABLE 4.5

CLASSIFICATION OF TOPICAL AREAS IN PSYCHOLOGY COVERED BY PsycLIT AND PSYCHOLOGICAL ABSTRACTS

ABSTRACTS

Note: This classification code system was designed to describe the content of the PsycINFO database, not the field of psychology.

2100 General Psychology
2140 History & Systems
2200 Psychometrics & Statistics & Methodology
  2220 Tests & Testing
    2221 Sensory & Motor Testing
    2222 Developmental Scales & Schedules
    2223 Personality Scales & Inventories
    2224 Clinical Psychological Testing
    2225 Neuropsychological Assessment
    2226 Health Psychology Testing
    2227 Educational Measurement
    2228 Occupational & Employment Testing
    2229 Consumer Opinion & Attitude Testing
  2240 Statistics & Mathematics
  2250 Research Methods & Experimental Design

2300 Human Experimental Psychology
  2320 Sensory Perception
    2323 Visual Perception
    2325 Auditory & Speech Perception
  2330 Motor Processes
  2340 Cognitive Processes
    2343 Learning & Memory
    2346 Attention
  2360 Motivation & Emotion
  2380 Consciousness States
  2390 Parapsychology

2400 Animal Experimental & Comparative Psychology
  2420 Learning & Motivation
  2440 Social & Instinctive Behavior

2500 Psysiological Psychology & Neuroscience
  2510 Genetics
  2520 Neuropsychology & Neurology
  2530 Electrophysiology
  2540 Physiological Processes
  2560 Psychophysiology
  2580 Psychopharmacology

2600 Psychology & the Humanities
  2610 Literature & Fine Arts
  2630 Philosophy

2700 Communication Systems

2720 Linguistics & Language & Speech
2750 Mass Media Communications
2800 Developmental Psychology
  2820 Cognitive & Perceptual Development
  2840 Psychosocial & Personality Development
  2860 Gerontology

2900 Social Processes & Social Issues
  2910 Social Structure & Organization
  2920 Religion
  2930 Culture & Ethnology
  2950 Marriage & Family
    2953 Divorce & Remarriage
    2956 Childrearing & Child Care
  2960 Political Processes & Political Issues
  2970 Sex Roles & Womens Issues
  2980 Sexual Behavior & Sexual Orientation
  2990 Drug & Alcohol Usage (Legal)

3000 Social Psychology
  3020 Group & Interpersonal Processes
  3040 Social Perception & Cognition

3100 Personality Psychology
  3120 Personality Traits & Processes
  3140 Personality Theory
    3143 Psychoanalytic Theory

3200 Psychological & Physical Disorders
  3210 Psychological Disorders
    3211 Affective Disorders
    3213 Schizophrenia & Psychotic States
    3215 Neuroses & Anxiety Disorders
    3217 Personality Disorders
    3230 Behavior Disorders & Antisocial Behavior
    3233 Substance Abuse & Addiction
    3236 Criminal Behavior & Juvenile Delinquency
  3250 Developmental Disorders & Autism
    3253 Learning Disorders
    3256 Mental Retardation
  3260 Eating Disorders
  3270 Speech & Language Disorders
  3280 Environmental Toxins & Health
  3290 Physical & Somatoform & Psychogenic Disorders
    3291 Immunological Disorders
    3293 Cancer

3295 Cardiovascular Disorders
3297 Neurological Disorders & Brain Damage
3299 Vision & Hearing & Sensory Disorders

3300 Health & Mental Health Treatment & Prevention
  3310 Psychotherapy & Psychotherapeutic Counseling
    3311 Cognitive Therapy
    3312 Behavior Therapy & Behavior Modification
    3313 Group & Family Therapy
    3314 Interpersonal & Client Centered & Humanistic Therapy
    3315 Psychoanalytic Therapy
  3340 Clinical Psychopharmacology
  3350 Specialized Interventions
    3351 Clinical Hypnosis
    3353 Self Help Groups
    3355 Lay & Paraprofessional & Pastoral Counseling
    3357 Art & Music & Movement Therapy
  3360 Health Psychology & Medicine
    3361 Behavioral & Psychological Treatment of Physical Illness
    3363 Medical Treatment of Physical Illness
    3365 Promotion & Maintenance of Health & Wellness
  3370 Health & Mental Health Services
    3371 Outpatient Services
    3373 Community & Social Services
    3375 Home Care & Hospice
    3377 Nursing Homes & Residential Care
    3379 Inpatient & Hospital Services
  3380 Rehabilitation
    3383 Drug & Alcohol Rehabilitation
    3384 Occupational & Vocational Rehabilitation
    3385 Speech & Language Therapy
    3386 Criminal Rehabilitation & Penology

3400 Professional Psychological & Health Personnel Issues
  3410 Professional Education & Training
  3430 Professional Personnel Attitudes & Characteristics
  3450 Professional Ethics & Standards & Liability

TABLE 4.5 (continued)

3470 Impaired Professionals
3500 Educational Psychology
  3510 Educational Administration &
    Personnel
  3530 Curriculum & Programs &
    Teaching Methods
  3550 Academic Learning &
    Achievement
  3560 Classroom Dynamics & Student
    Adjustment & Attitudes
  3570 Special & Remedial Education
    3575 Gifted & Talented
  3580 Educational/Vocational
    Counseling & Student Services

3600 Industrial & Organizational
  Psychology
  3610 Occupational Interests &
    Guidance
  3620 Personnel Management &
    Selection & Training
  3630 Personnel Evaluation & Job

Performance
  3640 Management & Management
    Training
  3650 Personnel Attitudes & Job
    Satisfaction
  3660 Organizational Behavior
  3670 Working Conditions & Industrial
    Safety

3700 Sport Psychology & Leisure
  3720 Sports
  3740 Recreation & Leisure

3800 Military Psychology

3900 Consumer Psychology
  3920 Consumer Attitudes & Behavior
  3940 Marketing & Advertising

4000 Engineering & Environmental
  Psychology
  4010 Human Factors Engineering

4030 Lifespace & Institutional Design
4050 Community & Environmental
  Planning
4070 Environmental Issues & Attitudes
4090 Transportation

4100 Intelligent Systems
  4120 Artificial Intelligence & Expert
    Systems
  4140 Robotics
  4160 Neural Networks

4200 Forensic Psychology & Legal Issues
  4210 Civil Rights & Civil Law
  4230 Criminal Law & Criminal
    Adjudication
  4250 Mediation & Conflict Resolution
  4270 Crime Prevention
  4290 Police & Legal Personnel

Source: American Psychological Association (1992). *PsycINFO user manual.* Washington, DC: Author.

TABLE 4.6

SAMPLE ABSTRACT PRINTOUT FROM PsycLIT

Media Type:	10 Journal Article
Title:	The method of reproduction and Mueller-Lyer changes.
Author(s):	Devane, Joseph R.
Institution:	State U New York, Coll at Cortland, US
Source:	Perceptual & Motor Skills
	1993 Feb Vol 76(1) 43–46
Year:	1993
ISSN:	0031–5125
Language:	Engl
Key Phrase:	method of reproduction, Mueller Lyer illusions, college students
Subjects:	MUELLER LYER ILLUSION; VISUAL PERCEPTION; ADULTHOOD
Classification(s):	23 Human Experimental Psychology
	2323 Sensory Perception—Visual Perception
Abstract:	In a 3-variable study of Mueller-Lyer decrement, each of 8 independent groups of 10 psychology students responded 30 times to 1 of the 2 Mueller-Lyer components by the method of reproduction. There were 3 independent variables in the 2 * 2 * 2 design: whether the stimulus figure had obliques turned in or out (In-Out), whether the stimulus figures included a horizontal line connecting the 2 sets of obliques, and whether the response was the drawing of a line or the placement of a dot. The mean of the initial Out response was significantly greater absolutely than that of the In response. Neither of the other independent variables produced a significant difference, although each entered into significant interactions. The In figure demonstrated illusion decrements across the 30 trials, but the Out figure demonstrated illusion increments. (PsycLIT Database Copyright 1993 American Psychological Assn, all rights reserved)
Age Group(s):	Adult
Doc Type:	10 Journal Article
Entry Month:	9309
Item Number:	80–32075

TABLE 4.7

INDEX PAGE EXCERPT CONTAINING THE ENTRY FOR PERCEPTION FROM PSYCHOLOGICAL ABSTRACTS

Müller-Lyer & other illusions, temporal integration, (Fren) 52

Müller-Lyer & Ponzo illusions, visual capture, 3993

perception of apparent movement, long-term perceptual memory, learning disabled 6–12 yr. olds, 9735

perceptual distortion in Ames room, sex & naiveté & stimuli, 1979

perceptual illusions & distortions, early history, 54

perceptual illusory change elicitation, isolated vowels as auditory stimuli, R. Warren's verbal transformation effect, 3992

perceptual moment vs. visual persistence, moment duration of time-dependent visual illusion, 10043

Poggendorff illusion, amputations & rotations & other perturbations, 6014

Poggendorff illusion, depth processing theory, 8022

Ponzo illusion & orientation change, assimilation theory & quantitative predictions, 10045

relative speed illusion, 7 & 9 & 11 & 13 yr. olds, (Fren) 2658

report of line drawings as upright vs. extended, extension cues in open & closed figures, relation to visual illusions, 8060

Sander illusion, relative space & component lines & assimilation vs. contrast effects, 10042

size difference illusion, perceptual set due to size relationship in drawings vs. actual objects depicted, (Russ) 76

spiral aftereffect duration, distance & retinal velocity, 8024

visual illusions of angle as application of Lie transformation groups, 53

---

search. *Psychological Abstracts,* an extensive collection of summaries of the periodical and book literature in psychology and related fields, is published monthly and found in the reference sections of libraries. The information available in *Psychological Abstracts* is similar to PsycLIT, except that it does not reference non-English journals. *Psychological Abstracts* is organized topically the same as PsycLIT (see table 4.5)—*except* that you must do a traditional search through a printed source. Unlike PsycLIT, of course, a search using *Psychological Abstracts* cannot be narrowed by continuing to add other terms as the search progresses.

If your college does not have PsycLIT, begin by looking up the *Thesaurus* term *Mueller Lyer Illusion* from Step 2 in the subject index of a particular volume of *Psychological Abstracts.* Each volume indexes citations published within a given year, so you will probably need to examine several volumes to get a sense of the literature pertaining to your topic. The specific *Mueller Lyer Illusion* entry in the index of volume 47 (January to June 1972), for example, directs the reader to the more general entry for *Illusion.* A copy of the subject index page containing entries under this term for volume 47 is shown in table 4.7. The number codes following the key term *Mueller Lyer Illusion* (i.e., 52, 3993) correspond to two research summaries.

If you chose to examine abstract 3993, for example, you would look it up in volume 47 of *Psychological Abstracts.* A copy of abstract 3993 is shown in table 4.8. As you can see, the entry begins with the code number, followed by the author's name and affiliation, the article title, and

---

TABLE 4.8

SAMPLE ABSTRACT FROM PSYCHOLOGICAL ABSTRACTS

3993. **Walker, James T.** (U. Missouri, St. Louis) **Visual capture in visual illusions.** *Perception & Psychophysics*, 1971(Aug), Vol. 10(2), 71–74.—Discusses visual capture, the resolution of visual-tactual conflicts in favor of vision. In each previous demonstration of this phenomenon, a distorted optic array, or some mechanical analogue for a distorted optic array, has produced a conflict between erroneous visual information and presumably veridical tactual information. 2 experiments with a total of 28 male and 28 female undergraduates are reported which demonstrate visual capture in the Müller-Lyer and Ponzo illusions in the absence of any distortions of the optic array. (15 ref.)—*Journal abstract.*

---

reference information where the source can be found (i.e., the journal, volume, issue, and page numbers). Following these important details, of course, is the summary of the work that will help you to decide whether to look up the article and read it.

I want to close Step 3 with an important point: Reading abstracts from PsycLIT or *Psychological Abstracts* is *not* research per se. It is a preface to research, a means of tracking down what you need. There is no substitute for actually going to the book stacks or the periodical section of the library, locating a reference, and then reading and thinking about it.

Step 4   After you search for useful article references through PsycLIT or *Psychological Abstracts,* should you rest easy? Are your library labors ended? No, not yet. There are still several valuable places to search for research materials to supplement the journal articles and improve the quality and scope of your project. The search activities that take place here in Step 4 will vary depending upon the resources available to you as well as the topical area you are searching. A library search, some additional computerized searches, and the use of materials close by and farther away will be presented. You could explore any one or a combination of these additional sources as you proceed.

On-line library searches   There is a very good chance that your college's library not only invested in computers for database searches but also that its card catalog is computerized. A card catalog that is now accessed from a computer terminal is referred to as an *on-line catalog.* There are some generic on-line catalogs available for libraries, but most have developed systems tailored to the needs of the institution and its collections. Thus, I cannot tell you about the particular abilities or limitations of your institution's system, but I can provide some observations about on-line catalogs and make a few suggestions about using them.

On-line catalogs tend to be user friendly, and usually they can accommodate both precise (e.g., specific book titles, author names, library call numbers) and more general (e.g., subject headings, subject keywords, title keywords, Library of Congress Subject Headings) information.

TABLE 4.9

SAMPLE SCREEN FROM RESULTS OF A LIBRARY ON-LINE CATALOG SEARCH

09 JUN 97	DIAL-IN REEVES LIBRARY—MORAVIAN COLLEGE	11:07 AM

Dial Pac

Press C for Copy status & Location Availability

AUTHOR	1) Cutting, James E.
TITLE	Perception with an eye for motion/
PUBLISHER	Cambridge, Mass.: MIT Press, c1986.
PHYS. DESC.	xiii, 321 p.: ill.; 24 cm.
BIB. NOTES	Bibliography: p. [289]–306.
SUBJECTS	1) Motion perception (Vision)
DYNIX #	116626

Press <return> to see Copy status:

09 JUN 97   DIAL-IN REEVES LIBRARY—MORAVIAN COLLEGE 11:07 AM

Dial Pac

Author	Cutting, James E.	
Title	Perception with an eye for motion/	Holds: 0

CALL NUMBER	STATUS	LIBRARY
1. BOOK STACKS	Checked In	REEVES LIBRARY—MORAV
BF245.C88 1986		

Choose a command:

On-line catalogs search for books and edited volumes, not periodical articles (although some on-line catalogs will tell you what periodicals are available at that library).

In the course of a bottom-up search, an on-line catalog will allow you to search a library's holdings by using key index terms. These index terms, however, are not necessarily those you found in the *Thesaurus of Psychological Index Terms* from Step 2; instead, you will want to select terms found under your topic's entry in the *Library of Congress Subject Headings* (LCSH; Library of Congress, 1995), a four-volume guide that will usually be located near the on-line catalog. Entries in the *Subject Headings* are alphabetized, include more specific search terms, and are cross-referenced with related terms in a manner similar to the *Thesaurus*.

Alternatively, of course, you can search by an author name. For instance, let's assume that I want to locate any books on perception written by the perceptual psychologist James Cutting. I enter his name in the author search directory of my college's library and locate his book *Perception With An Eye for Motion* (Cutting, 1986). Table 4.9 shows a printout of the computer screen from an on-line catalog search for this book in my college's library. As you can see, it includes Cutting's name, the book title, the publisher, a physical description of the book, and the fact that the book has a bibliography and that its LCSH is the perception of motion. The book's call number (i.e., its precise location in the library) is noted on a subsequent screen (see table 4.9). To save you time and effort, on-line catalogs indicate a book's availability (i.e., is it checked in or out?), as well.

ERIC   A second CD-ROM database worth exploring is called by the acronym ERIC, which stands for Educational Resources Information Center. ERIC is a bibliographic database citing research and technical reports, as well as several hundred education and education-related journals. Searching the ERIC database is somewhat similar to PsycLIT, although it will undoubtedly prove to be helpful if you seek the counsel of a reference librarian.

Other databases   Depending upon your library's reference resources, there are other social science databases you can search. The *Social Sciences Index* (SSI; H. W. Wilson Co., 1974–present), for example, reference periodicals from anthropology, economics, geography, law and criminology, political science, social work, sociology, and international relations. *Sociological Abstracts* (Sociological Abstracts, Inc., 1952-present) is a related database covering these same fields, as well as education, demography, race relations, and social psychology. Both *SSI* and *Sociological Abstracts* are available on *First Search,* an on-line database that is available at most colleges and universities. Ask a reference librarian if these three or any related databases can be accessed in your institution's library.

The Internet   Nothing is developing more rapidly and in so many different ways than the Internet. The Internet is a giant, computerized network of computer networks joining local, national, and international sources together. It includes sites for everything from education to commerce and contains information on an almost infinite variety of topics.

Of what relevance is the Internet to your research and writing in psychology? Access to the Internet is access to an endless chain of libraries, databases, discussion groups, homepages, and archives covering any number of academic disciplines, including psychology. Indeed, you can contact numerous psychology departments, participate in discussion groups on psychological topics great and small, and even send messages to psychologists at colleges and universities with ease. It is possible to search for information on virtually any topic, and a variety of on-line services now exist so that you can "surf the net" using a graphical interface; that is, portions of your computer screen remain the same while other parts of it change as new connections are made. You should be aware, however, that the Internet is *not* selective. It does *word searching* rather than index or term searching, so that virtually *any* occurrence of a word or phrase will be accessed—you will need to evaluate carefully what you find. To make using a search engine on the Internet easier, consult the engine's help screen for advice and pointers before starting a search.

Because the Internet is evolving so quickly, I can only recommend the few psychology websites shown in table 4.10. These websites and their addresses, which were identified by MacKenzie and Aguinis (1996), are categorized as either general or specialized in focus (note that some space is provided for you to record the addresses of other useful sites

TABLE 4.10

PSYCHOLOGICAL SITES ON THE WORLD WIDE WEB

General Sites for Psychology

PsychNET, the Internet Service of the American Psychological Association (APA): (http://www.apa.org/). The homepage of APA.

The American Psychological Society (APS): (http://psych.hanover.edu/APS/). The homepage of APS.

Psych Web: (http://www.gasou/edu/psychweb/psychweb.htm). This webpage at Georgia Southern University contains a great deal of psychology-related information available on the Internet.

Yahoo-Science: Psychology: (http://www.yahoo.com/Science/Psychology/). A good starting point for the beginner, as a detailed index of psychological resources is available.

PSYC SITE-Science of Psychology: Resources: (http://www.unipissing.ca/psyc/psycsite.htm). Another good place to begin. This homepage contains various links to psychological journals, abstracts, and list servers.

Special Interest Sites in Psychology

Clinical and Counseling Psychology: (http://server.bmod.athabascau.ca/html/aupr/clinical.htm). This website focuses on issues and resources in clinical psychology.

Cognitive and Psychological Sciences on the Internet: (http://www-psych.stanford.edu/cogsci/). This website focuses on issues and resources in cognitive science and psychological research.

The Industrial/Organizational Psychologist: (http://cmit.unomaha.edu/TIP/TIP.html). This website focuses on issues and resources in industrial/organizational psychology.

Links to Social Psychology Topics: (http://www.wesleyan.edu/psyc/psyc260/social.htm). This website focuses on issues and resources in social psychology.

Record Other Useful Psychology Sites You Locate in the Space Provided

http:// _____	http:// _____
http:// _____	http:// _____
http:// _____	http:// _____
http:// _____	http:// _____

Note: Entries in this table were taken from MacKenzie and Aguinis (1996).

you locate). Any one of the general entries is a good place to begin your search of the World Wide Web (www); if your interests are more focused, then one of the specialized sites, such as the one devoted to industrial/organizational psychology, may appeal to you.

A few interfaces, notably *Netscape,* and its servers, such as *Yahoo!* (see table 4.10) and *Infoseek,* are fine search tools for psychological topics. Another good strategy is to check the homepages sponsored by the *American Psychological Association* and the *American Psychological Society* (their respective addresses are provided in table 4.10). In the end, your best Internet strategy will be to learn what sources are accessible on your campus and then to spend a bit of time trying out whatever search engines are available. As you will soon see, the possibilities are virtually endless, and your Internet savvy will increase as you gain experience.

Using resources that are close at hand   Students often overlook two obvious resources for psychological references—their own textbooks and the psychology faculty at their institution. There is a good chance that a textbook you are now reading for another class (or read in the last semester or two) contains current references that would make a fine addition to your literature search and, eventually, a project paper. Comprehensive introductory psychology texts, for example, usually provide the classic or "greatest hits" references in the field. As a rule, introductory texts tend to be well referenced, although they often provide little more than a cursory review of any topic. For greater depth, you should consult an introductory level text targeting a particular subfield, such as personality, social psychology, or animal behavior. Concept coverage in such second-level books includes contemporary as well as classic references, and many authors thoughtfully include sections of recommended readings or even an occasional annotated bibliography.

You can also look in your own psychology department by consulting a faculty expert who teaches or researches in the area of your topic. For example, if your literature search deals with an issue in the domain of cognitive psychology, such as problem solving, then seek out the wisdom of the resident cognitive scientist. Faculty members are usually flattered to be asked to share their knowledge, and there is a good chance that one of your professors will be able to point you to a particular author or a cache of literature you did not previously locate.

Using resources that are farther away   Sometimes the references you need are not at hand or in your institution's library. There are three simple ways to proceed: using an interlibrary loan service, contacting relevant organizations, or writing authors. Your institution's library probably has cooperative loan agreements with a group of other educational institutions—in other words, libraries sharing resources with other libraries. If you need a reference that is not available in your library, ask at the circulation desk or in the reference department about how to obtain it using interlibrary loan. Let me issue a cautionary note: Be sure to order books or copies of journal articles well in advance of when you need them, since filling such orders can take weeks.

Rosnow and Rosnow (1995) identify the *fugitive* literature, a wonderfully clever description of reports or technical papers published by various private organizations or foundations, as well as local, state, or federal government agencies. These sources are fugitives because they are not readily located even when using the impressive arsenal of resources found in the average college or university reference library. Instead, you must access these sources by phone or through the mail, and request, for example, to be put on mailing lists or to be sent materials concerning your issue of interest. For example, one of my former students was writing her senior thesis on the impact of women's studies on the general curriculum. She found that contacting a variety of national women's organizations by sending a detailed form letter was invaluable for her research.

You can also contact certain psychologists about their most recent research, particularly when it is unpublished or "in press." If so, write to them and request *preprints* (unpublished article manuscripts) or *reprints* (published copies of articles) on a given topic, something academic psychologists do all the time. Sending a postcard or a short letter is sufficient, but be sure to explain briefly why their work is important to your own. You can usually obtain an author's mailing address from the author notes on a journal publication, or from the membership directories of the *American Psychological Association* or the *American Psychological Society*. Alternatively, you could save time by sending an author electronic mail over the Internet. E-mail addresses are increasingly published in author notes or can usually be found by searching the homepage of the author's institution.

Literature Chains: Existing References Contain Other References

Sources contain references to other sources, and as you search and research the literature, you should see a pattern emerge in the scholarship on any topic. What is the nature of this pattern? It is a chain of ideas that develops from a simple question early in the literature to a variety of related but more complex ones later. With diligence and a watchful eye on reference sections and bibliographies, you can easily follow a literature chain and locate resources to aid your research effort.

After your literature search is under way, take some time to scan the reference sections of the materials you collect. These existing references will contain many references in common, which is a reasonable (though not infallible) way to discern whether an article or book is worth reading. You should also be on the lookout, however, for less frequently cited gems from the literature or new, cutting edge perspectives that have not yet been adopted by many investigators. If you incorporate literature chaining into your bottom-up search strategy, it is highly unlikely that you will miss any important references.

Exercise 4.A: Keeping a Search Record

Because it is unlikely that you can accomplish a thorough literature search in one sitting, you will want to keep a record of where you already looked for sources. The record sheet shown in table 4.11 is easy to complete, and the information record will allow you to pick up the search between visits to the library. As shown in table 4.11, the topic of your search should be specified (e.g., *Perception*) and any key words or terms (e.g., *Illusion*) used for the search should be noted. Besides this information, you will need to write down the date of the search, the search tool used (e.g., PsycLIT), and a comment about what you found (e.g., "10 journal articles from 1982 to 1987"). Keep in mind, of course, that you can always print a copy of the search screen to supplement this record.

The comments you make regarding the results of your search using a particular database or tool are very important. If you find a relatively

| TABLE 4.11 | | |

REFERENCE SEARCH RECORD

As you conduct a search of the psychological literature, fill in the information here so that you will have a record of how you investigated various databases and reference sources.

Topic: _____

Key terms used: _____

Search Date	DataBase or Source	Comments
1.		
2.		
3.		
4.		
5.		
6.		
7.		
8.		
9.		
10.		

large number of article or book references, for example, then you will need to allot an appropriate amount of time to read through their abstracts carefully. If your search of a particular reference tool produces no results, however, you will want to consult a reference librarian or initiate another search using different terms. This record-keeping exercise will spare you the effort and time that repeating or re-creating a search can entail.

Using Library Resources: Befriend A Reference Librarian

If you cannot locate the resources you need in the library or if you do not understand how to use a particular library's tools, the solution is simple: Ask for help. Yet, students are sometimes reluctant to ask librarians for assistance, perhaps because they fear they will ask a wrong or even dumb question, or that they will appear unintelligent. To the contrary, one of the smartest things a researcher or a student can do is to cultivate a relationship with a reference librarian. Reference librarians are trained to find the things that are not readily found; indeed, the joy and satisfaction of their calling is the hunt for information that library patrons desire. Thus, keep in mind that libraries exist to share knowledge and that the librarian's role is to make that knowledge accessible.

HOW TO READ AN EMPIRICAL JOURNAL ARTICLE
OR BOOK CHAPTER

Whether they are teachers, researchers, or therapists, psychologists make careful reading a critical activity. But before you choose to read a source carefully, you must first determine if it is a good reference. Here are some guidelines (adapted from Toedter, 1996) that will help you select the best references from among those you find during a literature search. Because psychologists rely so heavily on empirical articles, these guidelines are weighted toward journals; however, criteria relevant to books and book chapters are also noted.

A good reference is one that

- *relates directly to the question you are trying to answer.* If you are studying how nonverbal communication affects teacher-student interactions, for example, then avoid references that examine cross-cultural examples of nonverbal communication. Instead, search for references that examine nonverbal communication in educational contexts.

- *is from a professional journal or book rather than from a publication written for the general public.* Choose a journal like *Cognition* over *Psychology Today* or *Newsweek*. Similarly, where books and book chapters are concerned, those written for scientific and professional audiences are more appropriate choices than more general or "popular" psychology references.

- *is a primary source.* Primary sources describe original research investigations, whereas *secondary sources* organize and analyze primary research done by others. To evaluate the quality of an empirical article (see Exercise 4.B on p. 128), for example, you need to thoroughly understand how the data were collected and analyzed. Thus, become knowledgeable by reading the original article—not a review of it.

- *provides help by addressing your topic using sound methodology or critical reasoning.* You cannot necessarily make this judgment by reading an abstract on PsycLIT or a summary from *Psychological Abstracts*. Good articles rely on high quality data, and good books and chapters synthesize such articles and take knowledge in new directions. Articles and chapters based solely on opinion, unsupported conjecture, or unscientific observations should be avoided.

- *comes from a good quality source.* American Psychological Association journals (see table 3.2 in chapter 3) and other select periodicals (e.g., *Science*) are always a good place to start. Quality journals are peer reviewed and accept a small fraction of the manuscripts submitted to them each year. Journals that are too specialized, narrow in focus, and limited in circulation (e.g., *The Icelandic Journal of Holistic Studies*) should be used with caution. Check with your instructor before using such references.

- *is written by an expert in psychology or a related field.* Consulting textbooks or your instructor about the expertise of an author is a good idea. Experts tend to publish in mainstream journals, for quality publishers, and in well-regarded anthologies and edited volumes.

- *is a reference that is cited by others.* Articles, books, and chapters that are frequently cited in other articles and books, literature reviews, handbooks, and textbooks are apt to be good options.

TABLE 4.12

CRITICAL QUESTIONS FOR GENERAL READING IN PSYCHOLOGY: WHAT TO LOOK FOR WHEN READING PUBLISHED RESEARCH

1. Is there a focused research question? Is it stated clearly?
2. Does the literature review provide enough context for the research question? Are important terms clearly defined?
3. Is the hypothesis easy to understand, one that logically flows from the research question and literature review?
4. Are the independent and dependent variables consistent with and appropriate for the hypothesis?
5. Is there a control group? If not, is its absence explained? Is the explanation tenable?
6. Could you precisely repeat the experiment by following the Method section? What details, if any, are missing?
7. Were the participants sampled, selected, and/or assigned randomly? Do they represent a larger, coherent population? Is the sample size sufficient to address the research question?
8. Are the results presented in a clear, orderly manner? Are the analyses appropriate and interpretable (see chapter 8)? Can you understand the textual description of the results, even if you do not understand the statistical analyses used? Do any accompanying tables and figures enhance or obscure the data?
9. Does the Discussion place the results into proper context (see 2. in this table)? Are any implications or generalizations convincing, or do they stretch credibility?
10. How could the research have been done better? What changes would you make—conceptual, methodological, or both?

- *is not from the same source as many of your other references.* Journals often have an editorial focus, one that emphasizes some topics while neglecting others. Whenever possible, opt for variety in your reading and writing by examining several sources.
- *is recent.* All else being equal, recent articles and books will include the most up-to-date scholarship (but keep in mind that the average publication lag for many journals exceeds a year from the date of acceptance). Scientific knowledge changes rapidly, and you should be certain not to miss any important advances by relying on out-of-date information.
- *is one you can get.* Try not to spend valuable time tracking down obscure journals or hard-to-find books. Use interlibrary loan services when necessary, but do not allow on-order references to delay your research and writing.

If you take advantage of these guidelines, you should have little difficulty culling good references from your literature search. The next step is to begin the process of reading and evaluating the materials you've gathered. Table 4.12 contains a list of critical questions for reading published research in psychology. These questions, tips really, will help you to develop a strategy for general reading in psychology. In other words, these are the usual questions you should ask yourself when reading published research. As you gain experience reading in the literature, you can add to this list; for now, you can refer back to table 4.12 as needed until its tips become second nature to you. Exercises 4.B and 4.C are designed to help you more intensively evaluate articles and book chapters, respectively, for research projects or course papers. But what about evaluating entire books?

As discussed earlier in this chapter, with some exceptions, whole books are not often used as key citations in psychology papers. Evaluating entire books can be done in one of two ways. First, you can read the book and then evaluate it holistically; that is, you give it a generally favorable or unfavorable overall evaluation. Books receiving favorable evaluations can be used. Of course, the particular information you draw from a book is likely to be relatively specific, and you will want to take careful notes on it (see Exercise 4.D). Alternatively, read select chapters from a book (sometimes all of them) and then evaluate each one by using Exercise 4.C.

Whether you are evaluating an article or a chapter, you should plan to read a reference at least twice. Your first reading should be to familiarize yourself with the reference and to evaluate it simultaneously using one of the two following exercises. Any subsequent reading of a reference will be to draw more meaning from it, to clarify or answer remaining questions, and to enhance your understanding of the author's arguments. The second reading is also the time to take detailed notes on it (see Exercise 4.D). Let's first turn to the evaluation exercises.

Exercise 4.B: Evaluating a Research Article

Research articles usually present data from one experiment (though multi-experiment papers—properly called "studies"—are becoming more common) to support an argument. The best time to evaluate an article is while you read it because its details will be fresh in your mind. There are really two stages of evaluation. First, you must determine what the author said. As shown in part I in table 4.13, this entails identifying the central point or hypothesis of a study, understanding the method, and then being able to summarize the study's findings and the author's conclusions about them. As you read an article, write down answers to these questions on a separate sheet of paper or in your research notebook. If you are using your own copy of the article, you can make notes in its margins or use a marker to highlight certain points.

Once you have read the article, you must write answers to the questions in the second stage (see part II in table 4.13). These questions require that you assess the author's conclusions in a critical manner, integrate them with your own thinking, and identify questions that occurred to you as you read. Your answers here will be invaluable in helping you understand the quality of the article and whether it will help you with your research project. Again, do not postpone answering these questions—do them immediately after your first

TABLE 4.13

EVALUATING A RESEARCH ARTICLE

Author of article: _____

Article title: _____

Journal: _____ Volume number: _____ Issue number: _____ Page numbers: _____

I. What the Author Said

Answer these questions as you read the article:
1. What is the central question addressed by the article? What is the study's hypothesis?
2. Briefly outline the most important procedures the author used to test the hypothesis.
3. Using words, succinctly summarize the *major findings* of the study.
4. What *major conclusions* does the author draw from these findings?

II. Integration and Evaluation

Answer these questions after reading an article:
1. *Assessment:* Do you think the author's conclusions are valid and reasonable? Provide an explanation. How do these conclusions relate to the methods used to test the hypothesis?
2. *Integration:* How does this research article fit into your research project? Does it support your project hypothesis or paper? Does it support other literature you are reviewing?
3. *What Questions Remain?* Are there important issues this article does not address or resolve? How do these issues relate to your research project or paper?

Note: This evaluation exercise was adapted from worksheets designed by Professor Craig Nelson (University of Indiana) and Professors Diane Zannoni and Dan Lloyd (Trinity College).

reading of the article. Later, after you decide if an article is useful, you can take more detailed notes on notecards (see Exercise 4.D).

Exercise 4.C: Evaluating a Book Chapter

Books and book chapters are usually more expansive in content and scope than empirical research articles. Although books and chapters also have a central theme or hypothesis, it is usually explored through a review of supporting studies and research sources rather than one or two empirical demonstrations. Thus, the evaluation process focuses more on understanding research that forms a consensus on some point. Please note that this exercise is meant to be used on a single chapter, so evaluation of a book could be done on a chapter by chapter basis. Two readings of a chapter—the first for this exercise and the second for note taking—are recommended.

As shown in table 4.14 there are three stages to chapter evaluation: getting an overview, determining what the author said, and integration and evaluation. Answers to the questions in each section should again be written on a piece of paper or in your research notebook. As section I in table 4.14 suggests, the reader's first step is to form an impression about what a chapter's message is likely to be. To do so, quickly peruse the chapter and any data displays, and then write a one sentence summary of the whole chapter.

TABLE 4.14

EVALUATING A BOOK CHAPTER

Author of the chapter: _____
Chapter title: _____ from the Book: _____
Chapter number and, if appropriate, volume number: _____ pages: _____

I. Overview

Answer this question before reading a chapter:
1. Read the chapter's title and section headings, as well as the headings on any tables or graphs. When you are finished, state in *one complete sentence* what you think the chapter is about.

II. What the Author Said

Answer these questions as you read a chapter:
2. As you read the chapter, write down and define any unfamiliar key terms or concepts.
3. As you read, write down the chapter's *major themes* and *key points.*
4. Write a complete sentence describing what information is being conveyed in each table or graph.
5. Create an outline of the themes and key points developed in the chapter (section headings are helpful in this regard). Use this outline to determine the author's main argument.

III. Integration and Evaluation

Answer these questions after you finish reading a chapter:
6. *Assessment:* Do you think the author's conclusions are valid and reasonable? Provide an explanation. Were there any controversial or contentious issues raised in this chapter? If so, describe them here.
7. *Integration:* How does the research reported in this chapter fit into your project? Does it support your project or paper? Does it support other literature you are reviewing?
8. *What Questions Remain?* Are there important issues this chapter does not address or resolve? How do these issues relate to your research project or paper?

Note: This evaluation exercise was adapted from worksheets designed by Professor Craig Nelson (University of Indiana) and Professors Diane Zannoni and Dan Lloyd (Trinity College).

In the second stage (see part II in table 4.14), the reader's activities begin with the familiar and the focused: Identify any novel terms or concepts and record the chapter's main themes and key points. To ensure your understanding of the chapter, however, you are also asked to describe the purpose of any tables or graphs and then to create an outline of the chapter in order to discern the author's main argument.

The evaluation and integration questions in section III of table 4.14 are the same as those used to evaluate an empirical article. Your critical and thoughtful evaluation of a chapter or book will help you decide what, if any, of its information can be beneficial to your work. Remember that it is best to answer this last set of questions immediately after you finish reading a chapter. If you wait too long to do so, you will be apt to forget details that could prove to be useful for your project or paper.

TABLE 4.15

KEY BIBLIOGRAPHIC INFORMATION FROM RESEARCH SOURCES

• Author(s), including first and middle initials
• Editor(s), if any, including first and middle initials
• Title of Source (including subtitle)
• Book Edition
• Complete Journal Title
• Volume Number for Journals and Books
• Issue Number for Journals
• Publisher for Books and Chapters
• Place of Publication for Books and Chapters
• Year of Publication
• For Journal Article and Chapters, all page numbers are needed.
• Date and Place of presentations, speeches, etc.

Note: The bibliographic information culled from a reference will depend upon whether it is a journal article, a book or book chapter, a report, newspaper article, etc. When in doubt, consult the *Publication Manual of the American Psychological Association,* fourth edition (APA, 1994).

KEEPING TRACK OF RESEARCH MATERIALS

Maintaining Key References

In the course of searching the literature and preparing to write a paper, you will need to keep a *bibliography*. A bibliography is a list of reference works, such as articles or books, about a particular subject or written by a particular author. For most psychology papers you will write, a bibliography will focus on a subject area (e.g., the modeling of aggressive behavior in childhood) and not a particular author (e.g., Albert Bandura).

There is one primary rule for keeping track of bibliographic sources: Maintain accurate information. As soon as you decide that a source will be useful for your work, immediately record all of its relevant bibliographic information. Table 4.15 shows the sort of bibliographic information that you should copy down from every source you use.

Please note that the type of information you take from a reference will depend upon whether it is an article, chapter, or book. Books published as part of a series are likely to have a volume number, for example, *Advances in Experimental Social Psychology,* Vol. 25 (Zanna, 1992); whereas those focused on a single topic will not, for example, *Rational Choice in an Uncertain World* (Dawes, 1988). Journals possess issue numbers as well as volume numbers (i.e., a volume of a quarterly journal has 4 issues per year; *Teaching of Psychology,* 1990, Vol. 17, Issues 1–4). Place of publication—a city and, if the city is small, the state it is in—is important for books and book chapters, but not for journal articles or other periodical references. When in doubt, record as much information about a source as you can, and later rely on APA style for references (see chapter 3) to report precisely what is necessary for a paper's References section.

You can write bibliographic information down on a notecard (see Exercise 4.D in this chapter), a list, or in your research idea notebook (see

Exercise 2.A in chapter 2). If you are far enough along, create a computer file of APA style references (see chapter 3) that can be updated as necessary. This reference file can eventually be merged into the file containing your paper. Alternatively, you might adopt the practice of scores of researchers who routinely photocopy the first page of an article, book chapter, or the title page of a book (Booth, Colomb, & Williams, 1995). Any bibliographic information missing from this photocopy (see table 4.15) is then written on it before it is filed away in a safe place for future use.

One final piece of information will complete the bibliographic information you gather: the library call number of the book, journal, or other source. Although you will not report the call number in any paper you write, having it at your fingertips means that you can go back to a library source for more information or clarification in a matter of minutes (Booth et al., 1995).

Why all the fuss about bibliographic materials? Quality research and scholarship in psychology depends upon attention to detail. If you lack accurate information for a source, you may never find it again. There is nothing more frustrating, time consuming, or disruptive than not being able to locate key reference information. Besides, when a paper is in its final stages, the last thing you want to do is retrace the search you did weeks or even months before. In sum, be sure to carefully document your bibliographic materials!

Organizing Materials

Student researchers need to know where all materials pertaining to a project or paper currently reside. Some people are compulsive, and their organizational prowess is a wonder to behold: Everything is labeled, filed alphabetically, and stored in the same place. References, notes, various paper drafts, and an up-to-date list of a project's next step can be accessed in a matter of seconds. Such people also tend to periodically purge unwanted clutter, old outlines, and stillborn thoughts, which means that their work areas tend to be pristine. Other individuals are much less precise in their organization. Their system often consists of little more than a growing clump of materials that they sort through when some piece of information is needed. Sometimes these clumps reproduce, so that the search for notecards or a copy of an article can become a small scale archaeological expedition. That is, different layers of different piles of materials must be sifted through before Troy—or the reference you desperately need—is located.

As a practical researcher, you should cut a middle path between these opposite organizational styles. That is, you should be able to locate materials that you need quickly but not with a ruthless efficiency indicating that your spare time is consumed with cataloging pencils and papers. This middle path should be one that allows you some flexibility within your organizational scheme. If you misplace a piece of information, for example, you should be able to retrieve it or a copy with relative ease. In whatever way your organizational style evolves, then, be certain that it works for and not against you.

In a related context, Taylor and Martin (1987) write of the research "pipeline," wherein a researcher can work on several different projects at various stages of completion at the same time. In a sense you already rely on this model by virtue of having to balance the demands of several college courses at once. In a similar way, the organization of your project should have a rhythm to it, so that when you are tired, bored, or finished with one piece of your project, there is another activity worthy of your attention in the pipeline.

NOTE TAKING

Taking notes on the materials you collect and read is an essential part of the research process. If you do not take notes carefully (or fail to take notes at all), then your research efforts will be wasted. The goal of note taking is a simple one: to create a written record of the main points of a book, chapter, or article that can be referred to as often as necessary. Note taking comes in two general forms, summarizing and paraphrasing.

A *summary* is a brief, encapsulated description of a reference. Summaries can be as short as one sentence or as long as a paragraph or two. What appears in a summary? A summary contains only the main points of a source or some part of a source. When writing these main points, however, you must be certain to use *your own words* and not those taken directly from a source. If I wanted to summarize the main points of the book *Shattered Assumptions: Towards a New Psychology of Trauma* (Janoff-Bulman, 1992), for example, I would be certain to highlight the author's central argument, or *thesis*, as follows:

> Traumatic experiences, such as rape, grief, or life threatening illness, shatter people's fundamental beliefs about the world around them: that the world is benign and meaningful, and that humans are worthy (Janoff-Bulman, 1992). Rebuilding a sense of control sometimes involves paradoxical and seemingly negative reactions to the trauma, including self-blame. A trauma's origin matters: if it was caused by others, people often view themselves in a negative light and see the world as a dangerous place. If nature is to blame, randomness and chance in the world create a sense of uncertainty. Thus, the nature of the experience, as well as people's interpretations of it, affect coping and long-term adjustment.

Why is writing a summary in your own words an important issue? For two reasons. First, you want to avoid committing *plagiarism*, which is presenting the work of another as your own (see the discussion of plagiarism later in this chapter). The second reason is equally important: You will actively learn something about a source by mulling it over in your head before jotting some summary thoughts down. If you passively copy the major points from a source, you will not learn them; indeed, you might as well just keep the original reference with you and skip note taking altogether.

BOX FEATURE 4.A

A Research Digression: First Things First

When students take notes, they often approach the task in a very passive, even linear way: They dive right in by reading the introduction to the article or the first chapter in the book. Rational? Yes. Efficient? No. Instead of beginning at the beginning, take a few minutes to flip through a source in order to develop some first impressions. Such impressions will help you identify issues to look for when reading, so that note taking will go more smoothly and efficiently. Here are a few helpful suggestions:

- When taking notes on an empirical article, begin by reading the Abstract so that you will know the study's purpose, hypothesis, method, results, and implications *before* you even start to read the introduction.
- When you take notes on a book or a book chapter, be sure to read the author's Preface. Why? Because authors usually lay out the goals of the work and reveal their intended audience there.
- When taking notes on a chapter in an edited book, peruse the Table of Contents so that you can get a feel for how the work you are reading fits into the framework of the book. Be sure to skim the Preface or Overview chapter, as well, because editors routinely provide chapter-by-chapter comments that provide a valuable context for the reader.
- Less useful contextual information is to be found in the Foreword to a book, as it is usually a short, complimentary piece written by a colleague of the author.
- Always check the date of publication for articles and books: How recent is it? Are the data new or several years out of date? If the work is dated, you could search for subsequent publications by the same author or for newer entries on the same topic.
- Try starting with the end of a source rather than the beginning. If you are reading a journal article, take a few minutes to read through the Discussion. As for books, there is much to be gained by a cursory glance at the last chapter where a work's main points are often tied together.
- Always skim the references or bibliography of any source. You will either be comforted by familiar citations or interested in new ones that can be added to your literature search. If no new references turn up, you might be wise to spend less time reviewing the source.

When you are summarizing a source, do so with a purpose in mind. Do you need to know the main points of an entire book or article, the method used in an experiment, the primary results, or the implications of the work for your own? In other words, fix the source's meaning in your mind as you take notes from it. Attention to such contextual detail will help you to record an appropriate, not excessive, amount of information in the course of your research.

A variation of summarizing is *paraphrasing*. Paraphrasing involves conveying the meaning of a passage in different words than those found in the original source. It is not the same thing as a summary because you are not necessarily trying to cover all the main points of a source, merely some key section or sections from it. Similar to good summarizing, paraphrasing is an active process requiring you to understand the material you are reworking or rephrasing.

Hult (1996) offers five excellent recommendations for paraphrasing material:

- Reorder the ideas within a source.
- Emphasize meaning by changing complex ideas into simpler ones.
- If an original source uses very technical jargon, translate it into a more familiar and concrete terminology.
- Alter the patterns of sentences.
- Try using appropriate synonyms in place of the source's original words (but avoid becoming dependent on a thesaurus).

Suppose, for example, that you were writing about the various and sundry definitions that have been offered for cognition. Here is an opening passage from *Cognition and Reality* (Neisser, 1976) and a paraphrase of it:

Original: "Cognition is the activity of knowing: the acquisition, organization, and use of knowledge. It is something that organisms do and in particular something that people do. For this reason the study of cognition is a part of psychology, and theories of cognition are psychological theories (Neisser, 1976, p. 1)."

Paraphrase: Knowing—acquiring, framing, and manipulating information—is the act that characterizes cognition. Living things, especially humans, perform this act. The human quality of thought makes it psychological, so cognitive approaches are inherently psychological approaches (Neisser, 1976).

As you can see, a good paraphrase maintains the ideas and integrity of the original passage, but without any loss of information. Remember, too, that paraphrased material must be cited properly (just as Neisser was credited at the end of the paraphrase). Paraphrasing should be used selectively or else it can become a crutch for your writing. Instead of thinking ideas through and writing them in your own way, you can become overly dependent on rephrasing the work of others instead of developing your own ideas.

Exercise 4.D: Using Notecards

Many researchers and students follow tradition and use notecards for their note taking. A notecard is nothing more than a lined or unlined index card. Some people prefer the standard 3×5-inch index card because it is compact and portable. Others prefer the larger 4×6-inch card because there is more room for detailed notes (Rosnow & Rosnow, 1995). The advantage of the notecard format is that it encourages the researcher to get down to the business of taking concise, systematic notes on sources (Booth et al., 1995). As a result, however, some researchers and students find notecards to be a tad too restrictive. They prefer to use their research notebook (see Exercise 2.A in chapter 2), a legal pad, or even a computer. All three of these alternatives afford the researcher a bit more space for notes than does either size of index card. Choose the alternative that you know will motivate you to take notes.

Preferences for cards or more writing space notwithstanding, the main point for note taking is content—what to write or not write down. What information should comprise your notes on a source? The typical format for notecards is shown on the opposite page. The author's name and the complete APA style reference appear across the top of the card (in fact, writing references at the top of notecards is a great way to learn how to write citations in APA style). Some researchers prefer to note keywords in the top right of the card, allowing the card to be mixed and matched with others in various categories. The main or center portion of the card will contain your summary of a source; a paraphrase of a section; a direct quotation (with accompanying page number); or your reactions, thoughts, or questions about a source. Some brief indication of the card's content (e.g., summary, paraphrase, questions) should be made in the bottom left corner of the card (see the illustration). If the source is a library book, then its call number should appear opposite this content notation, in the bottom right corner.

It is appropriate to use multiple cards for a reference if you are, for example, summarizing as well as reacting to it. As you can see in the illustration, the upper notecard summarizes a book, and the lower one consists of reactions to it. It could quickly become confusing as well as cumbersome if you tried to fit a summary, as well as thoughts and questions about a reading, onto the same notecard. Important detail, too, could easily be lost. Different entries for different purposes make outlining more efficient because you can try laying out ideas in a variety of ways before actually writing them into a developing paper. Notecards are another way to create and maintain your reference list. When you are not using them, however, notecards on the same source should be kept together (try using rubber bands or paper clips). These note-taking suggestions for using cards can easily be adapted to fit one of the alternative formats mentioned previously.

Avoiding Plagiarism: Document Sources and Don't Quote

After reviewing the importance of good bibliographic records and note taking, it is entirely appropriate to discuss ways to avoid *plagiarism*. As noted previously, plagiarism is taking credit for someone else's ideas—particularly written ones—by identifying them as your own. In academic circles, there is no greater sin than failing to cite the creator of an idea, thus effectively stealing that idea. I have some straightforward suggestions about how to avoid plagiarizing, but before I present them, we should review the two types of plagiarism that occur in college level work—accidental plagiarism and intentional plagiarism.

Accidental plagiarism occurs because of sloppy research habits and disorganization. Imagine that a harried student takes hurried notes on a research article by essentially copying material verbatim from it. In the process of doing so, he neglects to summarize, paraphrase, or identify these notes as direct quotations. Weeks pass and the verbatim material

Notes on Notecards

LAZARUS, R.S., & Folkman, S. (1984). Stress, appraisal, and coping. NewYork: Springer.

Presents A Transactional model of stress Focusing on The relationship between The person and The environment.
— Appraisal is cognitive AND relatively continuous
— coping responses Are understood as independent of outcome (e.g., health)

SUMMARY   BF575.575 L32 1984

LAZARUS, R.S., & Folkman, S. (1984). Stress, appraisal, and coping. NEW YORK: Springer.

- can the transactional model reasonably tested in one study? How?
- The book de-emphasizes physiological processes — but how do they fit into appraisal and coping?
- Do L. & F.'s recent writings update the model? How, specifically?

REACTIONS: QUESTIONS   BF 575.575 L32 1984

eventually finds its way from a notecard into the body of a paper, which is then submitted for a grade. Days later the student is called in for a private meeting with his professor, who accuses him of committing plagiarism. The embarrassed and understandably upset student explains the error as one caused by his accidental copying of reference material. Should the professor believe him?

Before answering that question, consider whether in the end accidental plagiarism is fundamentally different from intentional plagiarism. A second student has to write the same paper, so she collects some references and directly copies material from them. The copied material is then incorporated into her paper without attribution. She is fully aware of her actions but assumes that she will not be caught and, in any case, she is in a hurry to finish her work.

Do the situations differ? In terms of the students' intentions, yes, but not from the perspective of the evaluator. In fact, the situations are the same *except* that the intentional plagiarist knowingly copies verbatim material and consciously presents it as her own work. Unfortunately, the person doing the evaluation cannot tell who is telling the truth. Sadly, few plagiarists do tell the truth so that the accidental plagiarists among us are not likely to be given the benefit of the doubt. In the end, then, accidental and intentional plagiarists are both found guilty.

A practical researcher's focus, of course, should be on how to avoid plagiarizing in the first place. The first rule for avoiding plagiarism is simple: Be absolutely sure to keep an accurate bibliography and to document every source appearing in it. In the course of taking notes, be an active and not a passive filter of information by putting ideas into your own words. If you decide to use a quotation, put it into quotation marks (" ") on the note card, write down the number of the page where it came from, and label the card as containing a quotation.

The second rule is even simpler: Avoid quotations altogether. That is, don't write them down into your notes during the research phase and, even if you do, don't use them in your paper in the writing phase. Those are relatively strong suggestions that may fly in the face of popular wisdom about writing. Hear me out, however, before discounting this suggestion altogether.

In my teaching and research career, I have found that direct quotations are rarely necessary. When I read and grade papers, for example, I invariably find that students learn more and write better when they rely on their own interpretations of what they read. When quotations enter the picture, the writing around them often becomes stilted, as if student writers assume their comments will never be as definitive as those from a quotation (untrue!).

Where the quoting of psychological research is concerned, let's be honest: Unless a writer is taking issue with a definition, theory, or argument, there is no compelling reason to use a quotation. With all due respect to psychologists everywhere, writing in psychology is not like that found in great literature, fiction, and the classics, nor is it meant to be. It can be informative, convincing, even compelling, but the general goal is to educate rather than to entertain. Thus, we should aspire to good, even great writing, but in doing so we should avoid excessive quotation and the risk of plagiarizing the work of others.

SUMMARY

Surveying the psychological literature can be done well or it can be done very badly. Practical researchers approach the literature in organized and systematic ways. To this end, a bottom-up strategy was presented for systematically searching for journal articles, books, and book chapters. Because any search takes time and involves numerous steps, Exercise 4.A was included so that a record of resources could be kept. Once references are located, the next step is to determine which ones are most appropriate for your project. Exercises 4.B and 4.C, which are concerned with articles and books or book chapters, respectively, are designed to make the process of selecting useful sources easier. The importance of maintaining and organizing the selected sources was then discussed. The remainder of the chapter focused on how to take effective notes, and it drew a distinction between summarizing and paraphrasing ideas from research materials. Exercise 4.D offered guidelines for keeping and using notecards for note taking. The chapter concluded with advice on avoiding plagiarizing references in the course of research and writing.

KEY TERMS

bibliography (p. 131)
bottom-up search (p. 109)
computerized search (p. 114)
Internet (p. 121)
manual search (p. 115)

on-line search (p. 119)
paraphrase (p. 134)
plagiarism (p. 133, 136)
preprints (p. 124)
primary source (p. 126)

reprints (p. 124)
secondary source (p. 126)
summary (p. 133)
top-down search (p. 109)

SUGGESTED READINGS

American Psychological Association (1994). *Publication manual of the American Psychological Association* (4th ed.). Washington, DC: Author. Every psychologist's and practical researcher's Bible. Obtain a copy.

Booth, W. C., Colomb, G. G., & Williams, J. M. (1995). *The craft of research.* Chicago: University of Chicago Press. An excellent book offering insightful, down-to-earth advice about how practicing researchers in any discipline can do their work. I heartily recommend it.

Hult, C. A. (1996). *Research and writing in the social sciences.* Boston: Allyn and Bacon. A solid, interdisciplinary text focusing on how to conduct library research and to write research reports.

Meltzoff, J. (1998). *Critical thinking about research: Psychology and related fields.* Washington, DC: American Psychological Association. The first half of this book shows readers how to become informed, critical consumers of the psychological literature. Fictitious, flawed journal articles comprise the second half, allowing readers to hone their critical skills.

Sternberg, R. J. (1993). *The psychologist's companion: A guide to scientific writing for students and researchers* (3rd ed.). New York: Cambridge University Press. A prolific and consummate practical researcher provides chapter by chapter advice on everything from starting papers to writing lectures. This book really does appeal to student as well as professional audiences.

CHAPTER 5

Ethical Considerations in the Practice of Research

So act as to treat humanity, whether in thine own person or in that of any other, in every case as an end withal, never as a means only.
—Immanuel Kant (1785/1909)

This axiom, Kant's *practical imperative*, is a binding obligation for everyone, particularly those who study the human experience. In it, Kant identifies the key issue: How we think about and act toward individuals in our search for knowledge is fundamentally more important than any knowledge gained. Psychology has not been slow to embrace the imperative, although in its zeal to cover all aspects of the research enterprise, ethical considerations often end up as a side issue. To specifically avoid creating the impression that ethics in psychological research is anything less than a central topic, this chapter is devoted to creating a morally appropriate atmosphere through all phases of your research project.

Don't be put off by the word "moral." Practically speaking, there are right and wrong ways to treat research participants and to conduct psychological studies. These two issues—treatment and conduct—are intertwined in the topics presented here in chapter 5. As always, supporting exercises will make the material readily applicable to your own research. We begin with ethical overviews of human and animal research and then consider the crucial balance between participant welfare and scientific advancement. Important aspects of organized research, such as review boards and informed consent, are then presented, as are practical matters, including recruiting participants and keeping records. Advice on how to treat human and animal participants follows, as does detailed advice on debriefing human participants and maintaining an ethical stance outside the laboratory. The chapter closes with suggestions on using research to tell the truth in the course of advancing knowledge.

HUMAN AND ANIMAL RESEARCH

Human Research

The vast majority of psychological studies involve human participants, and few people question whether psychological research is worthwhile or of benefit to society. Questions are sometimes raised, however, about the ethical appropriateness of some psychological research. In particular, any ethical focus tends to center on the experience of research participants: Were they treated with dignity? Were they fully informed about the nature of the research and what they would experience? Were participant responses given in confidence and with assurance that they would remain anonymous? If introducing stress was necessary, did the investigators make certain that alternative methods were not viable? Did participants learn the scientific rationale for the research at its conclusion?

Sadly, history teaches us that clear ethical stances have not always been applied to research involving human participants. In fact, the first real code of biomedical research ethics was created after World War II during the Nuremberg War Tribunal (Sasson & Nelson, 1969). The Nuremberg Code was developed in response to the atrocities perpetrated by Nazi medical doctors on institutionalized persons and civilians imprisoned in concentration camps (Annas & Grodin, 1992; Barondess, 1996). Stated simply, civilians had no choice but to participate in the Nazi experiments; many died in the process, others were mentally or physically afflicted for the rest of their lives. The Nuremberg Code (Beals, Sebring, & Crawford, 1946–1949) created a basic set of principles emphasizing the rights of research participants, including that (1) voluntary consent is required, (2) full disclosure of the nature of the research occurs at the outset, (3) risks are to be avoided whenever possible, (4) participants should be protected against even minor risks, (5) only qualified scientists should conduct research, (6) participants can withdraw from a study at any time, and (7) researchers must terminate their work whenever continuation is likely to threaten the welfare of participants.

Since the Nuremberg Code was established, the American psychological community has done a great deal of soul searching regarding the ethics of research using human participants. A wide array of sources examine this issue in detail (e.g., Diener & Crandall, 1978; Kelman, 1968; Kimmel, 1988, 1991; Rosenthal, 1994; Rosnow & Rosenthal, 1997; Schuler, 1982; Sieber, 1982a, 1982b). The American Psychological Association (APA, 1982), which has a distinguished history of concern for research and professional ethics, carefully crafted 10 guidelines for psychologists who conduct research with human participants. These guidelines, which comprise the APA's ethical principle 9 (APA, 1990), are reprinted in table 5.1. As you read the guidelines, you will see that they are in keeping with the spirit of the Nuremberg Code. Whether or not you are planning to conduct research with human participants anytime soon, it is essential that you familiarize yourself with the contents of table 5.1. These guidelines are important to your development as a

---

TABLE 5.1

APA ETHICAL PRINCIPLE 9: RESEARCH WITH HUMAN PARTICIPANTS

A. In planning a study, the investigator has the responsibility to make a careful evaluation of its ethical acceptability. To the extent that the weighing of scientific and human values suggests a compromise of any principle, the investigator incurs a correspondingly serious obligation to seek ethical advice and to observe stringent safeguards to protect the rights of human participants.

B. Considering whether a participant in a planned study will be a "subject at risk" or "subject at minimal risk," according to recognized standards, is of primary ethical concern to the investigator.

C. The investigator always retains the responsibility for insuring ethical practice in research. The investigator is also responsible for the ethical treatment of research participants by collaborators, assistants, students, and employees, all of whom, however, incur similar responsibilities.

D. Except in minimal-risk research, the investigator establishes a clear and fair agreement with the research participants, prior to their participation, that clarifies the obligations and responsibilities of each. The investigator has the obligation to honor all promises and commitments included in that agreement. The investigator informs the participants of all aspects of the research that might reasonably be expected to influence willingness to participate and explains all other aspects of the research about which the participants inquire. Failure to make full disclosure prior to obtaining informed consent requires additional safeguards to protect the welfare and dignity of the research participants. Research with children or with participants who have impairments that would limit understanding and/or communication requires special safeguarding procedures.

E. Methodological requirements of a study may make the use of concealment or deception necessary. Before conducting such a study, the investigator has a special responsibility to (1) determine whether the use of such techniques is justified by the study's prospective scientific, educational, or applied value; (2) determine whether alternative procedures are available that do not use concealment or deception; and (3) ensure that the participants are provided with sufficient explanation as soon as possible.

F. The investigator respects the individual's freedom to decline to participate in or to withdraw from the research at any time. The obligation to protect this freedom requires careful thought and consideration when the investigator is in a position of authority or influence over the participant. Such positions of authority include, but are not limited to, situations in which research participation is required as part of employment or in which the participant is a student, client, or employee of the investigator.

G. The investigator protects the participant from physical and mental discomfort, harm, and danger that may arise from research procedures. If risks of such consequences exist, the investigator informs the participant of that fact. Research procedures likely to cause serious or lasting harm to a participant are not used unless the failure to use these procedures might expose the participant to greater harm or unless the research has great potential benefit and fully informed and voluntary consent is obtained from each participant. The participant should be informed of procedures for contacting the investigator within a reasonable time period following participation should stress, potential harm, or related questions or concerns arise.

H. After the data are collected, the investigator provides the participants with information about the nature of the study and attempts to remove any misconceptions that may have arisen. Where scientific or humane values justify delaying or withholding this information, the investigator incurs a special responsibility to monitor the research and to ensure that there are no damaging consequences for the participant.

I. Where research procedures result in undesirable consequences for the individual participant, the investigator has the responsibility to detect and remove or correct these consequences, including long-term effects.

J. Information obtained about a research participant during the course of an investigation is confidential unless otherwise agreed upon in advance. When the possibility exists that others may obtain access to such information, this possibility, together with the plans for protecting confidentiality, is explained to the participant as part of the procedure for obtaining informed consent.

Note: APA cautions that the 1990 *Ethical Principles of Psychologists* are no longer current and that the guidelines and information provided in "Principle 9: Research with Human Participants" are not enforceable as such by the APA Ethics Code of 1992, but may be of educative value to psychologists, courts, and professional bodies.

Source: Copyright (1990) by the American Psychological Association. Reprinted with permission.

> **BOX FEATURE 5.A**
>
> ## A Research Digression: What's in a Name?
>
> What's in a name? Quite a bit, actually. The way researchers write and talk about the people who take part in their research really does matter: Are they *subjects* or *participants?* Once upon a time the term *experimentee* was actually suggested (Rosenzweig, 1970, as cited in Martin, 1996), but, perhaps understandably, it was not greeted with any enthusiasm or much use.
>
> The APA (1994) recommends three good standards for deciding how to refer to people: contribution, specificity, and sensitivity. *Participants* is preferable to *subjects* because it implies an active rather than a passive role in scientific investigations. Using this animated term acknowledges contribution to a single piece of research and, more broadly, science. Naturally, other descriptive terms that enhance specificity, such as *college students, preschool children,* and *team members,* are also desirable. Impersonal, less specific terms, including *subjects* and *sample,* should be reserved for statistical matters, not people.
>
> As for sensitivity, people's preferences for titles that individualize them should be honored (Maggio, 1991). Avoid monolithic labels for people because it sanctions grouping them as objects (e.g., the aged, schizophrenics) and not as individuals. Labeling poses special problems where persons with disabilities are concerned, especially because they are often equated with their physical or mental conditions (Dembo, 1964; Wright, 1991). Instead of highlighting a disability, try to "put people first" when referring to these persons. Rather than "HIV+ patients" or "amputees," use "people diagnosed with HIV" or "persons with amputations." Another solution to the labeling dilemma is to rely on adjectives, as in "*gay* men," "*cancer* patients," and "*elderly* women."

student of psychology and a researcher, and familiarity with them will help you to understand the rest of this chapter.

There are a few good sources that can clarify or extend the guidelines presented in table 5.1. An extended discussion of the guidelines is available (APA, 1982), for example, as is a broader work discussing ethics for psychologists embodied in the APA's Ethics Code (Canter, Bennett, Jones, & Nagy, 1994). An excellent review of professional standards and ethical case examples is also available (Keith-Spiegel & Koocher, 1985). Later in this chapter, we will consider the practical side of how to treat human research participants ethically.

Animal Research

According to the 1979 issue of *Psychological Abstracts,* as few as 7 percent of the published articles used animals as research participants (Gallup & Suarez, 1980). Many individuals, including most psychology students, wonder why psychological research even uses animals at all. After all, what could studies using primates, rats, mice, pigeons, and occasionally cats and dogs, tell us about mind and behavior that could not be discovered in research employing exclusively humans participants? Gallup and Suarez (1985) provided a relatively extensive list of reasons animals are used in psychological research. A brief summary of that list follows so that you can begin to think about the relationship between the ethical standards of research in psychology and their link to the rationale for conducting animal research:

- *Control.* Laboratory experiments using animals allow for the controlled manipulation and measurement of factors that make behavioral results interpretable. Even the most carefully crafted research with human participants cannot approach the level of control achievable in animal research.
- *Objectivity.* The study of species other than humans verifies the objectivity and impartiality of the scientific method. If humans studied only other humans, such objectivity could be undermined by social relationships, cultural values, and other important but nonetheless complicating issues.
- *Developmental effects.* Behavior changes as a result of aging, and the process of change can be studied among animals with shorter life spans and in culture-free environments. The same research with humans cannot control for all potential confounds affecting the interpretation of results.
- *Genetic effects.* Genes clearly affect behavior. Animal research, which allows for selective breeding, can demonstrate genetic-behavior links with great clarity.
- *Methodology.* Animals do not speak, and as a result operational definitions and careful methodologies have evolved as a means to understand their experiences. Such rigorous techniques are often later applied to research with humans.
- *Complexity.* Basic elements and principles can be identified in the structure and function of animal behavior, where they might otherwise be lost amidst the complexity of human behavior.
- *Ideal case.* Humans lack many characteristics possessed by animals (e.g., night vision, homing ability, flight). To understand these extraordinary abilities, animals must be studied.
- *Heuristic value.* Animal experiments are very often the source of important hypotheses about human behavior. It is also true that animal studies have been helpful in elucidating basic behavioral principles (e.g., learning), as well as modeling and understanding psychological problems found in humans (e.g., drug addiction).
- *Practical value.* Animal research not only promotes understanding of emotional or behavioral problems in humans, it also expands scientific knowledge and technique that can benefit animals as well.

We might add a final, possibly implicit, point to this list:

- *Curiosity.* Animals are interesting to study in their own right. Careful observation leads to insights and understanding regarding animal behavior.

By presenting these reasons here, my intent is to *inform* you rather than to *convince* you about the virtues of animal research. You must decide on your own whether you believe psychological research using animals is ethically viable. In the course of making that decision, however, you should realize that the issue is complicated precisely because it involves a variety of scientific, societal, and human values that are sometimes at odds with one another. As an educated person who has a stake in the psychological enterprise, you must learn to weigh the costs and benefits of animal research, just as a similar balance must be struck where work with human participants is concerned. With these points in mind we now turn to consider the balance between participants and science.

BALANCING PARTICIPANT WELFARE AND SCIENTIFIC ADVANCEMENT

The investigator is responsible for balancing participant welfare with scientific advancement. Before one datum is collected, the experimenter must carefully weigh the *benefits* and the *costs* of conducting the research. Although such consideration is usually referred to as the *cost-benefit balance* or the *cost-benefit ratio,* no actual quantitative calculation is performed. Rather, any researcher must make a subjective assessment of relative costs and benefits associated with his or her research for the individuals taking part in it, for society at large, and for science (Fisher & Fyrberg, 1994). Careful examination of costs and benefits prompts one key question: Is the research worth doing in the first place?

There are usually some direct benefits associated with psychological research. For participants, these benefits include the educational experience and the self-knowledge gained by performing new tasks or learning new skills. On occasion, an experiment will contain a therapeutic component designed to treat some psychological or medical malady exhibited by participants. Once a project is over, others often benefit from the research; readers of the scientific literature (like yourself, for example) benefit, as do those who receive any treatments or applications derived from the work.

In general, though, the chief benefit of psychological research is the acquisition of new knowledge or the extension of existing knowledge. Sometimes the knowledge we gain has societal or therapeutic applications, but many times it does not (Keith-Spiegel & Koocher, 1985). In fact, the absence of any ready application is the norm, and researchers are usually content with just adding to the store of information about mind, behavior, and the natural world. Put simply, any knowledge is beneficial as long as no research participants are harmed in the course of obtaining it.

This latter concern leads to the notion of costs in doing—or not doing—research. The lesser costs associated with doing research are the investigator's time, money, and energy. Other costs are societal. If a given piece of research is not done, for example, perhaps its potential but untested implications for social well-being will be missed. Still greater costs, those that matter in the extreme, are those borne by the research participants. These particular costs are the *risks* associated with being a participant in a psychological project. There is some degree of risk in any study, but for convenience it is usually categorized as either *minimal risk* or *mental or physical risk.*

Minimal risk occurs by simple participation in any psychological study marked by the absence of or potential for mental or physical harm. Neither completing a short questionnaire on dormitory life on campus or describing study habits to an interviewer, for example, entails any apparent stress or discomfort for those involved. That is, it is extremely unlikely that any given person will become upset or threatened by questions on these topics—the possibility exists (e.g., a student might suddenly realize he does not study very much compared with others), but it is small indeed. Minimal risk is also associated with being assigned to the usually benign control condition of an experiment. Generally, most student research projects should fall under the heading of minimal risk.

In contrast, the increased possibility or reality of mental or physical harm is associated with the second category of risk. Mental risk, for example, entails asking people to disclose very private aspects of their lives, such as their sexual preference or experiences. Such disclosure can create anxiety ranging from the invasion of an otherwise private sphere of life to wondering what will be done with one's responses or who will read them. Mental risk is also present when a participant discovers at an experiment's conclusion that he was deceived regarding its true purpose, that things were not as they seemed. Physical risk occurs most frequently in biomedical research where research participants can be asked to expose themselves to illness (e.g., becoming infected with the common cold as part of a study on stress and susceptibility to illness; e.g., Cohen, Tyrell, & Smith, 1993) or to ingest medications. Some psychological research, however, can involve both mental and physical risk. When individuals are exposed to any stressful circumstance, from examining upsetting photographs (e.g., Neufeld, 1975) to taking part in an anxiety producing role-playing exercise (e.g., Haney, Banks, & Zimbardo, 1973), they can become both emotionally upset and physically agitated.

Student projects should not entail this second level of mental or physical risk or even its possibility. The costs to participants do not outweigh the advantages to science or education. How can we satisfactorily determine if costs and subsequent risks are too high for conducting some types of research? Although researchers are ultimately responsible for their work, fortunately, they do not usually make the decision to proceed without some ethical oversight from peers, the topic of the next section.

A Research Digression: Controversial Studies and Peer Reaction

Controversies can begin in or outside of a discipline, but they tend to center on perceived ethical violations. Some of the most frequently perceived ethical violations in the social sciences involve creating undue stress in research participants or inappropriately invading participant privacy. The research process does have a self-corrective element, however, in that controversial publications are often quickly followed by critical reactions from peer researchers. Such critical dialog is essential to improving the practice of research because it hones the ethical conscience of the members of a discipline.

Ethically minded critics, ethically guided criticism, and thoughtful readers all advance the cause and quality of psychological research. Investigators whose work creates controversies need not agree with their commentators; their substantive reactions and rebuttals both explain their intentions and aid science in the process. To provide you with an opportunity to learn from famous controversies, I provide some original references and peer commentaries and rebuttals below. My goal in doing so is not to suggest that there are absolute rights and wrongs in the studies cited here—indeed, the Milgram (1963) experiments and the Humphreys (1975) study are often labeled "classics"—but rather to invite you to see how perspective drives argument, research, and sometimes ethical stances. As you learn from investigators and critics, you must make up your own mind on the ethical status of research efforts.

UNDUE STRESS: OBEDIENCE TO AUTHORITY

Milgram, S. (1963). Behavioral study of obedience. *Journal of Abnormal and Social Psychology, 67,* 371–378.

Baumrind, D. (1964). Some thoughts on ethics of research: After reading Milgram's "Behavioral study of obedience." *American Psychologist, 19,* 421–423.

Milgram, S. (1964). Issues in the study of obedience: A reply to Baumrind. *American Psychologist, 19,* 848–852.

See also the following:

Orne, M. T., & Holland, C. C. (1968). On the ecological validity of laboratory deceptions. *International Journal of Psychiatry, 6,* 282–293.

Milgram, S. (1972). Interpreting obedience: Error and evidence. In A. G. Miller (Ed.), *The social psychology of psychological research* (pp. 139–154). New York: The Free Press.

INVASION OF PRIVACY: CROWDING AND BATHROOM BEHAVIOR

Middlemist, R. D., Knowles, E. S., & Matter, C. F. (1976). Personal space invasions in the lavatory: Suggestive evidence for arousal. *Journal of Personality and Social Psychology, 33,* 541–546.

Koocher, G. P. (1977). Bathroom behavior and human dignity. *Journal of Personality and Social Psychology, 35,* 120–121.

Middlemist, R. D., Knowles, E. S., & Matter, C. F. (1977). What to do and what to report: A reply to Koocher. *Journal of Personality and Social Psychology, 35,* 122–124.

INVASION OF PRIVACY: HOMOSEXUAL ENCOUNTERS IN PUBLIC RESTROOMS

Humphreys, L. (1975). *Tearoom trade: Impersonal sex in public places* (2nd ed.). Chicago: Aldine.

Sieber, J. E. (Ed.). (1982a). *The ethics of social research: Surveys and experiments.* New York: Springer-Verlag. (see chapter 1)

Warwick, D. P. (1973). Tearoom trade: Means and ends in social research. *Hastings Center Studies, 1,* 27–38.

INSTITUTIONAL REVIEW BOARDS (IRBs)

When psychologists conduct research in college or university settings, they are usually required to have their experiments reviewed in advance by an oversight panel. The name of this panel varies across institutions, but it is generically referred to as the *Institutional Review Board (IRB)* and its duty is always the same: to ascertain that research participants, whether human or animal, are treated in accordance with established ethical guidelines.

Please note that an IRB's role is *not* to assess the scientific relevance of the research proposals it reviews, nor is it supposed to make suggestions about improving methodology, tightening experimental procedure, or in any way challenging researchers' ideas. Instead, the IRB examines the ethical "bones" of the experiment. If deception is used, for example, then the IRB gives special attention to whether it could prove to be psychologically harmful to participants. Similarly, if research participants are placed at risk, either from some aspect of the study or because they belong to a protected group (e.g., children), the potential benefits from the research are weighed against this risk. Indeed, if any risk is present, an IRB will want to know if participants will be made aware of it in advance. For these and other ethically compelling reasons, most IRBs want assurance that participants can elect to terminate their participation in a study at any time (see the discussion of informed consent later in this chapter).

The use of animals in psychological research poses special concerns for IRBs. In fact, many institutions find it advantageous to maintain two panels: one for human research and another, which is often titled the "Animal Care and Use Committee," for animal research. The latter group assesses concern for the well-being of animal subjects in the course of a project, verifies the lack of alternatives to any pain and suffering, and ensures that the disposal of animals is performed humanely.

My assumption is that most readers are apt to conduct research with humans. With this in mind, Exercise 5.A on preparing an IRB form is geared toward research with human participants. If your work involves animal subjects, you should discuss the matter with your instructor, consult departmental regulations, obtain a copy of your department's IRB form for animal research, and carefully study the *Guidelines for Ethical Conduct in the Care and Use of Animals* (APA, 1993; see also the section on Humane Treatment for Animals later in this chapter).

Exercise 5.A: Preparing an IRB Form

IRB forms do vary across institutions, but the example shown in table 5.2 covers the essential ethical dimensions relevant to research with human participants. This particular form was developed for use in research conducted by undergraduate students; however, it shares many of the same features found in IRB forms that are used in faculty or sponsored research. Your institution probably already has a proce-

TABLE 5.2

A SAMPLE IRB REVIEW FORM FOR HUMAN RESEARCH PARTICIPANTS

Project Review Form

This form must be completed for any research activity that involves human participants. Please submit the completed application to your oouroo inotructor.

1. Name of student researcher(s) _____ phone: _____
2. Course _____
3. Instructor _____
4. Title of research _____
5. Semester _____
6. Does the research involve

persons younger than 18 years of age?	Yes	No
prisoners?	Yes	No
institutionalized individuals?	Yes	No
known pregnant women?	Yes	No
any other persons who are vulnerable to risk?	Yes	No

   If you answered "yes" to any of the above you must complete the long form for Human Subjects Approval.
7. Who, specifically, will your subjects be? _____
8. Does your study involve deception of subjects?   Yes   No

   If "yes," use the space below to describe the nature of this deception and your debriefing procedure.
9. Check any of the following that are true. The proposed research involves
   _____ only the use of educational tests (e.g., cognitive, diagnostic, aptitude, or achievement);
   _____ only survey or interview data;
   _____ no identification of the subject by name or number codes;
   _____ the participants being fully informed of the nature of the research project;
   _____ voluntary participation;
   _____ participation by random selection;
   _____ information that would place the subject at risk of liability if it became known;
   _____ information that could affect the participant's financial standing or employability;
   _____ information that deals with sensitive aspects of the participant's own behavior or feelings;
   _____ interviews or surveys of only elected or appointed public officials or candidates;
   _____ observation of public behavior;
   _____ collection or study of existing data, documents, records, or specimens.
10. Briefly describe your project, making sure to include study objectives and design, what will be required of subjects, and any procedures to reduce risks to participants.

Note: This form was specifically designed by the Moravian College Human Subjects Committee for use in undergraduate courses where research with human participants is conducted.

dure to ensure the ethical treatment of human participants, and it may be that completing some sort of IRB form is an integral part of it. If not, then minimally, you should review your project in light of the issues covered in table 5.2. Beyond such a review, however, I encourage you not only to complete this sample IRB form but also to form an in-class IRB (see the following Exercise 5.B).

As you can see, much of the requisite information in table 5.2 is self-explanatory, but several points do stand out. Item 6, for example, is important because any affirmative answer means that a longer, more detailed Human Subjects Review form must be completed. Why? Because interventions involving any of these groups require professional sensitivity, as well as assurance that they are not being exploited, mistreated, or otherwise coerced into participation. Affirmative answers to item 6 also mean that IRB members should exercise extra care and critical thought as they evaluate the potential risks and benefits of the proposed research. A closer evaluation of a proposal is also apt to occur if deception is used (see item 8 in table 5.2). When deception is employed, for example, then greater detail about how debriefing will proceed is required.

From a practical perspective, one of the virtues of completing an IRB form is that you have the opportunity to think about your research idea from a different perspective. Specifically, must a project be conducted as it was originally conceived? If you originally planned to use deception, for example, the process of completing an IRB form might lead you to recognize a nondeceptive alternative. Or, you might develop a powerful but ultimately stress inducing experimental manipulation, say, but your own concerns about an IRB review could motivate you to think of an equally compelling but less pressure-filled approach.

In fact, the perennial question to ask when considering the ethical appropriateness of a study is whether you would mind participating in it. That is, if you were a naive participant who signed up for a project similar to your own, would you have any qualms about participating? If the answer is "yes" or that you are uncertain, you should develop an alternative approach.

Feedback from an IRB is always helpful because a proposal is reviewed by impartial readers who are exclusively interested in its ethical soundness. IRBs are not antithetical to the research enterprise but instead are completely supportive of it. Under ideal circumstances, an IRB can be another source of quality peer feedback that can improve an existing idea (recall our discussions on the importance of peer comments in chapters 2 and 3). Keep the idea of quality commentary in mind as you read the next exercise, which involves forming an in-class IRB.

Exercise 5.B: Forming an In-Class IRB

Who serves on IRBs? Are they composed exclusively of philosophers, theologians, medical ethicists, and others who make moral issues their business? Not at all. Membership is invariably open to professionals with diverse interests and backgrounds. In academic settings, for example, it is not unusual to find panel membership drawn from a variety of disciplines, not just social or natural scientists with a vested interest in empirical research. Typically, noninstitutional members from the local community sit on IRBs, as well. Given their specialized needs, Animal Care and Use Committees have at least one panel member who is a practicing veterinarian.

TABLE 5.3

STEPS FOR DEVELOPING AN IN-CLASS IRB

Step 1—Each research team elects one member to serve on the in-class IRB.

Step 2—The new IRB members read and familiarize themselves with the ethical criteria pertaining to experimental research and professional behavior summarized at the start of this chapter and in the following APA publications.

American Psychological Association (1982). *Ethical principles in the conduct of research with human participants.* Washington, DC: Author.

American Psychological Association (1992). Ethical principles of psychologists and code of conduct. *American Psychologist, 47,* 1597–1611.

Step 3—Each research team completes an IRB form for their proposed project (see table 5.2) and submits a copy to the in-class IRB.

Step 4—The form is reviewed by the IRB. Approval must be by a unanimous favorable vote following discussion by the panel. When an IRB member is a co-author on a proposal under review, that individual is excused from the discussion and cannot vote. If the vote is unanimous and favorable, then proceed to Step 6; if not, then proceed to Step 5.

Step 5—When the initial review is not favorable, the IRB provides written comments and recommendations to the team, which is invited to resubmit an IRB form after addressing any points raised therein. The IRB is encouraged to ask research teams for additional information or clarification of procedures when necessary. Go back to Step 3.

Step 6—The IRB notifies both the research team and the course instructor in writing when a proposal passes review.

How does an IRB work? Some IRBs are institution wide, so that all research proposals are reviewed by one group. At larger institutions, there can be several independent IRBs with different research purviews. Many psychology departments have in-house IRBs for reviewing routine proposals using established procedures. When novel or controversial procedures are introduced, however, in-house IRBs usually defer judgment (and avoid conflicts of interest) by forwarding such proposals on to the institutional IRB.

Many undergraduate psychology departments rely on the goodwill and expertise of faculty members to read and review student IRB forms (recall the example presented in table 5.2) generated by classroom projects. Your own psychology department, for example, may have either a formal or an informal approach to reviewing student research proposals. But what if no IRB currently exists? With some supervision from your instructor, your class should create one to review course research proposals.

Table 5.3 outlines a list of recommended steps in developing an in-class IRB. These recommendations are meant to provide a modest framework for reviewing the ethical dimensions of your research projects and, as a result, they will need to be modified to fit the circumstances of your course, department, and institution, not to mention the projects themselves. Your instructor, too, will undoubtedly have suggestions to add to those found in table 5.3. As you plan and implement the in-class IRB, keep in mind that the group's purpose is distinct from traditional peer review, as the focus is exclusively on issues of ethical treatment.

The very heart of the work done by an IRB is ensuring that participants maintain the right to choose or to decline to be in any research. We now consider this right, called informed consent, in more detail.

INFORMED CONSENT

Informed consent is an idea with far-reaching implications for research, researchers, and most importantly, research participants. Quite simply, it is the experimenter's duty to inform research participants what they are in for by agreeing to participate in an experiment. In other words, before participants consent to be a part of any piece of psychological research, they must be informed about any aspects of the research that could alter their decision to participate.

A key element in informed consent is the participant's inviolable right to withdraw from a study—effectively withdrawing his or her consent—at any time, for any reason, and without any hinderance from the experimenter. Indeed, when a participant elects to withdraw, the experimenter should not question the decision or even ask for an explanation. This right to withdraw without penalty must be clearly explained to participants at the outset of any study.

Why would researchers knowingly choose to undermine their own work? The reason lies in unfortunate historical circumstances leading to the creation of the Nuremberg Code, which we discussed earlier in this chapter. In a real sense, experimenters are not undermining their own research by seeking informed consent; rather, they are allowing people to exercise their inalienable right to self-determination. The following passage from the Nuremberg Code illustrates this point well (Beals et al., 1946–1949; see also Katz, 1996):

> The voluntary consent of the human subject is absolutely essential. This means that the person involved should have legal capacity to give consent; should be so situated as to be able to exercise free power of choice, without the intervention of any element of force, fraud, deceit, duress, overreaching, or other ulterior form of constraint or coercion; and should have sufficient knowledge and comprehension of the elements of the subject matter involved so as to enable him to make an understanding and an enlightened decision. . . . The duty and responsibility for ascertaining the quality of the consent rests upon each individual who initiates, directs, or engages in the experiment. It is a personal duty and responsibility which may not be delegated to another with impunity.

In practical terms, relatively few participants ever withdraw from a study after their informed consent is obtained. Some observers might see such low attrition as evidence of the benign quality of the research process. Others, however, correctly point to the power of the experimental situation to preclude participant departure (e.g., Milgram, 1974; Orne, 1962). The truth of the matter is that most participants are compelled by trust and a desire to be helpful because they are receiving something, such as credit or payment, for their compliance. This should be sobering news to anyone who conducts social or behavioral research. Investigators are duty-bound to protect the rights and welfare of research participants, and they must be vigilant to avoid taking undue advantage of that participation.

Obtaining Informed Consent from Participants

Obtaining informed consent from individuals is largely dependent upon their legal status. Persons who are legally adults, for example, can speak for themselves and choose whether to take part in psychological research after learning an appropriate level of detail about it. Undergraduate students age 18 and above obviously fall into this group, and they can provide their own informed consent.

Other potential groups of research participants, however, must have consent supplied by another party. These groups, including children and legal minors, persons with mental disabilities, and prisoners, must legally and ethically have informed consent provided by either a legal guardian or some other authority (see APA, 1982). Does this mean that the judgment of legally incompetent participants should not be consulted? No. Members of these groups have wishes that should certainly be respected and considered in concert with those expressed by their parents or legal guardians. Under some circumstances, for example, children will be quite capable of making reasonable judgments about what is involved in a study and whether they want to participate in it. When any ambiguity regarding the participation or welfare of a special group is present, consulting an IRB for guidance can be helpful (APA, 1982).

Exercise 5.C: Writing an Informed Consent Form

Informed consent is an ethical demand placed upon all psychological researchers. If your psychology department already has a standard Informed Consent Form, then use it. If not, write up one of your own that incorporates the principles adopted by the American Psychological Association (1982) for the ethical treatment of human research participants. A sample Informed Consent Form that abides by these principles is shown in table 5.4.

The Informed Consent Form in table 5.4 assumes experimenters describe their studies and highlight participant rights in some detail before ever asking for signatures (see points *a* to *g*). When describing a study, however, *only the behavioral requirements*—what participants will literally do—should be noted. Thus, no mention of any hypotheses, or independent and dependent variables, should be made. If information about the study's actual purpose is revealed, participant responses can become biased, thereby corrupting the results. Further, if

---

TABLE 5.4

A SAMPLE INFORMED CONSENT FORM

Informed Consent Form

I, _____, have been supplied with the following information for a study entitled
_____:

   (a) the overall purpose of the study;

   (b) the role I am to play;

   (c) the basic procedures involved;

   (d) the setting and time requirement involved;

   (e) any possible risks or discomforts associated with participation;

   (f) my right to withdraw at any time with no negative consequences;

   (g) if the initial information is incomplete, my right to complete information following my
      participation.

In turn, I acknowledge my responsibility to

   (h) participate seriously and to the best of my ability

   (i) refrain from discussing the study with friends who may also be participating until all
      subjects have completed the experiment.

I agree with all of the above statements.

Signed: _____ Date:_____

Note: The above procedures are in accordance with the American Psychological Association's principles for the conduct of research with human participants. This form was designed for use in undergraduate courses where research with human participants is conducted.

participants know entirely what to expect, the experience will be boring, as experimental anticlimaxes are equally disruptive to the scientific enterprise.

Following a straightforward account of the study's procedure, I recommend that you introduce the concept of informed consent to your participants, answer any questions they have about it or the study's procedure, and only *then* give them the Informed Consent Form to carefully read and sign. As they read this form, note that participants are reminded of their duty to take the experiment seriously and to refrain from discussing it with others who may participate in the future (see points *h* and *i* in table 5.4).

One point in table 5.4, item *g*, merits further mention. The issue is identified as "incomplete information," which is a euphemistic term for deception. If any deceptive procedures were used, participants must be informed about their existence and the rationale for their use during the debriefing session at the experiment's conclusion (see later section Debriefing Human Participants).

When deception is unnecessary, however, it often pays to explicitly state in the Informed Consent Form that no "disguised procedures" will be used in a study (Sternberg, 1993). The reason for this blatant disclosure is because many people are uncomfortable with, even suspicious of, psychology experiments. More jaded participants assume they are somehow going to be duped or surreptitiously observed doing something foolish. This participant reactivity leads some researchers to eschew deception altogether. Any heightened awareness that is not linked to involvement in the experimental procedure is unnecessary, often counterproductive, and ultimately unfair to participants. Why not engage in a bit of truth in advertising and reduce discomfort by informing participants in advance when deceptive procedures are not being used?

What happens to the Informed Consent Form after it is signed? You retain it, filing it carefully—and separately—from all the other research materials from the study, especially the data. Why is the secure storage of Informed Consent Forms so important? Because all participants enjoy the rights of *confidentiality* and *anonymity.* These forms are now confidential documents, and any participant information—including identity—is private unless other agreements are made in advance (see guideline *J* in table 5.1). In most research projects, the principal investigator is the only person who, using a master key of participant names and numbers, could ever match an individual with his or her responses.

RECRUITING RESEARCH PARTICIPANTS AND ADMINISTERING CREDIT

In most psychology departments, recruiting participants for faculty and student projects is relatively easy because of the existence of a *Human Subject Pool.* In any given semester, the Human Subject Pool is usually comprised of the students enrolled in introductory level psychology courses. Students in these courses are encouraged to take part in a certain number of experiments being conducted by faculty, graduate students, or their fellow undergraduates. Participation is voluntary, leading to extra credit toward a course grade or even modest monetary remuneration. Some participants, of course, may choose to participate in experiments out of sheer curiosity.

For any number of reasons, however, students can decide not to be a part of the Human Subject Pool. If a student does not want to participate in any experiments, then he or she can forgo extra credit or payment. When participation is a course requirement, most instructors will have the student write an extra paper on a course topic. Availability of alternative activities is in keeping with the guidelines for the ethical treatment of human participants.

Most Human Subject Pools require a modest amount of bookkeeping to track which students participate, which choose alternative assignments, and who fails to follow either of these options. Beyond record keeping, the hallmark of the Human Subject Pool is usually a bulletin board in a public place within the psychology department. Any experiment currently being run is posted on a *research participant sign-up sheet,* which is a public invitation for students and interested others to take part in research. After reading what amounts to a brief overview of the

---

TABLE 5.5

A SAMPLE RESEARCH PARTICIPANT SIGN-UP SHEET

Impression Formation Study

As a participant in this study, you will describe what factors affect the impressions you form of other people. To do so, you will examine a series of photographs of men and women doing different kinds of activities. You will then be asked to rate the personality of each person appearing in these photographs.

The experiment will last approximately 30 minutes and is worth 1 experimental credit.

The experiment is being conducted by Susan Jones and Alice North. If you have any questions, please call Alice North at 444-4444.

If you sign up to participate, please come to Smoot Hall Room 27-A at one of the dates and times noted below. Please print your name and a phone number where you can be reached in one of the slots below.

Date: **Monday, October 7th**			**Tuesday, October 8th**		
Time	*Your Name*	*Phone #*	*Time*	*Your Name*	*Phone #*
3:00 P.M.			3:00 P.M.		
3:30 P.M.			3:30 P.M.		
4:00 P.M.			4:00 P.M.		
4:30 P.M.			4:30 P.M.		
5:00 P.M.			5:00 P.M.		

To remind yourself about your agreement to participate in this project, please tear off a slip of paper from the pad below and write down the date and time of the experiment.

[Slips of paper with "Impression Formation Study, Smoot Hall Room 27-A" would be attached here.]

---

experiment, interested individuals sign up for a convenient date and time. What follows is a straightforward exercise designed to help you create an effective sign-up sheet for your research project.

Exercise 5.D: Creating a Research Participant Sign-Up Sheet

Creating a research participant sign-up sheet is like reciting some of the basic points of reporting in a journalism class: Be sure to indicate whom, what, where, and when. A model sign-up sheet is shown in table 5.5 and much of its information is relatively standard. A *title*, for example, should convey something about the general area of your project, and it is usually followed by a *short paragraph* describing what participants are expected to do in the study. Following this short description is the *time* commitment required and the amount of *credit*, if any, participants will receive. Any restrictions on who can participate (e.g., only women, students with perfect 20:20 vision, unmarried persons) would also be mentioned here. The experimenter's *name*, the names of other project members, and a *phone number* where a contact person can be reached follow.

After this preliminary information comes the main point: specific *days*, *dates*, and *times* for participation. Interested passersby sign up for a convenient time and write down a phone number where they can be reached (for privacy reasons, some schools prohibit disclosure of phone numbers—follow the local rules on this matter). Beneath these slots is the *place* where the experiment will occur (be certain to reserve any experimental rooms well in advance of when you will be needing them).

There are two simple actions you can take to increase the likelihood that participants will remember that they signed up to be in your project. First, as noted at the bottom of table 5.5, you can provide slips of paper attached to the sign-up sheet noting where the experiment will take place (don't forget to provide additional space for participants to record the date and time they should show up). The experimenter's name and phone number on the paper could also appear on this slip. Second, using the phone numbers they provide on the sign-up sheet, give participants "reminder" calls the night before they are scheduled to participate. You will be pleasantly surprised at how readily these actions will substantially reduce attrition rates.

A final piece of advice: Check your sign-up sheets relatively frequently. Participants who change their schedules (or minds) will cross out their names, allowing other interested individuals to sign up in their places. Keeping track of course credit and a participant record are the next steps in conducting an ethical piece of research.

Course Credit and Record Keeping

Every experimenter is responsible for administering any credit for research participation and for keeping records of who actually took part in a study. Course credit is important because people who take part in experiments do so mainly to fulfil a course requirement or to obtain extra credit. Thus, it is advisable to give a form to participants when they finish an experiment so that they have proof they actually took part in it. Exercise 5.E discusses this issue in some detail and includes a sample form that you can adapt to fit your circumstances.

What about record keeping? What is the most practical way to keep track of research participants? I recommend simply holding on to the original research participant sign-up sheets (see Exercise 5.D) and making some notation next to the name of individuals who failed to appear at their scheduled times. You then file the sign-up sheet in a secure place (recall the discussion of informed consent and the careful storage of forms in Exercise 5.C). If a participant loses a credit slip you can simply verify his or her original participation by checking the original sheet and issuing a new credit slip.

Exercise 5.E: Creating a Course Credit Slip

There is a good chance that your psychology department already provides students and faculty conducting research with various Human Subject Pool forms, including credit slips. If so, then obtain as many of these forms as you need for your project. If not, then you may want to

---

TABLE 5.6

SAMPLE SUBJECT POOL INFORMATION/CREDIT FORM

Subject Pool Information/Credit Form

Date: _____

_____ has completed his/her participation in a study titled _____
and has earned the equivalent of _____ research credit(s). Course credit should be given,
as designated by the instructor of
Course title and number: _____
Name of Instructor: _____
Signed,
Experimenter(s): _____
(Student: Please submit this form to the appropriate person to receive course credit.)

---

create one based on the template shown in table 5.6 so that participants can receive one as they exit your study. The information shown in table 5.6 is relatively straightforward (i.e., date, participant's name, study title, credit earned, the course and its instructor's name, and the experimenter's signature). Any additional information required by the institution where you are conducting your research would also be noted in the body of this credit slip.

As experimenter, you must fill in the necessary information and then give a copy to each participant. Depending upon the folkways of your psychology department, participants then either give the form to the individual instructor identified on each form (see table 5.6) or submit it to some centralized location (e.g., a secretary, graduate student, or faculty member who maintains the Human Subject Pool).

There is sometimes a penalty for participants who miss their scheduled research time and fail to contact the experimenter in advance. If so, you are obligated to follow the local procedures when this happens. Generally, this responsibility entails submitting an absentee list to whoever maintains the Subject Pool. Some student researchers find this responsibility to be burdensome because they prefer not to keep such tabs on their peers. Instead, they should view the experimenter-participant relationship as contractual so that each party is responsible to the other (Aronson, Ellsworth, Carlsmith, & Gonzales, 1990). Thus, if experimenters exert time and effort to create interesting experiments affording credit opportunities, then participants should keep their appointments or make other arrangements well in advance.

What If No Human Subject Pool Exists?

If no Human Subject Pool exists, then you will have to be creative. By that I mean that you will need to develop effective ways to recruit people. A good way to begin is by placing attractive recruiting signs in prominent places on campus where potential recruits are likely to see them (naturally, the sign format should follow Exercise 5.D, though you may want to make it more eye-catching). Posting signs on bulletin boards in the psychology department, the student union, the main academic buildings, and in dormitories is a good bet. There may be college or university regulations governing the placement of signs, so be sure to consult the relevant campus authorities before posting any.

Even with an attention-getting poster announcing your project, however, a likely problem still remains: What is the incentive that will motivate people to sign up? In the absence of requirement or rewards, you and the members of your research team will need to rely on personal pleas. By personal pleas, I don't mean begging—but I do mean approaching people in public places, such as the library, the snack bar, or the student union, and asking them to take time from their busy schedules to help you with a class project. Be sincere, suggest that the experiment is a good study break, and perhaps provide some refreshments afterwards. Most important of all, look people in the eye and tell them how much their help will mean to the success of your project. You cannot be shy about asking friends to participate, either—anyone from fraternity brothers and sorority sisters to acquaintances in other classes is fair game.

Engaging in such vigorous but nontraditional recruiting practices means that you are placing a priority on participants over the desire for random selection. Any reduction in control or randomness threatens the ability to later infer cause and effect relationships among the variables (see chapter 1). Some sacrifices must be made, of course, and it is certainly not the case that the traditional sign-up sheets are ideal where randomness or control are concerned. If anything, traditional recruiting via sign-up sheets favors students currently taking psychology classes, which is, to be sure, not a random grouping. Nontraditional recruiting methods at least hold the promise of tapping some individuals, even subpopulations, who might not otherwise participate in any research, ever.

My point here is not to discourage budding researchers where random selection, control, and inference are concerned, but I do want to make it clear that *random assignment* to conditions within an experiment becomes crucial (see chapter 6). The overarching goal in a first research project is to conduct it from start to finish as best you can. If fate intervenes in the guise of problems or pitfalls, so be it. Becoming a good and practical researcher involves learning by doing, and that includes learning by working through less than ideal circumstances.

HOW TO TREAT RESEARCH PARTICIPANTS

Let's assume that you recruit the number of participants necessary for your project. As experimenter, how should you act toward them? The Golden Rule applies well here: Do unto research participants as you would have them do unto you. The experimenter's contractual obligation to human participants extends to the treatment they receive in the course of an experiment. You should treat them with courtesy, dignity, and respect. What follows are a few suggestions for you to keep in mind in your role as experimenter:

Be on time. It is rude to keep participants waiting or to keep them after the scheduled time has elapsed. When participants are late or fail to show up, for example, the experimenter's disgruntlement is justified; when the tables turn, similar frustration is acceptable in participants.

Establish rapport. Welcome participants to your study with a friendly smile and meaningful eye contact. Convey the impression that you are glad they decided to take part in your project.

Learn your lines. To be an effective experimenter, you must know the experimental script—exactly what you are supposed to say and do—in advance (see chapter 6). If you appear to be unrehearsed, uncomfortable, or otherwise unprepared, the participants will not take you or your project seriously.

Be interested. You must convey genuine interest in your research and to the reactions it elicits from participants. After you have run the tenth participant, the experience will be old to you but remember that it is wholly new to participant eleven. Maintaining a high level of engagement is important in every phase of the study, but especially so during debriefing where your integrity and the advancement of psychological knowledge are on the line (see later section Debriefing Human Participants).

Reduce residual anxiety. Always remind participants that their responses will be kept anonymous, grouped with those given by others and only reported in summary form. Should any particular response be presented in isolation from others, assure them that pains will be taken to disguise the source.

Show appreciation and courtesy. Be pleasant but not overly familiar with participants. The very term "participant" implies a degree of equality that was absent from the older term "subject" (see Box Feature 5.A). People, especially those who help you in your work, are not things. Thank them at appropriate intervals, and be sure that your comments are peppered with "please" and "you're welcome," as well.

Act professionally. You are not merely representing yourself in an experiment; you are also representing your research team, not to mention your course instructor, department, institution, and even the discipline of psychology. It is your responsibility to treat the participants ethically and to maintain confidentiality regarding any information they provide— and be sure to inform them of this fact at some point before the experiment begins (recall table 5.4).

Humane Treatment for Animals

Humane treatment is not limited to humans. To aid those psychologists who use animals in their research and teaching, the APA developed a separate set of guidelines for their care and use (APA, 1993). Despite claims to the contrary (e.g., Bowd & Shapiro, 1993), the humane care and treatment of research animals is of paramount concern to the field of psychology.

TABLE 5.7

6.20 CARE AND USE OF ANIMALS IN RESEARCH

(a) Psychologists who conduct research involving animals treat them humanely.

(b) Psychologists acquire, care for, use, and dispose of animals in compliance with current federal, state, and local laws and regulations, and professional standards.

(c) Psychologists trained in research methods and experienced in the care of laboratory animals supervise all procedures involving animals and are responsible for ensuring appropriate consideration of their comfort, health, and humane treatment.

(d) Psychologists ensure that all individuals using animals under their supervision have received instruction in research methods and in the care, maintenance, and handling of the species being used, to the extent appropriate to their role.

(e) Responsibilities and activities of individuals assisting in a research project are consistent with their respective competencies.

(f) Psychologists make reasonable efforts to minimize the discomfort, infection, illness, and pain of animal subjects.

(g) A procedure subjecting animals to pain, stress, or privation is used only when an alternative procedure is unavailable and the goal is justified by its prospective scientific, educational, or applied value.

(h) Surgical procedures are performed under appropriate anesthesia; techniques to avoid infection and minimize pain are followed during and after surgery.

(i) When it is appropriate that the animal's life be terminated, it is done rapidly, with an effort to minimize pain, and in accordance with accepted procedures.

Source: Copyright (1993) by the American Psychological Association. Reprinted with permission.

Table 5.7, which prescribes the behavior of psychologists who conduct animal research, is taken directly from the *Ethical Principles of Psychologists and Code of Conduct* (APA, 1992). Even if your own research interests do not extend to animal research, you should nonetheless familiarize yourself with the contents of table 5.7. If you intend to conduct research with animal subjects, this information is only a beginning. You will need to supplement table 5.7 with a variety of research sources dealing with the conduct of animal research (e.g., APA, 1993; Boyce, 1989) as well as the continuing debate surrounding it (e.g., Bowd, 1990; Feeney, 1987; Johnson, 1990; Miller, 1985; Plous, 1991, 1993; Sperling, 1988).

DEBRIEFING HUMAN PARTICIPANTS

Once the independent variables are manipulated, the dependent variables are measured, and the experiment proper ends, the researcher must perform the most important part of the procedure—the debriefing of participants. A *debriefing* is a postexperimental interview led by the experimenter, who asks a series of questions designed to learn participant reaction and assess suspicion. Why is debriefing so important to the experiment? Beyond the obvious benefits to research, a good debriefing also serves a valuable educational function because the participants learn the purpose of the piece of psychology in which they had a role.

Because it is the last component in any experiment, sometimes both the experimenter and the participant want a debriefing to be over quickly. Let me caution you to take your time so that you can review some valuable points with participants. First, you must establish your integrity and that of the scientific method underlying the research by presenting a detailed summary of the research. Second, participants need sufficient time to process information about the study, as well as to have any questions answered or concerns addressed. Third, experiments are like theatrical diversions, and those who witness them must be returned to the same psychological frame of mind they were in when their participation began. Thus, a careful debriefing can reduce discomfort and correct misunderstandings, if any exist. Fourth, the experimenter must repeat the guarantees of confidentiality and anonymity that were made at the start of the experiment. Fifth, the experimenter must ask participants not to tell their peers—other potential participants—about the study's specifics because the data will be biased and future participants will be bored because they will know the procedure in advance.

Sensitivity Regarding Deception

A thorough, detailed debriefing is also used to counteract any negative effects associated with the use of *deception*. Deception is the intentional withholding of information within the context of an experiment. As a research technique, deception generates considerable interest, even controversy, because it raises moral and ethical issues regarding the treatment of research participants (e.g., Baumrind, 1985; Bok, 1978; Kelman, 1967). Although it is associated with social psychology (e.g., Korn, 1997), this research technique is by no means exclusive to that field. Deception is usually used to elicit what are assumed to be truer verbal or behavioral responses than those that would occur if participants knew the real purpose of an experiment. As noted earlier, deception should only be used as a method of last resort (but see Christensen, 1988, for a different view).

There are two approaches to deception (Rosnow & Rosenthal, 1996). In *active deception,* participants are purposefully misled about the actual nature of a study. In Milgram's (1974) behavioral study of obedience, for example, the participants were deliberately led to erroneously believe that the "learner" was receiving a series of increasingly painful electric shocks. Other projects use cover stories to lead participants to believe one thing (e.g., "this experiment is on human memory"), although the study's true purpose is to examine some entirely unrelated process (e.g., susceptibility to use of social stereotypes). Active deception research routinely employs confederates or experimental "stooges," as well as placebos and false promises to create expectations in the minds of participants.

Passive deception occurs during the course of a study when some information is intentionally withheld from the participants. Many studies routinely give unlabeled personality inventories with no explanation, for example, and then use the responses to assign participants to particular experimental conditions. Surreptitiously watching adults shopping at the mall or children at play for purposes of observational research, and then failing to alert them of this fact, is also a form of passive deception. Researchers must be aware that deciding what constitutes public or private behavior is not always an easy task (Diener & Crandall, 1978).

When deception is used, the experimenter must be particularly sensitive to the feelings of the research participant. The rationale for its use must be disclosed, of course, but such disclosure must be done carefully and gradually, not abruptly. Participants must never feel that they have been duped or that they have behaved foolishly, nor should they ever leave the experiment with an overly self-conscious attitude.

Some participants, for example, believe that if they were successfully deceived their intellectual abilities must be questionable. Such beliefs are regrettable as well as incorrect, and the experimenter must eliminate them by expressing three points. First, the deception was probably effective because it was designed to be effective; participants were expected to find it convincing (Aronson et al., 1990). Second, the effectiveness of any experimental ruse is related to the unusual characteristics of the experimental situation and not personality traits or skills possessed by research participants. Third, if all participants were aware of a project's actual purpose, their reactions would not be spontaneous; that is, they might not behave the way they would in everyday life.

Exercise 5.F: Conducting a Debriefing and Creating a Debriefing Survey

Conducting a good and thorough debriefing following an experiment is more art than science. The person doing the debriefing interview is called upon to ask questions clearly, to listen carefully, to subtly gauge participant reactions without creating concern, and to gingerly probe for suspicion. As shown in table 5.8, the goals of conducting a debriefing include learning participants' *general reaction* to the study; verifying the effectiveness of the *cover story* or description of the research; determining to what degree participants *assessed the study's purpose* and, if so, with what accuracy; *assessing suspicion* and, if necessary, carefully identifying the nature and reason for the use of deception in your research; asking participants how to *improve the procedure;* and finally *concluding* the experimental session.

The questions provided in table 5.8 are meant to serve as a model for you to create your own *debriefing survey.* Depending upon the purpose of your research, you could have fewer or more questions. Ideally, you would *not* read these questions to the participant but have them more or less committed to memory. Remember, you want the debriefing to be smooth, professional, and friendly—not formal. As you ask questions and discuss a participant's responses, you can jot down brief summary notes on his or her debriefing survey. Avoid writing verbatim responses because they typically take too long to

---

TABLE 5.8

A SAMPLE DEBRIEFING SURVEY

Participant Debriefing Survey

Subject ID number: _____   Date: _____

1. *General reaction.* "What is your general reaction to the experiment? Did everything go well and make sense? Were all the instructions clear? Did you have any problems?"

2. *Recall of cover story.* "I know that the experimenter probably explained the purpose of the research to you. Do you remember what he or she said?"

3. *Assessing purpose.* "Do you have any idea what question(s) this research was trying to answer?"
   (Did the participant guess the correct hypothesis? Yes_____ No_____)

4. *Assessing suspicion.* "Many times participants are suspicious of psychology experiments. Did anything make you suspicious?"
   Yes _____ No _____
   If yes, what exactly made you suspicious?
   Experimenter: If deception was used, then explain how and why it was used, and the reason that an alternative to this deceptive circumstance was not available.

5. *Improving procedure.* "From your perspective as a participant, how could this experiment be improved? What changes, if any, would you make?"

6. *Conclusion and exit. Experimenter:* Thank the participant and then provide him or her with a copy of the *debriefing sheet* (see Exercise 5.G). Remind the participant to avoid discussing the project with others to (a) avoid biasing the data and (b) making it a less interesting exercise for future participants.

---

record and because detailed note taking makes participants self-conscious about their comments.

Interviews are not the only way to gauge participant reactions to an experiment. Some researchers prefer that participants write answers to questions similar to those shown in table 5.8 in a debriefing questionnaire rather than in the course of an interview. The obvious advantages of debriefing questionnaires include standardization of questions, ease of administration, and a time savings for the experimenter.

On the other hand, something is lost if a traditional dialog does not occur between experimenter and participant. The experimenter, for example, loses the opportunity to meaningfully probe for suspicion or to determine if the participant guessed the hypothesis. Neither is there a chance for the experimenter to "give psychology away" in the educational sense (Miller, 1969) by discussing the scientific goals of the research. For their part, participants lack an opportunity to ask direct questions, and there is a very good chance that they will not take a written debriefing as seriously as they would a flesh-and-blood interaction.

I am highly partisan on this issue. I believe absolutely that the experimenter has a responsibility to interview participants, not only to verify their psychological well-being after the study but as a professional

---

TABLE 5.9

A SAMPLE DEBRIEFING SHEET

Emotional Reactions to Music

Most of us realize that music elicits certain emotional responses while we listen to it. How many of us, however, actually sit and think about what the emotions are and why we have these reactions? This is the purpose of my honors project.

Each participant listened to eleven excerpts of musical pieces. There were two different tapes with the same pieces recorded in a different order to control for any effect the order of the music may have had on responses. From a list of ten emotions, some participants were asked to choose those emotions that best described their reaction to the music and also to rate the intensity of those emotions. Others were asked to come up with the emotion(s) they felt and to also rate the intensity of those emotions; an emotion word bank was provided to give these participants an idea of some emotion words. My intent is to see if all participants, regardless of their musical background, have the same or similar reactions to the same piece of music or if reactions are unique. For example, perhaps all (or a majority) of participants felt fear as they listened to the Bernstein piece, *Chichester Psalms.*

The main focus of my research is the difference in emotional reactions to music that may occur between musicians and nonmusicians. You completed a general information survey at the end of the study that I will use to determine your status as a musician or a nonmusician. The eleven surveys you completed after each piece will be used to determine your emotional reactions and the degree of those reactions. Using the general information surveys as well as the eleven surveys, I can evaluate whether there are differences between musicians and nonmusicians in their emotional reactions to music. I will analyze the eleven pieces used in the listening period using musical analysis. The analysis will help me to determine if there are any specific points in each of the pieces that may have elicited the emotional reactions you may have had.

If you have any questions, please ask me now or you may contact me later at 222-2222.

---

courtesy. As students of psychology, we must always remember that we owe research participants respect and a debt of gratitude.

Of course, participants will not necessarily recall everything they hear during the course of a debriefing interview. To fully reach an ethical closure to an experiment, researchers often provide participants with a short written summary of a project's purpose. Exercise 5.G provides a format for writing such summaries and includes a detailed example.

Exercise 5.G: Writing a Debriefing Sheet

At the conclusion of a debriefing session, it is often a very good idea to provide participants with a short account of the research in summary form. What level of detail goes into such a *debriefing sheet?* Really, just the basic facts. Imagine, for example, that you had only 1 minute to explain your project to a stranger—what would you say? A sample *debriefing sheet* from a project conducted by an honors student (Schaeffer, 1997) is shown in table 5.9. As you can see, a debriefing sheet not only reviews the basic idea behind the work and the procedure, it also draws the reader's attention to select independent and dependent variables. Debriefing sheets are really nothing more than an extended Abstract (see chapter 3) that is somewhat more detailed than usual. They serve a valuable educational function, however, in that participants can leave a study with the impression that their participation really mattered, that it helped the experimenter to learn something about human behavior.

ETHICS OUTSIDE THE LABORATORY

A variety of psychological investigations do occur outside the traditional setting of the campus psychology department. These other settings include (but are not limited to) community or professional organizations, hospitals or other medical offices, support groups, schools, and various other institutions. The research conducted in these settings may lack the control found in the laboratory (e.g., random assignment is neither possible nor ethical) but more than compensates by having a high degree of realism allowing for "natural manipulations" to observe cause and effect (McGuire, 1967). It may also involve an intervention that potentially affects the welfare of an individual or individuals, thereby raising ethical questions (e.g., Bermant, Kelman, & Warwick, 1978).

What is a researcher's ethical responsibility to participants when the research does not take place in a controlled setting? To adequately address this issue, we need to divide nonlaboratory research into two categories: situations where participants are aware they are taking part in a psychological study, and situations where they are unaware.

When participants are aware they are participating in some sort of study, it remains absolutely essential to obtain their informed consent. Please note that informed consent is necessary whether you are passing out detailed questionnaires or observing the daily routine in an office setting. In both these examples, you are effectively interrupting the normal course of people's lives and, typically, these people are not receiving even the modest compensation found in lab experiments. Minimally, then, you owe them not only a detailed explanation but also the traditional research escape clause so that they can elect not to provide informed consent.

As you can imagine, some settings can place a great psychological demand on people to participate. As a result, special informed consent forms tailored to settings must be written. Such forms differ from standard forms (recall table 5.4) in that they identify the unique aspects of settings and emphasize that refusal to participate will not affect the participants' current or future status on any key dimensions (e.g., employment, medical care, education). In professional settings, for example, this form must convince employees that the results of the research will not be used to compromise their jobs and that their responses will remain anonymous. Within medical settings, hospital patients or support group members must be told that the research will have no effect on the care or treatment they receive, nor will it affect their condition in any way (though it is sometimes appropriate to inform them that their responses may help others in the future). All of these points should be reiterated once more during a debriefing session immediately follow ing the intervention.

Does the research process change when participants are unaware that they are participating in research? The proper answer is an unsatisfying but duly cautious, "it depends," and we must keep in mind that withholding such information is a form of deception. Yet, if one were doing an observation in a public setting where it is normal to watch others—say, in an amusement park or on a beach—then obtaining informed consent is unnecessary. Similarly, there is no real danger of committing an ethical breach in the course of doing archival research with public records (e.g., city documents, newspaper articles) or private materials (e.g., diaries, letters, journals) that are now public.

There are clearly some ethically gray areas, however, as in the case of observing children playing on a school playground. Should you obtain permission from the school administration and the children's parents to simply watch them? Recalling that children constitute a special participant group, I would say "yes," but others might disagree and argue that this sort of observation is no different than any other. What about manipulating the mood of passersby by having some find a dime in the slot of a payphone and then subsequently staging a nearby pratfall to see if they are more likely to help a victim? Finding money in the payphone did lead to a greater incidence of helping than not finding money (Isen & Levin, 1972), but the ethical issue centers on the fact that the participants were never told they were a part of a study.

Should unaware participants be made aware of their unwitting research roles in such field research? Following the sage advice of Aronson et al. (1992), the researcher is responsible for weighing the effects of being told after the fact versus not being told at all. In the case of Isen and Levin's (1972) work, the participants were never at risk psychologically or physically, nor did they experience anything out of the ordinary—sometimes we do find money unexpectedly, just as we do offer a helping hand to strangers on occasion. It would probably have been somewhat puzzling, even disconcerting, to the participants if they were stopped for even a cursory debriefing. In other situations, however, researchers would appropriately elect to inform participants before they departed the field setting—it depends on the circumstances.

If you are contemplating any field project, it is important that you entertain alternatives, especially if your initial approach precludes informed consent. Before proceeding, be sure to enlist the viewpoints of your instructor, research team, and the in-class IRB. These colleagues may see ways to reduce any ethical problems arising from research out in the field.

BOX FEATURE 5.C

A Research Digression: Ethical Inquiry Outside a Vacuum

Ethical issues are engaging and involving, not just academic. They arouse passion, concern, and sometimes anger by forcing scholars, teachers, students, and citizens to take stands on questions affecting education, science, social policy, and—most importantly—the rights of the individual. *Ethical questions and our responses to them matter.*

To fully understand the essential role that ethical guidelines play in psychological research, you should consider possible situations that raise dilemmas, uncomfortable questions, and actual controversies. Following is a list of such situations that should give you pause—think about them, discuss them with peers, or debate them in class. As you become engaged with them, consider how well psychology's ethical guidelines help you to formulate answers. Are there any ethical matters psychology has missed?

- Where IRBs are concerned, is it ethical to approve experiments involving animals but to refuse to approve the same experiments when human participants are involved?
- Is it ethical to require college students to participate in research for course credit? If students refuse to comply with such requirements, is it justifiable to require them to complete alternative assignments?
- Suppose the psychological community decides not to conduct certain types of experiments or to pursue particular research questions. Does this decision pose any ethical problems for scientific inquiry? For education?
- Are there any circumstances where it is ethically sound *not* to debrief participants?
- Imagine that a dependent measure given in a study reveals that a participant is at risk for depression, but not (yet, anyway) depressed. What is the experimenter's responsibility? Should the participant be informed?
- Rigorous research in the health arena often necessitates that a control group be given a placebo (i.e., a pseudo-drug, one without any medicinal effect or benefit). In other words, some participants will intentionally *not* benefit from their participation in the project. Is this an ethical problem for the research and the researcher?
- Can we—should we—replicate research that has raised ethical concerns in the past (for examples, see Box Feature 5.B)? Is it ethical to refuse to allow such replications to take place?
- Traditionally, laboratory animals are euthanized at the conclusion of research projects. Should this tradition be upheld when classic experiments are replicated for classroom demonstrations? Should such demonstrations take place or simply be read about?

BEYOND ETHICS: TELLING THE TRUTH WITH RESEARCH

In concluding this chapter, it is important to realize that the ethical responsibilities of the researcher do not cease when he or she leaves the laboratory. The psychologist's ethic is not bound by time, place, or convenience (APA, 1992). Three remaining responsibilities of ethical researchers stand out, however: correctly interpreting psychological data, avoiding plagiarism, and maintaining study archives.

Correctly interpreting psychological data means that researchers are obligated to tell the truth about what they know. That is, data must be scrupulously collected without bias, appropriately analyzed using accepted techniques, and then carefully interpreted to link what is already known to what seems to be the case. Remember, knowledge is forged link by link, and truth holds these links together. When there is any shred of doubt—the results are uninterpretable, the statistical tests are not significant, an unknown factor or bias may have been at work, and so on—the researcher must firmly, openly, and honestly acknowledge it. To be less than honest with research is to risk letting half-truths, false information, innuendo, and incorrect facts become a part of the psychological literature. The need for honest presentation of psychological facts is crucial to what is written, spoken, or taught.

Honesty, then, should drive the public enterprise of psychology, but it must also drive the private exercise of psychology carried out by each one of us. Here we again raise the issue of plagiarism, a topic that was initially discussed in chapter 4. Conscientious researchers expend considerable effort to avoid using or writing down the ideas of others without proper attribution. Quotations are judiciously used, paraphrasing is noted. Researchers also do not plagiarize themselves. Data or text from one study cannot be used for another, for example, unless the use is made explicit and convincing to readers. This latter injunction is not very different from a rule that is common on most campuses, one you no doubt follow: You cannot submit a paper for credit if it is the same or highly similar to one submitted for another course.

Finally, we turn to the ethical example set by maintaining a study archive. As a student, you are probably used to keeping all the materials you use to write papers—notes, notecards, rough drafts, copies of articles— as many colleges and universities require these materials to demonstrate that your work is indeed your work. If not, adopt this habit immediately. A similar standard is held for research psychologists, who are encouraged to keep their original data, analyses, and other study materials available for perusal by other psychologists for at least 7 years. Such study archives protect against claims of plagiarism, as well as the charge that data were fabricated, deliberately "made up" by a researcher who was out to "find" some result. Study archives also provide an opportunity for other researchers to reanalyze existing data with new perspectives, theories, and techniques in mind. With this ethical encouragement, let me suggest you hold on to the fruits of your psychological labor after the results are analyzed, summarized, and submitted, as you and others may benefit from them again in the future.

SUMMARY

Ethical standards are an essential part of conducting psychological research and treating human or animal participants fairly. Some ethical standards are formalized. Exercise 5.A, for example, involved completing an IRB form, and Exercise 5.B provided recommendations for creating an IRB to evaluate it. Research participation involving humans was then characterized as a voluntary activity, one requiring a reasonable level of disclosure on the part of the investigator. This discussion of informed consent and related issues culminated with developing an Informed Consent Form (Exercise 5.C). Beyond these formal requirements, other aspects of experimental procedure were shown to have ethical overtones. The remaining exercises in the chapter pertained to the appropriate recruitment of participants through public sign-up sheets (Exercise 5.D), creating course credit slips (Exercise 5.E), leading a systematic debriefing interview (Exercise 5.F), and writing a short summary to give participants at the debriefing's conclusion (Exercise 5.G).

KEY TERMS

active deception (p. 162)
anonymity (p. 155)
confidentiality (p. 155)
cost-benefit balance (p. 145)
cost-benefit ratio (p. 145)
debriefing (p. 161)

debriefing sheet (p. 165)
debriefing survey (p. 163)
deception (p. 162)
Human Subject Pool (p. 155)
informed consent (p. 152)

Institutional Review Board
   (IRB) (p. 148)
minimal risk (p. 146)
passive deception (p. 162)
physical risk (p. 146)
research participant sign-up
   sheet (p. 155)

SUGGESTED READINGS

American Psychological Association (1982). *Ethical principles in the conduct of research with human participants.* Washington, DC: Author. A short and thoughtful explication of APA's Ethical Principle 9.

American Psychological Association (1992). Ethical principles of psychologists and code of conduct. *American Psychologist, 47,* 1597–1611. The updated ethics code for psychologists embodying values for the profession, scientific research, and most importantly, the protection of persons with whom psychologists work.

American Psychological Association (1993). *Ethical principles in the care and use of animals.* Washington, DC: Author. An extended discussion of the care of research animals and the responsibilities of researchers who use them.

Aronson, E. R., Ellsworth, P. E., Carlsmith, J. M., & Gonzales, M. H. (1990). *Methods of research in social psychology* (2nd ed.). New York: McGraw-Hill. This book is not solely for students of social psychology. The chapters discussing ethical issues in research with humans and how to conduct a debriefing are among the finest writings available on these topics.

Milgram, S. (1974). *Obedience to authority.* New York: Harper Torchbooks. Every person who performs psychological research with humans or wants to, or who worries about the ethical conduct of research, should read this book. A classic in social psychology, it speaks to the subtle but powerful authority of experimental settings and those who control them.

CHAPTER 6

Experimental Research

In many ways, the first half of this book has been preparation for this chapter, where the experimental approach to psychological research is reviewed in detail. The advantage of the experiment is clear: It allows the practical researcher to tease cause apart from effect and to effectively rule out competing explanations in favor of a sole account of some phenomenon. To get to that point, of course, the theoretical and practical sides of experimental research must be reviewed in detail, including the role of hypothesis testing, the manipulation of independent variables, the measurement of dependent variables, and the selection of an appropriate research design. A variety of exercises and suggestions accompany each of these topics, and such details add to the precision of your experiment and enhance its likelihood of success.

FORMULATING A TESTABLE HYPOTHESIS

Any experiment in psychology must have a *hypothesis*, the guiding force behind the research. As discussed previously, a hypothesis is a prediction, an educated guess, characterizing the relationship between two or more variables. In scientific investigations, there are two types of hypotheses: *null hypotheses* and *experimental hypotheses*. The null hypothesis is the "hypothesis of no difference." It assumes that the two groups being examined are the same (i.e., A = B) with respect to some behavior. Where experiments are concerned, the null hypothesis stipulates that there is no effect due to the manipulation of an independent variable. Consider an environment's effect on quality of learning, for example. If the issue is whether class size affects academic performance, a null hypothesis would be

> Students in small and large classes do equally well on in-class examinations.

In other words, the number of students in a class does not influence learning in positive or negative ways; crowding has no effect on academic performance. The null hypothesis, then, specifies an equality between the groups.

In contrast, an experimental hypothesis assumes that some difference exists between the two groups (i.e., A < B or A > B). The working assumption in experimentation is that some causal variable creates a difference between the groups. In the case of class size and academic performance, a researcher might assume that crowding does have a deleterious effect on how well students learn, such that students in larger classes might be expected to receive lower scores on examinations than those of students in smaller classes. Why? Well, perhaps students in smaller class sections receive more individualized instruction, have an opportunity for more discussion, and so on. Thus, an experimental hypothesis for this example could be

> Students in small classes obtain higher scores on in-class examinations than do students in larger classes.

Experimental hypotheses, then, highlight differences between groups or treatments. As an independent variable, class size—the number of students enrolled in a section—can be manipulated.

Experimental hypotheses come in two types: directional and nondirectional. Our class size example is a *directional hypothesis* because it specifically indicates how one group will differ from another—students in small classes will receive higher scores than those students in larger classes—as we saw, A > B. Researchers use directional hypotheses when they have a good idea of the character of the relationship between the variables of interest.

Researchers use *nondirectional hypotheses* when they are uncertain of the relationship between some variables. That is, they suspect that something is going on, but they want to hedge their bets by not specifying the relationship until they have an opportunity to examine it empirically. To carry our current example further, our nondirectional research hypothesis would be

> Students in small and large-sized classes will perform differently from one another on in-class examinations.

That is, A ≠ B.

Let's explore the characteristics of experimental hypotheses in greater depth.

Developing an Experimental Hypothesis

What are the characteristics of a good experimental hypothesis? A good hypothesis

- *is a clear statement, not a question.* This criterion may seem at odds with the fact that psychological research is all about asking questions, but hypotheses should firmly state what is being investigated. Consider a new example dealing with interpersonal communication:

  In everyday conversation, men talk more than women.

  For some readers, this hypothesis will be a surprise because the dominant stereotype is that women are more talkative than men (Tannen, 1990; see also, Swacker, 1975).
- *identifies specific relationships among variables.* Generally, the presence of one variable should cause some change in another. In a free conversation, then, male participants should "hold the floor" longer than female participants (e.g., Frances, 1979).
- *is based on a theory or existing knowledge.* In essence, there are no new ideas under the sun and, as discussed in chapters 2 and 4, the thought of prior scholars is an invaluable resource. There is ample evidence, for example, that men and women exhibit different communication patterns (Matlin, 1993).
- *is to the point.* Most hypotheses should be no more than a sentence or two in length. Great detail should be reserved for theorizing but avoided in the presentation of any hypothesis. Excess explanation, then, is unnecessary in explicating the relationship between gender and communication at the level of the hypothesis.
- *can be tested.* This criterion is the most obvious, but arguably the most important, one of them all. The hypothesis must lend itself to empirical study in either experimental or quasi-experimental research designs. Although we cannot literally manipulate gender, we can certainly observe how males and females communicate with one another—in both same- and mixed-sexed groups—and any differences will be informative.
- *can be readily understood by others.* Any good hypothesis should be easily understood by educated individuals. In our culture, gender differences are social fodder that we all understand and frequently think, talk, and even debate about with one another.

Operational Versus Descriptive Definitions

When psychologists decide to test a hypothesis in an experiment, they define it in two ways. The hypothesis is given a *descriptive definition* and then an *operational definition.* Descriptive definitions deal with relationships among variables in the abstract. For example, a personality researcher might theorize that people's level of self-esteem influences the likelihood they will procrastinate on important tasks. This researcher might hypothesize that individuals who possess more favorable self-images are less likely to put off completing difficult tasks because they are challenged, not threatened, by them. In contrast, persons with more negative self-beliefs might be anticipated to avoid doing, even thinking about, demanding activities precisely because their beliefs about themselves provoke anxiety. The descriptive definitions here center on self-esteem as feelings of self-worth and self-acceptance (e.g., Rosenberg, 1965) and procrastination as putting off demanding tasks in favor of those that are less anxiety-producing (e.g., Boice, 1996).

Operational definitions are concrete accounts of the relations among variables. Operational definitions represent the empirical aspects, the "operations," of the independent and dependent variables in a theory being tested. For example, the personality researcher might measure people's self-esteem using an existing, standardized scale (see Blascovich & Tomaka, 1991). As an independent variable, self-esteem would be operationally defined by an individual's score on a chosen scale.

Alternatively, self-esteem could be situationally manipulated in a laboratory setting through a transitory success or failure experience. Participants could respond to a false measure of general knowledge, and then half would be told that they "performed better" than 90 percent of the students who previously took the test. The remaining half, the failure group, would be told that they "scored worse" than 90 percent of prior test takers. Two levels of the independent variable of self-esteem—high and low—would be operationally defined by the performance feedback and the participants' reactions to it (naturally, the researcher would consider the ethical implications of this sort of manipulation; see chapter 5).

As the dependent measure in the study, procrastination could be operationally defined in any number of ways. In the context of a game where points could be earned, for example, the personality researcher might provide participants with an array of puzzles to solve. Participants would be told that correct solutions to the difficult puzzles earn more points than solving the less difficult ones. In operational terms, procrastinators would be more likely to work on easier puzzles of lower worth than on challenging puzzles leading to higher scores. The researcher could examine the average number of points earned per participant or, instead, the average number and difficulty level of the puzzles that were correctly solved.

Clearly, self-esteem and procrastination can be defined in descriptive as well as operational terms. Please understand, though, that there is no *absolute* or *ideal* operational definition for either variable. If anything, there are an infinite variety of possible operationalizations of these variables. Another researcher could develop an entirely different *empirical realization*—the translation of abstract concepts into operational procedures—of these ideas (Aronson, Ellsworth, Carlsmith, & Gonzales, 1990). It is the researcher's responsibility to determine which one seems to be of legitimate use within a particular experiment at a given time and place.

TABLE 6.1

DEVELOPING OPERATIONAL DEFINITIONS

Note: Each member of a research team should complete this exercise alone first, sharing his or her thoughts in a team brainstorming session later.

1. Briefly describe your *descriptive theory* in three sentences or less.
2. What is the descriptive definition of the independent variable(s) from this theory? The dependent measure(s)?
3. If you are using related, published research, what *operational definitions* have been used to examine these or similar variables?
   independent variable(s):
   dependent measure(s):
4. Do some *focused freewriting* about your theory: How could you create an empirical realization of your idea? After several minutes of freewriting, record the following operational definitions:
   Operational definition for the independent variable(s) identified in (2):
   Operational definition of the dependent measure(s):
5. The research team should discuss the operationalizations from (4) until a consensus among the members is reached. Record the final descriptions here.
   Independent variable(s):
   Dependent measure(s):

Exercise 6.A: Developing Operational Definitions

You may or may not be ready to write an operational definition for the variables you plan to use in your project. Nonetheless, it is a good idea to begin to write down relevant thoughts as they occur to you. Table 6.1 provides some space for you to do just that, and it contains several questions that can guide you toward developing good operational definitions. As you can see, the exercise uses techniques introduced earlier in this book, including focused freewriting (chapter 3), working with existing literature (chapter 4), and group discussion among research team members (chapters 1 and 2). If you are not yet ready to write down operational definitions for your research, you can return to this exercise when your project ideas are more fully developed.

RELIABILITY AND VALIDITY

Our understanding of descriptive and operational definitions—really, the abstract and the concrete relationships designated among variables—leads us to two key questions pertaining to the measurement of variables. Is our measurement of a variable reliable? Is the measure itself valid? Our review of the conceptual issues underlying these two questions will lay the ground work for subsequent discussions of manipulating independent variables and measuring dependent variables.

Reliability of a Measure

Reliability refers to the stability or consistency of a measure. Any instrument is deemed reliable if it consistently provides the same answer, result, or conclusion when measuring the same person, object, or construct on several occasions. Unless you are on a diet or you have been eating more than usual lately, for example, your bathroom scale should report approximately the same weight each time you use it, especially if you weigh yourself at the same time of day. An instrument is said to be unreliable if it provides different measurements at different times when the same object is being considered. Imagine that over a 3-day period your weight appeared to vary plus or minus 7 pounds from the first day's recorded weight, despite the fact that you weighed yourself first thing in the morning each time—you would probably not question your eating habits; rather, you would wonder how well the scale was calibrated.

Aside from the obvious variability in measurement, how else could we determine the scale's reliability? One way to assess the reliability of a measure is to compare its results with another measuring device, preferably one already deemed reliable. You could, for example, have your weight taken at your doctor's office on three consecutive days and then compare these weights with those taken at home. If the weight readings from the doctor's calibrated scale were similar to one another (some minor variability is normal) but rather different from your own scale's readings, you could rightly conclude that your own scale was not a reliable measure of weight.

Like the results given by a scale, we want the results of psychological measures to be reliable, that is, consistently trustworthy by being repeatable. Psychologists think of any measure as having two parts: a *true score* and *measurement error*. A true score is a genuine (though hypothetical) score on a given variable, such as some measure of a personality trait like shyness. A reliable measure of shyness would yield a score—usually called the *observed score*—approximately equal to a given individual's true score each time it was given. That is, the observed scores of one person based on different administrations of the shyness measure might vary slightly from one another, but they would presumably lie in the same range of values as the true score. An unreliable measure of shyness would result in a fair degree of measurement error each time—the observed scores would vary greatly from the true score, as well as one another—indicating that it was providing a relatively inconsistent assessment of a person's shyness; the true score was "missed" amidst all the variability. Again, please note that all measures will contain *some* degree of measurement error—it is simply the case that a reliable measure is apt to demonstrate less measurement error (i.e., difference from a true score) across administrations than would an unreliable measure.

Accepting the reliability of psychological measures is extremely important for psychologists, as countless standardized tests and personality measures are used in the clinic, the classroom, the laboratory, and out in the field. Most published tests and measures will include statistics indicating their reliability. These statistics are usually called *reliability coefficients*, which are based on the concept of correlation introduced in chapter 1 and discussed in some detail in chapter 8. If you create your own test or measure, then you will need to determine its reliability by using one of these coefficients. As you may know, correlations can range in value from -1.00 to $+1.00$; where reliability coefficients are concerned, higher values in a positive direction are desirable because they indicate greater consistency (i.e., typically above $+.70$ or $+.80$).

The most familiar example of reliability is *test-retest reliability*, which refers to how well performance on a measure at one point in time reflects performance on the same measure at a subsequent point in time. Reliability is determined by calculating a correlation coefficient between the pair of scores from each of the people who took the test at time 1 and again later at time 2. Test-retest reliability is an especially useful measure of consistency if the variable in question is one that should remain relatively constant across time. Variables that satisfy this criterion include most personality trait measures and various tests of intellectual achievement.

The test-retest method is not without its problems, however. One problem with giving a test twice is that people may recall what they said the first time, thereby artificially inflating the test-retest reliability coefficient. To avoid this problem, *alternate form reliability* is often employed. Instead of taking the same test twice, respondents take two different tests containing the same type of items at two different points in time. The scores on the two tests are then correlated.

Do researchers have to measure participant responses at two points in time to assess reliability? Not necessarily. Reliability can actually be demonstrated at one point in time if the measure in question contains multiple items (generally, any test's reliability is likely to be enhanced if it contains a large number of items). Approaches like this are called *internal consistency measures of reliability*. *Split-half reliability* is determined by correlating participants' total scores on the first half of a test with their scores on the second half of the test. *Odd-even reliability* is based on a somewhat similar procedure, except that reliability is found by correlating the total scores on all the odd numbered items with the total scores on the even numbered items. A final method of finding internal consistency reliability is *item-total reliability*, and it may be the most labor intensive approach. Scores on each item of a measure are correlated with the total score on the test. If, for example, the test had 50 items, then 50 correlation coefficients would be calculated. The average—that is, the mean—of these 50 correlations would be the reliability coefficient.

Construct Validity

Validity deals with whether an instrument is measuring what it is supposed to measure. A valid measure is one that truly measures or manipulates the construct of interest. As you will see in the remainder of the book, there are several ways to conceptualize validity. At this point in our discussion of experimental research, however, we need to be most concerned about what is called construct validity.

Construct validity addresses how well a researcher's operational definition of some variable captures the true nature and theoretical meaning of the variable. If a test is designed to measure problem-solving ability, for instance, then the test itself is the operational definition of problem solving as a variable. The test's construct validity, however, rests on whether—and how well—it measures the theoretical construct "problem solving."

Several types of validity help researchers forge connections between operational definitions and theoretical variables. The most common but least powerful form of validity is called *face validity*. It is called face validity because the measure seems to measure—"on the face of it"—what it is supposed to measure. In the case of problem solving, for example, a group of different sorts of puzzles (e.g., mathematical, verbal, spatial) are appropriate, even reasonable, operational representatives of problem solving, whereas a traditional spelling test does not seem to fit as well under this heading. Some readers may quibble over this distinction by arguing that spelling *is* a form of problem solving, especially when words are conceived as being based on linguistic root words, that smaller words often combine to form larger ones, and so on. If you thought of this argument, I agree with you and congratulate you on having demonstrated well why face validity can be problematic—different researchers can make different claims about what is (or is not) face valid. Thus, face validity is a first, if somewhat superficial, step toward establishing a measure's validity.

A second approach, one that is less dependent on opinion and more dependent on comparing a given measure with related variables, is called *convergent validity*. Specifically, convergent validity occurs when a measure of interest is found to be related to other variables in anticipated ways. Scores on the aforementioned measure of problem solving would be expected to be positively related to other existing measures of problem solving, for instance, but perhaps less strongly with existing measures of creativity. After continued research in developing the measure, an investigator might also find that high problem solvers tend to have high grades in math classes across their academic careers, are orderly and neat, prefer classical music to jazz, and usually finish even difficult crossword puzzles in a short period of time. As you can see, these varied measures and observations converge with one another, that is, they point to a common conclusion regarding problem solving.

Naturally, some variables will not be related to a given measure; indeed, some variables or other existing measures should be specifically predicted to be unrelated to it. This form of validity is called *discriminant validity*. A measure would be of no use to a researcher if everything related to it—instead, a good measure should discriminate between related and unrelated variables. Thus, scores on our hypothetical problem-solving measure would not be predicted to correlate positively with variables such as procrastination, geographical knowledge, and shyness, among others.

As methodological concepts, validity and reliability are critical to the creation, measurement, and manipulation of psychological variables, and to the accurate understanding and use of numerous psychological tests and measures. Here is a small thought experiment to conclude this section. Why is the following statement true? A reliable measure need not be valid, but a valid measure must be reliable. Answer: Consider a variation on the earlier faulty bathroom scale example—it may not provide a valid indication of weight, but it could provide the same (invalid) readings consistently.

MANIPULATING INDEPENDENT VARIABLES

A critical part of planning any experiment is determining what *independent variable* or variables will be manipulated. If you are working on a topic within an established area of psychology, then your literature search undoubtedly revealed a variety of variables that have been used by previous researchers (see chapter 4). As was discussed in chapter 2, for example, you can build upon prior studies by manipulating the same variables in similar or different ways. On the other hand, if your reading of the literature did not turn up many independent variables, then you will need to identify some and develop your own ideas about how they should be manipulated.

The most basic approach, of course, is to compare the *presence* of a variable against the effect of its *absence* on some dependent measure. Do people who exercise regularly get more hours of sleep per night than those who don't exercise? Does such exercise also result in a lower level of stress and fatigue? Alternatively, you could examine an independent variable in terms of some range of values, such that its impact could be meted out as high, medium, or low. For example, you could examine the effects of aversive noise (at 3 decibel levels) or ambient light (at 3 levels of illumination) on learning. Whether your independent variable of choice has 2 or more levels, be sure that the range between the values is sufficient enough to demonstrate behavioral differences. You will want to pilot test your study on a few participants before the actual data collection begins in earnest (see the subsequent discussion of pilot testing). Any demonstration of group differences through the manipulation of an independent variable must be done in a reasonable and judicious manner; metaphorically speaking, you do not want to "hit your subjects over the head" with a manipulation (this should be avoided in a literal sense, as well). A manipulation should not be so subtle so as to be missed, but neither should it be so strong that it appears to be obvious, if not ridiculous (e.g., Question: Are people more comfortable when the room temperature is 70 degrees F than when it is 97 degrees F? Answer: Yes! But so what?). As you continue reading this section, try to think about manipulating variables that capture participant interest as well as response between these two extremes.

Control Groups Are Essential

When students initially begin to think about issues surrounding research design and the interpretation of results, they often engage in a bit of one-sided thinking: They focus on the experimental level of an independent variable exclusively. As a result, they often pay little attention to the comparison level of the variable. I am quick to remind them that the comparison level, which constitutes the *control group*, is as important as the treatment level of a variable. As discussed in chapter 1, a control group does *not* receive the experimental treatment but is identical to it in all other respects.

Why are control groups so important? Because the basic requirement for a true experiment is an independent variable *with a minimum of two levels, one for the experimental condition and one for the control condition.* The control group is an essential part of any experiment because it allows the researcher to determine if the experimental treatment did, in fact, cause any observed differences in the dependent measure. Such differences cannot be assessed if there is no control group that did not receive the treatment. Thus, when examining the effect of any independent variable on behavior, an experimenter must always ask an important question regarding participant response: "Compared to what?" The behavior of the control group tests the null hypothesis, which must always be carefully examined before any conclusions about the effect (or non-effect) of some independent variable on some dependent variable can be drawn.

This important function of control groups may seem implicit, even obvious, to you. You would no doubt be surprised to learn, however, that many student and faculty researchers fail to examine the reactions of the treatment group with the control group. Only too late do they learn that the observed difference was not the one they predicted (i.e., the control group, *not* the treatment group, showed some change) or that both groups behaved similarly on the dependent variable (i.e., no group differences were found). When planning your research design and mulling over the anticipated results, then, you should cultivate the habit of regularly comparing the experimental group with the control group.

Exercise 6.B: Creating an Experimental Script

Experiments are like small bits of theater. The experimenter is the director, the participants are the actors, and there is a script—the experimental procedure—that contains the staging directions for both parties. A play is only as good as its script, and to a great extent this rule holds true for experiments as well. The detail of the script depends on the complexity of the research design. The goal of a good *experimental script* is to have the study run smoothly. If a study runs smoothly from start to finish, its rationale will be clear to participants, as will

TABLE 6.2

STAGES IN A TYPICAL EXPERIMENTAL SCRIPT

1. *Greeting.* The experimenter appears on time and makes the participant comfortable (see chapter 5). *The opening comments should always have the same content, but some ad-libbing is appropriate.*
2. *Rationale for experiment and explanation of the procedure.* The experimenter provides brief background on the study and what specifically will be required of the participant. *Consistent dialog is critical here, and it should be memorized.*
3. *Questions?* The experimenter must make certain that the participant understands the general idea of the research, the directions, and the role he or she is to play. *The experimenter should ask the same questions each time, but some ad-libbing is appropriate.*
4. *Experimental procedure and presentation of the independent variable(s).* The experimenter will guide the participant through the procedure that was described previously in stage 2 and then present the independent variable(s) at the appropriate moment. *Consistent dialog is critical here, and it should be memorized.*
5. *Administration of the dependent measure(s) and any manipulation check(s).* At some point after stage 4 the participant must complete the dependent measures (e.g., questions, rating scales) or perform some behavior that constitutes the main point of the study. Some means to verify that the independent variable was noticed by the participant is useful here. *Dialog is usually, but not necessarily, limited here.*
6. *Debriefing.* The participant is fully debriefed by the experimenter. If any deception was used, the participant's suspicion (e.g., awareness of the true hypothesis) is assessed. Ideally, the experimenter will follow a *debriefing sheet* tailored to the study (see chapter 5). *Dialog can be in the form of general questions but some ad-libbing is usually necessary. A verbal summary of the study is also provided.*
7. *Departure.* The participant leaves the experiment with a *credit slip,* if necessary, and a *debriefing form* (see chapter 5). *Dialog is a gracious thank you and a good-bye.*

instructions pertaining to the independent and dependent variables, and any potential sources of bias will be controlled.

What information is contained in an experimental script? Chiefly, two things: dialog and staging directions. The experimenter (or experimenters, as well as any confederates) needs to know what to say and when to say it (e.g., "Please let me know when you finish reading this booklet so that I can give you a questionnaire to fill out. In the meantime, let me know if you have any questions . . ."). Similarly, the experimenter needs to know what to do and when to do it (e.g., pass out the questionnaire after the participant finishes reading the stimulus materials). The easiest way to proceed is to break an experiment down into stages and then to write out whatever dialog and directions are needed within each stage.

Although every experiment may be different, some typical stages can be identified. As you can see in table 6.2, some stages have more standardized dialog than others, which rely on the experimenter to ad-lib or improvise comments. Remember that your goal is always to keep the conditions in your experiment as similar as possible, which means that improvisation should be kept to a minimum. Use table 6.2 as a guideline to develop your experimental script, and in doing so, keep in mind that after you have run the experiment a few times, both what you say and do will become automatic. Until that point, however, it is a good idea to have a script to remind you what should be happening next in the experimental procedure.

How do you begin an experimental script? Mentally walk yourself through the experiment from beginning to end. As you do so, think about how you would explain your actions to another person, someone who was not at all familiar with what you were doing. Jot down notes about what you would say and when you would say it. After you have a rough draft of the notes, sit down at a computer and begin to add detail to the dialog and the directions so that they form a script. Print out a copy of the script so that you (and any research team members) can review and edit it. Keep in mind that preliminary scripts are always rough, and that you can refine the dialog as you become familiar with it, as well as the procedure, during pilot testing.

Exercise 6.C: Keeping a Record of Experimental Conditions
One of the most important activities for psychological researchers is keeping careful track of participant information. If information regarding a participant's experimental condition, gender, and any relevant data are lost or misplaced, then it is highly likely that her or his responses to the dependent measure will have to be discarded, too. Why? Minimally, you will not know whether a participant was in the experimental or the control condition, so you will be unable to analyze his or her responses. Even if you do know the participant's experimental condition, this knowledge will not do much good if you lack accompanying detail about the person's other characteristics.

The best approach is to begin a careful record of participant information at the outset of an experimental session and to check it over at its conclusion. Table 6.3 shows a basic experimental record sheet for one participant. As you can imagine, the identification number assigned to a participant is extremely important and must appear on this record, as well as any other materials pertaining to a given participant. The other information that the experimenter supplies is meant to provide some context (e.g., date, starting and ending times) for that particular session. Depending upon when random assignment occurs, the information about the experimental treatment can be recorded either before or after the session. Any unusual events—if the participant asked a lot of questions or misunderstood the directions—can be recorded under the *Comments* section of the sheet.

As with all human participant information, please remember that the people's names should never appear on these records (see

TABLE 6.3		

A SAMPLE EXPERIMENTAL RECORD

Participant Record

Date _____

Participant identification number _____ Experimenter _____

Time of participant arrival _____
Time of departure _____

Experimental condition (circle one):   1 = control   2 = treatment
Participant's gender (circle one):   1 = male   2 = female
Comments:

chapter 5). The experimental record should be carefully stored with other materials until the data analysis of the study begins.

Exercise 6.D: Using a Manipulation Check

Outside of examining the results of an experiment after it is over—when it is too late—how can we determine if the independent variable was effective? Many researchers routinely use *manipulation checks* or supplementary measures that verify the effectiveness of treatment variables. Manipulation checks are administered to the actual research participants sometime after the independent variable and either before or after the dependent measure. For example, if you wanted to verify that unexpectedly receiving some free candy actually induced positive moods in an experimental group (e.g., Isen & Levin, 1972), you could administer a mood measure (e.g., Nowlis, 1965) shortly after the treat was provided. Alternatively, the same measure could be given during the debriefing session. This verification of the treatment's effectiveness is referred to as an *internal manipulation check* (Rosenthal & Rosnow, 1991).

Occasionally, some researchers will examine the effectiveness of a treatment variable by asking a separate group of participants to evaluate how they would react if presented with the same situation. Prior to data collection, pretest participants could rate possible tasks for their degree of pleasantness (e.g., listening to music) or unpleasantness (e.g., alphabetizing lists of words) within an experimental context (Dunn & Wilson, 1990). Such ratings constitute an *external manipulation check* (Rosenthal & Rosnow, 1991), and they allow researchers to verify that aspects of an experiment will create the desired impression on future similar participants.

Manipulation checks are very helpful because they allow researchers to learn if an experiment is being accurately perceived by participants. If not, then the procedure can be altered as needed.

TABLE 6.4

PLANNING A MANIPULATION CHECK

A general caution: Manipulation checks should be subtle, not obvious. Creativity is fine as long as it does not detract from experimental procedure.

1. Do you plan to use an _____ *internal* or an _____ *external* manipulation check?
2. If *internal,* will it be presented _____ before or _____ after the dependent measure?
3. If *internal,* will it be based on _____ self-report or _____ behavior?
    If self-report, consider embedding the manipulation check within a questionnaire. You could begin the debriefing with a very short questionnaire, one or two items of which could assess participant reaction to the independent variable.
    What type of self-report manipulation check is relevant to your project?
    If behavioral, select a measure that is conceptually consistent with the independent variable (e.g., interpersonal attraction could be measured by the distance between participants or how long participants gazed at attractive and unattractive photographs).
    What type of behavioral manipulation check is relevant to your project?
4. If *external,* be certain to recruit a pretest group that is similar to the study's actual participants.
    Who will your pretest participants be?
    What type of pretest manipulation check is relevant to your project?

Table 6.4 contains some questions that can help you plan your manipulation check, notably whether it is internal or external.

Practical researchers rely on manipulation checks as a means to maintain the integrity of project data. If the treatment variable was misinterpreted by a participant, the manipulation check will reveal the error—and those data can be legitimately dropped from the pool. Dropping any data is risky, of course, unless the criteria for doing so (e.g., "failure to follow instructions," "equipment or experimenter error") were established during pilot testing. It is too late, potentially biasing, and scientifically questionable to do so once actual data collection is underway.

Not all subfields within psychology use or need to use manipulation checks. Studies that rely on social or personality variables will probably need to verify the effects of treatment variables more often than those examining perceptual or cognitive effects. Intervention studies dealing with treatments designed to improve intellectual performance, educational effectiveness, or reduce problem behavior, however, should always contain some way to assess their efficacy. Performance on age-appropriate standardized tests, retention or graduation rates, and frequency of compliance with regulations (or recidivism rates) could constitute such efficacy measures.

Special Cases: Subject Variables

Not all variables that serve as independent variables can be manipulated. These *subject,* or *organismic, variables* are individual characteristics participants bring to an experiment that are beyond the control of the experimenter. Recall the gender and communication style example presented

TABLE 6.5

EXAMPLES OF SUBJECT VARIABLES

age	birth order
socioeconomic status (SES)	fraternity or sorority membership
intelligence	introversion-extraversion
self-esteem	year in school
marital status	health
race	religion

earlier in this chapter. Any person taking part in it could not be assigned to his or her gender, and yet psychological studies routinely compare male and female reactions *as if* gender were a causal factor. As previously noted in chapter 1, the experience of employed and unemployed persons on some psychological dimensions can be measured and compared, but the results are merely suggestive because it is not possible (or ethical!) to randomly assign people to either employment status. Additional examples of subject variables are shown in table 6.5.

Inferring causality is often a problem when subject variables come into play. What recourse is left to the experimenter? In the short run, a researcher can examine the role of subject variables from a correlational perspective. Thus, one could compare the academic performance of elementary schoolchildren who come from divorced or intact families while acknowledging that any number of variables could be contributing to any observed differences. In the long run, large groups of elementary schoolchildren could be tracked in the knowledge that, across time, a fair percentage of their parents will divorce (our societal divorce rate continues to hover around 50 percent). The academic performance of all the children could be examined longitudinally with special attention given to any changes observed among the children from divorced families. Of course, precise causal links will still remain unspecified, but researchers can nonetheless isolate reasonable candidates to explain the observed results.

Particular subfields of psychology are apt to be more concerned with subject variables than with others. To a large degree, personality psychology and abnormal psychology are predicated on the study of individual differences, many of which manifest themselves as subject variables. Social psychology, too, is selectively concerned with the manner and extent to which subject variables interact with situations (e.g., Aronson et al., 1990; Ross & Nisbett, 1991). Researchers in these subfields routinely identify subject variables that can either cloud or clarify the interpretation of research results.

What should practical researchers do when they are confronted with subject variables? Measure the influence of relevant subject variables in the course of the study. Some researchers seem to adopt a philosophy of "if it moves, measure it." It is not necessary to measure every possible variable, subject or otherwise, but it is prudent to somehow keep track of

---

BOX FEATURE 6.A

A Research Digression: A Variable by Any Other Name

Depending on the context, variables can have variable names, definitions, and functions. Independent and dependent variables have been discussed since the outset of this book, and some other variables have been introduced along the way. Still other variables are of particular concern to practical researchers, and three will be briefly reviewed here. Keep them in mind as you finalize your experimental design, and note that depending upon the circumstances, types of variables can be somewhat interchangeable.

A *moderator variable* is any variable that can conceal the true relationships among the variables being studied in an experiment. If you were studying how familiarity (as an independent variable) can lead to friendship (a dependent variable), for example, then you would certainly want to take into account the influence of physical attractiveness on both these variables. Why? Perhaps attractive individuals are sought out for friendship more frequently than are less attractive people, a plausible state of affairs that could wash out any effects due to familiarity. Physical appearance, then, *moderates* the relationship between familiarity and friendship.

The effects of other variables are often unpredictable in advance. These so-called *extraneous variables* can exert undue influence within experiments and should be monitored as much as possible. If you were studying how English-speaking elementary school students learn a second language (e.g., Spanish), then you would need to verify that none of the students already knew a second language or heard one spoken at home. Bilingual students—certainly Spanish speaking ones!—would probably have an easier time learning a new language because, unlike the monolingual students, they had prior experience with the development of new linguistic skills.

Control variables can be of concern to researchers because they can affect the dependent variable. If you were studying the relationship between student attrition (i.e., drop-out) rates and collegiate academic performance, you would not want to limit yourself to examining just the grades obtained in college courses. Instead, you would probably want to control for student academic performance before the first college year. Why? Some students' records were modest in high school, others were outstanding—in other words, their intellectual abilities were established prior to college. Therefore, any student's academic performance in college-level courses was determined, in part, by his or her achievement in high school. A researcher interested in collegiate attrition needs to remove or control for any student academic differences *prior* to college before drawing conclusions about how college performance is specifically related to attrition.

---

those that could contribute to the interpretation of the results (for a related discussion, see chapter 7). The independent variable record presented in Exercise 6.C can also be used to keep track of subject variables of interest.

ERROR

Because subject variables cannot be controlled by an experimenter, they can be a source of *error* within an experiment. Indeed, any aspect of a study that is beyond an experimenter's control can be said to contribute to error. Error refers to irregular variations in the measurement of some variable or variables within an experiment. Recall the distinction between a true score and an observed score that was introduced in our discussion of reliability: Error is the departure of an observed score for a given treatment condition from the true score for the condition. As we will see, individual departures from a true score can be attributed to any number of (potential) sources of error.

It's quite possible that you already have an intuitive understanding of error in psychological contexts, especially if you took the Scholastic Aptitude Test (SAT) more than once to improve your scores. In other words, you wanted to demonstrate to the college-of-your-choice that you could do better and that, in effect, at least one set of your scores was *in error*. Familiarity with the test (e.g., test-taking savvy, calmer nerves), you reasoned, would reduce the *error* in your score, thereby demonstrating your true academic ability.

There are two types of error that occur in the measurements taken during psychology experiments: *random error* and *systematic error*. Typically, random error involves minor, chance fluctuations around a true value. You may know, for example, that the correct answer to a question on a quiz is "c" but you unintentionally circle "b" instead—your answer was wrong but you *knew* the right answer. Your unaccountable slip of the pencil is an example of random error, as is *guessing* the correct answer to a question when you really don't know a right answer. Because they are due to chance, random errors tend to cancel each other out over many trials and multiple measurements. We hope that they register little influence in experiments, and in fact, random errors are sometimes referred to as *experimental noise*—distracting but not usually harmful.

But what if the errors do not cancel themselves out? What if the errors are consistent, even directional? In this case, we have systematic error. Systematic error introduces bias into an experiment, and it is the psychological equivalent of a butcher who consistently weighs meat by holding his thumb down on the scale—you get less but pay more for it. Systematic error, then, is usually directional in that the measurement is biased in either a positive or a negative direction away from some true value.

An example of systematic error would be unknowingly including a group of especially shy or withdrawn children in a project on peer friendship formation. After the observations were underway, the researcher could be puzzled as to why some children strike up friendships readily whereas others do so in hesitant, socially maladaptive ways. When it goes unchecked, such systematic error within a large portion of a sample is dangerous to the research enterprise, so be on the watch for possible sources of such error in your research design (see also, Box Feature 6.A).

Consideration of error in the research process is also relevant to hypothesis testing. When we test an experimental hypothesis we run the risk of committing what are called either *Type I* or *Type II errors*, which

TABLE 6.6		

TYPE I AND TYPE II ERRORS

	Actual State of Hypothesis	
Researcher's Belief	**Experimental Hypothesis Is True**	**Null Hypothesis Is True**
Experimental Hypothesis Is True	Correct Choice	Type I Error
Null Hypothesis Is True	Type II Error	Correct Choice

will be introduced here and then revisited in the context of statistical analysis in chapter 8. Type I errors occur when a researcher accepts the experimental hypothesis as true when in fact the null hypothesis is really true (i.e., you believe you found a difference between a control and an experimental group when, in actuality, the control and the experimental group did not differ for reasons having to do with the independent variable). See table 6.6.

Type II errors illustrate the opposite problem: The researcher accepts the null hypothesis as true when in fact the experimental hypothesis is really true (i.e., the experimental and control groups appear to be the same when they actually do differ from one another because of the independent variable). Table 6.6 illustrates the Type II error, where a researcher believes that the independent variable did not cause a difference, when in fact it did. Table 6.6 also identifies the correct choices that a researcher can make when his or her belief matches the actual state of the hypothesis.

Which type of error is worse? Many people are quick to respond that Type II errors must be worse. Imagine putting all that effort into a research project only to come up empty handed—your idea was actually correct, but your analysis wasn't sensitive enough to catch it! In practice, however, Type I errors are actually much worse because the researcher has faith in a result that is not true. Why does this pose a problem? Because once a researcher unknowingly publishes a false result, it becomes established wisdom within the psychological literature. Future researchers may unknowingly use the false result to build theories and test hypotheses, only to come up empty handed—and they may assume that the fault lies within their research, not with a previously published result. Type I errors are nefarious and incredibly difficult to eliminate once they become part of the literature, particularly because many researchers are reluctant to believe that published material can be fallible. The moral of the story is that it is better to miss good ideas (Type II errors) than to perpetuate potentially damaging results (Type I errors).

MEASURING DEPENDENT VARIABLES

When it comes to deciding upon a dependent measure—the variable that is assessed in an experiment—one is faced with the same sorts of choices

BOX FEATURE 6.B

A Research Digression: Realism in Experiments

HOW "REAL" IS AN EXPERIMENT TO ITS PARTICIPANTS?

Elliot Aronson and J. Merrill Carlsmith (1968) suggested that participants evaluate an experiment's realism in two distinct ways. In the first place, any experiment can be more or less involving for the people who take part in it. The tasks they must perform, for example, can be highly engaging so that they are drawn into them; that is, they attend to the experiment, taking it and its impact on them very seriously. Aronson and Carlsmith dubbed this *experimental realism*. The second type of realism is *mundane realism,* which refers to the similarity, even familiarity, of the experiment and its procedures to events that occur in the real world.

Experimental and mundane realism are independent, not opposite, concepts. Some studies can be high on one and low on the other, as well as high or low on both. A carefully controlled laboratory-based study may be barren of any resemblance to the real world, but it can still be challenging, interesting, and involving for its participants. On the other hand, a study in a field setting can mimic some aspect of everyday life in great detail but not be very engaging for those who happen into it. Consider these examples:

- In studies on the mental rotation of objects, participants judged whether two shapes were the same as one another, but viewed them from different perspectives. Participants' judgments were made as if they mentally rotated one of the shapes until its position matched (or not) the partner shape. Longer judgment times were associated with more disparate spatial orientations—and vice versa (Cooper & Shepard, 1973; Shepard & Metzler, 1971; see also, Shepard & Cooper, 1982). This series of clever experiments was very high on experimental realism but rather low on mundane realism.

- Can small favors lead to larger commitments? Apparently so, as demonstrated by homeowners who fell prey to the *foot-in-the-door phenomenon* (Freedman & Fraser, 1966). When researchers posing as driver safety volunteers got people to agree to a very small favor first (displaying a small "Be a Safe Driver" window sign), most subsequently agreed to perform a much bigger favor (posting a large, ugly "Drive Carefully" sign in their front yards). Compliance with the latter request was low *unless* researchers got a "foot-in-the-door" by getting people to agree to the smaller favor first. This classic study was clearly high in mundane realism—neighborhoods are often canvassed by salespeople, individuals collecting signatures on petitions, and the like—but rather low in experimental realism.

Realism, then, is in the eye of the participant, but it must still be evaluated by the researcher. Don't assume that laboratory studies are necessarily artificial or that field studies are automatically superior because they occur out in the real world. Evaluate every experiment—including your own—on both dimensions of realism.

surrounding independent variables. A host of examples can be found within the psychological literature relevant to your topic and many of them can be readily adapted to fit your particular purpose and setting. The option to depart from established tradition is available, however, and if you develop your own measure, you will need to be certain that it complements the variable you are manipulating (pilot testing what you measure is as crucial as what you manipulate). There are four classes of dependent measures you can choose from: behavioral, self-report, physiological, and behavioroid measures.

Behavioral measures are those that can be directly observed, especially concrete, readily codable behaviors (e.g., number of pauses during a speech, how long it took to answer a question, a recognition test of photographs, the physical distance between a participant and a confederate). Behavior—human or animal—comes in countless varieties, and it is no exaggeration to suggest that behavioral measures do, as well. Conceptually, however, behavioral measures should closely resemble the psychological construct they were designed to examine. If you want to measure the memory span of three-year-old children, use an age-appropriate recall task; to study helping behavior, create a situation where people have opportunity to lend aid (or not) to someone in need. In general, then, behavioral measures are usually seen as credible indicators of psychological states when they are used correctly.

Once a behavioral measure is chosen, a researcher must determine its level of specificity. A "gross" or global measure simply indicates whether some behavior occurred (e.g., did a participant respond aggressively to a staged insult?). Somewhat more refined measures will focus on the number of behaviors that take place (e.g., how many aggressive comments were made in response to the insult?), the reaction time involved (e.g., how quickly after the insult did an aggressive response occur?), and the time span of the behavior (e.g., how long did the participant display aggressive behaviors?). Naturally, some research will involve several different behavioral measures, some global in scope, others more refined. Other studies will be limited to one behavioral measure—it all depends on the hypothesis, the independent variable(s) involved, the findings of previous research, and the researcher's own judgment about how to best create a credible link between theory and result.

Self-report measures, sometimes referred to as verbal reports, are ubiquitous in psychological research. A standard self-report measure asks people to describe what they think or feel about some stimulus. Self-report measures come in many forms, from standardized personality inventories, rating scales, and surveys, to open-ended questions. Attitudes, mood states, emotional reactions, ratings of like or dislike, lists of thoughts, among many other possibilities, all can be assessed through self-report measures. Most self-report data are collected using paper-and-pencil measures; that is, participants are given some form or questionnaire upon which they write, circle, or check responses. Self-reports can also be gleaned from tape recordings, videotapes, and even phone or person-to-person interviews, of course; to reduce bias and experimenter error, however, most verbal reports are based on participants' written responses.

We should pause here for a moment and consider whether it is possible to directly observe *any* psychological states. In a literal sense, the psychologist never directly observes anything—knowledge about the actions, thoughts, and feelings of others is always indirect. Even behavioral dependent measures are indirect portrayals of an individual's psychology. Indeed, some authors argue that as a class, behavioral measures are conceptually indirect because the observer is always left trying to fathom what internal state led to the witnessed behavior (e.g., Martin, 1996). I understand but disagree with this characterization of behavioral measures because they are routinely preferred over verbal reports; in other words, most psychologists view what people *do* as more psychologically revealing than what people *say* led to their actions (Nisbett & Wilson, 1977; Wilson, 1994; but see Ericsson & Simon, 1993). As researchers, we are left knowing only how a participant behaves or how she says she feels; we do not have direct access to the actual motivation or cause of a behavior, nor do we ever "see" a feeling expressed by another, which means that our understanding is always limited and occasionally even suspect (e.g., Nisbett & Wilson, 1977). Again, the point here is not to question the credibility of the psychological enterprise but to remind ourselves that no dependent measure is ever truly direct and, therefore, entirely satisfactory.

What about *physiological measures?* Physiological measures usually involve indirect methods for measuring truly private, internal psychological states. Our knowledge of emotional states, arousal, and symptom reporting, for example, has been enhanced by reliance on physiological dependent measures (see, for example, Pennebaker, 1982; see also, Cacioppo & Petty, 1983; Cacioppo & Tassinary, 1990). If we are interested in the ways that fear can be induced in humans, then we may want to measure the resulting magnitude of the arousal associated with it. Instead of asking people if they were scared during a suspenseful film clip, we could use a physiological measure—accelerated heart rate—as an indicator of fear. Other indirect measures include respiration, blood pressure, pupil dilation, and galvanic skin response, an indicator of electrodermal activity.

Such physiological measures are quite objective but they pose some unique interpretive problems of their own in that they indicate change—accelerated or decelerated heart rate, for example—but not the reason for it. The researcher is left to develop a coherent, compelling, and ultimately convincing account of what precipitated the change in the physiological dependent measure. As you might imagine, these measures are sometimes deemed more controversial than either behavior or self-reports, and in many studies all three categories of measures are used.

Finally, we turn to so-called *behavioroid measures* (Aronson et al., 1990). Behavioroid measures are expectation-based in that they address "how will you act in the future" sorts of questions (e.g., Aronson et al., 1990). As part of a study on social compliance, for example, a participant might be asked to donate time at a local youth shelter. The researcher is interested in the participant's compliance or refusal with the request, not whether the volunteer work ever actually occurs. Behavioroid measures,

---

TABLE 6.7

A SAMPLE DEPENDENT MEASURE RECORD

Participant Response Sheet

Date _____   Participant identification number _____

Order of Stimulus Presentation	*Participant Rating (1–5)*	*Response Latency*
pretest item	_____	_____
_____	_____	_____
_____	_____	_____
_____	_____	_____
_____	_____	_____
_____	_____	_____

Comments:

---

then, are indicators of commitment. As dependent measures, they are usually administered late in a study, often during debriefing. Participants are told that the study is effectively over but that one final questionnaire requiring their attention remains. Asking participants to reflect on how they might react to some hypothetical event (e.g., "If your candidate lost the election, how would you feel about the economy?") can also constitute a behavioroid measure of sorts. Aronson and colleagues (Aronson et al., 1990, p. 272) point to the important difference between typical questionnaire items and a behavioroid measure for research participants: ". . . the latter has consequences . . . they cannot just check a scale and forget it, they are committing themselves to future behavior."

Exercise 6.E: Creating a Dependent Measure Record

Maintaining a careful record of participants' dependent measures is as important as tracking the experimental condition they are in (see Exercise 6.C). In many psychology experiments, the main dependent measure may be a self-report item embedded within something else, or it may be an observable behavior, or even performance on some task. As a result, it is likely that you will need to obtain the participant's response from an original source and then transfer it to a dependent measure record. A sample dependent measure record sheet is shown in table 6.7.

The sample sheet shown in table 6.7 is a very simple one. It contains space for a participant's ratings of five stimuli and the latency of response (the reaction time from presentation of a stimulus until a rating is made) for each. Both the ratings and the response latencies were obtained from a piece of experimental equipment. The experimenter simply copied the information from a screen between trials (a still more sophisticated procedure would save the data to a file on a computer diskette). Space for other measures, if any, can be made on the sheet, so some room for comments (see table 6.7) must be reserved.

Why bother with such duplication of information? Because a concise record of the participant responses is usually much easier to work with than the original measures themselves. Care must be taken when copying such information, of course; otherwise you risk making a mistake and introducing an unintentional bias into your results. Be sure to hold onto the original dependent measures from any study you conduct so that they can be double-checked as needed.

AVOIDING BIAS

Avoiding *bias* does not begin with keeping careful records. Concern about potential sources of bias in the experimental situation should be an ongoing concern through the life of any experiment. Pilot testing an experiment is one of the best and most straightforward means to avoid bias.

Pilot Testing

Pilot testing an experiment is the equivalent of running a dress rehearsal of a play. The experimenter has obtained permission to proceed from an IRB, collected all necessary materials for the study, as well as written a script, and is now ready to see his or her idea come to life. In running a pilot test, the experimenter runs through the procedure from start to finish with either an informed or a naive participant. Informed participants, usually a friend or colleague of the experimenter, know what the study is about and tend to focus on the clarity of the directions. Informed participants are essentially troubleshooters who can be especially helpful where methodological issues are concerned.

Using naive participants in a pilot study can also be advantageous because they are apt to be much more involved in the procedure than are informed participants. Their greater involvement is because they assume that their responses will be used as part of the research; that is, they remain unaware they are in a first pass of the experimental script until the debriefing. Similar to the informed subjects, they will also be able to pick out any aspects of the procedure that are not clear.

As a dry run of your ideas, then, pilot testing with either type of participant provides an excellent way to spot any flaws—and there can be many—in your research procedure (Sternberg, 1993). You can also determine if your experimental treatment is an effective one in advance of collecting the actual data (Aronson et al., 1990). Pilot testing is a great way to prevent the heartbreak of a good research idea that did not pan out empirically. The extra effort involved is worth it in the long run.

We turn now to the two main sources of bias within experiments, participant demand characteristics and the behavior of the experimenter.

Demand Characteristics

Concern about bias does not dissipate once a study is piloted on a few participants. The experimenter must also be concerned about participant reactions to the study's procedure. The chief source of concern involves experimental *demand characteristics.* Demand characteristics are those cues in any experiment that can lead participants to believe they either know the hypothesis or how they are supposed to behave in the course of the research (Orne, 1962). Given human nature, participants in any piece of research are apt to try to figure out what the experimenter "wants" them to do and why. Demand characteristics illustrate the quintessential human trait of curiosity, but they are obviously disruptive because they promote second-guessing, potentially leading participant attention away from the key variables of interest.

Demand characteristics manifest themselves in different ways. Some participants actively try to determine—and satisfy—the experimenter's expectations in a friendly but obedient manner. Such overly cooperative participants have fallen prey to the *good participant effect* (Rosenthal & Rosnow, 1991). Their actions often betray a desire to convince the experimenter—and perhaps themselves—that their actions are in line with those of healthy, psychologically normal, intelligent individuals. These good participants sincerely want to help researchers confirm hypotheses about human nature, never realizing that such cooperation is a bias that undermines the search for true cause and effect relationships. Even when it confirms a project's hypothesis, such data must be removed from the analyses because of their favorable bias.

The classic demonstration of the good participant effect was done by Orne (1962), who inadvertently discovered that nonhypnotized participants in his hypnosis research were willing to cheerfully do an endless series of meaningless tasks (e.g., adding thousands of rows of two-digit numbers) for hours at a time. Orne had specifically designed the tasks to be dull so that nonhypnotized participants would either refuse to do them or quit after a few minutes. As Orne (1962, p. 777) discovered, however, "Five and one-half hours later, the *experimenter* gave up!"

Other participants react to demand characteristics in anything but a compliant manner. Indeed, some participants actively try to disconfirm what they believe the research is intended to demonstrate. These participants are often fearful that experimenters will "read their minds" or otherwise discover something about their private psychological lives. Many arrive with heightened suspicion and the working assumption that psychologists routinely lie to research participants so as to conceal the purpose of experiments—sadly, their fears are often well grounded (e.g., Orne, 1962; see also chapter 5). To counteract these expectations, to assert individuality, or to demonstrate their negative opinion about the research enterprise, such participants often become unruly, unresponsive, and uncooperative—if not obstructionistic—during experiments. Such unhelpful participants must still be treated with courtesy (see chapter 5),

---

TABLE 6.8

WAYS TO REDUCE DEMAND CHARACTERISTICS

1. *Use effective cover stories.* A compelling explanation for the project's purpose will often satisfy participant curiosity.
2. *Have participants serve as "experimenter."* Participants who believe they are not "subjects" will be less suspicious of the study's intent (e.g., Aronson & Linder, 1965).
3. *Administer dependent measures outside the experimental context.* Tell participants they are participating in two separate experiments so they will not associate the independent variable in one with the dependent variable in the other.
4. *Avoid self-report measures.* Participants often give socially desirable responses that are less revealing than their behavior: Don't ask what they do, watch how they act.
5. *Study nonobvious hypotheses.* Hypotheses that are not intuitively obvious are less likely to be discovered by participants (e.g., Weber & Cook, 1972).
6. *Enlist participant assistance.* Tell participants that they will be most helpful to the research if they adopt an honest and unsuspicious attitude (e.g., Fillenbaum, 1966).
7. *Use bias-reducing research designs.* Assign treatment conditions in advance, making certain that neither the experimenter nor the participants themselves know which treatment is being tested (see Campbell & Stanley, 1966, for examples).
8. *Use involving activities.* If the experiment's procedure is sufficiently engaging, participants will have no time to be distracted by demand characteristics.

---

but their data should be carefully examined and discarded if the experimenter can determine they were actively trying to upset the proceedings.

How can the influence of demand characteristics be reduced? The best way to mollify the effects of either cooperative or uncooperative participants is to give them something to do or to think about once they arrive for an experiment; in short, keep them occupied. Table 6.8 summarizes many of the standard techniques for dealing with demand characteristics, the majority of which are drawn from Aronson et al. (1990). Which one, if any, you decide to use in your research will depend upon the nature of your study, its hypothesis, the materials you use, and so on. The suggestions outlined in table 6.8 are by no means exhaustive. Be advised, however, that some of these suggestions employ varying degrees of deception. Before you decide to use any deceptive methodology within an experiment, be certain that there are not more ethically compelling alternatives available (see chapter 5).

Experimenter Bias

Research bias does not only originate in cues that draw the attention of participants, it can also come from a surprising source—the experimenter conducting the research. *Experimenter expectancies* are the chief source of *experimenter bias.* This term refers to a researcher's beliefs about how participants will behave in a study, beliefs so powerful that the participants unknowingly confirm them. The experimenter is not aware that he or she is giving off subtle but biased cues that elicit the hypothesized responses or reveal the question being studied—all the experimenter knows is that the study is turning out as anticipated.

What makes experimenter expectancies so dramatic is the fact that they have been found to influence both human and animal behavior. The classic example of the transmission of human expectancies is a classroom study conducted by Rosenthal and Jacobson (1968). Elementary school-children were given an IQ test, and subsequently several children were randomly selected from different classes and identified to their teachers as "intellectual bloomers." This identification was an experimental ruse, of course, as they were randomly selected to receive this label. Months later a second IQ test was administered and, dramatically, the bloomers were found to have higher IQ scores than the other children, despite the fact they had merely been labeled for the teachers. Once planted in the minds of the teachers, however, the expectancies for success took root; that is, the children's intelligence per se did not change but the treatment they received from the teachers led them to meet the favorable expectations. This form of expectancy effect is powerful, and it has been replicated literally hundreds of times (Rosenthal & Rubin, 1978).

Favorable and not so favorable expectations can also influence the actions of animals. Some of the students in a laboratory class were told that their rat was bred to be "maze bright"; others were told their animal was "maze dull" (Rosenthal & Fode, 1963). As you may have guessed, the respective labels were randomly assigned, as the rats were not different from one another. Nonetheless, the rodents later confirmed the student expectations with aplomb: The "bright" rats learned the maze better and faster than the "dull" rats. How? Presumably the favorable expectations of the "maze bright" rats led their keeper students to work more closely and consistently with them than the students who expected little of their animals.

Can expectancy effects be reduced, if not eradicated? There are several reasonable ways to attenuate these effects. First, study procedures can be designed to keep an experimenter unaware of whether a given participant is in the experimental treatment or the control condition (e.g., one research team member randomly assigns participant groups, another conducts the actual experiment). This is the so-called "double blind" procedure. Second, any comments made by the experimenter in the course of a study must be carefully scripted and checked to verify that their use does not bias participant responses. Finally, written or tape-recorded instructions can be used during experimental sessions to reduce any undue influence on the part of the experimenter, as can interactive computer programs. Of course, these automated advantages must be weighed against the fact that participants will be somewhat less engaged in any study lacking continued contact with a flesh-and-blood experimenter.

SAMPLING AND ASSIGNING PARTICIPANTS

Sampling Issues

We introduced the concept of populations and sampling in chapter 1 and again in chapter 5 when we discussed recruiting participants. In brief, a sample is drawn from a larger population so that the former can be used to make inferences about the latter. To control for bias, researchers typically rely on random samples so that they can generalize from a sample at one place in time to its wider population at other points in time. If randomizing procedures are not used to draw a sample from a population, any effects obtained cannot be generalized beyond that sample's members.

There are two general categories of sampling within research—*probability sampling* and *nonprobability sampling*. Probability samples are desirable to researchers because the selection of research participants is determined by chance. Back in chapter 1, we discussed *simple random samples* that are drawn in such a way that every member of a population has an equal and independent chance of being chosen to be in the sample. Theoretically, the characteristics of a given simple random sample should closely match the characteristics of the population from which it was drawn.

A second, related approach is *systematic sampling*. A systematic sample involves selecting every *ith* case within a sample. If you were teaching a class of 60 students and you wanted to sample their opinion about your class style, you could systematically sample from the class list. You decide to sample the opinions of 10 students, and so you determine *i* by dividing 60 by 10, which is 6. You would then systematically sample every 6th name on your class list. To proceed, close your eyes and pick a starting point on the list—let's say you land on the 8th name—and then sample every 6th name after the starting point until you have 10 of them (i.e., students 14, 20, 26, 32, 38, 44, 50, 56, 2, and 8). Note that when you reach the end of a list you continue to count from the start of the list—after the 56th person, the next 6th person is number 2 on the list, and so on.

Systematic sampling is easy to do and quite popular among some researchers, but it is not without problems. Think about it: Is it truly random? No. Each member of the class population did *not* have an equal chance of being selected; by imposing some order, such as starting with person 14 (i.e., the starting point of name 8 + 6), you miss the chance to ever choose the 17th name or the 26th name, and so forth. Randomness is violated by the procedure's systematic nature, which in turn compromises a researcher's ability to generalize beyond the current sample.

Stratified sampling is a third type of probability sampling. The goal of obtaining a stratified sample is to accurately characterize a population by being concerned about portraying its subpopulations. Imagine that you were interested in examining the career goals of nursing majors. To do so, you would need to keep one major aspect of nursing students in mind—the interested majority continues to be female—so that a sample would be surveyed accordingly. In other words, care would be exercised to avoid oversampling male response, particularly if the nursing program at your institution had 200 students (say, 150 women and 50 men). To proceed, a researcher would create a list of males and one of females in order to randomly sample 10 percent from each (i.e., 15 female and 5 male students).

In contrast to probability samples, nonprobability samples are not random; that is, their members lack an equal and independent chance of being selected. You may be wondering why researchers use nonprobability samples. The answer is that such samples are reasonable ways to proceed with data collection when a probability sample cannot be obtained or when a researcher wants a quick answer to a question. We will consider two types of nonprobability samples—the *convenience sample* and the *quota sample.*

A convenience sample is aptly named: Participants are convenient to obtain. If you want to know how your dormmates feel about tuition increases at your school, go out your door and ask them. When a university Food Service wants to evaluate the quality of its daily fare, it must seek the opinion of the largely captive audience of student consumers. Convenience samples tell you what you want to know, but they are not random—nor are they apt to be completely representative of the population (e.g., perhaps some dormmates were out when you roamed the halls; maybe the food surveys were administered over a weekend when many students went home). As was noted in chapter 1, most psychology experiments—student as well as faculty—are actually based on convenience samples.

Quota samples highlight certain characteristics of interest to a researcher but they usually lack randomness and careful stratification. Imagine that you wanted to compare the experience of male and female athletes who participate in intercollegiate athletics at your school. Some sports have both male and female teams (e.g., soccer), whereas others are exclusively male (e.g., football) or female (e.g., field hockey). You decide to avoid worrying about some potentially relevant variables, such as the class composition of each team and its size, by simply interviewing 2 people—any 2 you happen to run into—from every team sport. In this quota sample, randomness and representativeness are sacrificed for inclusion of every sport and ease of information acquisition.

Can there be any middle ground between probability and nonprobability sampling? That is, can researchers capitalize on randomness of the former and ease of recruiting associated with the latter? Yes, a researcher can rely on what is called a *matching procedure.* Matching (also known as a *matched groups design*) involves creating comparable participant groups based on a pretest measure or some factor that is highly correlated with the dependent measure before an experiment begins. The goal of the matching procedure is to have the same type of participants assigned to each level of the independent variable. Of course, if the subject characteristic is not related to the dependent measure, then the matching procedure provides no experimental benefit.

A developmental psychologist might be interested in memory span declines associated with aging, and whether some tasks (verbal vs.

numerical) show steeper declines than others. The researcher could begin by recruiting some participants ranging in age from 18 to 90 years. These participants are then rank ordered from oldest to youngest by their age in years. Matched pairs of participants who are approximately the same age are then formed (the two 90-year-olds, the two 88-year-olds, and so on). The members of each pair are then randomly assigned to one of the experimental conditions. This combination of matching and random assignment is particularly advantageous when finding an adequate number of appropriate participants is difficult. On campus, recruiting college aged participants would be much easier than locating an equivalent number of middle-aged and geriatric participants.

Simple Assignment Techniques

Random selection and random assignment are two cornerstones of experimental design. When done properly, random selection allows researchers to generalize their results. In contrast, random assignment helps researchers to avoid confounding variables or creating biased participant groups. In practice, research conducted in college or university settings relies less on random sampling than on random assignment. Both randomizing procedures are desirable, but random assignment of participants to groups or experimental conditions is essential if causal inference about the effect of an independent variable on a dependent measure is to take place. Random assignment establishes equivalent groups, thereby eliminating most systematic biases and substantially reducing the influence of subject variables.

Procedurally, researchers recruit a convenience sample and then randomly assign each individual in it to a particular experimental group. The hope is that the researcher can place participants into these groups without bias. Because you are apt to use convenience sampling in your own research, we will discuss two simple ways to approach random assignment to experimental conditions. We will then consider an exercise on using a random numbers table for assigning participants to groups.

If you were testing participants one at a time in a two-group experiment—a control group and a treatment group—a simple possibility is to flip a coin before beginning each experimental session. If the coin comes up "heads," for example, then the participant can be assigned to the control group. If "tails" appears, then the individual can be placed in the treatment group. Assuming the coin you are using is a fair one, you can assume that approximately half of the available participants will be assigned to one group and half to the other.

Flipping a coin will not work, however, if you have more than two groups. A reasonable alternative for three groups is to write the condition numbers down on slips of paper ("1," "2," or "3"), say, 10 slips of paper for each of three groups. You then place the 30 slips of paper into a hat or some other receptacle, mix them up, and then draw one slip of paper—without replacing it—each time a new participant shows up for

---

TABLE 6.9

CONVENIENCE SAMPLE OF 20 PARTICIPANT NAMES

1.	Peter V.	11.	Tim T.
2.	Susan A.	12.	James G.
3.	Sarah S.	13.	Dave M.
4.	Tom A.	14.	Liz L.
5.	Bob B.	15.	Donna Z.
6.	Martha W.	16.	Arlen S.
7.	Roger H.	17.	Stacey B.
8.	Debbie O.	18.	Sharon P.
9.	Patti G.	19.	Paul A.
10.	George J.	20.	Pat B.

---

your study. Obviously, variations of this procedure can used for more than three groups.

Exercise 6.F: Using a Table of Random Numbers*

What if your research design involves running people in groups, not individually? Is there a straightforward way to assign them to experimental groups without bias? The easiest way is to recruit a sample of participants and then subsequently assign them to groupings. The following procedure is similar to one described by Salkind (1997). Let's assume that you need 20 participants for two groups of 10 each for a memory experiment. The three steps involved are these:

1. Recruit a convenience sample through the Human Subject Pool (or some other means) by posting a sign-up sheet with 20 slots.
2. Assign numbers to each member of the list (i.e., 1 to 20; see table 6.9).
3. Use a Table of Random Numbers to select 10 participants for the experimental group (the remaining 10 will comprise the control group).

Table 6.10 shows a page from a Table of Random Numbers. These random numbers were generated in an unbiased way so that any single-digit number from 0 to 9 occurs equally often throughout the table. After attaching names to numbers (the preceding step 2 and table 6.9), the random numerical entries in table 6.10 ensure that we will not select any one name over any other name.

To proceed, close your eyes and place an index finger anywhere on table 6.10. My finger lands on column 7 in row 20 containing the numerical string of 5-digits (94750). I decide to read downward in the first two columns of digits (i.e., starting with 94) with the goal of obtaining 10 numbers between 01 and 20. Does 94 fall in this range? No, nor do the next 7 two-digit pairs because out of range numbers are skipped. I

*Source: EXPLORING RESEARCH, by SALKIND © 1997. Reprinted by permission of Prentice-Hall, Inc., Upper Saddle River, 4E, NJ.

TABLE 6.10

AN EXCERPT FROM A TABLE OF RANDOM NUMBERS

00001	10097	32533	76520	13586	34673	54876	80959	09117	39292	74945
00001	37542	04805	64894	74296	24805	24037	20636	10402	00822	91665
00002	08422	68953	19645	09303	23209	02560	15953	34764	35080	33606
00003	99019	02529	09376	70715	38311	31165	88676	74397	04436	27659
00004	12807	99970	80157	36147	64032	00050	90951	10877	12171	76833
00005	66065	74717	34072	76850	36697	36170	65813	39885	11199	29170
00006	31060	10850	45571	82406	35303	42614	86799	07439	23403	09732
00007	85269	77602	02051	65692	68665	74818	73053	85247	18623	88579
00008	63573	32135	05325	47048	90553	57548	28468	28709	83491	25624
00009	73796	45753	03529	64778	35808	34282	60935	20344	35273	88435
00010	98520	17767	14905	68607	22109	40558	60970	93433	50500	73998
00011	11805	05431	39808	27732	50725	68248	29405	24201	52775	67851
00012	83452	99634	06288	98033	13746	70078	18475	40610	68711	77817
00013	88685	40200	86507	58401	36766	67951	90364	76493	29609	11062
00014	99594	67348	87517	64969	91826	08928	93785	61368	23478	34113
00015	65481	17674	17468	50950	58047	76974	73039	57186	40218	16544
00016	80124	35635	17727	08015	45318	22374	21115	78253	14385	53763
00017	74350	99817	77402	77214	43236	00210	45521	64237	96286	02655
00018	69916	26803	66252	29148	36936	87203	76621	13990	94400	56418
00019	09893	20505	14225	68514	46427	56788	96297	78822	54382	14598
00020	91499	14523	68479	27686	46162	83554	94750	89923	37089	20048
00021	80336	94598	26940	36858	70297	34135	53140	33340	42050	82341
00022	44104	81949	85157	47954	32979	26575	57600	40881	22222	06413
00023	12550	73742	11100	02040	12860	74697	96644	89439	28707	25815
00024	63606	49329	16505	34484	40219	52563	43651	77082	07207	31790
00025	61196	90446	26457	47774	51924	33729	65394	59593	42582	60527
00026	15474	45266	95270	79953	59367	83848	82396	10118	33211	59466
00027	94557	28573	67897	54387	54622	44431	91190	42592	92927	45973
00028	42481	16213	97344	08721	16868	48767	03071	12059	25701	44670
00029	23523	78317	73208	89837	68935	91416	26252	29663	05522	82562
00030	04493	52494	75246	33824	45862	51025	61962	79335	65337	12472
00031	00549	97654	64051	88159	96119	63896	54692	82391	22387	29529
00032	35963	15307	26898	09354	33351	35462	77974	50024	90103	39333
00033	59808	08391	45427	26842	83609	49700	13021	24892	78565	20106
00034	46058	85236	01390	92286	77281	44077	93910	83647	70617	42941
00035	32179	00597	87379	25241	05567	07007	86743	17157	85394	11838
00036	69234	61406	20117	45204	15956	60000	18743	92423	97118	96338
00037	19565	41430	01758	75379	40419	21585	66674	36806	84962	85207
00038	45155	14938	19476	07246	43667	94543	59047	90033	20826	69541
00039	94864	31994	36168	10851	34888	81553	01540	35456	05014	51176
00040	98086	24826	45240	28404	44999	08896	39094	73407	35441	31880
00041	33185	16232	41941	50949	89435	48581	88695	41994	37548	73043
00042	80951	00406	96382	70774	20151	23387	25016	25298	94624	61171
00043	79752	49140	71961	28296	69861	02591	74852	20539	00387	59579
00044	18633	32537	98145	06571	31010	24674	05455	61427	77938	91936
00045	74029	43902	77557	32270	97790	17119	52527	58021	80814	51748
00046	54178	45611	80993	37143	05335	12969	56127	19255	36040	90324
00047	11664	49883	52079	84827	59381	71539	09973	33440	88461	23356
00048	48324	77928	31249	64710	02295	36870	32307	57546	15020	09994
00049	69074	94138	87637	91976	35584	04401	10518	21615	01848	76938
00050	09188	20097	32825	39527	04220	86304	83389	87374	64278	58044
00051	90045	85497	51981	50654	94938	81997	91870	76150	68476	64659
00052	73189	50207	47677	26269	62290	64464	27124	67018	41361	82760
00053	75768	76490	20971	87749	90429	12272	95375	05871	93823	43178
00054	54016	44056	66281	31003	00682	27398	20714	53295	07706	17813
00055	08358	69910	78542	42785	13661	58873	04618	97553	31223	08420
00056	28306	03264	81333	10591	40510	07893	32604	60475	94119	01840
00057	53840	86233	81594	13628	51215	90290	28466	68795	77762	20791
00058	91757	53741	61613	62669	50263	90212	55781	76514	83483	47055
00059	89415	92694	00397	58391	12607	17646	48949	72306	94541	37408

continue to read down the column until I find 03, which corresponds to Sarah S. in table 6.9. Sarah S. becomes the first person assigned to the experimental group. I continue to select numbers until another 9 values between 01 and 20 are found. Reading down the same column to the bottom of the table and then up to the top of the page to the adjacent two-digit column (beginning with 95), I see that the remaining 9 numbers (and participants) are 13 (Dave M.), 18 (Sharon P.), 1 (Peter V.), 5 (Bob B.), 9 (Patti G.), 10 (George J.), 20 (Pat B.), 4 (Tom A.), and 11 (Tim T.). After this selection process, the remaining 10 names in table 6.9 are designated the control group. That is all there is to it.

Other random assignment variations work equally well. Rosenthal and Rosnow (1991), for example, suggest picking a row of digits in a random numbers table—say, 34072, 76850, and 36997 (see row 5, columns 3, 4, and 5 in table 6.10). Reading across, you can have any odd numbers (i.e., 1, 3, 5, 7, 9) assigned to the control group and even numbers (i.e., 0, 2, 4, 6, 8) assigned to the experimental group. This time Sarah S. (participant 3 in table 6.9) is assigned to the control group, Tom A. (participant 4) goes to the experimental group, and so on until all participants are placed.

Of course, if you have the luxury of being able to randomly sample from a population—you have a population of 90 people and you need a sample of 30 from it for your experiment—by all means take advantage of it. Simply pick a starting point and read down a two-digit column until you have 30 numbers corresponding to 30 numbers between 01 and 90. You can then use one of the random assignment procedures mentioned to create experimental and control conditions as needed. Always remember that any randomizing procedure will strengthen your research by reducing the chance of bias and strengthening your claims for generalizing any results you find.

RESEARCH DESIGN: FACTOR AND FACTORIAL

We will now consider some straightforward research designs that pull together many of the ideas discussed throughout this chapter and earlier in the book. The goal is always to choose a research design that will adequately address the question you set out to answer. Please bear in mind that this review of designs will be highly selective, as there are more designs and variations extant than it is possible to cover in an introductory book like this one. Although this parsimonious review is in keeping with the practical orientation of this book, you can always consult other references for more complex designs (e.g., Campbell & Stanley, 1963; Cook & Campbell, 1979; Kirk, 1995; Rosenthal & Rosnow, 1991).

One-Factor Designs: Posttest-Only and Pretest-Posttest

Many prior examples in this book have relied on a one-factor between-subjects design, where the effects of one independent variable with two

BOX FEATURE 6.C

A Research Digression: How Many Participants Do I Need?

This question plagues researchers everywhere. About how many participants are enough to test a hypothesis? The general rule for human research is "the more, the merrier," whereas animal research typically relies on fewer participants. The best approach to answer this deceptively simple question is to reflect on your available resources and the effect you are trying to demonstrate. There are two main resources to consider:

Availability of time. How large a block of time do you have to collect, analyze, and write up your data (see Exercise 1.A in chapter 1)? Will participants be run in groups (an efficient use of time) or individually (a less efficient use of time)? More time generally allows a researcher to recruit more research participants if they are available.

Availability of participants. Where will you obtain participants—a Human Subject Pool (see chapter 5) or another source? Will there be enough participants ready and willing to be a part of your study? The number of potential participants accessible to you will drive the number you eventually employ in your research, so plan accordingly.

Let's turn to the effect you hope to demonstrate, which, in part, will be affected by the participant samples you recruit and the research design you use:

Participant samples. Will the participant groups in your project be heterogeneous or homogenous? The less similar experimental groups are to one another, the fewer participants per group you will need. The more similar the membership of groups, relatively more individuals per group will have to be recruited.

Complexity of the research design. The number of independent variables you decide to manipulate will influence the complexity of your research design—simpler designs (i.e., 1 or 2 independent variables with 2 levels in each) need fewer participants than do more complex designs (i.e., 3 or more independent variables with 2 or more levels in each).

In general, the sort of study you are likely to undertake should have a minimum of 10 and a maximum of 30 per condition. There are quantitative techniques like power analysis available to help researchers more precisely determine the appropriate sample sizes needed to detect statistical effects of various levels of strength (Cohen, 1988; 1992; Rosenthal & Rosnow, 1991), but such techniques are beyond the scope of the current discussion (but see Box Feature 8.D).

or more levels on some dependent measure were examined. Traditionally, this simple design dominated psychological research, and its simplest case—a study with a control and an experimental group—constitutes the "true experiment" mentioned previously in this chapter. This design is frequently referred to as the *posttest-only design* because participant responses are measured only once, sometime after the presentation of an independent variable. A diagram of the posttest-only design is shown in the top half of table 6.11. If there is any problem with this design, it is that the researcher must assume that random assignment to the control or the experimental group is sufficient to make the groups equivalent before exposure to the independent variable. In practice, random assignment is both powerful and effective in this regard; on occasion, however, there are certain threats to group equivalence and a study's validity. We will review some of these threats in chapter 7.

TABLE 6.11

ONE FACTOR RESEARCH DESIGNS

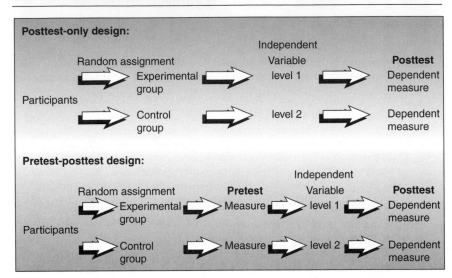

One way to address concerns about group equivalence directly is to employ what is perhaps the second most common single-factor design, the *pretest-posttest design.* This design is precisely the same as the posttest-only design except that a pretest measure is given *before* the independent variable is presented, thereby allowing the researcher to actually demonstrate group equivalence at the start. Thus, if posttest, not pretest, differences are found, the researcher can be very confident that the independent variable had an effect on participant responses (for a diagram of the pretest-posttest design, see the lower half of table 6.11). One worry associated with the pretest-posttest design is that participants will notice and react to the pretest. This genuine concern can be dealt with in several ways: disguising the pretest, administering it outside the context of the experiment, or making it appear to be just one of several questionnaires that must be completed before the study can begin.

There are both advantages and disadvantages to these two simple but true experimental designs. The advantages of these one-factor studies include that they are relatively easy to conduct and that their results are usually easy to interpret. One-factor studies are often used when little is known about an independent variable, so they are particularly suited to pilot projects or exploratory research. Such trial run studies are extremely helpful when it comes to designing more complex, multifactor studies.

As for disadvantages, one-factor studies can be limiting because they often portray more extreme ("either/or") sorts of differences when, in fact, many psychological effects are both subtle and complex. Two, three, or sometimes even four independent variables cannot convey enough rich detail about psychological experience. Why? Because psychological

TABLE 6.12		

THE BASIC 2 × 2 DESIGN

		Factor A	
		Level A1	Level A2
F a c t o r B	Level B1	A1B1	A2B1
	Level B2	A1B2	A2B2

events are rarely dependent on merely the presence or absence of one variable; life is more of a multifactorial than a single-factor design. Indeed, Martin (1996) notes that a chief drawback is the inability of single-factor designs to distinguish among competing theories with any complexity. The exercise of building psychological theories, then, is usually dependent on having more than one independent variable. As a result, many researchers resort to multifactor research designs.

2 × 2 Designs and Beyond

The main advantage of multifactor or, as they are called, *factorial designs,* is their ability to assess the effects of more than one independent variable on the same dependent variable. The most basic factorial design is called the *2 × 2 design* because it replicates the structure of the simplest one-factor study twice. Beyond providing the researcher with an assessment of how two separate independent variables affect an outcome variable, however, this factorial design has an added dimension—whether the two variables interact with one another. We will discuss the concept of *interaction,* a feature only factorial designs provide, in more detail later. Let's first consider the 2 × 2 design conceptually and then in the context of an example.

Why is it called a 2 × 2 design? Because it has 2 factors with 2 levels each. These factors and their cells are shown in table 6.12, where they represent 4 independent groups of research participants. A feature of factorial designs is that you can multiply the number of levels in each factor times the levels in the other factor(s) to determine the precise number of unique conditions (i.e., 2 × 2 = 4 cells). As you can see, factor A has 2 levels (i.e., A1 and A2), as does the second independent variable, factor B with levels B1 and B2. The resulting 4 conditions (A1B1, A2B1, A1B2, A2B2) are shown in table 6.12.

To review these ideas in an example, imagine that you were interested in how ease of imagery (Factor A) and frequency of words (Factor B) influence their recall (the dependent measure) in memory. You develop a list of abstract (A1) and concrete (A2) words, the idea being

---

TABLE 6.13

HYPOTHETICAL RECALL DATA AS A FUNCTION OF IMAGERY AND WORD FREQUENCY

		Imagery		
		Abstract (A1)	Concrete (A2)	Row means
F r e q u e n c y	High (B1)	8.0	15.0	11.5
	Low (B2)	5.0	6.0	5.5
	Column means	6.5	10.5	8.5

Note: Higher means reflect more words recalled.

that the former are less image provoking than the latter (e.g., Paivio, 1971; 1986). Coming up with an image of "democracy," for example, is somewhat more difficult than visualizing a "car." You review the lists of abstract and concrete words and then classify them based on the second factor—their relative frequency of use in spoken English. High frequency words (B1), such as "house," are encountered much more often than low frequency words (B2) like "zither." You then create four word lists corresponding to the 4 cells of the experiment: abstract high-frequency (A1B1), concrete high-frequency (A2B1), abstract low-frequency (A1B2), and concrete low-frequency (A2B2).

You then recruit 40 participants and randomly assign 10 to each of the 4 conditions. The participants listen to a list of 20 words, perform a distraction task (e.g., counting backwards from 500 by 6s) for a minute to wipe out the contents of their short-term memory, and then write down all the words they can recall. You then check their recall accuracy and calculate the mean number of words recalled in each of the 4 groups in the experiment. The hypothetical results from this experiment are shown in table 6.13.

A careful examination of the data in table 6.13 illustrates the benefits of factorial designs that go beyond the 4 cell means: One can readily see the independent effects of the 2 factors. Thus, you could average across the 2 levels of Factor B (word frequency) in order to examine the difference, if any, between recall for abstract versus concrete words (to do so, you would examine the means under columns A1 and A2). This is called a *main effect*. Because of their imagery provoking properties, concrete words were recalled more easily (with an average of 10.5) than abstract words (with an average of 6.5). If these means were the same or very similar to one another, then no main effect would exist. Similarly, you would also want to examine the main effect for relative recall differences

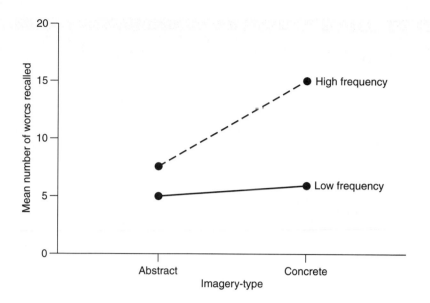

FIGURE 6.1
Graph Illustrating the Interaction between Imagery and Word Frequency on Recall.

between high and low frequency words by averaging across columns A1 and A2 in order to examine the row means for B1 and B2. The mean for the former (11.5) is higher than the mean for the latter (5.5). Note that we have not subjected these data to any statistical analysis, the only way to determine the actual presence or absence of a main effect; we are merely examining the relations among the variables disclosed by the magnitude and direction of the two possible main effects.

We now turn to the interpretive issue that makes factorial designs superior to single-factor designs, one that we held off discussing until now: the concept of interaction. An interaction occurs when the effects of one independent variable change at different levels of another independent variable. As with main effects, the only real way to determine if an interaction exists is by a statistical analysis of the data. There is a reasonable rule of thumb, however, that can be used prior to that point: If the data are graphed and the slopes of the resulting two lines visually differ from one another, then it is likely that an interaction is present. When the lines on a graph are parallel to one another (i.e., they do not and will never intersect), no interaction is present.

The interpretive power of interactions, of course, is what makes them an important tool for researchers. Figure 6.1 shows a graph of the four cell means from table 6.13. As you can see, the cell means have been graphed by placing mean number of words recalled along the y-axis and simply noting the imagery categories (i.e., abstract and concrete) along the x-axis. The hash-marked line illustrates the difference in recall for abstract versus concrete high-frequency words, while the straight line illustrates the relationship between these categories for low-frequency words. What do we know? The slopes of the two lines in figure 6.1 do differ, such that low frequency words do not appear to be recalled better

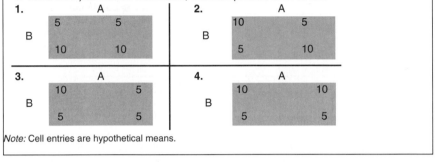

BOX FEATURE 6.D

A Research Digression: Identifying Main Effects and Interactions

The best way to become comfortable identifying main effects and interactions is to practice reading 2 × 2 data tables. Below are several examples to give you that needed practice. Determine if there is a main effect for variable A (column effect) or variable B (row effect) and then graph the data to determine if an interaction is likely to be present. Remember: Nonparallel lines (including lines that crisscross one another or could meet) denote an interaction, whereas parallel lines do not.

Note: Cell entries are hypothetical means.

Answers: 1. No main effect for A; main effect for B; no interaction. 2. No main effect for A or B; interaction. 3. Main effect for A and B; interaction. 4. No main effect for A; main effect for B; no interaction.

whether they are abstract or concrete. In contrast, recall increases dramatically for high-frequency concrete words relative to high-frequency abstract words. Thus, the effect of word imagery depends upon—interacts with—word frequency. Keep in mind that this hypothetical example and its data portray only one set of main effects and an interaction, and that many others are possible (see Box Feature 6.D).

Can we go beyond the 2 × 2 factorial design? Of course. You could add a third independent variable with 2 levels and end up with a 2 × 2 × 2 design, that is, three independent variables with 2 levels in each for a total of 8 conditions. Examining the effects of participant gender (i.e., male vs. female), interactive or otherwise, is common in such 8 cell designs. Do you see the pattern and logic of factorial designs?

Nor are researchers limited to variables with only 2 levels. Imagine an industrial/organizational psychologist who was interested in how management style and work group size affects how long it takes to reach a policy decision. This researcher envisions a 3 × 4 design: Management style has three levels (authoritarian, consensus building, and cooperative) and work group has four levels (a given group is comprised of 4, 6, 10, or 16 people). Participants would be randomly assigned to one of the 12 conditions, where they would be instructed to develop a policy in response to some hypothetical corporate problem. Each of the different sized groups would have copies of the appropriate management style guidelines available to it. Of course, the researcher might want to balance the gender of the groups by ensuring equal representation for males and females (gender, too, could serve as a third independent variable for a $3 \times 4 \times 2$ design).

As long as a project's design has a substantive rationale behind it, a factorial design is quite viable. Researchers must be aware, however, that adding independent variables increases a design's complexity. A $3 \times 4 \times 8$ design could be done, for example, but it would take significant planning and organization to create all 96 different treatment conditions. There is a more practical concern to worry about: participant recruitment. A researcher has to be very confident about locating the necessary number of participants (say, 10 per condition for a total of 960 altogether!) to fill out this challenging design. Moreover, this practical concern does not even address the analysis or interpretation of the resulting main effects and interactions in this complex design. Unless it is absolutely necessary, then, try to avoid adding too many independent variables with multiple levels to your research designs; Less can be more.

To avoid the problem of undue complexity in multifactorial designs, some researchers conduct several experiments on the same topic. You can conduct a variety of related experiments on the same topic that allow you to gradually converge on a particular hypothesis that accounts for some behavior. This package approach, called *converging operations* (Garner, Hake, & Eriksen, 1956; Martin, 1996), represents a workable truce between the desire for complexity and the restraint of practicality.

Other Design Options: Subject Variables Revisited

As we conclude our discussion of between-subject factorial designs, keep in mind that some designs contain independent variables that are manipulated as well as subject variables that are treated as independent variables, though such variables cannot actually be assigned different levels. These research designs are sometimes called *IV × SV designs* (independent variable × subject variable; Cozby, 1997). Gender, age, as well as any number of personality traits, cannot be manipulated (see table 6.5), but researchers can nonetheless see how participants hailing from these groups or possessing particular characteristics react to the independent variables(s) that is (are) manipulated. A basic design incorporating an independent and a subject variable will have one of each (e.g., a 2×2 design), though more complex designs are possible. Any main effects or interactions are explained in the usual manner; however, researchers should keep in mind that results involving subject variables are not causal, and therefore are open to alternative interpretation.

Within-Subjects Designs

Much of our emphasis has been placed on between-subjects research designs, but they are by no means the only option available to researchers. Another useful design is the *within-subjects* or repeated-measures design. In contrast to the between-subjects approaches where participants experience only one experimental treatment, within-subjects designs expose participants to every treatment. Instead of having multiple participant groups, only one group of participants takes part in a given study. As you might imagine, there are clear advantages to this approach, especially concerning time savings and fewer participants.

There is also a distinct methodological advantage in that random error resulting from individual differences or subject variables is substantially reduced because only one group of people participates throughout a study. How so? Because a participant appears in all experimental conditions, his or her unique variability can be statistically extracted from the experiment's random error. In a real sense, each participant serves as his or her own control group.

We could easily conduct the previously discussed imagery-word frequency experiment as a within-subjects design, such that one group of participants would have to listen to and then recall every one of the four types of word lists (see table 6.12). They would essentially do the earlier experiment 4 times instead of just once, which raises a methodological point. We would not want to have every participant learn and recall the same lists in the same order. Why? Because some people might actually obtain higher recall scores with practice (i.e., they do better after the second or third list than they would if they only did the task once). Other people might get tired across the trials so that their performance is relatively worse on the last list or so than on the first list. You can no doubt come up with other reasons why every participant should not do the same lists and recall tasks in the same order.

The appropriate course is to use what is called *counterbalancing* to eliminate any effects due to the order of presentation of stimulus materials. Experimental control is achieved by having everyone experience each stimulus, but the order of stimulus presentation differs for each participant (Campbell & Stanley, 1963). In the present example, each participant hears a different word list in a different order than the other participants. Counterbalancing evenly spreads any special effect of a particular stimulus order across all participants so that no confound due to ordering occurs. The top section of table 6.14 illustrates counterbalancing by using the same imagery words (abstract and concrete) and word frequencies (high and low) as before. This time, however, participants are randomly assigned to receive one unique order (see table 6.14). To have one participant be in every possible order (4! or $4 \times 3 \times 2 \times 1 = 24$), you would need only 24 participants—in the original study, 40 participants were used.

A compelling alternative to a full-blown, within-subjects research design is the *Latin square design.* Latin square designs control for most order effects economically, as only some of the possible combinations of treatment orders are run. The Latin square is useful when too few participants are available or when it is not possible to have every treatment order represented. A sample Latin square design based on the present example is shown in the bottom section of table 6.14. The partial counterbalancing

TABLE 6.14

WITHIN-SUBJECTS APPROACHES: COMPLETELY COUNTERBALANCED AND LATIN SQUARE DESIGNS

Counterbalanced Orders for 24 Participants in Imagery and Word Frequency Study

Participant List	Treatment Order	Participant List	Treatment Order
1	ABCD	13	CABD
2	ABDC	14	CADB
3	ACBD	15	CBAD
4	ACDB	16	CBDA
5	ADCB	17	CDAB
6	ADBC	18	CDBA
7	BACD	19	DABC
8	BADC	20	DACB
9	BCAD	21	DBAC
10	BCDA	22	DBCA
11	BDAC	23	DCAB
12	BDCA	24	DCBA

Latin Square Design for Imagery and Word Frequency Study

Group	Order of Presentation of Word Lists			
1	A	B	C	D
2	B	D	A	C
3	C	A	D	B
4	D	C	B	A

Note: A = abstract high-frequency words, B = concrete high-frequency words, C = abstract low-frequency words, and D = concrete low-frequency words.

strategy shown involves running 4 groups of participants, each of which receives the word lists in a different order (see the bottom of table 6.14). This strategy illustrates the rule of thumb associated with this particular research design: The number of orders in a Latin square is based on the number of conditions present. Thus, having four conditions means that four orders must be established (for ease of reading, the four distinct orders are referred to as groups 1 to 4 at the bottom of table 6.14). This particular Latin square design is by no means as involved as a completely counterbalanced design, yet it does have the virtue of having each of the four treatment combinations appear in each of the four order positions. Further guidelines for selecting or creating particular Latin square designs can be found in Winer, Brown, and Michels (1991).

Using a Latin square design, you can capitalize on the benefits of the within-subjects approach and still get away with 5 or fewer participants in each of the 4 groups (indeed, if need be, you could run only 1 person per group). It is essential, however, to have the same number of participants within each group (i.e., treatment order). In the Latin square shown at the bottom of table 6.14, there are 4 groups—if 5 participants took part in each group, a total of 20 would be needed to complete the design.

Not surprisingly, within-subject designs are perhaps more common in experimental psychology than in other areas. They are used much less frequently in social psychology, for example, because what a participant experiences in one condition of an experiment is very likely to effect his or her reaction to subsequent conditions. In other words, prior social experiences "contaminate" later ones (Aronson et al., 1990). In fact, using a within-subject design in social psychological research is risky because it invites participant speculation about the experimenter's intentions (recall our earlier discussion of demand characteristics) as well as potential carryover effects (see Box Feature 7.C).

Between and Within Factors Combined: Mixed Designs

Researchers sometimes combine the respective virtues of between- and within-subject designs in what is called a *mixed design.* Simply put, a mixed design contains both a between-subjects variable and a within-subjects variable; each participant group is exposed to one level of a first (between) independent variable, while all participants experience each level of a second (within) independent variable. Perhaps a researcher is interested in whether a particular vitamin enhances memory. With their consent, she randomly assigns 10 college students to receive either regular doses of the vitamin or a placebo (i.e., 5 people per treatment group)—the between-subjects factor. After a 2-week baseline period, the students then participate in learning sessions where they study educational material and are then tested on it. The sessions take place once a week for 14 weeks, so that the repeated testing sessions serve as the within-subjects factor (to control for any order effects, test orders would be counterbalanced for the 10 participants across the testing period). A diagram of this mixed design is shown in table 6.15. The advantage of a mixed design in this situation is that the effects of the vitamin—here, improved memory—can be compared between the groups and across time. One last point: Typically, the within-subject factors in mixed designs are temporal (e.g., hours, days, weeks, months, trials), but this is not a mandatory requirement of these designs.

SINGLE PARTICIPANT EXPERIMENTS

We are used to assuming that aside from case studies (see chapter 2), the bulk of empirical research in psychology is group-based research. In fact, there is a great research tradition using *single participant* or $N = 1$ *designs,* which examine the effect of an independent variable on the behavior of one organism, either human or animal. The behaviorist B. F. Skinner (e.g., 1953; 1956) is famous for having pioneered the use of single

TABLE 6.15

DIAGRAM OF A MIXED DESIGN

			Within-Subjects Factor—(Weekly Testing Sessions)
			1 2 3 4 5 6 7 8 9 10 11 12 13 14
		Partioipant 1	
		2	
	Vitamin	3	
	Group	4	
Between		5	
Subjects			
Factor			
		Participant 6	
		7	
	Placebo	8	
	Group	9	
		10	

participant designs using rats and pigeons, but the utility of these designs for achieving behavior change in humans caught on, so applications in clinical and educational settings, as well as experimental psychology, were developed. Several good references discussing the various features of these "small N" research designs are available (e.g., Hersen & Barlow, 1984; Kazdin & Tuma, 1982; Robinson & Foster, 1979; see also, Sidman, 1960).

Aside from usually having only one participant, single participant designs are within-subject designs (i.e., dependent measures are repeatedly assessed across time and the participant serves as his or her own control group) that lack random assignment. Generally, these designs measure a participant's baseline behavior, introduce an experimental treatment, and then continue to assess behavior. If any behavioral change occurs following the treatment, it is attributed to the manipulation of the independent variable.

To ensure this causal sequence is correct and not due to some uncontrolled influence, researchers often employ what is called a *reversal design*. It is called a reversal design because there is an attempt to "reverse" the behavior change by seeing if the participant's behavior will return to baseline once the independent variable is removed. The most basic reversal design is the *ABA design*, which looks like this:

A (Baseline period 1) → B (Treatment period) → B (Baseline period 2)

Please note that several assessment points would occur within each of the three periods, and that the resulting data from each would be plotted on a graph. If a participant's behavior returns to its pretreatment level, then the researcher has reasonable evidence to make claims about the efficacy of the treatment variable.

FIGURE 6.2
A Hypothetical ABA
Design

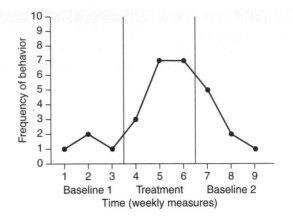

A hypothetical diagram showing data from an ABA design is shown in figure 6.2. The x-axis shows that dependent measures are administered across time (here, weekly) and the y-axis indicates the frequency of some desired behavior. As shown in figure 6.2, desired behavior occurs infrequently in the first baseline period, increases during the treatment period, and then tapers off once more in the second baseline period.

A study designed to modify problem behaviors exhibited by an elementary schoolchild illustrates well the effectiveness of the ABA design. During a baseline period, Hall, Lund, and Jackson (1968) observed a boy named "Robbie," who spent only 25 percent of a class spelling session studying—the other 75 percent was filled with disruptive activities, including fiddling with toys, laughing, snapping rubber bands, and so on. More than half the teacher's attention was directed at dealing with Robbie's antics, not teaching. The researchers designed an effective intervention where Robbie's disruptive actions were ignored while his attentive behaviors were praised; for every minute of continuous study, one of the researchers surreptitiously signaled the teacher, who would extend a compliment to the boy (e.g., "Good work, Robbie"). As expected, Robbie's studying increased substantially.

To verify that the intervention rather than an uncontrolled factor caused Robbie's improved behavior, a reversal was initiated—the teacher ignored Robbie 's performance, returning attention to the class at large. Over subsequent sessions, Robbie's studying dropped by half the amount that was gained when the intervention took effect. Naturally, the researchers and the teacher reintroduced the treatment during the class, and Robbie's academic performance improved once more. The addition of this second treatment period makes the design more convincing empirically—two documented behavioral changes, not just one, occurred—and the resulting design is often referred to as an *ABAB design*. Ethically, the ABAB design is often more compelling than the ABA design because the participant is left with some positive change when a study ends, not back at his or her baseline of problem behavior (Hersen & Barlow, 1984).

TABLE 6.16

A MODEL OF THE STANDARD EXPERIMENT

	Treatment of Participant Groups	
Sequence of Events	**Experimental**	**Control**
Random Selection or Recruitment	—	—
Greeting	Identical	Identical
Experimental Rationale	Identical	Identical
Random Assignment	—	—
Pretest measure (if necessary)	Identical	Identical
Independent Variable(s)	Different	Different
Manipulation Check	Identical	Identical
Dependent Measure(s)	Identical	Identical
Debriefing	Identical	Identical

There are a few advantages and one main drawback associated with single participant designs. The chief advantage was touted by Skinner himself: Behavioral change is obvious, easily plotted, and interpreted visually (recall figure 6.2) so that statistical analyses are unnecessary (though appropriate statistical techniques are available; see, for example, Kazdin, 1976; Kratochwill & Levin, 1992). A second advantage is one associated with case study designs: Rare or unusual behavior that cannot not be examined by traditional factor or factorial designs is accessible through single participant research. Finally, the independent variable can be introduced or altered at the researcher's leisure. In other words, single participant studies are extremely flexible—more data can be collected as needed, and the treatment itself can be changed or enhanced as necessary. Weighing against these advantages is one major drawback endemic to single participant designs: the inability to generalize beyond the behavior and results of one case. Different people may respond differently to the same treatment, a fact we cannot explore properly with only one person taking part in the research.

CONCLUSION: A MODEL OF THE TRUE EXPERIMENT

In closing this chapter, it is important to think about the sequence of events that takes place in most experiments. Table 6.16 shows a typical sequence of events for a single-factor experiment. Within each sequence, whether the treatment of the experimental and control group is identical or different is noted. This model is meant to be a conceptual guide, one that can be easily expanded to accommodate additional participant groups. Referring back to the model shown in table 6.16 should help you plan your own piece of research and allow you to check your understanding of much of what was discussed in this chapter.

SUMMARY

The experimental method is the defining feature of scientific research in psychology. The chapter opened with the necessity of formulating testable hypotheses, highlighting the important role of operational definitions (Exercise 6.A). Issues pertaining to the manipulation of an independent variable, the cause leading to an effect, and the usefulness of a control group were then considered. Specific exercises illustrated how to develop an experimental script (Exercise 6.B), keeping track of a participant's experimental condition (Exercise 6.C), and verifying the effectiveness of a manipulation (Exercise 6.D). The various types of error that can influence results or their interpretation were then discussed. A review of dependent variables, their measurement, and the creation of records to keep track of them (Exercise 6.E) followed. Practical ways to avoid bias, as well as advice on sampling, selecting, and randomly assigning (Exercise 6.F) participants to experimental groups were then presented. The chapter concluded by introducing common but useful experimental designs: single factor and factorial between-subjects designs, within-subject or repeated-measures designs, the mixed design, and single participant designs.

KEY TERMS

ABA design (p. 213)
ABAB design (p. 214)
alternate form reliability
   (p. 177)
behavioral measure (p. 190)
behavioroid measure (p. 191)
between-subjects designs
   (p. 202)
bias (p. 193)
construct validity (p. 178)
control group(s) (p. 180)
control variables (p. 186)
counterbalancing (p. 210)
convenience sample (p. 198)
convergent validity (p. 178)
converging operations
   (p. 209)
demand characteristics
   (p. 194)
dependent variable(s) (p. 188)
descriptive definition (p. 173)
directional hypothesis
   (p. 172)

discriminant validity (p. 178)
empirical realization (p. 174)
error (p. 186)
experimental hypothesis
   (p. 171)
experimental script (p. 180)
experimenter bias (p. 195)
experimenter expectancies
   (p. 195)
external manipulation check
   (p. 183)
extraneous variables (p. 186)
face validity (p. 178)
factorial design(s) (p. 205)
good participant effect
   (p. 194)
interaction (p. 205)
internal consistency
   measures of reliability
   (p. 177)
internal manipulation check
   (p. 183)
item-total reliability (p. 177)

IV × SV design (p. 209)
Latin square design (p. 210)
main effect (p. 206)
manipulation check (p. 183)
matched groups design
   (p. 198)
matching procedure (p. 198)
measurement error (p. 176)
mixed design (p. 212)
moderator variable (p. 186)
N = 1 design (p. 212)
nondirectional hypothesis
   (p. 172)
nonprobability sampling
   (p. 197)
null hypothesis (p. 171)
observed score (p. 176)
odd-even reliability (p. 177)
one-factor designs (p. 202)
operational definition (p. 173)
organismic variable (p. 184)
pilot testing (p. 193)

SUGGESTED READINGS

Aronson, E., Ellsworth, P. E., Carlsmith, J. M., & Gonzales, M. H. (1990). *Methods of research in social psychology* (2nd ed.). New York: McGraw-Hill. Although the book deals with social psychological research, it is nonetheless a lucid introduction to research with human participants. Separate chapters examine experimental design, and independent and dependent variables.

Campbell, D. T., & Stanley, J. C. (1963). *Experimental and quasi-experimental designs for research.* Chicago: Rand McNally. A short but detailed exposition of basic research designs. It remains an ideal reference tool for the strengths and weaknesses of various designs.

Rosenthal, R., & Rosnow, R. L. (1991). *Essentials of behavioral research: Methods and data analysis* (2nd ed.). New York: McGraw-Hill. An advanced introduction to behavioral research containing detailed discussions of experimental design, avoiding bias, sampling appropriately, and other issues involving human participants.

Rosnow, R. L., & Rosenthal, R. (1997). *People studying people: Artifacts and ethics in behavioral research.* New York: W. H. Freeman and Company. A concise but thorough discussion of how things can go wrong in behavioral research when unintended or uncontrolled variables, also known as artifacts, crop up. Strategies for overcoming artifacts and the interpretive problems they pose are discussed.

CHAPTER 7

Applied and Field Research

Different authors use different terms to describe research that takes place outside the laboratory. These terms can be rather arbitrary, but I have purposefully elected to use two oft-cited ones in the title of this chapter. Applied research and field research are distinct but complementary approaches to the study of behavior that lack the control associated with experimental research. By *applied research,* I refer to research that can improve the present situation or address some pressing difficulty. Applied research frequently encompasses approaches that are designed to modify or improve some existing circumstance (e.g., reducing cigarette or alcohol consumption, preventing sexually transmitted diseases). It does not necessarily permit a clear delineation between cause and effect, and so applied research is aimed at understanding a particular problem rather than adding to established knowledge (see table 2.2 for a comparison of basic and applied research). Some applied research is experimental, allowing causal inferences to be drawn, but much of it is nonexperimental. Still other applied approaches take knowledge from laboratory-based research and examine how it fares in the field.

As a term, *field research* encompasses anything that is not strictly a laboratory-based study containing the methodological necessities of experimental control, random assignment, participant recruitment, and so forth. There is no literal field or place of inquiry—any nonlaboratory situation lacking these traditional qualities to varying degrees, including offices, clinics, corporations, hospitals, and so on, qualifies as "the field."

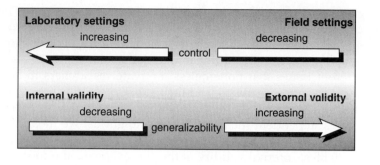

FIGURE 7.1
The Tradeoff
Continuum

Indeed, one could make the argument that there is no explicit field setting per se, only different settings with differing features of interest. A substitute term that has gained usage is *naturalistic research,* which is somewhat passive and noninterventionist. Field research, like much applied research, can be active and intervention-oriented, thus, my preference is to opt for the familiar term *field research.*

Critical readers may point out that applied research could easily be a subset of field research, and I would agree that this is generally true. Hedrick, Bickman, and Rog (1993, p. 1), for example, have explicitly stated that it is important to acknowledge that ". . . the environment of applied research differs substantially from basic research." In the main, that statement is true and it is in keeping with the orientation to field research just outlined. Some applied areas of psychology, however, such as industrial/organizational psychology and educational psychology, do rely on a mix of lab and field research in the course of building and testing theories. To acknowledge this reality, my admittedly idiosyncratic solution has been to treat applied and field research as largely separate from the traditional experimental approach espoused in chapter 6. To a degree, this solution plays off the basic and applied research continuum discussed in chapter 2, and the conclusion offered there should be kept in mind: Treat these distinctions as categories for methodological purposes, not as a means for determining the value of results.

VALIDITY AND CONTEXT

There is a fundamental tradeoff between research conducted in the laboratory and that done in applied or field settings. This tradeoff centers on control, the power to delineate and restrain influence within a research endeavor. As shown in the top-half of figure 7.1, laboratory settings offer researchers increasing amounts of control, whereas field settings offer correspondingly decreasing amounts of control.

At the same time, the magnitude of control available to the researcher affects the relationship between *internal* and *external validity.* Back in chapter 6, validity was defined as whether a given measure was actually tapping the psychological construct it was designed to measure. There is more to validity than this general orientation toward purported measurement, however. These two other types of validity—internal and external—are of concern in most research projects, and they address somewhat different issues that nonetheless motivate researchers to be wary about cause and effect relations, and their subsequent interpretation.

Internal validity refers to the unambiguous effect of an independent variable on a dependent measure. By unambiguous, we mean that the causal relationship is free of the influence of confounds or other uncontrolled variables. Internal validity is the *sine qua non*—the indisputable quality—of experimental research and a desirable feature of applied and field research. Conceptually, internal validity addresses a specific question: Are obtained results due to predicted relationships involving what was manipulated and subsequently measured, or were they caused by something else?

Internal validity is crucial in true experiments, where researchers can make causal inferences. It is desirable in nonexperimental research, as well—*that is, researchers would like to be able to make causal inferences*—but they rarely can do so because of the methodological limitations inherent in uncontrolled settings. Later in this section of the chapter we will review various threats to internal validity that, unless they can be ruled out, pose alternative explanations for observed results.

Where internal validity addresses the "inside" of the project, if you will, external validity is focused on the "outside" issue; that is, are the findings relevant to similar situations at other times and in other places? This criterion of generalizability is considered to be the important, even defining, feature of much applied and field research. This is not to say that generalizability is an unimportant aspect of traditional experimental research; after all, the methodological advantages associated with it allow researchers to extend results to other settings, times, and people, and much laboratory-based research does have clear relevance to everyday life (e.g., the study of basic processes in reading comprehension and problem solving are important for education). Yet, external validity can sometimes be less of a concern than internal validity where experimental research is concerned (see Box Feature 7.A). Nonetheless, external validity is the hallmark of any piece of research that attempts to address real world issues, including discovering solutions to social problems, improving psychological health and well-being, or improving education, to name but a few. Thus, when the external validity of a study is raised, the actual issue probably centers on the applicability of the results to understanding or addressing some general problem.

Let's consider an excellent example of applied research, one that illustrates the advantage of external validity. Langer and Rodin (1976) hypothesized that some of the psychological and physical debilitation associated with aging is due to loss of responsibility and choice—in a word, control—over daily decisions. To examine the benefits of inducing psychological control in a "virtually decision free" setting, Langer and Rodin created an intervention for some elderly residents of a nursing home. Some residents were given responsibility over decisions affecting their daily lives in the facility (e.g., aspects of self-care, layout of room furnishings, choice of when movies were shown), while a second group was reminded that staff members were largely responsible for their care. Both groups were also given houseplants as gifts; the former group was told it was their responsibility to care for their plants, whereas members of the latter group were told that nurses would care for the plants. Resident activity levels and the psychological outlook of both groups were measured for three weeks following the responsibility interventions. Members of the responsibility-enhanced group were more active and happier than the comparison group. An 18-month follow-up study extended these initial results, as the responsibility-enhanced group also showed substantial improvement in their physical health (Rodin & Langer, 1977; for related research, see Schulz, 1976; Schulz & Hanusa, 1978).

There are at least two main strengths in the Langer and Rodin (1976) study. First, knowledge regarding psychological control gained from laboratory-based research (e.g., Langer, 1975) was applied to a health-related issue in a field setting. Second, the results of the study appear to have a relatively high degree of external validity; that is, they appear to be applicable to the institutionalized aged at other times and in other facilities.

What about the study's internal validity? Can we be certain that the observed results were due to the intervention? Not completely, because we must acknowledge some inevitable methodological drawbacks that raise questions about the study's internal validity. True random assignment was impossible to achieve, for example, as residents were not assigned to either group individually but by floor. Some residents resided in the facility longer than others, potentially confounding well-being with the setting's familiarity, and so on. It is also true that no single independent variable was manipulated; instead, responsibility (or the lack thereof) was induced via several communications—a package of treatments, if you will. Langer and Rodin (1976) assessed the effectiveness of the whole package, so we do not know if the whole treatment or distinct pieces of it led to the results. Such multicomponent treatments are common in applied and field research, and they serve to highlight the unavoidable tradeoff between internal and external validity.

Trading Off Internal or External Validity

Conceptually, how should we view the relationship between internal and external validity? In much the same way we construed control in and out of the laboratory, except that now we are focused on the *tradeoff* between empirical certainty and applicability. As shown in the bottom of figure 7.1, as we increase the amount of internal validity in a given study, we are necessarily refining precision and our ability to tease apart cause and effect relations. At the same time, however, we are reducing our ability to draw broad conclusions about whether the results tell us anything about situations beyond the present one. The higher the level of control imposed within a research context, the more remote the results become from any possible real world situation; generalizability is sacrificed for heightened internal validity.

If we move more toward the external validity side of things in the bottom of figure 7.1, then we will necessarily leave the security of controlled settings to enter the open system of uncontrolled settings, where the ebb and flow of cause and effect are much harder to pinpoint with any real accuracy. Our description of topical issues will be rich and interesting, just as we will have much to say about general relations among variables in any real situation, but we will always have lingering doubts about what really caused the results we obtained in an applied setting. The loss of internal validity means that our research will be more relevant to the real world, but the drawing of precise conclusions must always be a tentative exercise.

In a sense we are left with a minor paradox characterizing the higher levels of either internal or external validity. As shown in figure 7.1, higher internal validity (i.e., more control) allows you to say a lot (verifiable results) about a little (one experiment); higher external validity allows you to say a little (verifiable results) about a lot (other situations, places, people, times). In short, there is always an imbalance between precision and generalizability.

What do practical researchers do about this imbalance? They acknowledge it and then embrace it. By acknowledging it, I mean that they are always aware of it in the planning and execution of a piece of research. Embracing the imbalance means that you vary your focus in subsequent pieces of research. Some of the very best researchers in psychology have a history of conducting pieces of research in the laboratory to determine a causal relationship among variables, only to test the veracity of results obtained in the lab by moving out into real world settings. New observations are made out in the real world, which are reexamined later in a new series of controlled laboratory studies. More data are collected, observations are refined, and the knowledge obtained in the impoverished but precise world of the lab is carried back to the harried but psychologically enriched real world (this is essentially a variation of the research loop of experimentation; see figure 1.2). Psychological knowledge is advanced through this continual back-and-forth or give-and-take between the laboratory and the world beyond it (Aronson, Brewer, & Carlsmith, 1985; see also, Aronson, Wilson, & Brewer, 1998).

A classic example illustrating the favorable symbiosis between the laboratory and the field is the research program that developed from the learned helplessness construct (e.g., Seligman, 1975). After experiencing uncontrollable events, humans and animals will stop trying to exercise

BOX FEATURE 7.A

A Research Digression: Defending External Invalidity?

Can research that is not generalizable beyond the setting where it was conducted still be meaningful? Many students, humanists, and not a few social scientists would answer in the negative, arguing that such work lacks relevance to "the real world." In recent decades, experimental psychologists have been singled out, even lambasted, for doing research that does not seem readily applicable to everyday life. One staunch experimentalist, Douglas Mook (1983), wrote a rather eloquent defense of "artificial" research settings and the results found within them, and practical researchers will do well to heed his cogent—if sometimes provocative—observations.

Mook advocates that sometimes an investigator simply does not need to worry about establishing external validity. When one is trying to test a hypothesis derived from a specific psychological theory, for example, Mook suggests that the external validity of any findings is irrelevant. Why? Because many experiments are conducted to determine if participants can be led to act in certain ways. For example, Milgram (1974) found that the authority of an experimenter and an experimental context was sufficient to promote obedient responses from research participants. Within an experiment supposedly on learning and memory, participant "teachers" were led to believe they were giving actual electric shocks to a participant "learner" when he gave incorrect answers. The learner, an accomplice of Milgram, never received any shocks but did give scripted wrong answers, complaints about the increasing levels of shock, and demands to be released from the study. Many observers criticized Milgram and his conclusions by arguing variations on one theme: The situation was artificial and not at all representative of real life.

Mook's response to such criticism is precise and direct: As predicted, the majority of the participants *did* gravitate to the highest levels of (false) shock even when the learner protested, cried out in pain, and, eventually, ceased responding. Milgram argued that the participants demonstrated obedience to authority. Whether they behave that way in the real world is a secondary issue to the question posed and effectively tested by Milgram's classic experiment. As Mook wrote in the article's abstract, "A misplaced preoccupation with external validity can lead us to dismiss good research for which generalization to real life is not intended or meaningful." This comment should be kept in mind by practical researchers who find themselves questioning the relevance of their investigations to anything beyond an intriguing idea or a compelling theory.

control in the situation; more disruptive still, however, they are apt to fail to exert control in new situations even when it is available to them. In short, they learn to be helpless by continually perceiving an absence of control. A student who does poorly in one class test after test, for example, risks generalizing that performance to his or her other classes. Perhaps you've seen peers who seem to spiral downward academically; they quit attending class, fail to seek help from faculty, and sometimes even withdraw socially.

The original research was done in the laboratory using animal subjects (e.g., Overmier & Seligman, 1967) and later humans (e.g., Hiroto & Seligman, 1975). Learned helplessness was subsequently linked with depression (e.g., Seligman, 1975), and the theory was then broadened to account for how people explain negative events (Abramson, Seligman, &

Teasdale, 1978). Certain types of causal explanations for negative events—said to be internal, stable, and global—were later identified as a risk factor for depression (e.g., Peterson & Seligman, 1984), as well as related real-life activities, such as poor academic performance (Peterson & Barrett, 1987) and health (e.g., Peterson, 1988; Peterson, Seligman, & Vaillant, 1988), among many others (see Peterson & Bossio, 1989; 1991, for reviews). Research that began in the controlled setting of the lab continues to bear fruit there as well as in the field. More recently, Seligman has extended the learned helplessness construct to more applied directions for the general public, including developing optimism (1990), raising optimistic children (1995a), and self-improvement (1995b).

Are there other research examples illustrating a favorable symbiosis between the lab and the field? Certainly. Individual differences in socioemotional development have been attributed to infant-parent attachment (Bowlby, 1969), a topic that has been studied in both the lab (Ainsworth & Wittig, 1969) and field (Ainsworth, 1963; 1967). Currently, the role of these affectional bonds in early nonmaternal care (i.e., daycare) and its developmental effects are being debated (e.g., Belsky & Rovine, 1993). Other interesting work links research on laboratory animals to human behavior. In the study of eating disorders, for example, certain gastrointestinal peptides discovered to limit food intake in laboratory animals (e.g., Gibbs, 1988) are now being used to treat obesity in humans (e.g., Pi-Sunyer, Kissileff, Thornton, & Smith, 1982). Similarly, a gene that exerts rather pronounced effects on the social behavior of mice may eventually provide a biological model for schizophrenia in humans (Wade, 1997). If you carefully scan the psychological literature, you will uncover many other examples tying lab and field results constructively together.

Project Contexts

What are the settings for applied or field research? What are the contextual issues—the necessary framework—that researchers must face? Table 7.1 includes several of the contextual features common to applied and field research. For ease of discussion, table 7.1 also includes the corresponding features found in basic research. As always, keep in mind that the dichotomy created here by using the labels "basic" and "applied" is really a false one. Although it is certainly easier to discuss these issues categorically, it is perhaps more constructive and accurate to think of them as being on a continuum.

The *place* where applied and field research is conducted was alluded to previously, but a bit more detail on this issue is appropriate here. Applied research is sometimes conducted on college or university campuses, but the overwhelming majority of the studies take place in state or federal agencies, local governments, private research institutes and foundations, various businesses and related organizations, and even in community settings. On-site research activities can involve searching

TABLE 7.1

CONTEXTUAL ISSUES AND THE BASIC-APPLIED DISTINCTION

	Basic	Applied
Place:	campus	government induotry health settings classroom
Topics:	self-initiated	client or issue-initiated
Focus:	disciplinary	interdisciplinary
Setting:	laboratory	field
Time:	low pressure, few deadlines	high pressure, many deadlines

Note: Based on Hedrick, Bickman, & Rog (1993).

through archives, examining public policy issues, surveying community attitudes, or tracing the impact of foundation grant money on particular social or educational issues, among numerous other possibilities.

Research is often desired by the people who work in these settings, but they are uncertain how to conduct it themselves and typically limited in terms of the resources (time, energy, money) they can devote to it. Researchers who offer their services, either in exchange for payment or access to data, must realize that these nonacademic settings are not usually organized in ways that make the running of a project smooth from start to finish. As a result, researchers who choose to work in field settings and on applied topics must learn tenacity tempered by patience and a strong willingness to cooperate with host organizations. The *setting* for field work does not often afford the familiar comfort, control, and expectations found in the psychology laboratory.

The *topics* of research projects that originate on campus tend to be self-initiated—the investigator develops the research question—which is less often the case for applied studies. In contrast, most applied research tends to be client-generated or issue-initiated in that some immediate question or ongoing problem requires attention. Many times, the precise question that needs to be addressed is not well understood by the client or host organization; that is, a general problem is certainly known but underlying issues are often vague. A neighborhood opinion poll concerning how police respond to domestic problems, for example, might reveal perceived benefits of intervention (e.g., decrease in incidents) as well as criticism about the forms such interventions take (e.g., arrests rather than warnings). Beyond addressing the perceived need presented by the host site, the applied researcher must also frequently explain the scope and implications of the issue to this organization as well (e.g., polling neighborhood opinion creates the expectation that concerns will be addressed, not just recorded).

A considerable number of these issues cannot be sufficiently addressed by a sole psychological researcher because the *focus* is necessarily broad, not specific. Much basic research in psychology is disciplinary, but applied work done in the field is rarely so narrowly focused. Instead, the issues often require a committed interdisciplinary focus where a team of researchers from different disciplines—say, for example, psychology, sociology, and medicine—combine forces and intellectual expertise to study a problem such as teen pregnancy in rural communities. Because many questions are interdisciplinary in nature, the use of a research team is advocated throughout this book. The difference between the sort of team we have emphasized and those found in applied or field settings centers on the usually diverse backgrounds of the latter's members—however, shared labor, discussion, cooperation, and planning are benefits, as well.

Finally, the availability of *time* serves as a major contextual difference found between basic and applied or field-based research. Students and faculty who conduct research often feel pressed for time and yet, in reality, there is usually an overabundance of it available. With effort and planning, most student projects can easily be completed within a typical semester (and in many laboratory classes, several studies can be completed in that time). Faculty researchers may feel pressured by their own agenda but for all intents and purposes, whether a study is or is not completed within a given time frame is really not at issue—there is rarely any external time pressure.

The same cannot be said of time pressure where applied projects and field situations are concerned: Host organizations usually have a question that must be addressed in a timely fashion. Deadlines are common, as research results have implications for planning, budgeting, hiring, resource allocation, and, of course, intervening into sensitive social or even economic arenas. Minimally, most organizations will want some idea of what was found by the research within some specified period of time—it may be weeks or even months, but not years.

In reviewing the contextual issues associated with applied and field research, you may jump to the conclusion that such research sounds too hard to accomplish because it places so many demands on the researcher. You might also conclude from the discussion that such research is exclusively for professionals, not undergraduate students. Neither of these conclusions is necessarily true, although it is the case that these contextual issues characterize applied research in general (Hedrick, Bickman, & Rog, 1993). Why? Because there is ample opportunity for student researchers to develop interesting applied studies that can be conducted in the field (or the lab) if the projects are attentive to alternative explanations (i.e., internal validity), organized and planned, appropriate in scale (remember "small is beautiful" from chapter 1), ethically sound, and engaging for participants. We will discuss these issues in the remainder of this chapter, but we first need to deal with the issue of competing explanations for results.

Threats to Internal Validity

Cook and Campbell (1979) developed a list of potential *threats to internal validity*. By "threat," they meant undesirable rival hypotheses or competing explanations that could account for the results in any piece of research. Because traditional experiments usually have both random assignment and a high degree of control (recall figure 7.1), these threats are less likely to account for obtained research findings. Naturally, however, conscientious researchers always assess whether threats to internal validity could potentially compromise the results of even the most rigorously designed experiment. Generally, however, threats to internal validity are more likely to surface in less controlled research, especially field studies. The field poses a different set of challenges than does the lab: Random assignment is often impossible to achieve, for example, and uncontrolled variables and extraneous sources of bias abound. For these and other reasons, it is necessary to rule out as many of these threats to internal validity as possible in planning and executing a field project.

Following are seven of the main threats to internal validity that are apt to occur in applied or field research. There are several others, discussions of which can be found in Cook and Campbell (1979) and Judd and Kenny (1981). Awareness of these main threats will help you to understand the subsequent discussion of quasi-experimental design, as well as related issues presented later in this chapter.

Ideally, any applied or field research design has a pretest measure before a treatment (if one is present) and a posttest measure. Why? Because randomly assigning participants to condition is not always feasible in applied or field research. As a result, pretest measures allow the researcher to establish a baseline, that is, a depiction of what the research participants were like at the outset of a project. In turn, posttest measures identify any changes from that baseline, changes that are attributable to a treatment or some other event, for example. Thus, some equivalence between groups can sometimes be established at the start of a project, just as any group differences can be assessed following a treatment.

Consider a study designed to help first-year students adjust socially, emotionally, and intellectually to college life. Once the members of the first-year class arrive on campus, some of them are given a series of pretest questionnaires to complete. Two groups are then formed, but not randomly. Instead, a residence life director places the students who arrive first into the experimental group; later arrivals are assigned to the control condition. In a subsequent session, the experimental group watches a videotape of upperclass students reflecting back on their adjustment to college, its grading demands, and social life. This attributional manipulation is designed to highlight common concerns first-year students share, concerns that dissipate as college becomes a stable and familiar setting (cf., Wilson & Linville, 1982; 1985). Participants in the control group watch a videotape of similar length promoting the virtues of the institution's undergraduate program; no mention of college adjustment is made.

During the next 9 months, the students are interviewed at periodic intervals and their academic performance is tracked. Toward the end of the year, a battery of posttest measures is administered to each of the groups. Did the attributional manipulation help students realize that college adjustment and concerns about academic and social life are temporary? Imagine that the informed group did show relatively higher grades, less attrition, and better adjustment across the first year than did the control group. Can we properly conclude that the attributional manipulation caused the between-group difference? Let's review the main threats to internal validity in light of this hypothetical study.

History   What happens to participants between a pretest and posttest? *History* is a threat when an observed difference is *not* due to an experimental treatment but is instead caused by some external uncontrolled variable(s) that influences participant behavior. What if some of the first-year students enroll in a study skills workshop during the project and neglect to inform the researcher? The extra experiences of these participants become confounded with the project treatment. As a threat, *history* is much easier to rule out in the lab than in the field because the time between the manipulation of the independent variable and presentation of the dependent measure is apt to be short.

Maturation   How do participants change between a pretest and a posttest? *Maturation* acknowledges natural changes occurring in participants, including aging, becoming experienced, getting hungry or tired, and the like. Most first-year students become savvy to the ins and outs of the college environment across that first year—in other words, they adjust to it. Such adjustment may be independent of any related treatment presented in an academic intervention project. Thus, a researcher risks concluding that a treatment led to change when normal maturation processes in the first-year students' experience (e.g., establishing a routine, learning to study, getting enough sleep) were the culprits.

Testing   *Testing* participants can change their behavior independently of any other manipulation, especially when they are repeatedly exposed to the same measures. Do participants complete the same measure or instrument more than once? If so, familiarity with the measure can lead to artificially enhanced performance or, at the other extreme, boredom, which leads to performance decrements. Students in the adjustment study might become "test-wise" by virtue of taking the same measures at frequent intervals across their first year in college.

Instrumentation   Are any changes in measurement introduced once a project is underway? Do the basic characteristics of the measuring devices change over time, as when the springs on a scale wear out? Once a project begins, researchers frequently adjust the measures to improve data collection. Perhaps the director of the First-year Students Adjustment Project decides mid-year to change the information used to assess students' stress and coping. Altering the standards being used could create illusory but apparently positive change, which is then erroneously attributed to treatment.

Selection Are the participants in the groups from the same or a different population? *Selection* bias is pervasive in field research when there is no random assignment (we will discuss this issue in detail later in this chapter). What if the preponderance of students who were very concerned about their academic performance during the first year in college ended up in the control group? In other words—and unbeknownst to the researcher—the between-group difference at the end of the year occurred because the control group was more anxious than the experimental group, not because the attributional treatment had any effect on the latter. An investigator risks concluding that group differences occurred due to a treatment when *a priori* individual differences are the actual cause; one group may have more anxious members than the other.

Mortality Why do some people drop out of studies? *Mortality* is a problem if different kinds of people elect to end research participation for unknown reasons. Perhaps some of the First-year Students Adjustment Project's participants become overloaded with school work and quit attending research sessions due to time constraints. If they fail to communicate this information to the researcher, what conclusions will be drawn about their withdrawal from the project? The problem is relevant to selection bias because the posttest group potentially differs from the pretest group, and the investigator does not know the reason for the differences.

Statistical regression Any time participants are selected because they exhibit extreme—that is, very high or very low—scores, *statistical regression* (regression to the mean) is a risk. What do we mean by statistical regression? At one time or another, everyone has had the experience of performing incredibly well or very poorly on some activity (e.g., on a test, in an athletic competition); subsequent performance, however, is rarely as good or as bad. It's almost as if individuals rebound by seeking their own average level of performance. Cook and Campbell (1979) argue that such extreme performances are atypical precisely because they are affected by chance (error) factors—across time and repeated performance of similar activities, people return to their more typical (i.e., mean) levels of performance. The problem is that when statistical regression effects occur, researchers can unknowingly risk attributing observed changes in participant responses to favored interventions because those responses are now in the direction of the mean, as well as the predicted effect.

Imagine that the participants in the first-year students adjustment study were recruited based on their (largely anxious) responses to the pretest questionnaires and that no control condition was formed. Instead, the researcher simply runs the experimental condition so that all the student participants were exposed to the attributional manipulation. Perhaps these recruited students were overly anxious about their first-year academic performance, but what happens if their heightened concern was of short-term duration? In other words, once the students quickly became settled into the relatively steady routines of college life, their anxiety about it would be somewhat reduced—they would appear less anxious, but *not* necessarily because of the experimental intervention. At the end of the year, the experimental group's relatively "successful" adjustment to college life is indicated by their responses to the posttest measures, yet that adjustment may instead be due to statistical regression, not the attributional treatment.

Keep these seven threats to internal validity in mind as you plan any research project. Although they are particularly relevant for applied and field studies, you should review any experiment you design with an eye to their potential influence, as well.

QUASI-EXPERIMENTS

We turn now to some common research designs that are used in applied and field research. Collectively, these designs are termed *quasi-experiments* because they lack a key aspect—typically, random assignment—associated with true experiments. Similar to true experiments, quasi-experiments often have treatments corresponding to independent variables, outcome variables serving as dependent measures, and many tools of the experimental trade, from manipulation checks to scripts. Researchers who conduct quasi-experiments, however, face one main obstacle that traditional experimenters do not: demonstrating that between-group differences are due to some treatment and not the fact that an experimental group and a control group (if one is available; see Box Feature 7.B) differ from one another *before* a treatment is even introduced. Overcoming this obstacle to accurate inference entails controlling for the main threats to internal validity we reviewed previously, as well as reviewing any results in light of the potential influence of any threats.

Cook and Campbell (1979) identified two chief classes of quasi-experiments: *nonequivalent group designs* and *time-series designs.* We will review some illustrative examples of each, but realize that there is a wide variety of quasi-experimental designs to fit different research needs and circumstances. Other such designs may be found in Cook and Campbell (1979).

Nonequivalent Group Designs

Nonequivalent group designs usually have two or more groups that are ideally measured both before and after some treatment. As noted previously, however, random assignment may not be possible in the field, so participant groups could differ from one another at the study's outset. In addition, a researcher may not be manipulating any variables but, instead, measuring participant reaction to some naturally occurring event (e.g., layoffs in industry) or intervention designed to introduce some particular change (e.g., making daycare affordable for working class families).

To compensate for the lack of a randomly assigned control group, many investigators using a nonequivalent group design employ what is called a *nonequivalent control group* or a *comparison group*. The nonequivalent control group is designed to approximate or match the characteristics of the treatment group, but the individuals included in it are not necessarily drawn from the same population as the treatment group. Indeed, without random assignment, we lack certainty that the two groups are equivalent; however, it is a given that potentially dissimilar groups are still compared (but see Box Feature 7.B).

The standard nonequivalent control group design includes a treatment group that receives a pretest and posttest, and between them is a naturally occurring event or an intervention serving as a treatment. A similar group of participants serves as the nonequivalent control group; they, too, complete the pre- and posttest measures but encounter no treatment or event. This design is diagrammed using Cook and Campbell's (1979) notation, where "O" represents an observation (i.e., pretest or posttest) and an "X" represents a treatment or event:

$$\frac{O_1 \quad X \quad O_2}{O_1 \qquad\quad O_2}$$

The broken line separating the two groups indicates that they were created in the absence of randomization. Cook and Campbell label this the Untreated Control Group Design with a Pretest and Posttest, and note that it is ubiquitous in social science research. If the control group can be demonstrated to share experiences in kind with the treatment group—and the pre- and posttest scores help in this regard—then the internal validity threats of history, maturation, testing, and instrumentation, are largely under control. Two main threats, selection and mortality, remain, however.

A quasi-experiment done by Baum, Gatchel, and Schaeffer (1983) illustrates well the use of several comparison groups when an actual control group was unattainable. The design Baum et al. used is called the Posttest Only Design with Nonequivalent Groups (Cook & Campbell, 1979; see also, Grady & Wallston, 1988). These researchers were interested in the stress reactions of people living near Three Mile Island (TMI) following the much publicized nuclear accident that took place there in the late 1970s. Because they were interested in people's reactions to a real and unforeseen disaster, no pretesting for group equivalency was possible. As a result, Baum and colleagues created three comparison groups comprised of individuals living near a functional nuclear power plant, a coal-fired power facility, and in a setting more than 20 miles from any power plant. These three groups were useful in ruling out alternative explanations and competing hypotheses to explain away the psychological

BOX FEATURE 7.B

A Research Digression: What If There Is No Control Group?

Not all powerful or meaningful research projects have control groups. Sometimes no plausible or reasonable comparison group can be found, especially if the event is out of the ordinary or, in the case of the Holocaust—the systematic extermination of European Jewry by the Nazis—horrific. Consider a study dealing with disclosure of trauma and health among a group of Holocaust survivors. Relying on a theory of inhibition and psychosomatics, Pennebaker and his colleagues (Pennebaker, Barger, & Tiebout, 1989) predicted that the more a group of survivors disclosed personally traumatic experiences (e.g., witnessing the execution of a loved one by the Nazis), the better their long-term health would be several months after the disclosure took place.

To test this prediction, Pennebaker et al. (1989) used a one-group posttest-only design (Cook & Campbell, 1979):

$$X \quad O$$

They videotaped 33 Holocaust survivors who talked about their personal experiences during World War II for a couple of hours (the tape was later coded for traumatic content by trained judges). As the survivors spoke, their skin conductance level (SCL) and heart rate (HR) were continuously monitored. Fourteen months later, the survivors were recontacted and asked to report on their current health. Controlling for any preexisting health problems among the survivors, Pennebaker and his colleagues found that higher degrees of disclosure during the interview were positively correlated with long-term health over a year later.

Who could have served as a control group? Pennebaker et al. note that they ". . . were unable to employ an adequate control group of Holocaust survivors who did not participate in the project" (p. 8). Was the study still worth doing? Emphatically, yes: The sample renders the study unique; the results were consistent with other evidence (e.g., Pennebaker, 1989; see also, Pennebaker, 1997), but more than that, the survivors had a chance to share their experiences, to open up to others, many for the first time. Their testimony was helpful to themselves, those close to them, and to those who believe that applied research can promote human welfare.

and physical reactions of the residents living near TMI. Diagrammed, the design looks like this:

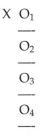

All four of the groups are tested at the same time, and only once, so that five main threats to internal validity—history, maturation, testing, instrumentation, and mortality—were controlled. Selection, however, continued to be a threat in this design, as it typically is in any study using non-equivalent control groups. When Baum and colleagues decided on the three comparison groups, they were specifically trying to rule out that selection bias had been a problem. (At their own risk, some researchers use a still weaker variation of this design by employing only 1 comparison group; see Cook & Campbell, 1979.)

Time Series Designs

A time series design employs multiple similar measures over time. Reactions from the same set of individuals could be collected on several occasions, for instance, or the same type of measures could be taken from the same sort of people in the same place. Thus, an educational psychologist could study the same group of third-graders for one academic year or subsequent groups of the third-graders in the same school for several years running. The term *interrupted time series* (Cook & Campbell, 1979) is often used because the treatment serves as an "interruption" in a series of observations, presumably creating observable changes in those dependent measures that follow the treatment.

A simple interrupted time series design looks like this:

$$O_1 \quad O_2 \quad O_3 \quad O_4 \quad O_5 \quad X \quad O_6 \quad O_7 \quad O_8 \quad O_9 \quad O_{10}$$

There is nothing magical about the 10 observation points, and a given researcher might increase or decrease their number. Note the lack of any control or comparison group, which creates the usual problems. The presence of multiple pre- and posttest measures, however, allows a researcher to reasonably rule out several of the main threats to internal validity, notably maturation and instrumentation (Grady & Wallston, 1988). Mortality and selection pose little threat, of course, if the same participants can be kept across the 10 points of measurement. What poses the greatest threat? History is a major threat here because quite a bit can happen in what is apt to be a fairly long period of time. Imagine, for example, if the data collection points were a month apart or longer—any number of locally or societally influential events can happen in a little less than a year's time.

The quintessential example of the interrupted time series design is an old one, but it is in many ways timeless. Campbell (1969) closely examined the effect of a particular legal reform, the 1955 crackdown on highway speeding in the state of Connecticut. After 324 traffic deaths in 1955, this crackdown was instituted; in 1956, there were only 284 deaths. Is it reasonable to attribute this 12.4 percent reduction in traffic deaths to police vigilance? Not really, as there could be any number of reasons—including the usual threats to internal validity—that could explain away the drop in highway deaths. To better explore these data, Campbell used the interrupted time series design and examined the deaths from the year 1951 to 1959 (see figure 7.2). As you can see, there *is* a drop in the

FIGURE 7.2

Connecticut Traffic Deaths from 1951 to 1959. *Source:* Campbell, D. T. (1969). Reforms as experiments. *American Psychologists, 24,* 409–429.

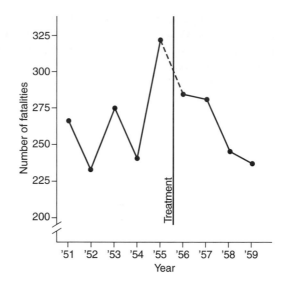

death rate, but it appears to be much less impressive when one considers the variability in the years leading up to the crackdown.

Undaunted, Campbell (1969) decided to employ an improvement on the basic interrupted time series design: the *interrupted time series with a nonequivalent no-treatment control group time series* (Cook & Campbell, 1979). In this case, a reasonable comparison group must be found and the resulting design looks like this:

$$O_1 \ O_2 \ O_3 \ O_4 \ O_5 \ X \ O_6 \ O_7 \ O_8 \ O_9 \ O_{10}$$
$$O_1 \ O_2 \ O_3 \ O_4 \ O_5 \quad \ O_6 \ O_7 \ O_8 \ O_9 \ O_{10}$$

Campbell chose an elegant solution to the dilemma of forming an adequate comparison group: He examined the highway death rates from 4 comparable states that lacked crackdowns during the same time period. As shown in figure 7.3, the death rates in the control states remained relatively *constant* across 8 years while Connecticut's fatalities appeared to decline relatively *consistently*. The result? Campbell concluded that the crackdown did indeed have some effect on the decline in highway deaths, but the point would have been less persuasive—*and less valid*—without the quasi-experimental advantage provided by the time series design.

SURVEYS

A *survey* is a general examination of a topic and, in psychology, survey research tends to rely on self-report measures in the form of questionnaires or interviews (recall that, as a research approach, questionnaire research was introduced in chapter 2). Using a direct method, survey questionnaires can be administered to and then collected from groups of people. Following an indirect approach, questionnaires can be mailed to

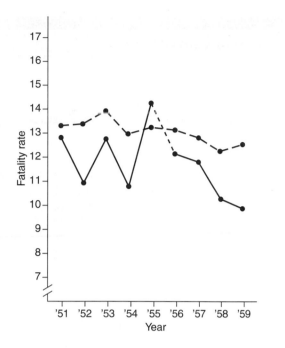

FIGURE 7.3
Traffic Deaths from 1951 to 1959 in Connecticut and Four Control States. *Source:* Campbell, D. T. (1969). Reforms as experiments. *American Psychologist, 24,* 409–429.

potential respondents, some of whom will choose to complete it and mail it back to an investigator. Interviews, too, can be direct, as in a face-to-face situation where an interviewer solicits responses from interviewees using a standardized questionnaire. The same procedure can be done in an indirect manner during a telephone interview.

As an applied approach, survey research is usually targeted at understanding a particular question (e.g., who will win the election?) or problem (e.g., alcohol or drug use), or examining the experiences of certain groups (e.g., teens, widowers, people with AIDS). The setting for exploring these or related issues is almost always out in the field.

The two main approaches to survey research are cross-sectional or longitudinal in nature. A *cross-sectional design* involves collecting information from one or more participant groups at one point in time. This design provides a "snap shot" of a sample's opinion on some topic. If you were interested in how middle-class couples were likely to react to a tax increase, then you would draw a sample within a particular income bracket (say, annual household income of $40,000.00–$50,000.00) and administer a survey once.

In contrast, a *longitudinal design* entails surveying the same group or groups more than once. This repeated-measures approach to surveying allows investigators to assess change across time. You could survey the same middle-class couples before *and* after the tax break, perhaps over a period of several years, to assess not only their opinions on a tax increase but also how it has affected related aspects of their lives (e.g., retirement planning, social mobility, employment status).

TABLE 7.2

STEPS IN CONDUCTING A SURVEY

Step 1—Decide on a topic and define a sample
Step 2—Draft and critique the initial pool of survey items
Step 3—Pilot test the survey
Step 4—Revise the survey items based on Step 3
Step 5—Write the survey instructions and the demographic measures
Step 6—Administer the survey to the sample

Many students elect to conduct survey studies for their research projects in lieu of experiments or quasi-experiments. A chief reason for doing so is to better understand issues affecting on-campus attitudes or community reactions to current social issues. Table 7.2 contains six steps that should be followed in order to conduct a quality survey project. We will review each step in turn, discuss some characteristics of quality surveys, and then review an exercise on writing good survey questions.

In *step 1*, an investigator decides on a topic and defines a sample to survey. Let's assume that you decide to examine student attitudes toward a perennial collegiate lightning rod—alcohol consumption. Opinions about drinking on college campuses are diverse; some people believe too much "partying" goes on and that it is detrimental to academics as well as to social life; others treat such activity as a normal part of student life; and still others do not worry about the issue at all.

To better understand the diversity of opinion, you decide to survey a sample of undergraduate students at your institution. How would you sample this diversity of opinion? Simply by choosing one of the probability or nonprobability sampling procedures discussed in chapter 6.

Step 2 involves writing drafts of questions that will be used in the survey (specific recommendations for writing survey items are provided in Exercise 7.A). As you begin the writing process, you need to decide what types of questions to ask. There are two classes of questions that correspond to the distinction between open and closed systems first introduced in chapter 2: open-ended and closed-ended questions. *Open-ended questions* are those questions that allow respondents to provide detailed answers. For example, you might ask, "Why do college students drink alcohol?" Respondents can write everything from a few words ("beer tastes good") to several paragraphs in response ("College is a time to explore and try new things, and alcohol is a part of that. At my first college party I . . ."). The advantage is that you will have a great deal of rich, interesting comments; the disadvantage is that such comments are difficult to summarize and analyze because they are qualitative, not quantitative (the pros and cons of these two categories are reviewed in chapter 2). A good rule of thumb is to use open-ended questions to elicit information that can later be used to create closed-ended items, which are easy to analyze and summarize.

On the other hand, a researcher could conduct a *content analysis* of open-ended responses, a technique that was briefly introduced in chapter

2. A content analysis is really a class of techniques for drawing inferences about message characteristics, including oral and written communications (Holsti, 1969; Viney, 1983). It is generally associated with the latter, as researchers derive coding systems for scoring and then interpreting archival materials. When applied to open-ended responses (which are, in a sense, archival), content analysis is a useful tool for categorizing participant responses. Once categories are established and the necessary coding takes place, researchers can use frequencies and other descriptive statistics to portray the quality and character of the responses.

Closed-ended questions provide respondents with a limited number of response alternatives that may be categorical or numerical. The simplest categorical response format is the *yes-no question:*

Do you ever drink alcohol (check one)?
___ Yes   ___ No

An example of a broader categorical response follows:

Where do you drink alcohol (check all that apply)?
___ at parties
___ at home
___ at bars
___ in my dorm/apartment
___ other _____

The preexisting categories make it easy for the researcher to quickly tabulate responses and determine what percentage of people drink alcohol at social functions, and so on. Note that a closed-ended question with a category for "other" can still leave respondents with the opportunity to leave an open-ended (albeit brief) response.

Numerical questions can ask respondents to report a whole number in answer to a question, as in the following:

On average, how many alcoholic drinks do you consume per week? _____

Answers to this sort of question provide numerical data that can easily be converted to an average (3.5 alcoholic drinks per week), a range of values (between 2 and 5 alcoholic drinks per week), a percentage (77 percent of the sample said they drank alcohol weekly), or to frequencies (20 respondents consumed 1 drink, 43 consumed 2 drinks, etc.).

Numerical questions can also be composed of several types of rating scales that allow respondents to indicate their opinions regarding some topic. One of the most common rating scales, the *Likert-type scale* (Likert, 1932), allows respondents to rate their degree of agreement or disagreement with opinion statements. For instance, an opinion could be as follows:

Today's college students tend to abuse alcohol.

Strongly Disagree	Disagree	Uncertain	Agree	Strongly Agree
(1)	(2)	(3)	(4)	(5)

This fixed-alternative format requires that respondents simply circle one of the options, such as "Agree," that most closely corresponds to their level of agreement with the item. Likert's innovation was the development of a scaling method where each level of agreement was later assigned a weight, as shown here by the numbers in parentheses. The weights for several similar items can then be summed and averaged to form an index of opinion toward alcohol use. If a respondent answered four Likert-type items by circling "Agree," "Agree," "Strongly Agree," and "Uncertain," the corresponding weights would be 4, 4, 5, and 3. The average of these weights is 4.0, a score that could be used to indicate this respondent's agreement with the general tone of the questions.

There are any number of variations on the Likert-type scale, but space constraints prevent a more detailed review. Many rating scales simply have two labeled end points, or anchors (e.g., "Very Favorable" and "Very Unfavorable"), and a series of numbers between them. Instead of circling a word, respondents circle a number corresponding to their feelings on the continuum between the anchors. For example, consider this item:

> The legal age requirement for drinking alcohol should be lowered from 21 to 18.
> Approve 10   9   8   7   6   5   4   3   2   1   Disapprove

Once you have drafted a set of questions for your survey, you can go on to pilot testing them in *step 3*. Pilot testing the items will help you avoid any ambiguity where the content of the survey is concerned. As advocated in chapter 6, have several people who are similar to members of the sample who will eventually take the survey complete the items. When they are finished, ask them if the questions were easy to understand, and then rewrite any that were not clear. Also ask whether the scope of the questions was broad enough, if any topics or issues were forgotten, and so on. Such careful, conscientious pretesting will save time and improve results in the long run.

Implementing revisions or item-adjustments from pilot testing constitutes *step 4* in the survey construction process. Some items may need to be pilot tested more than once, so be sure to allow enough time for the revision process here to take place.

In *step 5*, the investigator must write instructions for the survey and decide on any demographic measures to be included. The instructions are meant to provide some context for the people completing the survey. Why is the survey topic important? Why should participants take it seriously? Clear sets of instructions anticipate readers' questions before they are asked. Detail is important, too. A mail-in survey will naturally have more detailed instructions than one administered by an interviewer; the latter group can ask the investigator questions directly whereas the former group cannot.

Surveys should always include demographic information so that a descriptive portrayal of the survey sample is possible. Typical demographic items ask participants to indicate their sex, age, marital status, religion, yearly income, education level, and profession or college major. Do not underestimate the importance of demographic information, as it can help the researcher to see unexpected relationships in the survey data or to rule out rival hypotheses (see Exercise 7.B). Failing to measure key demographic variables (e.g., sex) can render the results uninterpretable.

The final step in conducting a survey entails actually administering it to the sample. *Step 6* can be a relatively long or short step depending on the circumstances. If the survey is done on campus in classrooms, for example, then data collection should be short and swift. On the other hand, if a mail-in survey or telephone interviewing is used, then it may be several weeks or months before all of the data are collected and the analyses can begin.

Characteristics of Good Surveys

When constructing a good survey, it is important to pay close attention to a few guidelines. First, be aware that *language matters*—the way a question or statement is phrased can be as important as the clarity of its content. Using biased words leads to receiving biased responses (Judd, Smith, & Kidder, 1991; Schuman & Presser, 1996). In the Likert-type rating scale reviewed previously, the word *abuse* is a strong one. Would we get the same responses if the statement were rephrased "Today's college students *consume too much* alcohol"? Possibly not. Both attitudinal statements will elicit reactions, but the former has a relatively stronger value judgment embedded in it (see Box Feature 7.C). Very often, it is a good idea to ask the same sort of question in several different ways so that any fine shades of meaning become apparent. Any words or phrases that provoke strong emotional reactions (e.g., *liberal, right wing, socialist, bureaucrat, communist*) should be avoided (Judd, Smith, & Kidder, 1991; see also, Schuman & Presser, 1996).

Second, *length matters.* All else being equal, shorter surveys are apt to elicit better responses and more respondent cooperation than longer ones. If a questionnaire is too long, even the most conscientious respondents can become bored and careless with their answers. To alleviate this problem, place more important items early in the survey and less critical ones later. If respondent interest wanes, only the later items will be adversely affected. Because they are both simple and quick to answer, it is usually safe to save demographic questions for the end of the survey instrument.

Third, *self-report data are always suspect.* Indeed, there is compelling evidence that people do not have access to the cognitive processes they use to make some judgments (Nisbett & Wilson, 1977; Wilson, 1985), rendering aspects of questionnaire research potentially problematic. This issue remains a controversial one, as other psychologists argue that self-reports are quite valid under some circumstances (Ericsson & Simon, 1980; 1993). The moral: Although questionnaires can reveal important psychological data, they are only one tool for the practical

---

BOX FEATURE 7.C

A Research Digression: Carry-Over Effects and Questionnaires

Answers to attitude questions in surveys can vary markedly depending upon preceding items in a questionnaire. Thus, the order of questions can matter a great deal in terms of what responses people give to them. In survey research, this is known as a "carry-over effect" (Tourangeau, Rasinski, Bradburn, & D'Andrade, 1989; see also, Tourangeau & Rasinski, 1988). Carry-over effects pose problems because an answer to one question can bias answers to subsequent questions.

Consider two questions from a telephone survey, both of which concern abortion:

"Please tell me whether or not you think it should be possible for a pregnant woman to obtain a legal abortion if there is a strong chance of a serious (birth) defect in the baby."

"Please tell me about whether or not you think it should be possible for a pregnant woman to obtain a legal abortion when the woman is married and does not want any more children."

Schuman and Presser (1996; see also, Schuman, Presser, & Ludwig, 1981) found that when the birth defect question came first, it *reduced* the number of pro-choice responses to the item about married women. When the second question came before the first, however, it received a more favorable endorsement for the survey's respondents. A clear reason that carry-over effects can be so detrimental is that they can change how respondents think about target issues rather than reveal their actual opinions. In some cases, people may provide responses that are inconsistent with their beliefs or, as is often the case in longitudinal surveys, with an attitude given at an earlier time in response to the same question.

---

researcher. Whenever possible, the results of questionnaire studies should be bolstered by behavioral data.

Fourth, *good, reliable, and well-constructed questionnaires are not easy to develop.* This overview of survey research is meant to whet your appetite rather than to address all the pertinent issues involved in questionnaire construction and administration. If you decide to conduct a questionnaire or survey, you should consult appropriate references containing important information, which space considerations preclude discussing here (e.g., Converse & Presser, 1986; Eagly & Chaiken, 1993; Judd, Smith, & Kidder, 1991; Oppenheim, 1966; Schuman & Presser, 1996; Schwarz, Groves, & Schuman, 1998).

Exercise 7.A: Writing Good Survey Questions

If you decide to do a survey study, this exercise is designed to help you do step 2 in table 7.2. When writing questions, one can follow general guidelines to increase the chance that the survey will be a success. Table 7.3 contains a list of guidelines that you or a research team should follow when writing, revising, and refining items. To get started, I recommend that you use freewriting (chapters 2 and 3), brainstorming techniques (chapter 2), or a combination of both to

TABLE 7.3

GUIDELINES FOR WRITING GOOD QUESTIONNAIRE ITEMS

1. Use everyday language that is straightforward and familiar (e.g., *new* not *novel*, *use* not *utilize*, *aid* not *facilitate*).
2. Make certain the questionnaire is reading-level or age appropriate (e.g., a survey designed for college students should *not* be given to middle school students).
3. Keep each item short and concise: "What are your hobbies?" rather than "When you are not doing homework or chores around the house, what do you like to do in your free time?"
4. To avoid *nay-saying* or *yea-saying*, phrase some items negatively ("I never have enough free time") and others positively ("Leisure time is important to me").
5. Do not use *double-barreled* items, which ask for two responses at once ("I agree that students should volunteer in the community and plan a meaningful career of service").
6. Do not write *leading questions* because they bias respondents ("A majority of people believe that taxing welfare is a good idea. What is your opinion?").

generate an initial list of survey items. You can then critique this item pool (the Research Topic Critique questions in table 2.4 can be modified with survey research in mind), and then revise, add, or drop items as necessary before pilot testing them (see step 3 in table 7.2).

Keep one final point in mind when writing survey items: No single questionnaire can address every point of interest regarding a topic or completely portray people's opinions about it (Schuman & Scott, 1987). Survey research is an ongoing process, and reviewing the results of one set of questions invariably leads to another set of questions for a future study. Political polls, for example, are an ongoing proposition, as public opinion reacts to various social, political, and economic events. As always, the most constructive approach is to ask a lot about a little and to treat survey research as one of several ways to understand a psychological topic.

What if you decide not to write your own items? An alternative approach is to rely on a variety of existing psychological measures or questionnaires. To borrow from Sudman and Bradburn (1982), who strongly endorse the words of the humorist, Tom Lehrer,* for this situation:

Plagiarize, plagiarize
Let no one else's work evade your eyes
Remember why the good Lord made your eyes
So don't shade your eyes
But plagiarize, plagiarize, plagiarize
Only be sure always to call it, please—
Research

Certainly, there is an advantage in doing so where a savings in time and adequate phrasing are concerned (all kidding about plagiarism aside, be certain to cite all sources properly; see chapters 3 and 4).

Source: Copyright 1953, Tom Lehrer. Used by permission.

BOX FEATURE 7.D

A Research Digression: Research as Community Service

Applied or field researchers often share their results with the people who took part in the research. This form of "giving psychology away" is a means to promote human welfare and well-being (Miller, 1969). It is also a community service, a way to thank as well as educate the people who took part in it. Learning whether one's peers responded similarly to a questionnaire, for example, promotes social comparison (Festinger, 1954). Evaluating one's beliefs, abilities, or situation by comparing oneself with similar others can be a powerful and positive influence (e.g., Taylor & Lobel, 1989).

I recently wrote about factors affecting well-being following limb amputation. The study's participants were members of a national amputee golf association, many of whom started playing the game after losing a limb to disease or trauma. The participants completed a mail-in survey (50 percent response rate) on psychosocial adjustment to limb amputation. The results revealed that finding positive meaning following disability, being optimistic, and perceiving control over disability were associated with lower levels of depression and higher levels of self-esteem. These results were published in a journal piece aimed at a professional audience (Dunn, 1996), but before it appeared, I wrote a shorter article tailoring the results to the needs and interests of the study's participants. The latter article appeared in the sponsoring organization's membership magazine (Dunn, 1994).

Especially where health-related research is concerned, efforts should be made to communicate results back to the research settings where the data were collected (Adler, Taylor, & Wortman, 1987). Reporting results back to an audience or organization is more than a courtesy; it is an obligation for psychological researchers (Adler et al.). Through sharing my project's results, I was able to thank and perhaps even help the individuals who supported and cooperated with the work.

Because such measures have been used in prior research, it is also the case that their validity and reliability are already established.

A good place to begin a search for established measures is your department. Find out if a collection of psychological tests and measurements is maintained. Otherwise, there are published collections of measures of personality and social psychological measures (e.g., Robinson, Shaver, & Wrightsman, 1991), political attitudes (e.g., Robinson, Rusk, & Head, 1968), and occupational interests (e.g., Robinson, Athanasiou, & Head, 1969) to call upon. Naturally, the literature search techniques provided in chapter 4 can also help you locate many psychological tests and measures published in periodicals.

A Gentle Warning: An Advantage Can Sometimes Be a Disadvantage

The main advantage of survey research, and no doubt a reason for its relative popularity among students and faculty, is the ease with which a project can be conducted. You draw up a list of questions, ask people what they think, and then analyze their responses in short order. What could be easier? This advantage can quickly become a disadvantage, however, if a researcher becomes too dependent on questionnaire methodology to understand one or, worse, several psychological topics. Ultimately, over-reliance on any one psychological method is extremely limiting, which is precisely why so many researchers and theorists advocate the use of multiple methods to understand a given phenomenon (e.g., Campbell & Fiske, 1959). The take-home message on survey research is a practical one: use questionnaires selectively and wisely, and try to support any conclusions with behavioral evidence from the lab or the field.

REMAINING PRACTICAL CONCERNS IN APPLIED AND FIELD RESEARCH

Sampling Revisited: Issues and Biases

The question posed by your research can define the population you will use in an applied or field project. If you are interested in relative use of employee assistance programs (EAPs) for stress reduction, for example, then you will find yourself working with the Human Resources departments of local corporations or larger businesses. The resulting population of people you will be drawing from is likely to be comprised of educated men and women in their mid-20s or older, and chances are they are middle to upper middle class in terms of socioeconomic backgrounds. They will differ from many of their corporate counterparts because they have an EAP available for dealing with the stress they feel in the workplace or from a hectic lifestyle outside it. Similarly, a close study of the effectiveness of youth programs on preventing adolescent delinquency and crime will entail visits to community and church organizations. Who will be in your sample? Teen and preteen boys and girls who have elected to take part in various after school or weekend programs, but assuredly not all of the teens in the community.

In both of these examples, the research question framed the setting where the research would occur. In turn, the setting attracts certain types of people—here, employees or teens—who will end up being recruited to participate in the research. Both of these examples illustrate a *selection bias*, one of the main threats to validity plaguing research that lacks adequate control groups. There is danger of a selection bias anytime a research question, a setting, or even a particular methodology constrains the sorts of people who will be able to take part in the research. Studies conducted in emergency rooms, for example, tend to have a high rate of economically disadvantaged participants (Grady & Wallston, 1988), just as traditional laboratory-based research tends to attract college student volunteers who may be unlike older, noncollege-educated adults in many demonstrable ways (Dawes, 1991; Sears, 1986; see also, Guthrie, 1998; Smart, 1966). On the other hand, some effects are not disrupted by nonrandom samples. Perception research, for example, is probably not adversely affected when limited sampling is employed.

Practical researchers worry whether any selection biases will affect a project's hypothesis or participant reaction to independent variables (if any) or dependent measures. In part, then, selection as a threat to internal validity remains an ongoing concern. Are only anxious employees or sociable teenagers, for example, taking part in the research? Attention must also be paid to external validity: Will any findings be useful for understanding employees or teenagers at other places and other times? Or are the results limited to the present two samples? Some attempt should be made to measure any social, demographic, or other variables that could potentially impact on theory, method, or any variables involved.

Applied and field researchers also need to worry about *response rate* and controlling *attrition,* two facets of mortality, a second, aforementioned threat to internal validity involving loss of participants or their data. Agreeing to participate and actually doing so have direct consequences for participant mortality and, therefore, the quality of a project's sample. A field researcher wants every person approached to agree to participate, but fate is rarely this kind. People refuse to participate or they drop out of a study for any number of reasons.

To calculate response rate, divide the number of people who agree to participate by the number of people who were actually approached (i.e., if 20 consented to take part in your project and 30 were approached, your response rate would be 20/30 or 67 percent). When a sample is carefully selected and randomly assigned to various conditions, it is very important to maintain a high response rate or the assumptions (and utility) of randomness are violated. Similarly, adequate response rates from mailed surveys or direct requests for help from a sample of convenience are 50 percent or higher, but researchers generally settle for much lower yields. Topically specific surveys (e.g., standardized testing in the public schools) sent to individuals with vested interests (e.g., teachers, school administrators, school board members) will have much higher return rates than general questionnaires (e.g., values toward public education) sent to larger groups (e.g., local taxpayers).

In many field settings, of course, it is not logistically possible to determine actual response rate (e.g., how many people saw your recruiting poster at a support group meeting or in the Student Union?). Practical researchers make every effort to maximize participant responses in a project and to discern why some people declined to take part in it. If a survey is not anonymous, then a researcher can sometimes contact nonrespondents to learn why they never returned the measure (and doing so often prompts them to send it in). When participants are assured of their anonymity, however, there is no way to determine who failed to return the surveys and why.

Attrition depends on the length of your project, and most student projects, even those dealing with applied issues in the field, tend to be cross-sectional and therefore not very time consuming. If you were doing a study across the course of several weeks or even a few months, however, you would probably lose people at each subsequent point of data collection. Why do people drop out? Usually because of some form of

TABLE 7.4

RECORDING VARIABLES POTENTIALLY RELEVANT TO SELECTION BIAS, RESPONSE RATE, AND ATTRITION

Listed below are common variables associated with selection bias, response rate, and attrition in applied and field studies. Identify, discuss, and then keep record of any that might apply to your project sample:

age
gender
education
health or disability issue(s)
socioeconomic status (SES; income, social class)
religious affiliation
political party affiliation
personality characteristic(s) (specify):
characteristic(s) of the field site (specify):
characteristic(s) of the population sampled (specify):
other:
other:

---

response burden, or how much effort is entailed in continuing to participate in a project (remembering an appointment or just getting to yet another project meeting is burdensome to many people). Although participant loss is annoying because the response rate drops across time, there is a still more serious concern: Is there some uncontrolled but systematic factor that is causing the attrition? Researchers usually go to great efforts to determine if there are measurable differences between those who complete a project and those who drop out; this possibility reinforces the necessity of carefully measuring potentially related variables.

Exercise 7.B: Keeping a Record of Potentially Related Variables

The problems posed by the potential for selection bias, low response rate, and attrition all point to an important aspect of much applied and field research: keeping record of potentially related variables. This is an important issue precisely because many applied or field projects involve little or no variable manipulation but usually have a considerable amount of variable *measurement*. Some projects have an intervention component, but others simply monitor an event as it naturally occurs. Two earlier exercises dealt with the importance as well as utility of maintaining accurate records of independent variables (Exercise 6.C) and dependent measures (Exercise 6.E). This exercise extends the logic of these exercises a bit by trying to identify those variables that could (a) create alternative explanations for any obtained results or (b) mask differences among participant groups (see also, Box Feature 6.A).

Table 7.4 contains a list of variable categories, any of which could be relevant to understanding the behavior or attitudes of the participants in applied or field projects. Following instructions provided back in chapter 2, the process of identifying potentially related variables can be done as a brainstorming activity. Either on your own or with your research team, review the list in table 7.4 and try to decide if any variable (or a combination of variables) could selectively motivate some people to take part in your study; to selectively encourage others not to take part; and to encourage initially interested participants to drop out across time. (Note that space is provided at the bottom of table 7.4 for you to generate any variable categories unique to your project.)

Once you have identified a variable(s) you believe could potentially explain the results or mask differences, you will need to measure it. The easiest way to proceed is to record the value of the variable(s) on each participant's independent variable (Exercise 6.C) or dependent measure (Exercise 6.E) record sheet. You will recall that each sheet has additional space for this or any other information deemed noteworthy. During the actual data analysis portion of the study, you can then check to see if any of the potentially related variables make interpreting the results any easier.

Besides keeping track of potentially related variables, of course, you should maintain accurate and up-to-date records on response rate and attrition. Your goal in such additional record keeping is to make certain that no systematic biases caused a decline in response rate or an increase in attrition. To track response rate, simply note how many male and female participants were approached about the study, and then indicate of those persons how many agreed to participate and how many refused to do so. (Such information is routinely reported in percentage form in the Method section of APA style papers.) As for attrition, keep records on how many male and female participants began a project and then indicate which, if any, men or women dropped out of the study (i.e., did not show for every participant meeting beyond the first one). Try to identify what factors—individual or situational—led to the attrition. If possible, contact any individuals who dropped out of the study to ascertain their reasons for doing so, or use the list in table 7.4 to generate possible explanations.

Field Sites and Gaining Permission

What is a reasonable site for field research? Students often want to conduct a field study but they are not sure where to go about doing it. Sometimes it can be difficult to think of off-campus settings, as students are accustomed to doing research in the lab or classroom. Table 7.5 contains some common field settings that readily lend themselves to student research. Most of these sites are germane to research with humans, but animal behavior, for instance, can be studied in the zoo with relative ease. The examples listed in table 7.5 should help you to begin thinking of potential research sites. Note that there is extra space at the bottom of this table so that you can write in other possibilities as they occur to you.

TABLE 7.5

COMMON FIELD SETTINGS APPROPRIATE FOR STUDENT RESEARCH

shopping malls	daycare centers
zoos	public or private schools
restaurants	airports, bus or train stations
corporate settings	hospitals
nursing homes	medical or dental offices
small businesses	religious organizations (churches, synagogues)
public streets	museums
theaters	
other:	
_____	_____
_____	_____

How do researchers go about obtaining permission to conduct research at these field sites? Is it always necessary to obtain permission? To begin the process, you must determine whether your study will be done within a public or a private setting, such as an organization. Table 7.5 contains examples of both; a street is a public place, for example, whereas a nursing home is apt to be private. Some settings—such as an airport terminal—contain elements of both a public and a private setting.

Research done in public settings does not always require obtaining permission from any office or authority. If you were conducting an observational study in a public place on your campus, such as the quad, then you might not need to obtain permission from the college administration. Why? Because observing students is something anyone on a campus *does* by virtue of being there; watching people is not the same thing as becoming involved in their affairs, nor is it an out of the ordinary event in everyday life. On the other hand, if you were to go beyond observation by creating some sort of intervention—administering an opinion survey or somehow involving passersby in an activity—then you would need to seek permission from the appropriate campus offices (e.g., the Dean of Students) before collecting any data. To be sure, interrupting people as they go about their daily routine is a modest intervention, but it is an intervention nonetheless, and the affected individuals would not stop at that place and time if you were not conducting a study there.

When you are planning to conduct research in any private context, especially within an organizational setting, it is essential to obtain permission to do so. If you were interested in interviewing parents who take their children to a particular pediatrician about childhood health issues, for example, then you would approach the head physician at the practice. You could not simply show up in the practice's waiting room one day, clipboard in hand—parents and the practice would be confused, if not upset, by your presence and lack of ethical acumen. Similarly, a study of stress and coping among law enforcement officers would entail meeting with the chief of police prior to interviewing field officers, and so on. Receiving formal permission often involves nothing more than a short letter of agreement, but some sites have a relatively lengthy protocol they (and, therefore, you) need to follow before permission to collect any data is granted. (Related issues, seeking Institutional Review Board [IRB] approval for off-campus research and tailoring informed consent forms to particular groups, are discussed later.)

Once you know whether permission is likely to be a necessary prerequisite for starting your research, how do you go about obtaining a positive response from the appropriate authorities? You must be sensitive to the folkways and function of the people in the setting you decide to approach. In general, the rule here is to do your homework before meeting with the person(s) in charge of the site. Schedule an appointment and then be prepared to discuss some issues that are peculiar to applied and field research (Grady & Wallston, 1988). Keep in mind that it is your responsibility to develop a good answer to a deceptively straightforward question: *Why* should a busy organization cooperate with your research? To be persuasive as well as convincing, be sure to discuss the following:

- *the practical or clinical relevance of the research.* Even if your project addresses a theoretical question, it should also have some useful implications or applications. In succinct terms, explain how your research can help the organization directly or potentially provide better service to its clients. In particular, any application of the research that could positively impact on the health or well-being of clients should be presented.
- *sensitivity.* The staff will want assurance that data will be collected and disseminated in ways that maintain confidentiality where the organization and the individuals it services are concerned. You will need to demonstrate that the research is socially sensitive to the feelings and the needs of the group (e.g., children, persons with disabilities, senior citizens) it will involve. If the project deals with issues pertaining to sexual preference or practices, for example, are the questions phrased in ways that invite rather than inhibit participant response? Is other personal information sought in a professional, nonjudgmental manner? In short, are participants apt to feel neutral or even positive about taking part in the project?
- *open collaboration.* Some organizations want to do more than promote research—they actually want to take part in making it happen. Such help can be modest, as when members of an organization's staff collect information from records or make a few phone calls for the investigator; other help is effectively collaborative, where the members of the staff approve, modify, or add to a research procedure. Collaboration can actually improve a project a great deal, but the primary researcher must be prepared to alter the planned research to satisfy the desires of the host organization. Flexibility should be your watchword!
- *how the research will help you.* Most organizations will want to know precisely how a piece of research will help an investigator. Is it part of

a larger project? Is it a new idea or one based on prior research? Are you doing the research as part of a class project, to satisfy a course requirement, or just out of idle curiosity? Be open with the host organization about how the research will help you, as your honesty and enthusiasm may influence the decision to allow the project to go forward.

* *a clear plan.* What exactly do you need from the host organization and when do you need it? Your goal here is to be minimally disruptive. Be specific and detailed about the entire procedure, and do not be surprised if the organization's director asks for a project time line (Exercise 1.A). Remember: The organization is doing you a big favor by allowing you access to its resources or client base, and it is no doubt appropriately concerned about the disruption a time-consuming research project could pose to its services. To return the favor, you must be flexible and willing to compromise your research plan to fit the organization's needs.

Once you meet with the site sponsor and discuss these points, you may want to offer to write a short research proposal. Such a proposal contains a detailed description of the research procedure you plan to use, copies of any measures that will be employed, as well as a rationale containing the hypothesis you hope to test. Alternatively, you could offer to give a short presentation on your research to the organization's staff. Hearing you speak will allow the staff members to get to know you and give them an opportunity to ask questions or express any reservations about the project.

Working with Protected Groups

Back in chapter 5, we noted that particular vigilance must be exercised to protect the rights of certain groups of potential research participants. Researchers must be careful not to exploit the goodwill of participants, nor should they coerce them into taking part in any piece of research. Accidental exploitation or coercion take on a special meaning if participants believe that their failure to comply with a research opportunity will have adverse consequences. Patients in health settings, for example, may assume that they could be denied treatment or attention if they refuse to take part. Prisoners could assume that obtaining probation or special privileges in the prison could be compromised. Parents may fear that their children will "miss out" on an educational experience if they do not sign the research consent form, and so on.

Through no fault of the researcher, participants and their families or guardians may perceive a subtle authority behind an invitation to take part in an applied or field study; in fact, they can feel that refusal is *not* an option available to them. The lesson to be learned here is that prospective participants for applied research will not necessarily see research from the point of view of the investigator, so it is crucial for investigators to try to put themselves in the position of the potential participants. Vigilance, care, and sensitivity are called for in order to avoid coercive influences or the appearance of inducements to participate.

Applied projects in the field typically have great relevance to the experiences, if not lives, of those who are considering taking part in them (see Box Feature 7.D). As a result, IRBs are very demanding when it comes to reviewing and approving off-campus studies that rely on non-student populations as a source of participants; acknowledged risks are very carefully weighed against potential benefits before approval is granted. Understandably, however, the physical and psychological welfare of these atypical participants overrides all other concerns, and the issue of informed consent and the option to refuse to take part in a study take on special meaning. Beyond following suggestions for gaining permission to work with a particular participant population from a sponsoring organization, a special informed consent form should be developed.

Exercise 7.C: Creating a Special Informed Consent Form

How does a consent form tailored to fit the needs of an applied population differ from the standard consent form (see table 5.4) presented in chapter 5? As you can see in table 7.6, a consent form tailored to a special population in the field is more detailed than the forms used for traditional laboratory-based research. By special populations, I refer to traditionally protected groups, such as children, persons with mental illness, prisoners, and individuals who have either acute or chronic illnesses. I am also referring to any group of people recruited from local communities or businesses, really anywhere beyond the traditional confines of Human Subject Pools or other campus and university settings.

Table 7.6 is meant to serve as a template for applied populations, every one of which will have special points of concern regarding the research procedure, varied views on what constitutes benefits or risks, and issues of confidentiality. You, as investigator, must add additional details (see the *italicized* sections of table 7.6) to the information already provided so that the consent form is appropriate and tailored to the need of the special population participating in the research. (Be sure to determine if your institution has its own required consent form before adopting the one shown in table 7.6.)

Your completed consent form, as well as the study's procedure, must be carefully reviewed by an IRB (see chapter 5). The involvement of an IRB, its neutrality and dispassion, are essential to applied research, as the excitement of "fielding a study" can all too easily lead even the most principled researcher to overlook subtle threats to informed consent (Grady & Wallston, 1988). Finally, as noted in table 7.6, each participant must be given a signed copy of the consent form; the original form is retained and securely filed by the investigator (see the discussion of confidentiality of records in chapter 5).

TABLE 7.6

SAMPLE INFORMED CONSENT FORM FOR SPECIAL POPULATIONS

Consent Form

I, [*Participant writes his or her name here*], am being asked to participate in a study entitled [*project title*]. This project is being conducted under the supervision of [*Your name*] of [*Your institution*]. The project was approved by [*Your institution's*] Internal Review Board and by the [*Sponsoring Organization's name and/or Contact Person*].

From this project, we hope to learn [*in lay terms, explain the project's purpose and why the participant's involvement is needed*].

As a participant in this research, I will be asked to [*explain the procedure to the participant: What will he or she do? How long will the study last? Write a concise but informative description that avoids technical terms or descriptions*].

I understand that there are benefits as well as risks associated with this research. I know that the benefits are [*describe any direct (e.g., learning about the self, the research issue) or indirect benefits (e.g., potentially helping others, society)*. I know that the risks are [*describe any potential psychological discomfort. Alert the participant if there are no apparent risks*].

I understand that the investigators will take every precaution to safeguard the confidentiality of the information I share with them. I know that my responses will be reported in summary form, that my identity will be concealed, and that my name will never be used. [*If your research involves the possibility of obtaining information that you are obliged by law or ethics to disclose (e.g., knowledge of child abuse, the threat a participant poses to self or others), add a sentence specifically identifying the limits of confidentiality.*]

If at any time I want more information about this project, I can contact [*Your name*] at [*Your institutional address and phone number*]. I understand that if I encounter any problems in participating in this research, I should notify [*Your name*] and [*the name of a contact person at the Sponsoring Organization*].

I understand that I have the right to refuse to participate in this study. I also understand that if I do agree to participate, I still have the right to change my mind at any time and that I may quit whenever I wish. I understand that my refusal to participate will not negatively affect [*identify whatever treatment or support the participant receives from the Sponsoring Organization and any related details*].

My signature below indicates that I have given my informed consent to participate in the above described project. My signature also indicates that

- I have been given the opportunity to ask any and all questions about the project and my participation in it, and that all of my questions have been answered to my satisfaction.
- I have read this consent form and been given a signed copy of it.
- I am at least 18 years old.
- I am legally able to provide consent. [*If not, then add space below for a parent or guardian's signature of consent.*]
- To the best of my knowledge and belief, I have no physical or mental illness or weakness that would be adversely affected by my participation in the described project.

Signature of Participant	*Date*
Signature of Witness	*Date*

Note: The information required in italicized sections should be completed by the investigator(s).

Starting Early

Although they vary greatly from one another, nonlaboratory projects share one defining feature: They take quite a bit of time to get started. As we discussed previously, studies in the field require the cooperation of some sponsoring organization. Such cooperation often can be obtained only after many levels of the organization's hierarchy have had a chance to review the proposed research.

The same problem can happen within the research hierarchy on your campus. The IRB's review of any study using special populations or field methods is apt to take somewhat longer than average for several reasons. First, the IRB will want to make absolutely certain that the procedure is ethically sound. Second, the IRB will want to verify that the special population and the sponsoring organization truly understand what will occur during the research process, and why. Finally, there may be concerns that are unique to the site and population under study, and such concerns are sometimes not apparent until after a preliminary review of an IRB form. Even the most thorough researcher can miss points of concern, and it is the IRB's job to identify such concerns before they turn into real problems (see chapter 5).

Data collection in the field is often a protracted, occasionally even problematic, process. If information is being gathered through a mail-in survey, for example, there is no assurance that every completed survey will reach the investigator—even the best intentioned participant can forget to put one in the mail. When data are gathered during the course of a support group or other organizational meeting, the researcher can't always be sure if all the group members are present and accounted for, so repeat appearances at future meetings are often necessary. Participants' changes of heart cannot be overlooked, either; sometimes people who were initially enthusiastic about your work suddenly become reluctant to participate in it. Practical researchers remain gracious when this happens, avoid trying to persuade participants to change their minds yet again, and continue their quest for a reasonable number of participants.

What else should the investigator do? Begin the process of soliciting sponsoring organizations and thinking about how to recruit special participant populations sooner rather than later. Write and submit an IRB form and a draft of the tailored informed consent form as soon as possible. Getting an early start on an applied or field project is absolutely necessary, as many sponsoring organizations place the research under considerable time pressure while at the same time their hierarchical structure of review and consent keeps things from getting underway. All one can do is try to adopt the stoic (and eminently practical) perspective that such setbacks are commonplace (and they are!) and continue with the important job of research. Finally, have all project materials ready to begin data collection at a moment's notice—the moment you gain an organization's permission to proceed with your research.

EXTERNAL VALIDITY AS OPPORTUNITY

The focus of this chapter has been taking the research enterprise out of the heavily controlled environment of the laboratory and moving it out into the world. In quasi-experiments, for example, precision is reduced but empirical richness and diversity are increased; put another way, rigor's loss is vigor's gain (e.g., Kelman, 1968). Practical researchers are not put off by the challenges of applied work or the field: The opportunity to grapple with external validity, to see whether one's ideas can account for thought and behavior in everyday circumstances, is not to be missed. So if you can, get out there and extend what you know about psychological research and methodology to other people, places, and times.

SUMMARY

This chapter drew distinctions among laboratory-based, applied, and field research. The relationship between internal and external validity was then clarified, and the inevitable tradeoff that occurs when empirical certainty is favored over applicability (and vice versa) was discussed. Contextual issues for research projects (e.g., place, topic, setting) and threats to internal validity apt to occur in real world contexts were then reviewed. Representative examples of quasi-experiments, some non-equivalent control group designs and time series designs, were then presented. Due to its popularity, extended coverage was given to survey research, including a review of the steps involved in developing a questionnaire and an exercise devoted to writing quality items (Exercise 7.A). The remainder of the chapter focused on practical concerns in applied and field research, including potential biases in sampling, maintaining records of potentially related variables (Exercise 7.B), gaining permission to conduct research in a field setting, and developing a consent form for special participant groups (Exercise 7.C). The chapter concluded with the recommendation to view external validity as an opportunity for, not a detriment to, research.

KEY TERMS

applied research (p. 218)
attrition (p. 244)
closed-ended questions (p. 237)
comparison group (p. 231)
cross-sectional design (p. 235)
external validity (p. 219)
field research (p. 218)
history (p. 228)
internal validity (p. 219)
instrumentation (p. 228)
interrupted time series designs
   (p. 233)

Likert-type scale (p. 237)
longitudinal design (p. 235)
maturation (p. 228)
mortality (p. 229)
nonequivalent control group
   (p. 231)
nonequivalent group designs
   (p. 230)
open-ended questions
   (p. 236)
quasi-experiments (p. 230)

response burden (p. 244)
response rate (p. 244)
selection (p. 229)
statistical regression (p. 229)
surveys (p. 234)
testing (p. 228)
threats to internal validity
   (p. 227)
time series designs (p. 230)
yes-no question (p. 237)

SUGGESTED READINGS

Cook, T. D., & Campbell, D. T. (1979). *Quasi-experimentation: Design & analysis issues for field settings.* Boston, MA: Houghton-Mifflin. A classic text containing many research designs applicable to applied research questions and investigations outside laboratory settings. Drawbacks to these designs, especially helpful where internal validity is concerned, are discussed.

Judd, C. M., & Kenny, D. A. (1981). *Estimating the effects of social interventions.* Cambridge: Cambridge University Press. An advanced-level text exploring the strengths and weaknesses of experimental, quasi-experimental, and nonexperimental research designs.

Schama, S. (1992). *Dead certainties (unwarranted speculations).* New York: Vintage. A history book—yes, a history book—that elegantly illustrates how difficult but exhilarating it can be to break through the ambiguities of human behavior. Psychologists stand to learn a great deal about interpreting events in the real world from historians like Schama.

Sudman, S., & Bradburn, N. M. (1982). *Asking questions: A practical guide to questionnaire design.* San Francisco: Jossey-Bass. A clearly written, highly useful, and readily accessible introduction to questionnaire and survey research.

CHAPTER 8

Planning Analysis and Displaying Data

Any practical researcher must be well acquainted with basic statistical analysis and ways to properly display data. The statistical analysis of psychological data helps researchers discern what behavioral differences or consistencies occurred within a study, what manipulation worked, as well as what observations are unusual or unexpected. Creating an effective tabular or graphic presentation of relations within the data, too, is important because interested parties should be able to grasp a project's main results with relative ease. Results should always be clear, not complicated.

The purpose of this chapter is to conceptually review basic statistical issues with an eye toward planning analyses in advance and knowing which statistical test to apply under what conditions. To achieve these ends, we will discuss descriptive and inferential statistics, as well as scales of measurement, and then briefly comment on several of the most common statistical tests used in psychological research. In turn, the planning of analyses—an excellent way to locate any flaws in the logic underlying an experiment or its design before any data are collected—and the interpretation of results and their meaning are considered. Special attention is then placed on the effective communication of results to others. Ways to develop effective tables and figures, as well as the virtues of holding onto data, close the chapter. The role of statistics as a tool within psychological research must be understood, however, before any other issues can be considered.

STATISTICS AS A TOOL

What is a *statistic?* A statistic is a piece of information that is expressed in numerical form (e.g., the average work day is 8 hours in length). The academic discipline of statistics concerns itself with the collection, classification, analysis, and interpretation of such numerical information. In the field of psychology, statistical analyses are used to interpret the results of experiments and applied or field studies. Whether the term is used to refer to specific analyses or particular results, statistics are *not* as important as the variables or psychological phenomena they help to explain. Instead, they are useful tools—the means that allow researchers to accomplish their tasks and to make sense out of research on behavior.

If you have not yet taken a statistics course, you should at your earliest opportunity. There is no adequate substitute for taking a statistics course either in or outside the field of psychology. Properly taught, statistics should introduce you to new ways to think about the world, including how to predict events and isolate biases within it. By and large, most statistical analyses do not entail a great deal of math, especially if you focus on the inherent logic behind quantifying relationships among variables and remember the role of some frequently used Greek symbols (they are only stand-ins for simple, familiar mathematical functions). In my experience, many "statistics shy" students can have an "is that all there really is to it?" sort of experience if they approach analyses with diligence, effort, and an open mind (see Box Feature 8.A).

Please be aware that I am not going to teach you to actually *calculate* any statistical tests in this chapter; rather, my purpose here is to convey information designed to help you *choose* the right statistical test. Some basic statistical tests will be presented, but only in brief, conceptual discussions (Appendix B contains directions for performing their calculations). To apply more advanced tests to a data set or to analyze complex research designs, you will need to consult your professor or a good statistics text.

One other point: Computers have revolutionized the analysis of data. Many of you will have access to fast, efficient statistical software that makes doing calculations a breeze. Although I do not advocate one program or package over another, I urge you take full advantage of available software—but *not* before you learn (or, for the experienced among you, refresh your memory) about what is actually entailed in the calculation of both descriptive and inferential statistics. Having a program do the heavy work is fine, but it is no substitute for understanding (a) where the numbers came from and (b) what they actually mean. Keep these two issues in mind as we proceed with this discussion.

BOX FEATURE 8.A

A Research Digression: Familiarity with Statistics Breeds Content

Are you a *statisticophobe?* Statisticophobes display anxiety about learning statistical analyses (Dillon, 1988). Here is a simple test to determine if you are a statisticophobe. Read and complete the following statement:

"When I look at this equation: $t = \dfrac{\overline{X}_1 - \overline{X}_2}{S_{\overline{x}_1 - \overline{x}_2}}$

I feel _____."

Dillon (1988) reports that students often report feeling everything from "unsure" and "uneasy" to "nauseous," "doomed," "overwhelmed," and even "like running over to the registrar's office to change my major." If you answered the above question using these or similar terms, then you are in good company—many psychology students feel uncertain about statistics. In Dillon's teaching experience, few students express confidence about the equation at this first encounter (if you were confident or curious about the equation, then you are on the right track already).

To use Dillon's (1988) term, many people can be classified as statisticophobes because they are somewhat anxious about statistics. Yet they shouldn't feel that way about statistical analyses, nor should you. Why not? *Simply because you should never be bothered by something you don't understand until you've taken the time to try to understand it.* This equation—it's the *t*-test, by the way—is either unfamiliar to you or you've forgotten that you're already acquainted with it (if you are interested, you can look it up in Appendix B). In other words, it is too soon for you to be anxious about it. This anticipatory fear, not statistics per se, causes some students to have difficulty thinking about statistical issues in psychology.

So, give statistics a chance and yourself a break. As you carefully read the remainder of this chapter and get used to the ideas in it, the role of statistics within psychology will begin to make more sense to you. If this does not happen right away, you have several options available to you: You can ask your instructor or a peer for help, take a look at books on math anxiety (e.g., Tobias, 1978), consult a good introductory statistics text, or read the contents of Appendix B. Remember, familiarity with statistics breeds content.

REVIEW OF BASIC STATISTICAL ISSUES

Descriptive and Inferential Statistics

There are two main categories of statistical procedures: descriptive statistics and inferential statistics. *Descriptive statistics* describe and summarize available information about samples by reducing large amounts of numerical data into a more meaningful and manageable form. The main use of descriptive statistics is to present the characteristics of a sample drawn from some larger population. Descriptive statistics *describe* a sample by highlighting characteristic indices such as number (e.g., how many people answered the ad?), range (e.g., what are the lowest and the highest ratings on the scale?), frequency (e.g., how often was the answer "no"?), and, of course, average (e.g., what was the mean rating of liking for the target person?).

Inferential statistics go further and tell about relationships in a set of data, allowing a researcher to make inferences about a population based on what is known about it from sample data. For example, is a given sample apt to have been drawn from one population or another? The chief purpose of inferential statistics is to aid researchers in testing the null hypothesis, the hypothesis of no difference introduced in chapter 6. If the null hypothesis is not a compelling explanation for the obtained results of an experiment, and its theory and design are sound, then there are grounds for arguing that the independent variable caused the observed change in the dependent measure. That is, the difference between the sample means is not due to chance, suggesting that some true difference exists between the corresponding populations. Still, at base, statistical inference is based on one main idea: Are the results of any experiment due to chance, or not?

Inferential procedures test for hypothesized relationships within a data set (e.g., Did an experimental drug alleviate the allergic reaction better than traditional medication?). The use of these tests hinges on certain assumptions—notably probability, the likelihood that certain events will occur given the constraints imposed by an experiment. Because it is unlikely that any given experiment will be repeated over and over again so that observed results can be verified many times, inferential statistics allow investigators to draw conclusions about results *as if* the experiment were to be conducted many times over with many different participant samples. Researchers *infer* what is likely to be a plausible explanation given the available evidence (all the while realizing that any conclusions drawn are tentative).

A second and by now familiar assumption is that any control and experimental groups are as equivalent as possible prior to the manipulation of the independent variable. As discussed in previous chapters, this group equivalence is achieved through random assignment to condition and the careful control of any relevant variables that could affect the behavior of research participants. We will return to inferential statistics later when we review how to select the appropriate statistical test for a particular data set.

Scales of Measurement

When we collect responses to any dependent measure for future analysis, we can rely on one (or more) of four main scales of measurement. In practice, the field of psychology uses *nominal, ordinal, interval,* and *ratio scales* within research projects. Your choice of scale will determine what sort of statistical test you can perform on the data you collect.

Nominal scales   Nominal scales name, classify, or label things but they have no mathematical qualities. When you categorize people as being "male" or "female," for example, you are relying on a nominal scale.

Ordinal scales   Items that can be ranked or ordered based on some underlying dimension can be understood using an ordinal scale. If we watch a series of student speeches and then select the individuals who gave the best, second best, and third best talk, we are effectively ranking three people as 1, 2, and 3. Notice that while we can agree that speaker 1 gave a better presentation than speaker 2, the ordinal ranking does not indicate *how much better* because the intervals between ranks are not necessarily comparable. Other examples of an ordinal scale include the order in which people finish a race or one's class rank in high school (e.g., 26th out of 85).

Interval scales   When intervals are meaningful, measurable, and equal, then you are probably using an interval scale. The best example of an interval scale is the Fahrenheit scale for measuring temperature. The temperature difference between 75 and 80 is 5 degrees, the same interval difference that exists between the cooler temperatures of 50 and 55 degrees. Interval scales also have one other defining property: They lack a true zero point. When it is 0 degrees outside it is cold, but temperature does not cease being meaningful at this point because it can get colder still (i.e., below zero). Many psychological and educational tests rely on interval scales, notably the rating scales that are so common in research projects, scores on various intelligence tests, or the number of correct answers given within some problem-solving task.

Ratio scales   As you might guess, the ratio scale picks up where the interval scale left off. Ratio scales rank responses, contain equal and meaningful intervals between points, and can have true zero points, though they may never occur. When measuring reaction time in a memory experiment, for instance, zero responses *are* possible, though highly unlikely to occur.

What are the consequences of this combination of features in ratio scales? Where measures such as age, time, distance, weight, volume, amplitude, and intensity are concerned, there are very real consequences. Traveling 30 miles is twice as far as going 15 miles, for instance, and it is also possible not to move any distance at all; if you stay put, you can say you went 0 miles.

You can clearly see a progression from the simplest scale (nominal) to the most complex (ratio), from the least information to the most. In terms of dependent measures and data analysis, psychologists are apt to rely more on interval scales than any of the others. Although it is true that ratio scales provide a bit more information, there are few cases in the study of behavior where a true zero point occurs.

TABLE 8.1

A COLLECTION OF 11 HYPOTHETICAL TEST SCORES

97 $N = 11$
92
89
87
87
85
83
79
78
75
62

sum of x = Σx = 914

$M = \bar{x} = 83.09$ $mdn = 85$ mode = 87

range = 97 − 62 = 35

variance = s^2 = 89.49

standard deviation = $SD = s = \sqrt{s^2} = 9.46$

Measures of Central Tendency

The first goal in the analysis of any data sample is to determine the most representative score—the *central tendency*—of a *distribution*, or set of scores. There are three common measures of central tendency: the *mean*, the *mode*, and the *median*. Table 8.1 contains a simple distribution of 11 hypothetical test scores, which range from a low score of 62 to a high score of 97 (the highest one could score on the test is 100).

Mean   The mean is the arithmetic average, and it is calculated by summing a set of scores (*x*s) and dividing by the number of scores (*N*). The formula for the mean looks like this:

$$\bar{x} = \frac{\Sigma x}{N}$$

where $\bar{x}$ (x-bar) is statistical notation representing the mean and Σ (sigma) is a Greek letter used to signify "the sum of *x*," or the total of all the test scores. As shown in table 8.1, the sum of *x* is 914, and when this sum is divided by the *N* of 11 test scores, the resulting mean is 83.09. In psychological reports, the mean is symbolized as *M*, and it is based on either an interval or a ratio scale of measurement.

Mode   The mode is the most frequent observation within a distribution. Unlike the mean, the mode is not calculated, but it is determined from data using frequency as a guide. An examination of the sample distribution in table 8.1 reveals that 87 is the mode because it occurs twice, whereas the remaining numbers each occur only once. Make no mistake here: The mode is the *number* that occurs most frequently (i.e., 87) and not the *number of times* it occurs (i.e., 2). Because it focuses on only this one aspect of central tendency, its use is limited.

Median   The median is the value that divides a distribution in half, such that 50 percent of the scores appear above it and 50 percent are below it. A median can be identified in data using ordinal, interval, or ratio scale data. In table 8.1, the median is 85 because 5 scores fall above it and 5 are below it (in an odd number of ranked scores, then, identify the number that is literally the midpoint of the others). If there had been an even number of scores, then the median would be calculated by taking the average of the 2 scores in the middle of the distribution, if there were 12 observations in table 8.1—say, there was an additional test score of 98—then the median would be $(85 + 87) \div 2$, or 86.

Which is the best indicator of central tendency? It depends on the data and their purpose. The mean, for example, is affected by extreme scores; very high or very low scores can inflate or deflate the average. For this reason, researchers are usually concerned about the shape of a distribution of data, an issue addressed in some detail later. Demographers report *median* income in the United States rather than *mean* income, as the latter is apt to be biased by the relatively small number of people who make large amounts of money each year. How so? Well, most American households actually earn less than \$36,000 a year, but imagine how the earnings of individuals who make hundreds of thousands of dollars, even millions, during this time could cause the average to creep upward. Indeed, calculating the mean of the distribution of household earnings could point to an income level that would not accurately represent the experience of most citizens—it would be much too high. In contrast, the median is insensitive to extreme scores—it is the midpoint of any distribution—so it is not as affected by income disparity and should be a better reflection of the financial experience of most people.

Nonetheless, psychological research is highly dependent on examining average behavior, and a casual perusal of most major journals will reveal that the bulk of reported statistical analyses focus on establishing mean differences between or among groups. Why is psychology so focused on averages? One answer is statistical: Most psychological variables are normally distributed or "bell-shaped," thereby rendering the mean the best measure of central tendency. Another is interpretive in that psychological research hopes to portray the thoughts, feelings, and actions—the behavior—of *people in general.* The best portrayal of this generality is the average, precisely because it captures how most people in a sample thought, felt, or acted with respect to some measurable dimension. In essence, then, the mean is the best, most reliable estimate we can make regarding any individual's behavior within a psychological context.

It is also true that a mean can be calculated only when an interval or ratio scale is used. Either one of these scale types takes advantage of more of any available information than either nominal and ordinal scales of measurement.

Measures of Variability

The second goal in the analysis of any data set is to determine how the observations spread around a mean. Are the observations clustered close to the mean, for example, or are they spread relatively far apart from it and one another? The dispersion of observations within a data set is called its *variability,* and there are three descriptive statistics that are commonly used to index it: range, variance, and standard deviation (calculation procedures for the latter two indices are shown in Appendix B).

The *range* of a distribution is obtained by subtracting the lowest score from the highest score, and it characterizes the difference between these two ends of the distribution. The range of the test scores in table 8.1 is 35 (i.e., 97 – 62). The range provides only a very simple account of dispersion—the high and the low of a distribution—as it is insensitive to the observations between the extremes. A range can be determined from ordinal, interval, or ratio scale data.

A second indicator of dispersion is called *variance.* Variance (symbolized s^2) is a number that represents the total amount of similarity or dissimilarity of scores within a sample or distribution. Consequently, the larger the number representing the variance, the greater the spread of the scores. Because this discussion is conceptual, the calculation of variance does not concern us now. The variance of the test scores shown in table 8.1 is 89.49. By examining table 8.1, one can clearly see that this relatively large number indicates a fair amount of spread in this sample of data. Notice that the closest score to the mean of 83 is 85, the next 87, and so on.

As a statistical concept, variance has a great deal of utility because it can be partitioned or divided into different parts. Why does this characteristic matter? Because it allows psychologists to identify factors that influence the variability associated with the measurement of variables. When we discuss individual performance on a given standardized test, for example, variation can be explained by pointing to a given child's innate intelligence, the different educational opportunities different children experience (i.e., public versus private schooling), genetic determinants, and even measurement error (e.g., some children are not feeling well the day of the test, others are rested, etc). These and other factors explain the dispersion of observations around some central point.

There is still a better and more useful indicator of dispersion, the *standard deviation,* which is an index of variability around the mean value of some distribution of data. The standard deviation indicates how close observations cluster around the mean and, advantageously, it is expressed in the variable's original unit of measurement. As a result, it lends itself to meaningful probabilistic interpretations of the distance between a given observation and the mean.

Conveniently, the standard deviation is obtained by taking the square root of the variance. The square root of 89.49, for instance, is 9.46 (see table 8.1). In statistical notation the standard deviation is symbolized *s* (remember, it is based on the square root of s-squared) and in psychological writing it is written as *SD*. Both the standard deviation and its parent, variance, can be determined using data from interval or ratio scales.

As for interpreting the clustering of observations around a mean, a smaller standard deviation suggests relatively uniform responses. A larger standard deviation, however, points to less regularity in participant response; in other words, people's scores place them further out from the mean value. Using the data in table 8.1, the standard deviation indicates that most of the test scores fall 9.46 units above and below the mean of 83, that is, between the scores of 73.54 and 92.46.

If the mean is the best estimate we can make about any individual observation in a distribution, then the standard deviation is a reasonable way to index the error—the discrepancy or inaccuracy in a measure—associated with using the mean as an estimate. If the scores in a distribution were identical to one another, for example, then there would be no error. Why? Because everyone would be giving the same (i.e., mean) response. In this case, there would be no variability, either, so that the standard deviation would be 0. As the standard deviation increases, then we have a sense of how much error is associated with the mean, that is, the similarity (or dissimilarity) of people's reactions within a sample.

Hypothesis Testing and Statistical Significance

Research can never prove that any given hypothesis is really true, only that under certain conditions it can be shown to be false (recall the discussion of falsificationism and philosophy of science in chapter 1). In keeping with this idea, the two types of hypotheses associated with research, the null hypothesis and the experimental hypothesis, were introduced in chapter 6. These hypotheses and the logic underpinning them are relevant to our discussion of statistical issues. Why? Because the inferential statistical tests used to assess differences pit obtained data against the null hypothesis.

As you will recall, the null hypothesis anticipates that an independent variable will *not* have an effect on a dependent measure. In statistical terms, this means that the population mean of one group (A) is equivalent to the population mean of the other group (B), that is, A = B. Do *not* assume that the sample means for groups A and B should literally be *equal* to one another because any observable, superficial differences are attributable to random error. At the theoretical level, however, the population means that the sample means *represent* are equal to one another. Under these circumstances, the researcher is said to *retain the null hypothesis* (i.e., to acknowledge that the independent variable did not have any effect on the dependent measure). Please note that the statistical analysis does *not* demonstrate the A = B is literally true; rather, the research has failed to show that it is *not* true in this instance.

What about the experimental hypothesis, which tests the investigator's prediction? The experimental hypothesis anticipates that the independent variable *will* have an effect on the dependent measure. As noted back in chapter 6, that effect can be either directional (A > B or A < B) or nondirectional (A ≠ B). Thus, the responses of groups A and B are different from one another, presumably because of the influence of the independent variable; the population mean of group A is *not* equal to the population mean of group B. When a statistical difference is found to exist between A and B, a researcher is said to *reject the null hypothesis.* By showing that the null hypothesis is incorrect, the experimental hypothesis is accepted as correct for the time being (remember the research loop of experimentation from chapter 1, where one study leads to another and theory revision is ongoing). Rejecting this hypothesis of "no difference" is a statistical way of saying that something occurred, that the independent variable had an effect on the dependent measure.

But what statistical difference allows a researcher to reject the null hypothesis? One where the difference between two sample means is too great to be due to chance alone. Some systematic influence, it is hoped the independent variable in the experimental hypothesis, is the cause. If so, then the sample means are said to be *significantly different* from one another.

What is *statistical significance?* A difference between means is said to be statistically significant when there is a very low probability that the observed results are due to random error. A significant result is one that is very unlikely to occur if the population means are actually equal to one another. In lay terms, the difference is seen as a reliable one because behavior within the respective groups differed due to some experimental intervention.

Significance can be illustrated in still more concrete terms by pointing to what are called *levels of significance,* which are associated with all inferential tests. Statisticians and researchers generally assume that a significant difference between group means occurs when the likelihood that the difference is due to chance is less than 1 in 20. Thus, if an experiment were run 100 times, you would expect to obtain the same results by chance—*not* because of any independent variable—5 times or less. An observed difference is not assumed to be meaningful or reliable unless it reaches this 5 percent or, as statisticians say, *.05 level of significance.* Some researchers apply even more stringent demands, accepting a result only when it could be due to chance once in 100 trials (or the 1 percent or *.01 level of significance*). When the .05 or .01 level is reached or exceeded (i.e., the probability of a difference being due to chance is lower still), a given finding is said to be statistically significant.

Most psychological researchers rely on the .05 level of significance. I am sure that if you have spent any time reading journal articles (by now,

A Research Digression: Results Are Significant or Nonsignificant, *Not* Insignificant

SIGNIFICANT? WHAT EVER DOES *THAT* MEAN?

Many students are understandably confused about how to properly use and interpret the word *significant* in a research context. Confusion about its correct use is not surprising, however, because this statistical nomenclature is a departure from the everyday meaning of the word. In data analysis, a significant effect is *not* an important, consequential, or meaningful effect, nor even particularly large—rather, it is one that is statistically reliable or trustworthy.

A significant result is one that provides a researcher with enough evidence to reasonably reject the null hypothesis. Commenting on the term *significant,* Wright (1997) wisely suggests that the word *detected* would have been a better, less confusing choice. A low *p*-value (e.g., *p* < .05) allows us to claim that an effect has been detected (Wright, 1997).

When writing up results for the first time, novice researchers often make the mistake of noting that ". . . the result of the statistical test was insignificant" or the ". . . main effect was very significant." In the first place, the result of a statistical test is never *insignificant,* a word that means trifling, petty, or not worth noting. Why? Because it always tells you something, in this case that a difference was *not* detected. In the second place, a statistical test is either significant (a difference is detected) or nonsignificant (no difference is detected); it is not hugely significant, wildly significant, or for that matter, depressingly insignificant. Remember, reliable relationships are either *detected* or *not detected* in a data set.

you should have spent a fair amount of time doing so for your research project), you have seen what are called *p,* or *probability values,* attached to various statistical tests. These *p*-values are written as *p* < .05 and *p* < .01 to signify that an observed outcome has less than a 5 percent or 1 percent chance of occurring when the null hypothesis is true. In statistical contexts, the value of *p* is often referred to as α ("alpha") or even an α– level.

Always watch the notation carefully: If you see *p* > .05, for example, then the results are *not* statistically significant. Any result falling between the .10 and .06 levels of significance is said to be marginal and should be interpreted with caution (see Box Features 8.B and 8.C for related discussions). Marginal results are suggestive, not definitive, and they can be unreliable. Any result that is *p* > .10 is treated as *nonsignificant* (i.e., a researcher cannot be confident that the independent variable had any effect on the dependent measure).

The two types of errors that can be made doing hypothesis testing need to be reviewed with statistical significance in mind (they were introduced conceptually in chapter 6). A Type I error occurs when an investigator incorrectly rejects an actual null hypothesis. If the null hypothesis *is* true, then the probability of making a Type I error is equal to α; if *p* < .05 is the significance level, then there is a 5 percent chance of rejecting a true null hypothesis. A researcher would be making a Type I error if she concluded that a dietary supplement helped people to lose unwanted pounds when, in reality, it had no effect on weight loss. In contrast, committing a Type II error entails incorrectly failing to reject a false null hypothesis. In other words, a researcher concludes the absence of an effect (i.e., accepting the null hypothesis) when one is, in fact, present. If a group of educators concluded that a new battery of reading tests did not reliably differentiate slower from faster learners—when it actually did—they would be making a Type II error.

In practice, Type I errors are the more avoidable of the two because a more stringent level of significance can be used for hypothesis testing. Using .01 instead of .05 decreases the likelihood that you will incorrectly reject a null hypothesis. The downside is that you are working against yourself by making a significant difference more difficult to detect. The probability of making a Type II error cannot be determined as readily; as you decrease the chance of making a Type I error, you automatically increase the likelihood of making a Type II error. Why? Because increasingly stringent significance levels (.01 or even .001) make observing any reliable differences difficult, so incorrectly accepting the null hypothesis becomes a probable event. In short, increasing statistical rigor is a good idea but there can be diminishing empirical returns if such rigor is over applied (cf., Box Feature 8.D).

This section must end with two important reminders about proof in research and avoiding over analyzing data. Neither the process of hypothesis testing nor statistical tests or summaries ever really *prove* anything (recall falsificationism and related views on the philosophy of science from chapter 1). Rather, any conclusions we draw from a data set must be carefully understood in terms of probability—what is likely to be true under the circumstances—and not as being absolutely correct or true. There is no truth per se, only our thoughtful consideration of evidence demonstrating a probable link between an independent variable and a dependent measure.

You should also keep in mind that it is possible to be too rigorous in your analysis of a data set. Coupled with ingenuity and a little time, anyone can sit down with a computer program or calculator, some data, and then run any number of analyses until some result—any result—is found. In research circles, this is pejoratively known as "going on a fishing expedition" because the researcher keeps casting around until some finding is "caught." Running unwarranted, unplanned, exotic, or unduly complicated analyses also capitalizes on chance, meaning that any significant relationships revealed in this way are apt to be false (recall the previous discussion of Type I errors).

Parametric versus Nonparametric Tests

For the most part, hypothesis testing in psychology and the other social and behavioral sciences relies on *parametric statistics*. Parametric statistics

BOX FEATURE 8.C

A Research Digression: Significance Testing Is Dead! Long Live Significance Testing!

As this book was being written, a long ignored debate in research circles was beginning to once again have its 15 minutes of fame. The status and utility of null hypothesis significance testing has been debated for years, but only recently has that debate been taken seriously by the psychological community (Loftus, 1993; 1996; Shrout, 1997). One group of vocal methodologists has even advocated putting a ban on significance testing—imagine, no more *p*-values! No doubt some student veterans of both statistics and research methods courses (and a few psychology faculty, as well) would welcome such a ban with open arms.

Why do away with null hypothesis testing? Because most researchers are not using it correctly and misinterpreting its applicability to obtained results, among other, more technical reasons (see Loftus, 1996, for a detailed discussion). Worse still, most students, too many psychologists, and the average person on the street equate the term *statistical significance* with words like *important, meaningful,* and *truthful*. (If you are harboring this illusion, go back and re-read the section on null hypothesis testing and significance, as well as Box Feature 8.B, where the term is appropriately linked with the *reliability* of research results; see also, Cohen, 1994; Rosnow & Rosenthal, 1989; Scarr, 1997.)

The debate over significance testing has great merit if only to remind otherwise intelligent people that a test statistic is mute when it comes to deciding whether a theory is sound, clever, and reasonable. We are not doing psychology any favors (or for that matter, science) if we routinely confuse statistical significance with *practical significance* (i.e., what a result means and its implications for understanding behavior); people, not statistical tests, theorize about behavior. It is entirely possible to have a significant result that is, in the end, not terribly meaningful (e.g., Abelson, 1995).

What are the alternatives to significance testing? One easy one encouraged by Geoffrey Loftus is to graph or plot research results (means, standard deviations) and interpret what you see in light of the hypothesis. A glance at a graph should be sufficient for relationships in data to stand or fall on their own without having to resort to inferential statistics (other alternatives can be found in Abelson, 1997; Harris, 1997; and Loftus, 1996). Although the jury on significance testing is still out, awareness of the debate can only promote better psychological research.

---

are statistical formulas that assume that certain specific characteristics are true of any population from which samples are drawn. Such assumptions must be met in order for the results of any statistical test to be deemed valid. One of the most common assumptions for parametric tests is that the distribution of scores from which a sample is drawn must be *normal* (though some parametric tests are said to be "robust," or capable of dealing with nonnormal data).

A *normal distribution* is a hypothetical frequency distribution of scores that is bell-shaped or unimodal, and a large portion of these scores appears at or near the midpoint of this distribution. Normal distributions are symmetric on either side of this midpoint, as shown by distribution

FIGURE 8.1

Different Types of
Frequency
Distributions

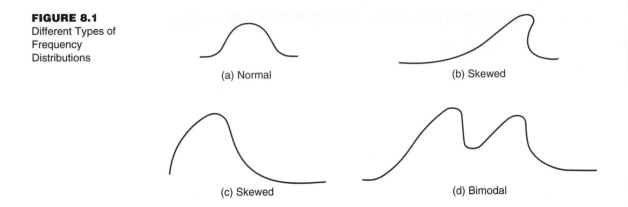

(a) Normal   (b) Skewed

(c) Skewed   (d) Bimodal

(a) in figure 8.1. A frequency distribution that is truly normal has a mean, median, and mode with the same value. These characteristics of the bell-shaped curve are important to statisticians and psychologists alike because they provide good ways to represent variables (Runyon, Haber, Pittenger, & Coleman, 1996). In addition, the normal distribution is expressed as a mathematical function, giving it considerable utility for addressing research questions (for discussion of its mathematical properties, see Runyon et al.).

Various frequency distributions deviate from the standard normal distribution, however. When a distribution is asymmetrical—statisticians say *skewed*—it has more observations in one of its tails than the other (see distributions [b] and [c] in figure 8.1). If you plotted the IQ scores of a class of gifted children, for example, relatively few would have low scores and a skewed distribution would be expected (i.e., scores would be compressed in the higher end of the distribution); in contrast, the distribution of scores in an average class would be more likely to approximate the normal curve. Occasionally, a distribution can be described as being *bimodal* because it has two areas that contain a high frequency of observations (see distribution [d] in figure 8.1). When students perform either very well or very poorly on the same exam, instructors will often describe the distribution of scores in the class as being bimodal.

When a set of data violates certain statistical assumptions and its appearance is skewed or otherwise nonnormal, then a different class of inferential statistics is sometimes used. *Nonparametric statistics* make almost no assumptions about data or the population from which the observations were drawn. They serve as a statistically powerful option when parametric tests cannot be used, as frequently happens when researchers are confronted by unavoidably small sample sizes. Later in this chapter we will consider the *chi-square* (χ^2) *test*, the most common nonparametric test that is used to interpret nominal or categorical data. The definitive source for nonparametric or "distribution-free tests of significance" is Siegel and Castellan (1988), but many texts, such as Runyon et al. (1996), provide solid overviews of selected tests and guidance about when to use them.

A Short Intermission: The General Linear Model

When data are collected in an experiment and subsequently analyzed, a researcher makes assumptions about the composition of each observation. Presumably, any individual observation is made up of three components: the mean of the theoretical population from which it was drawn, the effect due to a level of the independent variable (which can be positive or negative), and random error. These three components comprise what is known as the *general linear model (or GLM)*. As you are well aware, randomization within experimental designs allows researchers to avoid biases and to estimate random error, or any information not attributable to the effects of the independent variable.

You should be aware of a second major approach to research and analysis that we alluded to in chapter 7 when the importance of measuring uncontrolled variables was discussed. It is possible to use advanced correlational techniques to analyze data that were not collected in an experiment or with any randomizing procedure. The specific technique is called *multiple correlation*, a complex but useful procedure most students encounter in advanced statistics or research methods courses. All you need to know for present purposes is that with multiple correlation, one can measure participants on some uncontrolled variable and then statistically remove its influence on a dependent measure. This statistical control allows researchers to isolate potential cause and effect relations in less than ideal research conditions.

As a researcher in training, you should be aware that a variation of the *GLM* unifies the statistical advantages of experimentation with those of statistical control. The resulting approach is a special case of multiple correlation; indeed, all descriptive and inferential statistics, along with the logic guiding them, can be subsumed into this *GLM*. *GLM* is discussed in advanced methods texts after the two traditional approaches are covered (see, for example, Winer, Brown, & Michels, 1991; Kirk, 1982). Some psychologists (e.g., Vadum & Rankin, 1997) believe that as *GLM* becomes increasingly popular among researchers and teachers, it will appear in introductory books, as well.

SELECTING THE APPROPRIATE STATISTICAL TEST

Planning Analysis: Do It Before, Not After

When I was a graduate student, I noticed a curious form of self-defeating behavior. Graduate students in and outside of psychology would come up with very clever research designs to tease apart relationships underlying big questions in the social sciences, but more often than not one problem remained. Many otherwise bright and talented students did not think beforehand about how they would go about analyzing the data from these clever experiments until *after* it was collected. Others have witnessed this same scenario, as well (e.g., Martin, 1996; McKenna, 1995).

Failure to plan analyses *before* collecting data is all too common. It usually happens for one of two reasons. First, many people approach statistics with fear and loathing, feelings that behaviorally manifest themselves as avoidance: "If I don't think about it, then maybe it will go away" (perhaps you've engaged in this sort of wishful thinking where statistical analyses are concerned). The origins of such feelings vary, but most center on a general discomfort with mathematics (for help, see Tobias, 1978) or having endured a class that did not present the field of statistics in a very favorable light. "Statisticophobia" is a common—though by no means terminal—affliction (Dillon, 1988; recall Box Feature 8.A).

Second, many people see data analysis and data display as little more than afterthoughts associated with research projects, something to do "later." They are not put off by the numbers or the analyses; they are just more interested in running the experiment. Like Scarlett O'Hara, the heroine of *Gone with the Wind*, they decide to worry about data analysis "tomorrow."

Sympathetic as I am to both perspectives, neither is sufficient cause to forego learning to use statistics properly and to neglect planning statistical analyses in advance. Indeed, you should always think about your analyses in some detail before you actually begin to run a project. Then, once you have the data in hand, you can begin the statistical analyses almost immediately and without worry.

Exercise 8.A: Developing an Analysis Plan

Once a study is designed, it is the researcher's responsibility to develop an *analysis plan*. An analysis plan characterizes variables collected within a study and identifies specific statistical tests appropriate for their analysis. Having an analysis plan increases the chance that meaningful results will be found because the research design is matched to the analyses from the outset. As shown in table 8.2, the first three steps in an analysis plan deal with activities done before any data are collected, and the next four cover what the investigator does with the data once they are collected.

Step 1 has two parts to it and each hinges on the quality of the dependent measures used in the study. First, decide whether your dependent measure will collect *continuous* or *discontinuous* data. Continuous data have values that occur at any point along a scale, and psychologists typically rely on equal-interval measures to approximate them. Examples of continuous scales include scores on a personality measure, the temperature outside, grade point average (GPA), and a preference rating on a Likert-type scale. Continuous data are usually analyzed by parametric statistics.

In contrast, discontinuous or "countable" data have gaps where no real scaleable values occur, and such data tend to be nominal or category based. You could calculate the average number of books bought per course in a given semester, for example, but an answer like 3.5

TABLE 8.2

A BEFORE AND AFTER DATA COLLECTION ANALYSIS PLAN

Before

Step 1—Determine the Quality of the Dependent Measure(s):
    a. continuous or discontinuous data?
    b. independent (administered once) or correlated (administered more than once)?
Step 2—Choose the Appropriate Statistical Test to Analyze the Data
    a. go to table 8.3 and answer the series of questions within it.
Step 3—Begin Project and Collect Data

After

Step 4—Summarize Data and Perform Descriptive Statistics
    a. copy data onto record sheets or enter into a computer file.
    b. for continuous data, calculate means and standard deviations.
    c. for discontinuous data, calculate frequencies or percentages.
Step 5—Perform Statistical Analyses Based on a Test(s) Chosen Back in Step 2
Step 6—Interpret Result(s)
    a. follow Exercise 8.B.
    b. create a data display (i.e., table, figure, graph) if necessary.
    c. determine if any post hoc analyses are necessary (if so, go back to step 2 or step 5).
Step 7—Integrate the Results into a Paper or Research Presentation
    a. see chapters 3 and 9.

Source: Adapted from McKenna (1995).

books would mean that there were 3 or 4 books in each—you cannot buy half a book (the other familiar example in this vein is the nuclear family with 2.5 children!). Discrete answers to any questions, such as "yes" and "no," constitute discontinuous data and are typically recorded as whole numbers (i.e., 1 = "yes", 2 = "no"). Because the range of responses for discontinuous data is limited, such data are usually analyzed by nonparametric tests.

The second half of *step 1* asks the researcher whether the dependent measure is *independent* or *correlated*. "Independent" in this context means that the responses of one group of participants (the control group) were *not* influenced by those given by another group (the experimental group). In general, independence means that a between-groups research design was employed (see chapter 6). A correlated dependent measure is one that the same group of participants is exposed to more than once, such that their responses are *not* independent of one another. In a within-subjects design, for instance, participants may rate the same stimulus materials twice (i.e., before and after the presentation of the independent variable), so that any later reactions are *dependent* on their initial reactions (see chapter 6). Such before and after ratings are said to be "correlated" with one another because the response on the first measure is necessarily associated to the response on the second.

Step 2 in the analysis plan involves actually choosing the appropriate statistical test to analyze your data. This step is critical to the analysis plan. To simplify the choice process, table 8.3 contains a series of straightforward questions to help you narrow your search for the proper statistical test that will best fit your research design. Once you identify the statistical test you should employ to analyze the data from your study, you can read about it in the next section of this chapter or consult a statistics text.

Step 3 in table 8.2 involves the activities and exercises that have been presented in the earlier chapters in this book: starting the project and collecting data. This step entails everything from developing a contract for your research team to debriefing the research participants after you have run them through their paces.

Once all the data from the participants are collected, the researcher moves on to *step 4*, where the data are summarized and descriptive statistics are performed (see table 8.2). The first activity in *step 4* involves copying the data in one of two ways. If the data are going to be analyzed by hand, then they need to be carefully copied onto record sheets that will allow you to work with the numbers easily (graph paper is excellent for this purpose). If the analyses are going to be done by computer, then the data will need to be entered into some spreadsheet program or into a format appropriate for the statistical software you plan to use.

In the second part of *step 4*, means and standard deviations need to be calculated for all the continuous dependent measures and by the different experimental groups (levels of the independent variable), if any. To get an idea of whether the relationships in the data are in the hypothesized direction, you will want to examine the means and standard deviations *before* doing any statistical analyses. Checking the data at this point also allows you to determine if they were coded and copied correctly, if the numbers are within the appropriate ranges of value, and so on—this is a chance to get a "feel" for your data (cf., Tukey, 1977).

When discontinuous data are collected, means and standard deviations are not usually appropriate summary statistics to perform. Instead, as shown by the third part of *step 4*, it is a good idea to calculate frequencies or percentages for each category within a nominal or ordinal dependent measure (e.g., how many people agreed or disagreed with a statement, what percentage of respondents were female graduate students). Naturally, these discontinuous data should also be carefully scanned for any coding errors or out of range values.

After the data are examined and summarized, *step 5* involves performing the appropriate statistical test on the dependent measure(s). This step is based on the test chosen back in *step 2*, which in turn was determined by carefully answering the step-by-step questions listed in table 8.3. Again, analyses can be done by hand with a calculator or with the aid of a computer program.

Step 6 is important because it deals with the interpretation of the results from the research project and the creation of any needed tables, figures, or graphs. The importance of interpreting results is discussed in Exercise 8.B, followed by a separate chapter section devoted to data display.

It is also here in *step 6* that you will determine if any post hoc or "after the fact" analyses are necessary. These analyses are unplanned because secondary hypotheses will only occur to you after you have the benefit of examining the data. As a result, interpret the results of such analyses with caution, taking care to make their post hoc nature known. When post hoc analyses are necessary, briefly loop back either to *step 2* (if a new analysis must be determined) or *step 5* (if a similar analysis can be performed) to complete them.

Table 8.2 concludes with *step 7,* the integration of results into either a psychology paper or a presentation. Sharing research results either in writing (see chapters 3 and 9) or in a spoken presentation (see chapter 9) is an important obligation for any researcher.

Review of Some Common Statistical Tests

Table 8.3 was introduced above in *step 2* of the analysis plan. As you can see, table 8.3 is a step-by-step guide that will narrow the search to the appropriate statistical test for your research design and its data. Each test will be reviewed in order of its appearance in table 8.3.

Chi-Square (χ^2)   The chi-square is a nonparametric test that can be used to analyze nominal data only. The chi-square can be used to test hypotheses about one variable ("Are self-described liberals more likely to be registered as Democrats than Republicans?") or about whether two variables share some relationship with one another ("Does a child's gender influence the selection of aggressive or nonaggressive toys in a free play period?"). The chi-square test compares the observed frequency count collected in a study with a theoretical frequency count expected by chance. In a one-variable, two-group case, such as "yes" or "no" answers to a question, the expectation would be a 50:50 split. An independent variable is likely to have created a significant difference the more the observed data depart from expectation (say, 70:30).

Analysis of Variance   The analysis of variance (ANOVA) is a parametric test used to analyze either interval or ratio data when there are more than two groups in a research design. The test statistic resulting from the ANOVA is the *F*-ratio, a number representing the ratio of between-group variance divided by within-group variance. Between-group variance is due to the influence (if any) of the independent variable plus random error (variance *not* due to the independent variable), whereas within-group variance is a result of variation of performance of the participants in each treatment group. Ideally, a researcher wants a relatively large amount of between-group variance (i.e., the independent

TABLE 8.3

CHOOSING A STATISTICAL TEST

Step 1—Are participants randomly assigned to groups in your study?
   a. if yes, go to *step 3*.
   b. if no, go to *step 2*.
Step 2—Are participants randomly selected from some population?
   a. if yes, go to *step 3*.
   b. if no, go to *step 10*.
Step 3—Is at least one independent variable being manipulated in your study?
   a. if yes, then go to *step 4*.
   b. if no, then go to *step 9*.
Step 4—Are your data continuous?
   a. if yes, then go to *step 5*.
   b. if no, do a nonparametric test like the *chi-square*.
Step 5—How many independent variables are manipulated in your study?
   a. if 1, then go to *step 6*.
   b. if 2 or more, do a *factorial analysis of variance*.
Step 6—How many levels does the 1 independent variable have?
   a. if 2, then go to *step 7*.
   b. if 3 or more, then go to *step 8*.
Step 7—What are the two levels like?
   a. if different participants in each group, do an *independent t-test*.
   b. if the same participants completed a dependent measure twice, do a *correlated t-test*.
Step 8—Were the same participants exposed to every level of the independent variable?
   a. if yes, then do a *one-way repeated-measures analysis of variance*.
   b. if no, then do a *one-way analysis of variance*.
Step 9—Were two (or more) measures per participant collected outside an experimental design?
   a. if yes, then use the *Pearson product-moment correlation*.
   b. if no, go to *step 10*.
Step 10—Inferential statistics are not appropriate. Try presenting the results in a graph, table, or diagram.

Source: Adapted from McKenna (1995).

variable had an effect) and a small amount of within-group variance (i.e., participants behaved similarly within each group); dividing the former by the latter leads to a larger F-ratio, and thus a significant result.

A one-way ANOVA determines whether there are any significant between-group differences among 3 or more groups representing the levels of an independent variable. When only 2 groups are present, the results of an F-test are almost identical to a t-test (discussed later). A social psychologist might examine the effect of emotional induction on person perception, such that one subject group was put in a bad mood (failure feedback), a second was put in a good mood (success feedback), and a third group served as the control group (no feedback). The dependent measure could be a series of rating scales used to evaluate a target person whom the members of each group were introduced to earlier in the experiment. The researcher's hypothesis could be that a positive mood would lead to more favorable ratings (i.e., a higher group mean) than the no mood control condition. In turn, the negative mood group could be predicted to have a lower mean rating than either the positive mood or the control groups.

A one-variable repeated measures (also known as within-subjects) ANOVA examines the reaction of the same group of participants at three or more points in time, and each point represents a different level of the independent variable. A researcher might be interested in knowing if practice in solving certain types of puzzles increases people's performance across time. In other words, does performance improve significantly with each subsequent exposure to the puzzles? Participants' performance scores would be collected at three (or more) points in time and then analyzed by a one-way repeated measures ANOVA, the result of which would reveal any main effect for practice.

A two-way ANOVA examines factorial effects, that is, how two (or more) independent variables affect one dependent measure simultaneously. In a two-way design, each independent variable can have two or more conditions. This statistical test is used to analyze the results from the classic 2×2 design introduced back in chapter 6. A researcher might be exploring the effects of noise (controllable versus uncontrollable) and time pressure (pressure versus no pressure) on problem solving (how many problems are completed correctly). Three separate F-tests result from a factorial ANOVA, two for the resulting main effects and one for the interaction (see chapter 6). The main effect for noise indicates whether more problems are solved when noise is controllable or uncontrollable, and the effect for time pressure examines the number solved when pressure is present or absent. Do noise and time pressure interact so that the level of one variable depends upon the level of the other? The interaction effect is the hallmark of factorial designs, so you may wish to review the relevant discussion in chapter 6.

The *t*-Test   The *t*-test (sometimes referred to as Student's *t*) is used to determine if the mean of one group is significantly different from that of a second group. As you might guess, it is ideal for testing whether the mean of an experimental group differs from that of a control group. Similar to the F-ratio discussed above, the *t*-value is based on the ratio of between-group variability (attributable to an independent variable and random error) divided by within-group variability (performance variation of participants in both groups). A smaller *t*-value or one close to 0 indicates that the sample means are similar to one another (i.e., they are from the same theoretical population). As the disparity between the sample means increases, the likelihood of obtaining a significant *t*-value (i.e., rejecting the null hypothesis) grows.

Consider a simple two-group experiment dealing with subtle, interpersonal physical contact—touching—which is known to increase positive feelings for others. Crusco and Wetzel (1984; see also, Hornik, 1992) had waitresses who worked in a diner test whether they had the "Midas touch," the social psychological observation that people will tip better when they are unobtrusively touched. Calculating what percentage of a bill a tip represents indicates its relative size (i.e., was the service appreciated to a greater or lesser degree relative to the meal's cost). When returning the change from a bill, the waitresses gently touched half the paying customers on the hand; for the remaining customers, the change was put down on the table without physical contact. Crusco and Wetzel found that customers who were touched left a higher tip (based on percentage of their bills) than the no touch control group, a result that could be readily verified by then employing the *t*-test for independent groups.

What about the *t*-test for correlated means? The same logic used for the *t*-test for independent means applies, except that a correlated *t*-test determines whether reactions to a dependent measure change from one point in time to another. With one salient difference, the example cited earlier for the repeated-measures ANOVA will suffice to illustrate the correlated *t*-test: Participant reactions can be assessed only *twice* (remember that the *t*-test compares only 2 means). Thus, does participant performance on certain types of puzzles increase with practice, from an initial exposure (time 1) to a subsequent exposure (time 2)?

Pearson Product-Moment Correlation   The Pearson product-moment correlation, or *r* for short, is a statistic that is used to analyze data from interval or ratio scales. The correlation coefficient indicates the strength of association between 2 variables, and its values can range between −1.00 and +1.00. In practice, pairs of observations are taken from each research participant—one for each of the two variables—and they are correlated. The closer a correlation is to 1.00 (in the positive or the negative direction), the stronger the association between the variables. How strong is a correlation? Disregarding the plus or minus sign, values between 0.00 and .20 are described as weak; between .30 and .60 are moderate; and .70 and above are strong. Coefficients at or near 0.00 indicate that there is no association between the variables.

Correlational relationships are often examined using a *scatterplot,* a graph of data where the position of each observation is determined by its value corresponding to the variables on the *x* and *y* axis. Scatterplots visually illustrate positive, negative, or zero correlations between (usually independent and dependent) variables (see figure 8.2). A positive correlation indicates that the value of each variable moves in the same direction (e.g., higher grades are linked with more hours of study, lower grades with fewer; see graph [a] in figure 8.2). In contrast, graph [b] shows a negative correlational relationship, where as one variable decreases in value, the other increases in value (e.g., lower grades are linked with more frequent campus parties, or vice versa). A correlation of zero indicates that there is no discernable association between the independent variable and the dependent measure. As shown in scatterplot

FIGURE 8.2
Scatterplots Illustrating
Correlational
Relationships

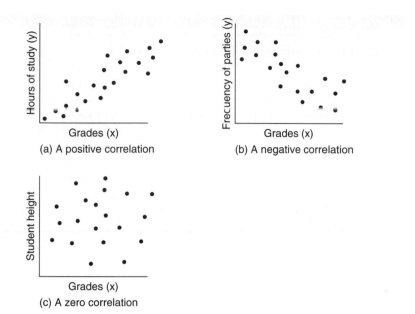

(a) A positive correlation

(b) A negative correlation

(c) A zero correlation

[c] in figure 8.2, grades do not appear to correlate in any noteworthy pattern with the heights of those being graded.

Remember the dictum introduced in chapter 1: Correlation does not imply causation. Correlation coefficients and scatterplots often point to suggestive or intriguing relationships between variables (age and IQ are positively correlated), but such relationships must be explored through the experimental process before any definitive conclusions can be drawn (after all, IQ does not continue to increase across the entire life span).

Concluding Comment on These Common Tests

This review and the contents of table 8.3 are highly selective, as there are other useful parametric and nonparametric tests available to the psychologist. If you develop a research design that does not appear to fit the steps outlined in table 8.3, don't give up. Instead, consult a good statistics book, your instructor, or a knowledgeable peer in order to see if there is a test to fit your specific needs.

WHAT DO THE STATISTICAL RESULTS MEAN, ANYWAY?

Many people assume that analyses are more important than results, especially because the numbers associated with statistics lend an air of technical credibility to the process. Not so. Doing the appropriate analysis correctly is both important and necessary, of course, but the whole point of the research enterprise is to *understand what the results reveal about some aspect of human (or animal) behavior*. In short, how did participants behave in the course of the study? Despite conventional wisdom,

A Research Digression: Power and Effect Size

Research is all about power; that is, *statistical power,* which is the ability to achieve your research goals (Aron & Aron, 1997). Technically speaking, statistical power refers to the probability that a given project will obtain a significant result if the experimental hypothesis is actually true. Naturally, researchers want to avoid making Type I errors (i.e., finding a significant result when the experimental hypothesis is actually false) in the process of maximizing power.

How can a researcher maximize power in a given study? A researcher can control power by deciding how many people will take part in it; all else being equal, the more participants, the greater the power. The drawback to this strategy is obvious: Recruiting many participants and shepherding them through a study takes a great deal of time and effort. Researchers must frequently balance an increase in power with the practical matter of locating adequate numbers of participants (see Box Feature 6.C). Other ways to increase power include making independent variables more salient to participants; increasing the reliability of dependent measures (e.g., adding more items to a test or questionnaire, measuring responses more than once); and making certain the research procedure is standardized—precisely the same—across groups except for the presentation of the independent variable.

Power does not depend exclusively on the number of available participants, salience or reliability of variables, or standardized procedures, however. It also depends on a related concept, *effect size.* The strength of association among variables or the magnitude of an experimental effect is called *effect size.* In concrete terms, effect size is determined by how far apart group means are predicted to be and how much variance is anticipated within each group (Aron & Aron, 1997). When an effect size is large (i.e., the means for each group are far apart and within group variance is low), then fewer research participants are needed. Smaller effect sizes (i.e., means are close to one another and within group variance is large) require larger respondent samples in order to detect reliable differences.

Fortunately, effect size is easily calculated (Appendix B contains effect size calculations for most inferential tests discussed in this chapter; see also, Cohen, 1988, 1992; Kraemer & Thiemann, 1987; Rosenthal, 1991; Rosenthal & Rosnow, 1991). Many researchers routinely report effect sizes in their published work so that readers will know the magnitude of a given treatment effect and how difficult it was to obtain useful information when planning related research. Similar to Pearson's *r,* effect size is reported as a coefficient ranging between 0.0 and 1.00, where a higher value indicates that an independent variable had a stronger influence on a dependent measure. The convention is to describe an effect size of .20 as small, .50 as medium, and .80 as large (e.g., Cohen, 1988).

then, interpretation and meaning are much more important than whether a result is significant at the $p < .01\ or\ .05$ level (cf. Box Feature 8.C; Cohen, 1990).

It is also true that some research results are more meaningful or persuasive than others. Using the acronym MAGIC, Abelson (1995) suggests five particular qualities to keep in mind when evaluating whether a set of results adequately supports a study's hypothesis. MAGIC stands for *magnitude, articulation, generality, interestingness,* and *credibility.* Table 8.4 defines and summarizes each of these criteria by posing questions researchers

TABLE 8.4

THE MAGIC CRITERIA FOR MAKING PERSUASIVE ARGUMENTS ABOUT RESULTS

Magnitude. Statistically speaking, how strong are the results? To what degree do the observed results support the hypothesis? Magnitude addresses the question of effect size, which is discussed in Box Feature 8.D

Articulation. How clearly, concisely, and cogently are the results described in words? As long as important detail is not lost, shorter explanations are generally better explanations. Too many *ifs* and *buts* or extraneous qualifications will erode readers' confidence in any conclusions drawn.

Generality. Are the results applicable to other settings? Are they broad or narrow in scope? This criterion emphasizes the role of external validity (see chapter 7) in the interpretation of statistical results.

Interestingness. Will psychologists and other parties care about the results? Will they be surprised? Will established findings need to be reexamined in light of the results? Abelson (1995) advocates that for results to be interesting, they should alter what people currently believe about important topics.

Credibility. Are the results believable? Are they methodologically sound and do they hold together in support of a theory? Interested parties will scrutinize the research and offer constructive (or not-so-constructive) criticism depending upon the credibility of the data.

Source: Adapted from Abelson (1995).

should ask themselves when reviewing their results. Read table 8.4 now and plan to refer back to it when you put your research results into words, the topic of Exercise 8.B. The *MAGIC criteria* represent idealized aspects of research projects, so each one will not necessarily apply to any given study. Nonetheless, Abelson's points offer guidance about how to think about results and the effects they are likely to have on an audience of readers or listeners.

Exercise 8.B: Putting Statistical Results into Words

Table 8.5 is a template designed to help you put statistical results into words by following a two stage process. *In the first stage, a researcher needs to consider the properties of the statistical test and how that test links up with the dependent measure.* Let's complete table 8.5 by reviewing some possible results of the study on the Midas touch discussed earlier in the section on the *t*-test.

At the top of table 8.5 (*step 1*), the appropriate statistical test is identified along with the numerical relationship it will test. Imagine that eight customers who were touched on the hand left an average tip of 18 percent of the bill and that another eight who were not touched left only 14.75 percent. Did touching matter? In other words, is an 18 percent tip reliably different than a 14.75 percent tip? We know that the independent *t*-test indicates whether a difference exists between two different groups on some measure of average

---

TABLE 8.5

PUTTING STATISTICAL RESULTS INTO WORDS

Stage I

Step 1—Statistical Test—(Check one):

		tests for the following:
chi-square	____	categorical difference(s)
factorial ANOVA	____	mean difference(s)
independent *t*-test	____	mean difference
correlated *t*-test	____	mean difference
repeated-measures ANOVA	____	mean differences(s)
one-way ANOVA	____	mean difference(s)
Pearson *r*	____	correlation
other	___	_____

Step 2—Perform the Actual Statistical Test identified in *step 1.*

Step 3—*Statistical Notation*—(Fill in each blank):
    a. Test (e.g., *t, F, r*)   _____
    b. Degrees of freedom (*df*)   _____
    c. *Write the critical value (from a statistical table or computer printout) for the test statistic here: _____
    d. *Write the specific test value (based on calculation or computer printout) here: _____
    e. Circle one: Based on the analysis, can you *accept* or *reject* the null hypothesis? *(Is the value recorded in (d) *greater than or equal to* the value in (c)? If (d) > or equal to (c), circle *reject;* otherwise, circle *accept*.)
    Circle one: Obtained significance level: < .10 < .05 <.01 < .001 other: _____

Step 4—*Describe the numerical relationship in words* (if means are used, be sure they are in the direction specified by the hypothesis):

Stage II

Describe what the results mean conceptually:

---

performance (here, the average gratuity left to a waitress when she gently touched or did not touch a patron), so it is the appropriate analysis. You would then place a check mark on the line next to the *independent t-test* in table 8.5.

Next, you would carry out *step 2:* Perform the required statistical analysis identified in *step 1.* Doing an analysis is beyond the scope of our discussion, but we will assume that a *t*-test on the average tips for each of the two groups was performed. The hypothetical results of this study will be used to complete the remainder of table 8.5.

Once *step 2* is completed, you would proceed to *step 3* in table 8.5, which covers *statistical notation* and how to write it out for inclusion in a professional report. To begin, the abbreviation for the statistical test, such as t (for a t-test) or F (for an ANOVA), is recorded. Because you are doing an independent t-test, you would write t on the line.

Below this entry, you would need to write down the number corresponding to the *degrees of freedom* for the test (note that the F test has two numbers for degrees of freedom whereas most other tests, including the t-test, have only one). Degrees of freedom, sometimes abbreviated *df*, are numbers based on the size of the study. These numbers, which are determined during the calculation of any test statistic, can also be found on the printout from any data analysis done by computer. To continue this example, we will assume the t-test had 14 degrees of freedom, and so the number "14" would be written into table 8.5.

The next necessary entry in table 8.5 is the *critical value* for the test statistic. Critical values are obtained from statistical tables (see Appendix C) or from a computerized statistics program, and they serve as guides to whether a result reaches significance. The critical value for a t-test with 14 degrees of freedom is 1.761, and formally it is written thus: $t(14) = 1.761$. Below the critical value, the actual test statistic from an analysis—done by hand or computer—is recorded. Let's imagine that the t-value (also with 14 degrees of freedom) from the Midas touch experiment was 5.51, which is formally written out thus: $t(14) = 5.51$.

Following these values, it is necessary to note whether the null hypothesis was accepted or rejected, followed by the obtained significance level of the test statistic (in this example, $p < .05$). Practically speaking, did the value of the test-statistic from the study (here, 5.51) exceed or equal the critical value (here, 1.761)? The former clearly exceeds the latter, and so the null hypothesis is *rejected*. So you would circle "reject" as well as "< .05" that appears beneath it. (Be sure to remember that this significance level also points to the probability of making a Type I error.)

Consider the MAGIC criterion of *articulation* for *step 4,* the final section of table 8.5. The goal is to report the main result in one clear sentence:

> Restaurant patrons who were touched left a significantly higher tip (M = 18.0 percent) than patrons who were not touched (M = 14.75 percent).

Note that the condition means were included here for accuracy. This sentence can then be altered somewhat for inclusion in the Results section of a paper:

> As predicted, restaurant patrons who were touched left a significantly higher tip (M = 18.0 percent) than patrons who were not touched (M = 14.75 percent), $t(14) = 5.51$, $p < .05$.

When reporting the results of a *t*-test, it is often easier to provide the means and the actual statistical information inside a sentence instead of in a table. As you can see, a reader knows what happened behaviorally (how much each group tipped in terms of average percentage) and statistically (there was a significant between-group difference) because the information is right there in the sentence. One other suggestion: Be sure to report a result in words *before* citing the values of the test statistic and significance level. If readers encounter the statistic first they will not have a context for understanding what it explains.

The second stage in putting results into words involves going beyond the face value of the results. This stage (see Stage II in table 8.5) is usually more relevant for writing a paper's Discussion section than the Results (see chapter 3), but it depends on the scope of the project, the complexity of the results, and so on. In other words, what else do we know besides the fact that one group tipped more than the other? Well, we need to consider what role touching plays in social exchanges like the one examined in the study. Prior research found that cursory, quick interpersonal touch is usually not even consciously registered by people (e.g., Crusco & Wetzel, 1984; Fisher, Rytting, & Heslin, 1976). Although some favorable feelings were triggered in the patrons, feelings that led them to leave a larger tip for their server, the effect is seemingly subliminal (e.g., Nisbett & Wilson, 1977). Such nonconscious emotional reactions are interesting but beyond the scope of the current tipping results.

Does this mean that the researcher should avoid speculating about such reactions? Absolutely not—speculation is encouraged as long as the researcher acknowledges that the present data point to possibilities for future studies, not definitive answers now.

DISPLAYING DATA

Above all else show the data.
—Edward Tufte (1983)

Displaying data entails creating a table, a figure, or perhaps a graph illustrating some important result from an experiment. The main purpose of any data display is information reduction, or conveying a large amount of information in a concise manner. Only the most important result or results should be presented in a table or a figure, so any paper or presentation should have very few such displays. There are two reasons for this rule. In the first place, too many tables or figures can be distracting, even tiresome, so that readers will pay little attention to them. The second reason represents the pragmatic side of the publishing industry: Graphical images are sometimes very expensive to reproduce and should therefore be used sparingly.

TABLE 8.6

TIP PERCENTAGES BY TOUCH CONDITION AND GENDER OF CUSTOMER

Gender	Touch			No Touch		
	M	*SD*	*n*	*M*	*SD*	*n*
Males	17.25	.98	4	15.0	1.10	4
Females	18.75	1.5	4	14.5	.58	4

Note: The higher the number, the higher the tip expressed as the percent of a restaurant bill.

For ease of understanding, I will follow the *Publication Manual's* (American Psychological Association, 1994) distinction between tables and figures. A *table* contains precise quantitative data exclusively. Any other representation, including graphs, histograms, line graphs, diagrams, photographs, and the like are collectively referred to as *figures*. Because they contain precise numbers, tables implicitly invite careful study. Readers may need to pause for a bit because a little effort may be needed to interpret their contents. For example, table 8.6 illustrates a fairly standard display of means and standard deviations broken down by experimental condition and gender (these hypothetical data are based on the Midas touch study). In contrast, figures should be constructed so that readers can take in the relationships they portray with a brief glance or cursory examination. Figures are often used to illustrate interaction effects in factorial designs, for example (recall figure 6.1).

There are four common errors people make when creating data displays (Sternberg, 1993; Tufte, 1983; see also, Tufte, 1990; 1997). The first error is *redundancy*. Many researchers needlessly duplicate the material appearing in a table, figure, or graph. If the means and standard deviations are reported in the text of the Results section, for example, then why duplicate the values in a table in the same section? Needless redundancy wastes precious page space, is costly, and annoys readers.

A second error is *linkage between text and graphics*. Very often well-done tables are included in papers, but authors make little or no attempt to draw the readers' attention to them. Indeed, sometimes important data are included in such tables but they bear no resemblance to what is discussed in the Results section. Readers are left wondering why such information was included or whether a relevant discussion was somehow inadvertently dropped from the text. Firm, even obvious, links must be forged between the text and any tables or figures.

Having *minimal or no discussion of a table or figure* is a third common error. Some authors will insert a well-constructed table or figure into the text, but then add only the most indirect reference to it, such as "see table 5." Such short directives are fine, but not if the surrounding text does not lead the reader through the table entries or explain what the graph or line figure demonstrates. Graphics should supplement the

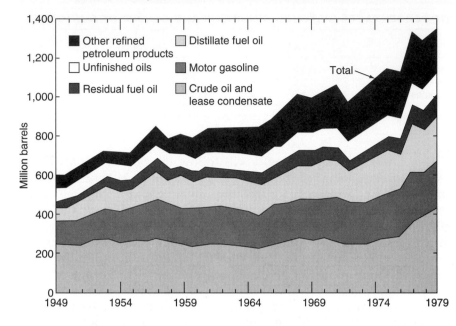

written text in an effective way but under no circumstances should they stand alone from it.

The fourth and final error is the frequent use of *chartjunk* (Tufte, 1983). In Tufte's view (1983, p. 107), "The interior decoration of graphics generates a lot of ink that does not tell the viewer anything new." Scientific results do not benefit from excessive ornamentation; in fact, any extraneous information only makes it more difficult for readers to see the conclusion the table, figure, or graph is supposed to convey. Busy pie charts, colored bar graphs, overly detailed tables, and stylized figures have no place in presentations of psychological data. Unfortunately, the increasing plethora of graphics programs makes chartjunk easy to produce—but avoid being seduced by such convenience. Data and their realized relationships, not the background on which they appear, matter.

An example of chartjunk from a governmental publication is shown in figure 8.3. Note the overuse of distracting graphic textures in figure 8.3, visual "noise" that impedes the flow of information to the reader (Tufte, 1983). Much less busy, easy to comprehend data displays are shown in figure 8.4. Figure 8.4 shows two clear and representative graphs from the field of psychology. These graphs contain only essential information—the data can speak for themselves.

The single best source of advice on formatting tables and figures of psychological data is the *Publication Manual* (American Psychological Association, 1994). It provides sound and practical advice for creating these data displays, and a wide range of examples are included. Table 8.7 is a

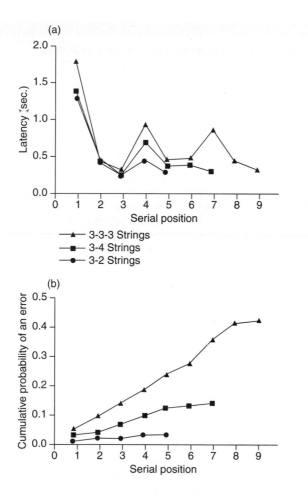

FIGURE 8.4
Sample Figures from
Psychological
Research. *Source:*
Anderson & Matessa
(1997).

distillation of some of the more useful advice from the *Publication Manual* as well as some common sense observations on data display. Be sure to consult table 8.7 when considering creating any data display. Other accessible sources for guidance include Sternberg (1993) and a book by Wallgreen and colleagues (1996).

CODA: KEEPING DATA AND ANALYSIS RECORDS

Once the data are analyzed and written up for presentation or publication, what then? Should researchers discard all their raw data, the independent variable and dependent measure record sheets, any printouts or analyses done by hand? No, never! Researchers work long and hard on their projects, so the last thing they should do is to throw away the tangible results of that labor. There are several compelling reasons to hold onto data, including ethical guidelines, the sharing of ideas, and theory building through meta-analyses.

TABLE 8.7

TIPS FOR CREATING EFFECTIVE TABLES AND FIGURES

- Less is more; use tables and figures sparingly and only when necessary.
- Tables contain precise numbers, whereas figures can graphically illustrate numerical relationships, patterns, or trends.
- A good rule-of-thumb is to rely on a table when four or more means (or other observations) must be reported.
- When reporting means (*M*s) in a table, be sure to report the accompanying standard deviations (*SD*s) and number of observations (*n*s) per condition, as well.
- Double-space all the information in a table, including the title and any numbers or notes.
- Make certain that any lines or bars in a figure are clearly labeled.
- When graphing any result, place the dependent variable on the vertical or *y-axis* and the independent variable along the horizontal or *x-axis*.
- When using APA style, insert tables and figures on separate, sequentially numbered pages following the Reference section. In student papers, however, tables or figures can appear in the body of the text.
- Discuss tables and figures in the text.
- Explain any abbreviation or symbol appearing in a table or figure in a note underneath it.
- Give all tables and figures brief but explanatory titles.

Source: Adapted from the *Publication Manual* (American Psychological Association, 1994).

How can maintaining an archive of data involve ethical guidelines? The American Psychological Association advocates that researchers keep their data in case other interested researchers would like to review it. Other researchers have the right to verify that both a project's methodology and the data analysis were carried out in a correct and rigorous manner. Most individuals who ask for such information are likely to be interested in replicating the work, not challenging its conclusions. Authors are expected to comply quickly and fully with such requests, being careful, of course, to continue to maintain the privacy and anonymity of the original research participants. The minimum recommended time for holding onto data, as well as procedural details, instructions, and any analyses, is 5 years after they appear in print.

Some scholars will want to conduct a *secondary analysis* of the results. Secondary analyses are undertaken when a researcher has a different idea about how data and prior results could be reinterpreted in light of other data or newer theorizing. These sorts of analyses should be encouraged in the discipline of psychology because the relatively slow process of careful theory building is often neglected in favor of conducting more studies to collect more data. Expanding knowledge is a laudable exercise, of course, but the creation of interpretive frameworks for the results must keep apace with such expansion.

Sharing data or any part of the research enterprise with other interested investigators is an important duty—really an obligation—of any psychologist. As noted earlier in this book, very few ideas in psychology or any academic field are novel. The bulk of research incorporates the ideas and insights of previous generations of researchers, as well as the

BOX FEATURE 8.E

A Research Digression: A Cautionary Tale on Caring for Data

Shelley E. Taylor (personal communication, March 13, 1997) believes in caring for data, the fruits of the psychologist's labors. Now a social and health psychologist at the University of California at Los Angeles, Taylor experienced a freak accident as an undergraduate working on her senior honors thesis. She had collected data from dozens of research participants and was storing it in piles on the floor of her dormitory room. The semester wore on and the data began to gather dust, and in a "fit of cleanliness," she put all the data on her bed as she planned to vacuum the room. In Taylor's words:

> First, though, I had to go to class, and while I was at class, my dorm caught on fire. The firemen succeeded in keeping the building from being a total loss, but most of the rooms were filled with a foot or more of water from the hose spraying for the next several days, until we were allowed back in. Had my data still been on the floor, I would have lost every bit. As it was, I lost only the first page of data on each of four subjects at the top of the four piles (very little missing data indeed, given what could have happened).

This experience made a great impression on Professor Taylor, and she handles her data with extreme care, making certain that multiple copies are made of it as soon as possible. Freak accidents aside, the lesson is clear: Handle data with care or you risk losing the information you worked so hard to collect. You may not need to make multiple copies of what you collect (though maintaining the original data separate from the dependent measure sheet is a good idea; see chapter 6), but you should take the effort to store it carefully.

views of contemporary investigators. Making data, methodology, and measures available to others aids the research process and promotes what is arguably the most important aspect of science—the notion that inquiry is a shared process, that true understanding of mind and behavior results from pulling together the small advances found in disparate studies. This sharing of information helps to develop, test, revise, and occasionally discard theory.

There is one final, innovative reason for sharing data with other investigators: a statistical technique called *meta-analysis*. Meta-analysis effectively performs an analysis on a set of studies purporting to examine the same effect or phenomenon. In other words, where an experiment examines consistency in the response of individuals taking part in it, a meta-analysis examines the collective consistency of individual experiments dealing with the same topic. For example, a meta-analysis might examine the effect of divorce on children's academic achievement, gender differences in nonverbal communication, or the effect of any given therapy on alleviation of depressive symptoms. A meta-analysis does not replace the role of individual experiments; rather it provides researchers with a systematic way to summarize what is known about focused research questions that appear in the psychological literature (for specific examples of meta-analysis, see Eagly, 1978, on sex differences in influenceability; Greenberg, Bornstein, Greenberg, & Fisher, 1992, on the utility of anti-depressant medications).

As a statistical technique, meta-analysis takes into account the effect sizes or significance levels associated with each separate study. The chief advantage of meta-analysis is that it synthesizes research, that is, merges separate findings into a complex whole. As Rosenthal and Rosnow (1991, p. 140) put it, meta-analysis is the "analysis of analyses." Demonstrating that an effect is valid and reliable across a variety of studies done at different times and places, by different investigators, and with different participant samples, is an undeniable strength. Meta-analysis also helps to build theory by demonstrating consistency in findings; firm conclusions about one aspect of a research topic invite, even direct, future speculation about others. Many good references on the technique and its usefulness to psychology are available (Cooper & Hedges, 1994; Glass, 1976; Glass, McGaw, & Smith, 1981; Judd, Smith, & Kidder, 1991; Rosenthal, 1991; Rosnow & Rosenthal, 1996).

SUMMARY

This chapter contains a condensed review of basic descriptive and inferential statistics. It adopted the stance that data analysis is simply another practical tool for the researcher. The importance of planning before executing statistical analyses was emphasized throughout the chapter. Accordingly, Exercise 8.A provided guidance on developing an analysis plan. Five basic inferential statistical tests—with guidance about when to use each—were presented. A second exercise illustrated how to put statistical results into words, thereby clarifying their meaning for written and oral communication. The remainder of the chapter provided helpful suggestions about creating tables, figures, and graphs that conveyed results clearly, simply, and without undue embellishment. Finally, the importance of keeping data—to share with others or for reanalysis in the future—was discussed.

KEY TERMS

analysis of variance
  (ANOVA) (p. 273)
analysis plan (p. 270)
bimodal distribution (p. 268)
central tendency (p. 260)
chartjunk (p. 284)
chi-square test (p. 268)
continuous data (p. 270)
correlated measure (p. 271)
critical value (p. 281)

degrees of freedom (p. 281)
descriptive statistics (p. 257)
discontinuous data (p. 270)
distribution (p. 260)
effect size (p. 278)
general linear model (GLM)
  (p. 269)
independent measure (p. 271)
inferential statistics (p. 258)
interval scale (p. 259)

MAGIC criteria (p. 279)
mean (p. 260)
median (p. 261)
meta-analysis (p. 287)
mode (p. 260)
multiple correlation (p. 269)
nominal scale (p. 259)
nonparametric statistics
  (p. 268)
normal distribution (p. 267)

ordinal scale (p. 259)
parametric statistics (p. 266)
Pearson product-moment
  correlation (p. 276)
range (p. 262)
ratio scale (p. 259)

scatterplot (p. 276)
secondary analysis (p. 286)
skewed distribution (p. 268)
standard deviation (p. 262)
statistic (p. 256)
statistical power (p. 278)

statistical significance (p. 264)
t-test (p. 275)
variability (p. 262)
variance (p. 262)

SUGGESTED READINGS

Abelson, R. P. (1995). *Statistics as principled argument.* Hillsdale, NJ: Erlbaum. Clever, often humorous, always insightful, this book teaches students and researchers to think coherently about using and interpreting statistics in psychological research. Advanced but accessible to interested readers.

Runyon, R. P., Haber, A., Pittenger, D. J., & Coleman, K. A. (1996). *Fundamentals of behavioral statistics* (8th ed.). New York: McGraw-Hill. Arguably the most lucid statistics text for undergraduate students in psychology and related fields. As a reference work, it contains clear and detailed procedures for analyzing data from simple to moderately complex two-factor designs.

Siegel, S., & Castellan, N. J. (1988). *Nonparametric statistics for the behavioral sciences.* (2nd ed.). New York: McGraw-Hill. The one and only reference for choosing appropriate nonparametric statistical tests for research.

Tufte, E. R. (1983). *The visual display of quantitative information.* Cheshire, CT: Graphics Press. An elegant and educational lark promoting clear communication with numbers, graphs, and pictures.

CHAPTER 9

Presenting Research

Although it is very enlightening and personally satisfying, the process of conducting research is not meant to be an end in and of itself. You must share what you learn with others, as disseminating knowledge is an integral part of science. This point was first made back in chapter 3 when APA style was introduced. In this chapter, we consider two approaches to sharing the results of research with others: oral and written presentations. Oral presentations are variously called papers, speeches, or talks; written presentations are usually research summaries that appear in the form of conference proposals or journal articles.

Practical researchers know that the way research is presented can be as important as the content of the research. Why? Even when an audience is motivated and attentive, if the research is not conveyed well in either spoken or written form, the ideas contained in it will be transitory— and quickly forgotten. This chapter contains ideas to help you create a memorable presentation of psychological research suited to either formal or informal settings. In addition, forums for submitting and presenting research are reviewed, and some final advice about writing and submitting an APA style article based on your research project is discussed.

WRITING: A BRIEF REPRISE

In chapter 3, I suggested that readers of this book should treat writing as both a first and a last consideration in the research process. In some ways, this chapter deals with the end of the research process: sharing what you have written with others. Just don't assume that such sharing is restricted to APA style articles.

Although journal style articles are an important as well as a traditional mode for communicating results, writing is a necessary part of oral presentations, as well. As you will see, skills such as outlining, drafting, and sharing preliminary work with peers can also be useful when putting together a presentation. Indeed, the writing process can help to refine the main ideas that form the core of a spoken presentation. Writing, then, remains an ongoing and unrestricted activity that is as important to the later stages of research as it was to the earlier part of the process—and it should remain your first and last consideration.

GIVING A RESEARCH PRESENTATION

Speaking Before an Audience

Think about the teachers who really made an impact on your learning or left a lasting impression in your memory. Invariably, such individuals were good, even polished, public speakers. How did they get that way? Many people persist in maintaining the erroneous belief that good speakers are born rather than made, that oratorical skills cannot be learned. Let's dispel this myth once and for all. Public speaking is like any other craft in that it requires patience, practice, and reliance on some practical rules of thumb.

Here are several rules of thumb routinely used by seasoned speakers. They are well worth emulating as you prepare a research presentation. A good speaker

- *does not read a presentation.* There is nothing more boring than listening to another person read from a prepared text. The written word is not, after all, the spoken word. A presentation should have some degree of spontaneity in it, so *talk*—don't read. In this vein, many speakers recommend striving for a conversational style (e.g., Martin, 1996).
- *tells the audience why the topic is interesting.* If you are not enthused about your work, the audience will not be enthused about your presentation. Why did you select this topic over others? Why does it matter to you? Why should it matter to your listeners? Engage your audience by letting them know why you pursued your topic in a research project.
- *is organized.* Good presentations have well-developed, even obvious, outlines. An outline is hierarchical: Main points are highlighted and secondary points support them. The audience should always know where you are and where you are heading.
- *uses time wisely and effectively.* Every available minute is used for the presentation, although time for questions and answers is always re-

served at the conclusion (with the proviso that finishing early is more acceptable than finishing late, thereby taking precious time away from other speakers).

- *uses many examples.* Without illustrative examples, technical or conceptual material will go right over the head of even the most interested members of your audience. A judicious use of examples will liven up a presentation the same way it does written prose (cf. chapter 3).
- *summarizes main points throughout a presentation.* Tell the audience what the presentation's purpose is at the outset, remind them again as you cover your main points during the talk, and then close with a final summary. Don't say the same things the same way at each point; rather, get a general point across each time so that the audience can link the details of your presentation to it.
- *is confident and authoritative.* Appearing confident involves conveying a sense that you know what you are talking about. Being authoritative builds on this confidence by demonstrating your range of knowledge regarding a topic. Note that exuding confidence or being authoritative is not the same thing as being authoritarian, arrogant, or condescending, three attitudes that will ensure a presentation's failure.
- *speaks at a reasonable pace.* Practice slowing down if you speak too rapidly. If you have the reverse problem, then try to pick up the pace. Practice in front of a friend and ask for comments, or record (or videotape if you dare!) your presentation and then listen to yourself. It can be sobering but very helpful.
- *is animated.* Don't be wooden or hide behind a podium. Be expressive and move around a bit. Your animation will involve your audience and make you more accessible to them.
- *maintains eye contact with the audience.* Pick a friendly face or two to speak to in the audience. You will quickly lose audience interest if you look down at your notes too much or if you stare off into the distance; instead, create a rapport with the people you are addressing by looking at them.
- *is not overly dependent on visual aids.* Avoid using too many crutches, such as complex and colorful overheads, charts, figures, and tables. A few high-quality overheads are fine, but good speakers know their goal is to educate rather than to distract an audience with too many props. Remember, the audience is there to see you, not your slides. The same logic holds true for handouts, which are riskier to use—people are apt to read them instead of listening to the presentation.
- *rehearses the talk.* Winging a presentation is never a good idea, especially because the audience is apt to recognize that you seem uncertain about the points you want to make. Unrehearsed presentations also tend to be peppered with awkward pauses and silences, rustling papers, and overuse of "um," "ah," and "er, well," and the phrase, "you know." Rehearsing means going over the outline a sufficient number

BOX FEATURE 9.A

A Research Digression: Beginnings and Endings

Good research presentations are based on good outlines, main points, and supporting details, but they also depend on a strong beginning and a clear closing. As you outline and write a presentation based on your research, be sure to give special attention to how you begin and end it. What follows are a few objectives to keep in mind as you put your presentation together.

Start out strong, or well begun is half done. Stephen E. Lucas (1995), a specialist in communication, suggests that there are four objectives that presenters need to establish shortly after they begin speaking:

- Gaining the audience's attention and interest.
- Disclosing the presentation's topic.
- Appearing credible and full of goodwill.
- Leading into the body of the presentation.

When developing the presentation, work on the body first, and a good opening may come to you. It is especially important to *know* your opening; ideally, then, avoid relying on notes so that you look directly at the audience as you start to speak.

End well. Conclusions, too, should be developed after the body of the presentation, but keep an eye out for interesting ways to end during outlining. Your objectives, however, at the end of a presentation are clear-cut:

- To alert the audience that you are ending.
- To reiterate the main point(s) from the presentation.

Lucas (1995) advocates that speakers end with a bang, not a whimper: Remember, the final impression you make in a presentation is apt to be what sticks in the minds of the audience. To end well, don't be abrupt and avoid tired phrases, such as "In conclusion. . ." or "In summary. . . ." Of course you are concluding and, yes, summarizing is a part of that—but do it, don't talk about what you are going to do. Your ending, like your opening, should be smooth and known by heart, not read from notes.

As a final courtesy to your audience, it is entirely appropriate to briefly thank them for showing interest in your work—just be sure to look at them as you do so.

of times so that it becomes a guiding mental framework for your presentation. Moreover, rehearsal will help you to anticipate logical questions from an audience, which can then be built into the presentation.

- *is open to comments, questions, and even criticism.* A good presentation is like a good conversation where give-and-take occurs between the participants, and a quality talk invariably generates interest and curiosity from listeners. Good speakers welcome audience responses because they often extend the presentation's message to related points, clarify content, or raise unexamined issues. Speakers often receive helpful suggestions, sometimes even citations, that improve their work. Try not to react defensively, and adopt the accurate view that both speaker and listener benefit from constructive criticism.

TABLE 9.1

ESSENTIAL STEPS IN SPEECH PREPARATION

Step 1—Select and then narrow the topic
Step 2—Identify the main idea
Step 3—Consider the audience
Step 4—Collect the presentation materials
Step 5—Outline and expand the material
Step 6—Rehearse the presentation; return to step 5 as necessary

Note: Adapted from Gronbeck, McKerrow, Ehninger, & Monroe (1997).

Presenting a Paper: KISS Revisited

How to begin? Remember the modified KISS ("Keep it simple, student") rule from chapter 2? Well, it is quite applicable when it comes to presenting research.

When presenting a research paper to an audience for the first time, inexperienced speakers often make fairly predictable mistakes. For example, there is a tendency for novice speakers to overdo it. Why? Because first time speakers make the mistake of assuming that every detail of the research project—from the genesis of the idea to the most minor result—must be mentioned in a presentation. Alternatively, novices often skip over some points in favor of others. Martin (1996) notes that discussion of experimental procedure is often rushed, if not sacrificed, to get to the results. This assumption is understandable, perhaps, but it is also true that adequate understanding of the results is dependent upon the procedure's clarity in the mind of the listener.

Do as the modified KISS rule advocates: Keep your presentation simple, straightforward, and understandable. To begin, follow the essential steps in preparing to present a speech outlined in table 9.1, which is adapted from Gronbeck, McKerrow, Ehninger, & Monroe (1997). Steps 1 and 2 should already be done if your presentation is based on a research project. Certainly, you will not want to present all the detail from your research project or any existing paper based upon it. Paper presentations must be very focused, and you will need to be selective about what you end up discussing.

Step 3 involves identifying your listeners and the venue for the presentation (we will discuss details regarding formal and informal venues below). Whom you speak to will determine a great deal about the way you present. If you are speaking to an audience that has background knowledge of your topic, omit a general explanation. If the audience lacks such knowledge, then provide an overview of the topic.

Collecting materials for the presentation (step 4) should not prove to be difficult. It is likely that you have written a detailed course paper or a concise lab report that will prove to be a very useful resource. If neither of these is available, you should still have the materials from your experiment or project to call upon. Any notes pertaining to the methodology and the results themselves will be especially important for the next step. (If your presentation is not based on any empirical research you have conducted, use the guidelines presented in chapter 4 and conduct a search of the psychological literature pertaining to your topic. The bibliographic materials you collect will help you do the next step in developing a presentation.)

Step 5 entails writing an outline (see Exercise 3.A), which you may already have if you used one during the course of writing a project paper. An outline from such a paper is apt to contain more detail than a presentation requires, so it may have to be simplified accordingly. If no outline presently exists, then develop one based on the suggestions made in Exercise 3.A. Do not simply take an existing project paper and try to edit it down—presentations lifted from such papers tend to be heavy and dry because detail tying the points together well is necessarily discarded. Start new or work from an outline so that you don't rely on canned phrases taken from a paper—a presentation should have a spark of its own.

Once you have a working outline, you should flesh out the main points by writing down what you intend to say. Following APA style, you will want to have concise notes on the study's purpose, the hypothesis, the method used, the results and whether they support the hypothesis, and the implications of the results. Once you have these supporting notes for the outline, go back over them. You will begin to see gaps where additional detail is needed, as well as information that can be omitted.

Finally, step 6 entails a rehearsal of your presentation. As was noted earlier, a tape recorder can help in this regard. The best approach, of course, is to have a real audience listen and react to what you say. Feedback at this stage is extremely useful because it will allow you to tailor your presentation appropriately and to anticipate the reactions, even needs, of your future audience. Once you have rehearsed the presentation sufficiently, it is time to perform the actual paper presentation within its intended venue—either a formal or an informal paper presentation.

Formal Paper Presentations   Formal presentations at conferences and similar settings tend to be about 15 to 20 minutes in length, which, as any regular presenter will tell you, is not much time (others, of course, see it as a virtual eternity). As a rule, you should plan to present your general topic and specific question examined within the first 2 minutes or so of your talk. You should then turn to the methodology, highlighting the participants and procedure (about 5 minutes). The remainder of your time should be spent carefully reviewing the results, their meaning in light of the hypothesis, and how well they link up with existing literature (about 5 minutes). The final 3 minutes or so should be spent considering the implications of the findings, and then on to questions from the audience (usually around 5 minutes).

Informal Paper Presentations   Most informal presentations occur in the classroom. If you have the opportunity to give a class presentation on your research, then by all means do it. Speaking before your classmates is good experience because they are apt to be a welcoming and interested audience (and in all likelihood, you will be in the audience when they present). Part of your class grade may depend on giving a presentation of your work, for example. If so, your professor undoubtedly has a set of presentation guidelines concerning what is expected, how long a talk should last, and so on. Such in-class presentations are also a good opportunity for students to learn what their peers have been working on; even in the most small and intimate of classes, there will be several students or research teams working in relative ignorance of the others.

What if no class time has been allotted to research presentations? Take the initiative and ask your professor to provide an opportunity for students to present their work. Alternatively, you might want to consider organizing a student research symposium, the subject of Exercise 9.A.

Exercise 9.A: Organizing a Student Research Symposium

A *symposium* is a meeting held to discuss a particular subject, such as the psychological research conducted by the members of your class. Recruit an interested group of peers from your research methods class (say, the members of several research teams) and organize an after-hours symposium. All that is needed is a place for the presentations, an agreed upon length for each talk (again, no more than 15 or 20 minutes is a good rule), and time for questions following each presentation. If possible, it's a good idea to organize the presentations using some framework, such as the topical area (e.g., memory) or the research locale (e.g., the lab or the field). Here are a few rules of thumb to make the symposium run more smoothly, but be sure to tailor them to fit your particular needs:

Form a committee.   Holding a student symposium is not a tremendous amount of work if several volunteers are willing to help, but some organization is involved. I recommend that you convene a group of interested individuals, including a faculty sponsor, and discuss when, where, and how you might do it. Use the questions in table 9.2 to guide your discussion. Good luck!

Ensure participation from classmates.   Creating an opportunity for student presentations is great, but only if you get enough students or research teams to agree to present their work. Before proceeding any further, be sure to get a sufficient number of individuals to commit to presenting at the symposium. The number here will vary, but I would suggest that you have at least 4 to 6 presentations before going to the trouble of organizing a paper session.

Plan ahead.   Location is everything. If your classroom is available and commodious, by all means use it—but be sure to reserve it. You might consider obtaining a room or rooms for presentation in a more central location, such as your institution's Student Union.

TABLE 9.2

PLANNING A STUDENT SYMPOSIUM: ISSUES FOR DISCUSSION

1. *Will there be any interest in a symposium?*
   If so, who will present?
      Class members? Research teams?
      Other potential presenters?
2. *When should the symposium be held (i.e., day, date, and time)?*
   Where can it be held?
      A classroom? A seminar room or other campus site?
   Who will make and verify room reservations?
   What other materials are needed?
      A projector and podium?
      Refreshments for speakers? The audience?
      Other needs?
3. *Who will attend?*
      Classmates? Students from other classes?
      Faculty members from Psychology and/or other departments?
      Other potential audiences?
4. *How will advertising be done? Who will be responsible for it?*
      Posters? Notices and/or e-mail?
      The campus newspaper?
5. *Who will serve as the moderator?*

Again, reserve the space ahead and confirm its availability before the presentations.

Regardless of the facility's location, you will need to have an overhead projector, a screen, and a podium available; a pitcher of ice water and glasses for the speakers is also a nice touch. You might also consider serving modest refreshments for the presenters and the audience after the presentations are over or, if you are ambitious, host a celebratory dinner.

Appoint a moderator.   Every symposium must have a master of ceremonies, someone to introduce the speakers and their topics and keep things moving. Credibility and experience may point to having a faculty member moderate, but I think that student symposiums should be run by students. After all, moderating a paper session is good experience for a student because it is another form of public speaking.

The main responsibilities of a moderator include keeping time and monitoring the question-and-answer session following each talk. By keeping time, I mean making certain that each presentation starts and stops no later than the established times. The moderator must keep an eye on the clock and subtly alert the speaker at the half-way point, the final two minutes, and when the presentation *must* end. He or she then initiates the question period, concluding it when the next speaker must be introduced.

Advertise.   Invite students from other psychology classes and encourage faculty to attend. Consider asking students and faculty from related departments that have an interest in psychological issues (e.g., biology, sociology, philosophy) to participate, as well. Post announcements around the campus, take advantage of electronic mail, and invite the campus newspaper to cover the symposium (or at least to announce it among upcoming campus events). If there are any colleges or universities adjacent to your own, send a symposium announcement to their psychology departments as well as any student psychology organizations (e.g., Psi Chi chapters).

Support peers and generate knowledge, not competition. No matter how great or small the student symposium, keep in mind that its goals are to give support to student research and researchers, as well as to expand psychological knowledge. The audience and the participants should be courteous to all speakers by conveying interest and respect. Questions and discussion from the floor should be encouraged. Speakers should be supportive of one another's efforts, so that the event is a chance to learn about disparate ideas and approaches in psychology, and not a competition to see whose project was the most impressive.

Concluding Comments on Giving a Paper

Ralph McKenna is a social psychologist who is singularly concerned with having students benefit from conducting research and sharing it with others. In a recent book, McKenna (1995, p. 259) offers what I think is sage advice when preparing to give an oral presentation:

> I tell my students about the 15 minutes of intense boredom surrounding the modal convention presentation. I suggest that instead of reading a completed manuscript, which I find deadly, they work from notes and be themselves, whether the presentation is in our class or at [a] student symposium. If they are able to relate to the audience on a personal level, honestly reviewing the research process and its outcome, then their presentations should be well received, maybe even memorable.

These are words to think about, and perhaps live by, when preparing to give a paper presentation.

Poster Sessions

The advantage of *poster sessions* over traditional paper presentations is one-on-one contact between researchers and people who are interested in their work. Compared to paper presentations, poster sessions are informal affairs. Presenting research during a poster session is often more appealing to student researchers because it has a lower threat value than speaking before an audience. Presenting a poster involves writing a very short research summary of a study (i.e., besides the one-paragraph Abstract, each section of the APA style paper is short—preferably less than one typed page in length) and mounting it on poster board. (Having hard copies for interested individuals to take with them is a good idea, as well.) Researchers stand at the ready by their posters to discuss their

BOX FEATURE 9.B

A Research Digression: Stage Fright Is Common

Even the most practiced speakers get butterflies in the stomach before a talk—or even a new semester. In fact, most people endorse "giving a speech" as being very high on their list of greatest fears (Goleman, 1984). Other research on public speaking reveals that fully 76 percent of experienced speakers have stage fright before their presentations (Hahner, Sokoloff, & Salisch, 1993). As a result, some students of public speaking suggest that nervousness is a positive sign that the presenter is getting "psyched up" (Lucas, 1995). Ironically, it follows that being too calm, cool, and collected prior to speaking is not a good portent for a speaker.

Let's proceed with the assumption that a bit of anxiety is normal, perhaps even desirable, and address a second issue: How should a speaker handle this requisite case of the jitters? Here are a few pointers from Lucas (1995):

1. Approach presenting as a novel activity; as you grow accustomed to it, it will no longer be anxiety producing to you.
2. Like any acquired skill, giving presentations involves trial and error. As you gain experience, you will get better and better at doing it.
3. Talking about topics you care a great deal about, such as your research, minimizes nervousness about speaking in front of groups.
4. Your physical and mental condition matter. Get a good night's sleep prior to a presentation by avoiding partying or cramming for a test.

Some parting wisdom: Check out the room where you will speak in advance. When presenting in an unfamiliar place, plan to arrive a few minutes early so that you can get a feel for it. You will want to set up and make sure any equipment you need (e.g., microphone, overhead projector) is available, anyway. While you prepare, take a look around the room and get a feel for where you will stand, whether you can move around as you speak, and how close you will be to the audience. Such minor preparation will reduce your uncertainty about the setting and increase your comfort before you start to speak.

work as interested conferees mill about the room, reading individual posters and asking questions. It is a very good idea to have a very short oral summary (two or so minutes) prepared, as some viewers will still want to hear your ideas instead of reading them.

Posters have one other distinction that you should capitalize upon: They are visual. People who are interested in your work will read the short summaries, but you should also give them something to look at beyond the text. Graph the results, for example, or have a display or even photograph of the stimulus items you used. If you employed a survey or a particular personality inventory, then post a copy or, better yet, a sample of representative items. Naturally, your data should be the focus of the poster, but creating an attractive, ambient background for them is fine. Exercise a bit of decorum, however: Don't get carried away and hang up a light display around your poster or have the summaries mounted on paper that is a color not-found-in-nature (it has been done, believe me).

TABLE 9.3

UNDERGRADUATE RESEARCH CONFERENCES IN PSYCHOLOGY

Arkansas Symposium for Psychology Students
Carolinas Psychology Conference
Delaware Valley Undergraduate Research Conference
Great Plains Students' Psychology Convention
ILLOWA Undergraduate Psychology Conference
Lehigh Valley Undergraduate Psychology Research Conference
Michigan Undergraduate Psychology Paper Reading Conference
Mid-America Undergraduate Psychology Research Conference
Minnesota Undergraduate Psychology Conference
Southeastern Undergraduate Psychology Research Conference
University of Winnipeg Undergraduate Psychology Research Conference

Information about the dates and times of these conferences is published in the *APA Monitor*, *Eye on Psi Chi*, and in the February issue of the journal *Teaching of Psychology*.

Poster sessions held at larger conferences tend to be thematic (e.g., sleep disorders, behavior modification, recovered memories), but those held at student conferences or in a classroom context need not be. In fact, both presenters and attendees probably learn much more about many different approaches to psychological research in a poster session than in more traditional speaking venues—the low pressure setting lends itself to friendly speculation and informal inquiry.

FORUMS FOR RESEARCH: WHERE CAN YOU PRESENT?

Many students want the experience of giving a presentation off campus. In doing so, they have an opportunity to meet other students who are interested in sharing the fruits of their research experiences in psychology. They also want to explore another role filled by the professional psychologist, that of academic citizen. Beyond campus, there are two main places to present your research: at specially organized undergraduate conferences and at regional or national professional conferences that hold special sessions for students.

Undergraduate Conferences

Undergraduate psychology conferences are usually organized exclusively for students to present their research and to hear the presentations of others. Many of these conferences will invite a prominent researcher to give a keynote address. Undergraduate conferences have grown in popularity in recent years, and table 9.3 contains a list of some of the larger and more enduring student conferences. Each conference is likely to have a slightly different set of guidelines for submission (for discussion of the general requirements, see Exercise 9.B), so you will need to contact the school or organization hosting a given conference for important details.

TABLE 9.4

PROFESSIONAL CONFERENCES WITH PSI CHI STUDENT SESSIONS

Psi Chi, the National Honor Society in Psychology, offers student paper and poster sessions at the following regional and national conferences:

Regional

Eastern Psychological Association
Midwestern Psychological Association
Rocky Mountain Psychological Association
Southeastern Psychological Association
Southwestern Psychological Association
Western Psychological Association

National

American Psychological Association
American Psychological Society

Dates, times, and submission requirements for the conference sessions can be obtained from *Eye on Psi Chi,* the society's quarterly periodical, or by contacting

Psi Chi National Office
407 East Fifth Street, Suite B
Chattanooga, TN 37043-1823
(423) 756-2044
E-mail: psichi@psichi.org

Table 9.3 also includes sources where the specific conference dates and locations can be found.

Professional Conferences

Professional conferences differ from undergraduate research conferences in that they are organized for academic psychologists and practitioners. Across time, many of these conferences have embraced student involvement by allowing Psi Chi, the National Honor Society of Psychology, to host special paper or poster sessions for its members. Table 9.4 contains a list of the regional and national conferences that routinely sponsor Psi Chi sessions. Besides presenting their own work, a decided benefit for the students who attend these conferences is the opportunity to attend other sessions devoted to topics that interest them, as well as to hear prominent scholars discuss their latest research. If you are interested in participating in the Psi Chi sessions at one of these conferences, contact the Psi Chi National Office for more information (see the bottom of table 9.4).

Exercise 9.B: Answering a Call for Papers: Writing a Conference Abstract or Proposal

How does one begin the process of conference participation? By answering a *Call for Papers.* What is a *Call for Papers?* It is an invitation to submit your work to a conference. Most *Calls* appear in psychological

TABLE 9.5

A SAMPLE CALL FOR PAPERS FROM AN UNDERGRADUATE RESEARCH CONFERENCE

MORAVIAN COLLEGE   BETHLEHEM, PENNSYLVANIA

The Lehigh Valley Association
of Independent Colleges

announces the

**SEVENTH ANNUAL LEHIGH VALLEY
UNDERGRADUATE PSYCHOLOGY CONFERENCE**

to be held at

MORAVIAN COLLEGE

SATURDAY, APRIL 4, 1992

**FEATURED SPEAKER
DR. BARRY SCHWARTZ**

Professor of Psychology, Swarthmore College

CALL FOR PAPERS

- Two double-spaced typewritten copies of an abstract, 100-150 words, showing title of paper, author(s), institution, and name and signature of faculty sponsor should be submitted.

- The Conference will include paper presentations and poster sessions.

- Abstracts are to be mailed to Drs. Dana S. Dunn and Stacey B. Zaremba, Psychology Department, Moravian College, 1200 Main Street, Bethlehem, PA 18018 **no later than March 6, 1992.**

- You will be notified of your acceptance. If your abstract is accepted, it is understood that you are commited to present your work.

GENERAL INFORMATION

- Registration is at 8:30 a.m. and presentations begin at 9:00 a.m.

- Pre-registration fee $5; registration at door, $6.

- Abstracts will be published in a *Proceedings* booklet.

- Directions to Moravian College and information about accommodations will be forwarded to the authors of accepted abstracts.

ANY QUESTIONS?

Call 215-861-1316

---

periodicals or, even more typically, in poster form. You are apt to see *Calls* posted on one of the bulletin boards in your institution's Psychology Department. A sample poster from an undergraduate conference held at my institution a few years ago is shown in table 9.5. This particular poster included specific information about the *Call for Papers*, general information about the conference, specification of its time and place, and an announcement that a featured speaker was invited.

Some *Calls* are tailored to specific topical areas within psychology; others are broad invitations open to any area of inquiry. Those aimed at student audiences are usually of the latter variety (see table 9.5). As will be discussed shortly, *Calls for Papers* usually request interested students or researchers to submit either a short abstract describing the research or a longer, somewhat more detailed proposal. Many student conferences require faculty sponsorship, so be certain to have a faculty advisor read and approve any submitted materials (the submission form will have a place for your advisor's signature).

One word of advice: Submission deadlines are to be taken very seriously. *Be sure to allocate enough time to complete all the submission requirements.* If you wait until the last minute and send your work in late, it will probably be rejected out-of-hand. Deadlines are not meant to be punitive; rather, they are typically used to deal with a huge volume of submissions. So, avoid heartache and unnecessary rejection by submitting on time.

Conference abstracts. Many conferences, especially those aimed at undergraduate students, want to receive only a short summary of your research in answer to a *Call for Papers*. This summary is really no different than—indeed, it is usually called—an abstract. Similar to the information provided in table 9.5, most such abstracts are no more than 100 to 150 words in length, although the *Call for Papers* will specify the desired length. *Whatever that length turns out to be, do not exceed it.* Your Abstract should follow the basic format discussed in chapter 3 (see p. 81–82), except that you should add your name and the college or university you attend beneath it. Keep in mind that an abstract needs to be general enough that naive but interested readers (and conference organizers) can understand what you did, what you found, and why.

Besides submitting a few copies of your Abstract to a conference, it is likely that you will need to indicate whether you prefer to be part of a paper or a poster session. Consider the respective virtues of each type of presentation format and select the one you believe will represent your research in the best light. Normally, you will also include a self-addressed stamped envelope with the submission materials so that the conference organizers can let you know if your work is accepted for presentation.

Conference proposals. Other conferences want to see more detail about your research than is available in a short abstract. *Calls* usually provide necessary details regarding what should appear in such proposals; general practice dictates a Title, Abstract page, one page containing the Introduction and the Method, and one page that includes the Results and Discussion sections. A page for references, and any needed for figures or tables, follow—in short, your proposal will be around 5 pages in length.

When writing your proposal, rely on the modified KISS rule and highlight only a few key points (Taylor & Martin, 1987). Even the most interested reviewer looks for the big picture, which can all too easily become lost in overly complicated discussion. Stay focused, be brief, and write only what is absolutely necessary to convey the main ideas of your research.

Finally, do not be fooled by the term "proposal" and assume that the *Call for Papers* is seeking incomplete (i.e., "proposed") work. Finished products are preferred; those nearing completion are sometimes acceptable. Conference organizers want presenters who will actually present their work. If your research is not at a stage where you can guarantee you will have data to present, don't submit.

Concluding comments on answering a Call for Papers. If you submit your work and it is accepted, you *must* go and present it. It is very bad form not to do so. Sometimes people submit a presentation topic and then change their minds about attending the conference. This sort of behavior is unprofessional and unacceptable because it disrupts the work of others, organizers as well as fellow submitters. If you go to the trouble to submit a proposal, and the conference organizers and reviewers go to the trouble to read, review, and accept your work, then be courteous and fulfill your obligation. When personal circumstances absolutely prevent you from attending a conference, notify the conference organizers and arrange for someone else to present your paper or poster for you.

Journals: Undergraduate and Professional

Psychological journals are a third forum for the presentation of your research. Students sometimes wrongly assume that submitting research for publication may be a goal well beyond their reach. Undergraduate research is usually published in one of two places, student journals and in mainstream psychology journals.

Undergraduate Journals Over the last several years, journals specifically aimed at publishing undergraduate scholarship have begun to appear. Occasionally, for example, psychology departments at colleges and universities have published "in-house" periodicals containing student work. These local publications are an excellent way for students to take a first stab at presenting their written work to an audience beyond the classroom.

More recently, however, several national student journals in psychology have sprung up. Table 9.6 contains the names and addresses of four such journals you should consider as publication outlets for your research. Similar to "in-house" journals, these national journals are meant to be a first outlet for students, as they are devoted exclusively to undergraduate research in psychology. To their credit, these journals tend to adopt the style and standards found among respected mainstream journals in psychology. That is, they seek to publish original work; they adhere to APA style and format; a peer review process is often employed and an editorial board exists; communication regarding manuscript content occurs between author and editor; and some maintain author anonymity during the review process.

TABLE 9.6

PUBLICATION OUTLETS FOR UNDERGRADUATES

Each of the following journals publishes undergraduate student research. Write each one to learn specific submission requirements and procedures.

Journal of Undergraduate Studies
Department of Psychology
Pace University
861 Bedford Road
Pleasantville, NY 10570

Modern Psychological Studies: A Journal of Undergraduate Research
Department of Psychology
University of Tennessee at Chattanooga
615 McCallie Avenue
Chattanooga, TN 37403–2598

The Journal of Psychology and the Behavioral Sciences
Department of Psychology
Fairleigh Dickinson University
Madison, NJ 07904

The Psi Chi Journal of Student Research
Psi Chi National Office
407 East Fifth Street, Suite B
Chattanooga, TN 37043–1823

Most of these journals will include a *statement of purpose,* which serves to disclose the publication's mission and to help potential authors decide whether to submit their work. Keep in mind that these journals are appropriately student-centered. As one of the journals, *Modern Psychological Studies,* remarks in its statement of purpose:

. . . we at *MPS* wish to emphasize to fellow undergraduates that

- we are capable of doing meaningful quality work and of communicating that work to interested students and professionals.
- we are capable ourselves of directing the meandering focus of the psychological profession.

A journal will also typically include a list of *submission guidelines.* These guidelines serve to describe the sorts of manuscripts being sought by the journal (e.g., empirical, theoretical, literature reviews), what the preparation of the manuscript entails, and occasionally a sponsoring statement from a faculty advisor. A copy of these guidelines usually can be found in a copy of the journal (check your library) or can be obtained by contacting the journal's editor (see addresses noted in table 9.6).

Professional Journals Increasingly, research by undergraduates is appearing in major psychology journals, some of which specifically

---

BOX FEATURE 9.C

A Research Digression: Negotiating Authorship, or Who's on First?

Solo researchers do not have to negotiate authorship, but what about members of research teams? Who should be listed as the first (or last) author? Should team members be listed alphabetically, by the amount of their contributions (and who is a fair judge of that!?), or some other scheme? What if two people shared the work and their last names begin with the same letter? Worst of all, what if a student collaborates with a faculty advisor on a project: Should the student give the faculty member primary authorship, or vice versa? Believe it or not, this issue stirs up strong emotions in students and faculty, each of whom can have different points of view on the matter (Ross & Sicoly, 1979; Taylor & Martin, 1987).

In song and story, of course, academic life is supposed to be above the petty jealousies and competition that occur outside the college's hallowed halls and ivied walls. Don't believe it. Understandably, people want credit to equal perceived effort, so the issue of order of authorship—whose name is listed first, second, and so on, beneath the title of a paper, poster, or publication—can be a problem *unless* it is handled properly.

Where graduate students are concerned, APA's ethical standards actually stipulate that when data are primarily from a student's masters thesis or doctoral dissertation, that student should receive first authorship. Many faculty members who direct undergraduate honors theses, independent studies, and the like, follow this quite reasonable practice even though it is not mandated by the APA. Where undergraduate research is concerned, then, be aware that faculty advisors can accept or decline first authorship on any resulting works at their own discretion.

Traditionally, first authorship is reserved for the individual who developed the research idea in the first place. Many times, this person is easily identified, but other times, the project is truly a group effort and no one can remember who came up with what innovation when. Very often, the hardest worker is easily recognized. Sometimes, though, idiosyncratic solutions are used; occasionally, the Author Notes of a publication will reveal that the order of authorship was determined "at random" or that "the authors are listed alphabetically because contributions were equal."

Naturally, the way out of these and other odd exercises is to discuss the authorship issues early, during a project's planning stage. Certainly, the issue of authorship should be considered at the same time a team's research contract is developed (see Exercise 1.B). Guidelines on this matter can be found in sections 1.03 and 6.05 of the *Publication Manual* (American Psychological Association, 1994; see also, American Psychological Association, 1992, section 6.23). In any case, remember that open communication and honesty are critical to the research process!

---

welcome undergraduate or graduate student submissions as part of an award competition (e.g., *Personality and Social Psychology Bulletin*). This is a very good sign because it suggests that students are forming close research collaborations with their faculty advisors and that they are addressing timely questions. Indeed, these student papers are often co-authored by faculty advisors.

Each professional psychology journal will contain a *statement of purpose* as well as *submission guidelines* to guide you. Share this information with your faculty advisor and listen carefully to his or her counsel about whether and where to submit your work.

Be aware that competition for acceptance in a professional journal is stiff, as the rejection rate for submissions can reach or even exceed 90 percent. Nonetheless, if your academic advisor believes that your project is worth a shot, all that you have to lose is the cost of postage and the time associated with refining the manuscript for submission; the former is not much and the latter is good practice. Whatever the outcome of your effort, you can learn quite a bit about academic publishing and get high-quality feedback on your project from an editor and peer reviewers. Such advice is invaluable for revising your current work and planning future research.

Submission Suggestions   How long should a manuscript be when it is ready for submission to an undergraduate or professional journal? At the risk of appearing glib and unhelpful, the answer is this: as long as it needs to be. The faculty member supervising your research or who taught the class where the work was produced should be able to give you suggestions about appropriate length. I would urge you to strive, however, for a total of 15 to 20 double-spaced, wordprocessed APA style pages.

When you take into account the space allotted to APA style considerations, the space reserved for actual text is fairly small. As a result, you must use the space wisely and well, which means that your prose must be concise. You will want to revisit the directions for drafting and writing an APA style paper in chapter 3 (see especially table 3.5), just as you will need to seek peer feedback on any draft(s) you produce before you submit them to a journal (see Exercise 3.B).

Some readers will no doubt want to submit a course paper presenting an original experiment or the results of a replication study to a student journal. Resist the temptation to slip the paper into an envelope and mail it off to the journal right away. Instead, review and incorporate any of the suggestions or corrections marked on the paper by faculty members. If any fatal flaws in the logic of the experiment's design, your argument, or the results were identified, then you will need to address them in a revised version of the manuscript (depending on the scope or depth of this criticism, you may decide against submitting the manuscript for publication).

Even if these issues can be easily addressed in a revision, you should still carefully re-read the paper yourself. As you do so, try to read it from the perspective of a naive but interested reader: What aspects of the text require additional explanation? Are some parts of the text overly detailed? If so, can they be summarized succinctly, edited back, or even removed? Be certain that the Method section is sufficiently detailed so as to allow an undergraduate peer to replicate the result you obtained. Have you come across any new references since the paper was first written? If so, will their inclusion improve the paper? Finally, have a peer read the final draft before you send it off so that you can be sure the writing was pitched to the appropriate audience.

Best of luck on submitting a manuscript, but be aware that your work is not necessarily over even if (or optimistically, *when*) it is accepted for publication. It can take some time to hear from the journal—patience is the great unsung virtue of the practical researcher—and there may be a revision process where an editor has you make some alterations to the manuscript. Such alterations can be cosmetic or substantive; the former fit your work into the journal's existing style or tighten your prose, the latter involve satisfying suggestions offered by peer and/or faculty reviewers. If revisions are required, accept the suggestions gratefully and incorporate those that improve the paper (you will find that most do!). Consult the editor about those you find inappropriate, keeping in mind a publishing maxim: Reviewers are usually right; editors always are.

Once you have navigated these shoals, you will have the printed work—your words and ideas—in hand, and you should be justifiably proud of yourself. Your pride in this accomplishment is especially meaningful when you consider the median career publication rate for academic psychologists, which is zero (Boice & Jones, 1984). In other words, fully half of all academic psychologists have never written a book or a book chapter or published an article (see also, Sax, Astin, Arredondo, & Korn, 1996). By taking the initiative and exerting some effort, you can join a select group of individuals who care about expanding knowledge about psychology. So get started, write up your research, and plan to earn hearty congratulations for a job well done.

CONCLUSION

Students of psychology—and I include faculty here, as well—often forget that the presentation of results represents a creative process. As we explore a topic by reading about it, thinking about it, and conducting experiments or other research concerning it, we alter our understanding of it. This alteration is to be expected, even welcomed, because it means that psychological knowledge is not static.

As you prepare to speak or write about your research project, I recommend that you keep in mind the wise observation of Graham Wallas (1926, p. 106):

> The little girl had the making of a poet in her who, being told to be sure of her meaning before she spoke, said, "How can I know what I think till I see what I say?"

SUMMARY

For scientific knowledge in the field of psychology to flourish, presenting results and sharing ideas remain essential activities. These activities form scholarly communication, which ensures that knowledge does not remain isolated or that it is available to only a select few individuals (Hills, 1983). Learning to speak well and to write well advances these goals. Scholarly communication in psychology is not limited to professors and practitioners; rather it must be undertaken by interested students, as well, who will appreciate the opportunity to present in the classroom, at conferences, or even to publish what they have written.

KEY TERMS

Call for Papers (p. 301)
conference abstract (p. 303)
conference proposal (p. 303)

journals' statement of
  purpose (p. 305)
journals' submission
  guidelines (p. 305)

paper presentation (p. 294)
poster session (p. 298)
symposium (p. 296)

SUGGESTED READINGS

Gronbeck, B. E., McKerrow, R. E., Ehninger, D., & Monroe, A. H. (1997). *Principles and types of speech communication* (13th ed.). New York: Longman. In print since 1935, this classic text covers the principles of speech and communication, emphasizing ways to improve the public speaking skills of students.

Lucas, S. E. (1995). *The art of public speaking* (5th ed.). New York: McGraw-Hill. A concise and practical guide to public speaking, one that relies on step-by-step instruction to plan, research, and deliver presentations to audiences.

Sternberg, R. J. (1993). *The psychologist's companion: A guide to scientific writing for students and researchers* (3rd ed.). New York: Cambridge University Press. One chapter provides savvy advice on winning acceptances from psychology journals, and another, the book's last chapter, contains brief but helpful suggestions on writing and presenting a lecture.

CHAPTER 10

Closing Thoughts and Future Directions

Traditional endings in research methods books are rarely satisfying. In fact, few research methods text books in psychology actually even have concluding chapters. Most end rather abruptly, making no mention of the fact that the pedagogical portion of the book is finished; the reader is alerted to this fact by running into the appendices. If any attempt at closure occurs, it is apt to be very, very short.

I hope to change this tradition. Although this chapter is briefer than the others in this book, there is more than a professional farewell here. Indeed, this chapter has three important purposes: to tie material from earlier chapters together, to revisit the role of questions in psychological research, and to motivate you to reflect on the importance of what you have learned. At the same time, of course, it should satisfy the innate desire for closure.

Exercise 10.A: Bringing It All Together —A Checklist for Research Projects

Back in chapter 1, the five stages of a typical research project—the *idea stage*, the *implementation stage*, the *analysis and interpretation stage*, the *writing stage*, and the *presentation stage*—were introduced. In subsequent chapters, the various activities occurring in each stage were articulated in detail. The whole purpose of this text has been to present practical perspectives and supporting exercises designed to make research activities accessible, efficient, and ultimately effective. Many readers no doubt felt somewhat daunted by the amount of preparation a solid, theoretically grounded research project requires. In the end, however, such background effort invariably results in a better piece of research.

Nonetheless, we must acknowledge that there are quite a number of discrete activities to manage in the course of any research project. A checklist can often be used to plan a research project, to note completed activities, and to identify those still requiring attention. Table 10.1 is offered as a way to keep track of many of these activities, and specific exercises, tables, figures, and conceptual issues from earlier chapters are indicated throughout this checklist. Although it is quite detailed, please be aware that the checklist in table 10.1 cannot catalog every conceivable part of a given project; some projects will require greater levels of detail, others much less. Nor does table 10.1 indicate the amount of conceptual as well as practical overlap that occurs among these activities. Yet, having this checklist as both guide and record should help solo investigators and research teams alike organize what needs to be done to create a good piece of research.

Similar to several previous exercises, tables, and figures in this book, table 10.1 is meant to be consulted often during the course of a project. It is also true that you should loop back within and between any one of the five stages as a project progresses. Practical researchers should rely on this checklist for guidance, planning, or organization at every stage in the life of a project. Please note that there is also space provided at the bottom of table 10.1 where any unanticipated, project-specific issues can be recorded.

TABLE 10.1

A CHECKLIST FOR RESEARCH PROJECTS

1. Idea Stage
_____Create a realistic project time line (Exercise 1.A) (p. 22)
_____Decide whether to collaborate or to work alone
    _____Develop a peer research contract (Exercise 1.B) (p. 32)
_____Keep a notebook of research ideas (Exercise 2.A) (p. 58)
_____Freewrite to generate and refine ideas (Exercise 2.B) (p. 61)
_____Brainstorm to generate project ideas (Exercise 2.C) (p. 62)
_____Search the psychological literature
    _____Keep a search record (Exercise 4.A) (p. 124)
    _____Evaluate selected articles (Exercise 4.B) (p. 128) and books (Exercise 4.C) (p. 129)
    _____Use notecards (Exercise 4.D) (p. 135)
_____Develop a hypothesis and determine research design
    _____Will the study be an experiment, or an applied or field study?
_____Develop operational definitions for independent variables and dependent measures (Exercise 6.A) (p. 175)
_____Develop an analysis plan (see Exercise 8.A) (p. 270)
    _____Choose appropriate statistical tests in advance (see table 8.3) (p. 274)

Continued

TABLE 10.1 (*Continued*)

2.Implementation Stage

____Identify participants

____Will they be treated ethically?

____Prepare an IRB form (Exercise 5.A) (p. 148)

____Form an in-class IRB if no formal committee exists (Exercise 5.B) (p. 150)

____Write an Informed Consent Form (Exercise 5.C or 7.C) (p. 153 or p. 250)

____Recruit participants

____Create a research participants sign-up sheet (Exercise 5.D) (p. 156)

____Create a course credit slip if none is available (Exercise 5.E) (p. 157)

____Decide how participants will be assigned to conditions (Exercise 7.B) (p. 245)

____Prepare to carry out the study

____Create an experimental script (Exercise 6.B) (p. 180)

____Create a record of experimental conditions (Exercise 6.C) (p. 182)

____Consider developing a manipulation check (Exercise 6.D) (p. 183)

____Create a dependent measure record (Exercise 6.E) (p. 192)

____Consider threats to internal validity

____If applicable, keep a record of potentially relate variables (Exercise 7.B) (p. 245)

____Pilot test the experiment

____Plan the debriefing

____Create a debriefing survey (Exercise 5.F) (p. 163)

____Write a debriefing sheet (Exercise 5.G) (p. 165)

____Collect the data

3.Analysis and Interpretation Stage

____Implement the analysis plan (see Exercise 8.A) (p. 270)

____Code and analyze the data

____Put the results into words (Exercise 8.B) (p. 279)

____Create any necessary data displays (tables, figures, graphs)

____Store the data and analyses

4.Writing Stage

____Write an APA style summary of the research

____Do an outline (Exercise 3.A) (p. 96)

____Receive peer feedback on your draft (Exercise 3.B) (p. 102)

____Revise the draft based on peer comments

____Provide feedback to peers (Exercise 3.C) (p. 104)

____Consider submitting the paper for publication in an undergraduate journal (see table 9.6) (p. 305)

5.Presentation Stage

____Develop a presentation based on the study

____Organize a student research symposium (Exercise 9.A) (p. 296)

____Answer a "Call for Papers" (Exercise 9.B) (p. 301)

Other Project Issues:

ASKING THE RIGHT QUESTIONS IN PSYCHOLOGICAL RESEARCH

. . . a firm grasp of methodology can free researchers to pursue interesting questions of substance. But it can also result in their becoming fixated on questions of methodology at the expense of questions of substance.
—Robert J. Sternberg (1997, p. 14)

Sternberg's (1997) message here should give us some pause—or should it? We have spent quite a bit of time reviewing the theory and practice of research, but we still need to remind ourselves that methodology, regardless of its utility, is not the main point of the research enterprise. As Sternberg frames the issue, we need to remind ourselves what makes research worth doing in the first place.

Some suggestions in this vein were made at the start of chapter 1, and by now you should have a clearer vision of the research process, one that implicitly incorporates many of those points. With your recently acquired knowledge of psychological methods, it is equally important to consider *what sorts of research questions are worth asking.* Healthy skepticism, a habit I hope you have been cultivating in the course of this book, invites critical evaluation of research you generate as well as that created by peers or found in the psychological literature. In the future, as you think about research, be sure to balance the desire for methodological rigor gained here (and in any future psychology courses you take) with concern about quality and scope of the questions being asked.

Sternberg (1997, p. 14) offers five questions students (and, I think, their instructors) should ask themselves as they evaluate any research questions:

1. Is the question scientifically important? Why or why not?
2. What is the question's scope? Does it seek to explain a great deal or comparatively little?
3. What are the best and worst possible outcomes we might predict for the research?
4. If successful results are produced, how much of a change will they contribute to psychological theory or empirical knowledge?
5. Is there reason to believe that readers will be interested in the results? Why?

There are no doubt many other questions to ask and profit from answering. Yet Sternberg's (1997) point is clear: As producers and consumers of psychological knowledge, we should seek substance in our reactions rather than dwelling on small flaws or minor criticisms. Errors must be identified in any work, of course, but sometimes great ideas or insights contain imperfections that do not—must not—reduce their potential to teach and advance inquiry. I hope that you will try to address Sternberg's valid concerns and at the same time cultivate your own views on what constitutes good, even great, research in the field of psychology. In the end, such concern has practical effects that benefit the greater psychological community.

THE PLACE OF RESEARCH: SKILLS ACQUIRED, SKILLS APPLIED

Can a thorough understanding of research methods in psychology benefit students outside of this or other courses in the future? Yes. Some students who use this book are probably planning to attend graduate school in psychology or a related discipline. These individuals may be thinking about an academic or practitioner career, or one where research abilities of one type or another are important. Others are considering professional school options, preparing for a career in the law, business, or even medicine, among others. These individuals, too, have a sense that research skills are useful and readily applicable to a variety of professional settings. Still other students are planning to enter the working world immediately after graduation from college. The latter group is composed of people with varied interests; some know that research skills will help them, others are not sure, and a few may be indifferent about the issue.

No matter what path you follow in or outside of college settings, an understanding of the research process will benefit you. Anyone would be hard pressed to point to a profession that could not—or does not—profit from individuals who are trained to conduct and interpret research findings. Whether you study or help people, the two sides of the psychological coin, or if you decide to teach, manufacture or sell things, provide a service, or take part in political or bureaucratic enterprises, your experience with the research process will further the cause of whatever profession you join. In the words of Booth, Colomb, and Williams (1995, p. 3), "In any field, you will need the skills that only research can help you master, whether you expect to design the production line or to run it."*

Beyond this practical side, there is a personal advantage associated with the research process. You will never work so well, think so systematically, or understand and learn about a topic in such depth as when you research it. The skills you have acquired through reading this text and, I hope, conducting your own piece of research should not be underestimated. Think about it: You can now conduct a research project from start to finish, from problem conceptualization to analysis and write-up. Between those poles, you now know how to collect information, search the relevant literature, evaluate, critique, and extend it by conducting your own independent work.

Still, readers may wonder, does exposure to principles of research methodology in general have any lasting effects? Certainly it does. People's inferential reasoning is enhanced by such exposure; research shows that people can reason in the abstract about everyday life events, and not only about the concrete examples usually studied within classroom settings (e.g., Fong, Krantz, & Nisbett, 1986; Nisbett, Fong, Lehman, &

*Source: Booth, W. C., Columb, G. G., & Williams, J. M. (1995). *The Craft of Research.* Chicago: University of Chicago Press. Reprinted with permission.

Cheng, 1987; see also, Nisbett, Krantz, Jepson, & Kunda, 1983). Students who major in the social sciences, for example, improve their reasoning abilities in research methodology and statistics across four years of college (Lehman & Nisbett, 1990). Indeed, students in psychology and its sister disciplines—sociology, anthropology, economics, and political science—show greater improvement in these two areas in that time frame than their student counterparts in either the natural sciences (e.g., physics, biology) or the humanities (e.g., English, history) (Lehman & Nisbett, 1990).

Taking a course in research methods in psychology has been found to affect students' reasoning about real-life events as well as psychological phenomena in the short run, as well. VanderStoep and Shaughnessy (1997) tested groups of students enrolled in Research Methods and Developmental Psychology, respectively, at the beginning and end of a semester. The students answered a 7-item measure designed to elicit their understanding of various methodological (e.g., selection bias, spurious causal relations) and basic statistical concepts. The questions were written in lay rather than methodological or statistical terms, and each one provided the participants with choice among four or five alternatives.

See how well you do on this sample item from VanderStoep and Shaughnessy (1997, p. 123):

> Suppose it were discovered that students who majored in math, engineering, or computer science scored higher on tests measuring "problem-solving" ability at the end of 4 years of college than did students who did not major in these fields. How would you interpret this information?
>
> a. Physical science training has positive effects that improve complex reasoning ability.
> b. Math, engineering, and computer science majors have more class assignments that require students to use complex reasoning.
> c. Physical science majors may differ on many other things besides problem-solving ability, and they would have scored higher at the beginning of their freshmen year as well.
> d. It is likely that physical science students will score lower on tests of *verbal* ability.

Which alternative did you select? If you chose "c" you were correct. Based on the available evidence, this answer illustrates that the relationship between one's choice of major and future problem-solving abilities may not be causal (i.e., the lack of any pretest scores precludes drawing any causal conclusion).

A graph of the pretest and posttest scores for both participant groups is shown in figure 10.1. Students enrolled in Developmental Psychology received an average of 2.38 at the start of the term and 2.84 at its conclusion. In contrast, the Research Methods students began with a score of 3.0 and ended up with an average of 4.97. The data analysis revealed that the Research Methods students showed greater improvement than did

FIGURE 10.1

Mean Performance for Students Enrolled in Research Methods or Developmental Psychology. *Note:* Means are based on number correct on a 7-item measure (see VanderStoep & Shaughnessy, 1997).

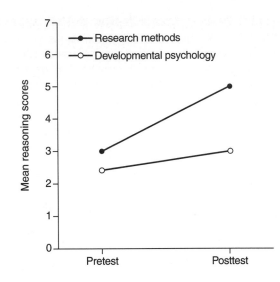

A Research Digression: "No Pressure—Just Lovely, Interesting Discussions"

The best way to appreciate research is to appreciate the things taking place around you. Psychology—a systematic study of mental life and behavior—is just one of those things. Cultivate your ability to notice things in the tradition of the late physicist, Richard P. Feynman (1988, pp. 15–16), a man who surely knew a great deal about psychology:

My father taught me to notice things. One day, I was playing with an "express wagon," a little wagon with a railing around it. It had a ball in it, and when I pulled the wagon, I noticed something about the way the ball moved. I went to my father and said, "Say, Pop, I noticed something. When I pull the wagon, the ball rolls to the back of the wagon. And when I'm pulling it along and I suddenly stop, the ball rolls to the front of the wagon. Why is that?"

"That, nobody knows," he said. "The general principle is that things which are moving tend to keep on moving, and things which are standing still tend to stand still, unless you push them hard. This tendency is called 'inertia,' but nobody knows why it's true." Now, that's a deep understanding. He didn't just give me the name.

He went on to say, "If you look from the side, you'll see that it's the back of the wagon that you're pulling against the ball, and the ball stands still. As a matter of fact, from the friction it starts to move forward a little bit in relation to the ground. It doesn't move back."

That's the way I was educated by my father, with those kinds of examples and discussions: no pressure—just lovely, interesting discussions. It has motivated me for the rest of my life, and makes me interested in *all* the sciences. (It just happens I do physics better.)

May you have lovely, interesting discussions about behavior that prove to be as revealing.

TABLE 10.2

DISTINCTIVE SKILLS OF PSYCHOLOGY STUDENTS

Literacy—Able to write in several literacy formats (e.g., essays, reports, concise pieces).

Numeracy—Can interpret data summaries and understand probability statements.

Computer literacy—Able to use computers, can select appropriate software.

Information finding skills—Know traditional and contemporary (e.g., CD-ROM) library search skills.

Research skills—Familiar with experimental, observational, applied and field research techniques.

Measurement skills—Trained to operationalize independent and dependent variables, and capable of designing questionnaires and other measurement tools.

Environmental awareness—Understand that settings (work, home, school, leisure) affect people's behavior.

Interpersonal awareness—Aware of appropriate communication skills and sensitive to sources of conflict.

Problem-solving skills—Trained to systematically analyze and solve intellectual and practical problems.

Critical evaluation—Able to constructively use skepticism to evaluate inquiry and action in research and life.

Perspective—Appreciate that people have different points of view.

Higher-order analysis—Can extract general principles or spot patterns in human behavior by engaging in deeper analyses.

Pragmatism—Realize that no experiment is perfect, that successive approximation to truth is useful.

Note: Skills relevant to research methods are *italicized*. Skills list adapted from Hayes (1997).

those enrolled in the other course of study (see figure 10.1). The authors concluded that exposure to research methods in psychology can promote people's ability to think more critically about real-life events (Vander-Stoep & Shaughnessy, 1997).

Does learning about research methods and psychological issues more broadly provide students with other distinctive skills? Again, the answer is definitely "yes." Students who major in psychology develop skills in at least thirteen different areas, which are briefly summarized in table 10.2 (Hayes, 1997; see also, Hayes, 1996). Several of these skills are clearly based on or related to research methods and the experience of conducting projects (for your convenience, these particular areas appear in *italics*). Hayes (1997) argues that studying psychology provides students with different forms of expertise, a claim few other academic disciplines can make. So, whatever your future holds, the time spent learning about the field of psychology, and its methods, will serve you well.

LOVING THE RESEARCH PROCESS: A RESPONSIBILITY

Has this book inspired you to enjoy conducting research? Perhaps that is too strong a word and too great a hope for a first encounter with research methods in psychology. I am confident, however, that the contents of this book pushed you to think a bit and gave you some direction, as well as increased your appreciation of the methodological side of the study of behavior. More than that, I hope that you will learn to love the research process in the future.

Love the research process? That's right, love it. The word *love* may seem odd in this context, but it is not out of place if you consider research to be an enterprise that generates passion and commitment: the formation of good, clear research questions, the creation of a hypothesis to test the question, the development of a study design to complement the hypothesis, and so forth. These acts require both effort and time, but above all they invite a belief in possibilities—questions leading to answers and, at the same time, new questions. A research endeavor can be done mechanically, of course, but when it is done with enthusiasm and direction, the labor can become one of love.

As with any love or strong feeling toward any activity, there is an accompanying responsibility. You are intellectually, even morally, responsible to use the research knowledge and skills you have acquired to deal with life both in and beyond the classroom. Asking the right questions, being rigorous in searching for answers, and appropriately using research methodology to make proper inferences are the duties of all researchers, especially practical ones. You should bring the same level of critical sophistication to the evaluation of information in the campus newspaper or the evening newscast as you do a published journal article or the idea for a study being contemplated by a peer. The tasks vary in scope, but your engagement with them should be active.

I will close this book by citing the words of Tarfon, the rabbinic sage who said, "You are not required to complete the work, but neither are you at liberty to abstain from it." I hope that this book helps you to fulfill your responsibility as a practical researcher and that your love for research as product and process will continue to grow in the future.

SUMMARY

This concluding chapter began with a practical checklist for research projects (Exercise 10.A). Applicable to experimental or field research, the checklist should be consulted in the course of any project. The chapter closed with a recommendation to love the research process and to responsibly consider its products.

KEY TERM

checklist for research projects (p. 311)

SUGGESTED READINGS

Brannigan, G. G., & Merrens, M. R. (Eds.). (1993). *The undaunted psychologist: Adventures in research.* Philadelphia, PA: Temple University Press. Fifteen notable psychologists discuss their lives, intellectual development, and sometimes serendipitous—but always interesting—research findings. This book is inspiring and easy to read.

Feynman, R. P. (1988). *What do you care what other people think? Further adventures of a curious character.* New York: W. W. Norton and Company. A character with a great deal of character discusses science and its relation to life.

Keller, P. A. (Ed.). (1994). *Academic paths: Career decisions and experiences of psychologists.* Hillsdale, NJ: Lawrence Erlbaum Associates, Inc. Thirteen autobiographies by academic psychologists who describe diverse intellectual journeys and work in different types of institutional settings. A good introduction for students who seek a behind-the-scenes view of the lives and careers of academic psychologists.

Sample Student Manuscript Written in American Psychological Association (APA) Style

Consecutive numbering begins on the Title page; a short heading appears to the left of the page number.

Running head: HUMOR AND SPATIAL REASONING

The running head is flush left, and the abbreviated title appears in capital letters.

APA titles are short but descriptive, and typically no more than 15 words in length.

A Funny Thing Happened:

Humor's Influence on Spatial Reasoning

Barbara Loecher

Moravian College

The author's name appears above an institutional affiliation.

APA style papers appear on 8½ × 11 inch white paper.

Abstract

This experiment tested the hypothesis that humor can enhance problem solving, and that its effect on this ability is more marked than positive affect generally. To test this hypothesis, a spatial reasoning test was given to three groups of participants—a control group, a group in which positive affect had been elicited with a gift of candy, and a group that had just reviewed seven cartoons that were judged humorous in a pretest. Performance was compared to see whether the group who reviewed the cartoons scored significantly higher than the other two. Contrary to expectations and previous research, there were no significant differences among the groups' average scores. Possible explanations for the lack of between-group differences are discussed.

The Abstract appears separately on page 2 of the APA style paper.

The Abstract is not indented.

The hypothesis is presented in the Abstract.

The margins are at least 1 inch on each side.

The left margin of an APA style paper is always even, but the right margin remains uneven.

A Funny Thing Happened:

Humor's Influence on Spatial Reasoning

When people laugh at the punch line of a joke, they feel good. At the heart of most humor is an incongruity waiting to be discovered. In essence, "getting" humor involves recognizing the incongruity and resolving it. To this extent, getting humor is similar to solving problems (e.g., Belanger, Kirkpatrick, & Derks, in press). In a related way, other research has found that positive affect enhances creative problem solving (Isen, 1993; Isen, Daubman, & Nowicki, 1987). Favorable moods can be elicited by having research participants watch a humorous film (e.g., Isen & Gorgoglione, 1983, as cited in Isen et al., 1987) or by giving them an unexpected token, such as a gift of candy.

Positive mood appears to have a number of effects on cognition, and to have effects different from those associated with generalized arousal (Isen, 1993). For instance, positive affect aids in recall of positive information (Isen, Johnson, Mertz, & Robinson, 1985). Whether encouraged by a humorous film, or by a gift of candy, positive affect appears to enhance the ability to recognize relationships among things that are not obviously related, to integrate ideas, and to think more flexibly (Isen, 1993; Isen et al., 1987).

Could humor have additional effects on cognition—apart from the effects of a happy mood? Might people perform significantly better on cognitive tests when amused, than when feeling happy because, for instance, they've been given a small gift? Studies suggest that the cognitive processes that come into play when someone gets humor may prime the brain for certain problem-solving tasks (Belanger et al., in press; Derks, Gillikin, Bartolome, & Bogart, in press; Rauscher, Shaw, & Ky, 1995). Indeed, mentally processing humor triggers a specific sequence of electrical changes in the brain. About 300 msec after a person reads something that makes him or her laugh, for example, a positive wave sweeps the cortex. In turn, it is followed about 100 msec later by a negative wave (Derks et al.). These changes sweep the entire cortex, and involve neural networks that handle both sequential-verbal and pattern recognition tasks.

A sequence of positive and negative waves is also associated with complex information processing. A negative wave at 300 msec is associated with categorization, and a negative wave at 400 msec, with a disruption and then a possible extension of categorization. Humor processing, then, appears to activate a variety of neural networks throughout the cortex, just as other types of complex information processing tasks do (Derks et al., in press).

Related research suggests that cognitive processes that activate certain neural pathways might prime the brain for other cognitive tasks involving those same pathways (Belanger et al., in press; Rauscher et al., 1995). Rauscher and her colleagues found that listening to complex music—a Mozart piano sonata—resulted in short-term improvement in performance on a spatial reasoning test (Rauscher et al., 1995). In contrast, listening to a relaxation tape prior to taking the test had no effect on performance, nor did sitting in silence before taking the test. Since the researchers found no difference in pulse rates before and after each listening condition, arousal did not seem to be the contributing factor (see Rauscher, Shaw, & Ky, 1993).

It is possible that humor processing, which also appears to activate complex neural networks, may produce similar effects. That is, humor may have an effect on cognition that is distinct from—and

---

Standardized units of measurement are abbreviated.

After a first citation within a paragraph, no date is necessary.

Citations by different authors appear in alphabetical order by first author's last name.

stronger than—the effect of positive mood more generally. Humor processing may prime the brain for other complex cognitive tasks by activating neural pathways involved in the completion of those tasks. If so, people would be expected to score relatively higher on certain types of cognitive tests immediately after being amused by something than if they received a small, unexpected gift (a standard mood induction technique) before such tests. To test this hypothesis, a spatial reasoning test was administered to three groups of participants: a group that took the test immediately after reviewing seven cartoons that were judged humorous in a pretest, a second that took the test immediately after getting a gift of candy, and a control group.

> The hypothesis is clearly stated prior to the method section.

Method

> Sections of the APA style paper appear with no page breaks.

Participants

> First-level headings are centered but *not* underlined.

Participants were 17 (8 males, 9 females) staff members in the editorial and design departments of a publishing company, and 13 (7 males, 6 females) college students who received extra credit toward their psychology course grades.

> Second-level headings appear at the left margin and are underlined.

Design

Participants were assigned randomly to one of the three treatment groups—the control group, the candy group, and the humor group. The control group took a spatial reasoning test without any prior treatment. The candy group took the test immediately after receiving a gift—a bag of candy—found to induce positive affect in other studies (e.g., Isen et al., 1985). The humor group took the test immediately after reviewing seven cartoons judged humorous in a pretest.

> e.g. ("exempli gratia") means "for example."

Procedure

Each of the three groups solved 18 problems from the Paper Folding and Cutting section of the Stanford-Binet Intelligence

Test (Thorndike, Hagen, & Sattler, 1986). These were the same problems Rauscher and her colleagues (1985) used to test the effect of music on spatial intelligence.

Following the procedure used by Isen and her colleagues (1985), participants in the candy group received 15 pieces of assorted wrapped hard candy in a small, sealed plastic bag, immediately before they took the test. Members of the group were told that the gift was a token of appreciation for their participation—and assured the students in the group that they would earn extra credit for their participation, as well. To avoid confounding the results with any changes in blood sugar levels, group members were asked to put the candy aside so they could eat it later (Isen et al., 1985).

The humor group took the test immediately after reviewing seven cartoons from <u>The New Yorker</u> magazine. Each of the cartoons had been pretested by a sample of ten men and women drawn from the same population as participants in the study. In the pretest, cartoons were rated on a scale of 1 to 5, where a score of 1 indicated the cartoon was <u>not funny</u> and a score of 5 indicated it was <u>extremely funny</u>. All cartoons selected for the study had a mean score of 3 or higher.

In a manipulation check, participants in the humor group were invited to jot down a word or two describing their reactions to the seven cartoons immediately after reviewing them. Following Isen and colleagues (1985), participants in this group were informed that the cartoons were for use in an unrelated study, and that only their general reactions to the cartoons were of interest. Members of this group were told not to try to memorize anything from the cartoons, that they should simply review them, jot down a few words, then turn to the spatial reasoning test.

All participants were then informed that it was important that they do their best on the test. Isen has found that positive affect influences performance on a task <u>only</u> when participants are interested in the task or think it important (Isen, 1993).

After finishing the test, participants were debriefed in accordance with the American Psychological Association's Ethical Principles for the treatment of human research participants. All participants were asked to avoid discussing the study with others until all testing was completed.

Results

Based on results of earlier studies, participants who took a spatial reasoning test immediately after reviewing a series of cartoons that were judged humorous in a pretest were predicted to score higher than those who took the test immediately after receiving a gift designed to encourage positive affect (Belanger et al., in press; Derks et al., in press; Isen et al., 1987; Rauscher et al., 1995). It was assumed that those who took the test after receiving a small gift, in turn, would score higher on spatial reasoning than those who received no treatment (Isen et al., 1987). Unexpectedly, the study's results did not support this hypothesis.

Table 1 presents the data showing the mean scores participants earned on the spatial reasoning test—the 18-question Paper Folding and Cutting section of the Stanford-Binet Intelligence Scale (Thorndike et al., 1986). There were no effects due to gender, so this variable will not be mentioned further. Participant scores on the spatial reasoning test were analyzed using a one-way analysis of variance (ANOVA), which indicated that there were no significant differences among the three groups, F (2, 27) = .274, p > .05.

An abbreviation is spelled out the first time it appears.

Non-significant results must also be provided.

Insert Table 1 about here

As can be seen in Table 1, the mean score for the group that reviewed cartoons immediately prior to the test was higher than both the mean score for the group that received candy and the mean score for the control group. Contrary to expectation, however, the mean score for the candy group was lower than that for the control group.

The manipulation check administered to the humor group also showed some unexpected results. In a pretest, the stimulus cartoons were judged humorous but responses to the manipulation check revealed that only six of the ten participants in the humor group reported that the cartoons were, in fact, funny. The other four used words like "confused" and even "mad" to describe their responses.

Discussion

Although previous research suggests humor can enhance creative problem solving, and that humor's effect on problem-solving ability may be more marked than that of positive affect in general (Belanger et al., in press; Derks et al., in press; Isen et al., 1987; Rauscher et al., 1995), the results of the present study did not confirm these observations. Participants who reviewed cartoons before taking a spatial reasoning test did not earn a significantly higher mean score than those in the positive mood or no treatment control groups.

There are several reasons that no between-group differences materialized. First, it may be that the groups in this study—which included ten participants each—were too small. Studies positing links among humor, positive affect, and enhanced problem solving typically include larger numbers of participants in each group (e.g., Belanger et al., in press; Isen et al. 1987). Second, the results may also have been confounded with the humor group's unexpected responses to the cartoons. In a manipulation check, few participants in the humor group reported being amused by cartoons that were judged humorous in a pretest. Finally, the results could have been influenced by unexpected responses to the candy gift intended to evoke positive affect.

The latter explanation raises an interesting possibility. Though the difference was not significant, the mean score of the candy group was lower than that for the control group. Had this study included a larger number of participants in each group, this difference might have reached significance, thereby contradicting prior research on positive affect and problem solving (e.g., Isen, 1987). Though Isen has found that a bag of 15 pieces of candy invokes positive affect, it may not have done so in this study because the populations from which participants were drawn may have been significantly different from the general population and its attitudes toward candy. Half of the participants in the candy group were employees of a company that publishes books and magazines about health and fitness. Many of the people who work at this company are extremely careful about what they eat—and are particularly diligent about cutting back on fat and sugar. These participants may not have been pleased to get the candy; indeed, they may actually have been disappointed (D. S. Dunn, personal communication, April 20, 1997).

An example of how to cite a personal communication.

In light of research that suggests positive affect—whether encouraged by humor or other means—can improve problem solving, and studies that suggest humor processing may prime the brain for cognitive tasks in ways that positive affect does not, further study of humor's effect on problem solving is warranted. A larger-scale, more tightly controlled study to determine whether humor has an effect distinct from that of positive affect would be particularly appropriate.

Recommendations for future research are noted.

References

Belanger, H. G., Kirkpatrick, L. A., & Derks, P. (in press). The effects of humor on verbal and imaginal problem solving. HUMOR: International Journal of Humor Research.

Derks, P., Gillikin, L. S., Bartolome, D. S., & Bogart, E. H. (in press). Laughter and electroencephalographic activity. HUMOR: International Journal of Humor Research.

Isen, A. M., Johnson, M. M. S., Mertz, E., & Robinson, G. F. (1985). The influence of positive affect on the unusualness of word associations. Journal of Personality and Social Psychology, 48, 1413–1426.

Isen, A. M., Daubman, K. A., & Nowicki, G. P. (1987). Positive affect facilitates creative problem solving. Journal of Personality and Social Psychology, 52, 1122–1131.

Isen, A. M. (1993). Positive affect and decision making. In M. Lewis & J. M. Haviland (Eds.), Handbook of emotions (pp. 261–277). New York: The Guilford Press.

Rauscher, F. H., Shaw, G. L., & Ky, K. N. (1993). Music and spatial task performance [Letter to the editor]. Nature, 365, 611.

Rauscher, F. H., Shaw, G. L., & Ky, K. N. (1995). Listening to Mozart enhances spatial-temporal reasoning: Towards a neurophysiological basis. Neuroscience Letters, 185, 44–47.

Thorndike, R. L., Hagen, E. P., & Sattler, J. M. (1986). Stanford-Binet Intelligence Scale. (4th ed). Chicago: Riverside Publishing Co.

The References section begins on a new page.

The first line of a reference is indented 5 spaces.

Journal article.

Chapter in an edited book.

Letter to the editor.

Author notes, if any, appear on a separate page following the references section.

Author Note

This project was conducted to fulfill a course requirement in Statistics and Research Methods of Psychological Inquiry during the spring semester of 1997. Copies of the stimulus cartoons shown to the humor group may be obtained from the author.

Tables are numbered, double-spaced, and are flush with the left margin.			

Table 1

Mean Scores on Spatial Reasoning Test by Condition

Condition	$\underline{M}$	$\underline{SD}$
Humor	15.3	2.5
Positive Affect	14.3	3.6
Control	14.6	4.3

Tables are clear and concise.

Subgroups are referred to by lowercase n.

Any tables or figures must appear on separate pages.

Note: $\underline{n}$ = 10 per condition. Higher scores reflect better performance on the spatial reasoning test.

Statistical Analyses

This appendix is designed to help you perform the statistical analyses discussed in chapter 8. What follows are formulas for some basic descriptive and inferential statistics often used in psychological research. Neither this appendix nor the discussion in chapter 8, however, is a substitute for a basic statistics class or a comprehensive statistics text. Please also be aware that other useful statistical tests are not included here. You should consult your course instructor or a good introductory statistics book if you cannot locate the appropriate test for your data in this appendix.

Before you read this appendix, be sure that you carefully read chapter 8. In particular, pay attention to the properties of the four scales of measurement—nominal, ordinal, interval, and ratio—which are reviewed there. Before doing any calculations, be sure to scan the Before and After Data Collection Analysis Plan (table 8.2) and Choosing a Statistical Test (table 8.3). Table 8.3 is especially important, as it will help you to determine which statistical test is the right one for your data.

This appendix is long on calculation but short on background. In other words, I will not be explaining the origin of or much statistical theory behind any given test, but a description of what the test tells you and the circumstances to which it is applicable can be found in chapter 8. I assume at least modest familiarity with algebraic symbol manipulation and the logic of statistical analysis in that I will not be explaining why various steps are necessary within any given formula. The examples are short and to the point. If your own data set is a relatively small one, then you can follow the steps outlined for a given test and do the necessary calculations by hand. If you have a large data set or a more complex research design, then you should locate a user friendly computer program—there are many good ones available on main frame systems or PC software (e.g., SPSSx, SAS,

TABLE B.1

DESCRIPTIVE STATISTICS FOR A SET OF 10 OBSERVATIONS

X

1   mode = 3

2

3   median = 4.5

3

4   range = 8

5

6

7       $\text{mean} = M = \bar{x} = \dfrac{\Sigma X}{N} = \dfrac{48}{10} = 4.8$

8

9       $s^2 = \dfrac{\Sigma(X-\bar{x})^2}{N-1} = \dfrac{\Sigma X^2 - N(\bar{x})^2}{N-1}$

$\Sigma X = 48$

$\Sigma X^2 = 294$ $= \dfrac{294 - 230.4}{9} = \dfrac{63.60}{9} = 7.067$

$N = 10$

      $s = \sqrt{s^2} = \sqrt{7.067} = 2.66$

Minitab)—and let the program do the analyses for you. Remember, it is the planning and the interpretation the practical researcher brings to results that matter!

Whether you do calculations by hand or by computer, be aware that statistical formulas often contain frequently used symbols that indicate routine calculations, procedures, or assumptions. The most common **statistical symbols** are the following:

X, Y = a score, an observation, or an ordered pair

N = the total number of scores

Σ = to sum or add the available scores

X^2 = "X-squared" (multiplying a score by itself)

$\sqrt{X}$ = the square root of X

DESCRIPTIVE STATISTICS

Measures of Central Tendency

Mode The mode is the most frequently occurring score in a set of data. When examining a data set, simply count the number of times each score appears, and then select the score that occurs with the greatest frequency. The mode of the 10 observations in table B.1, for example, is 3. As you can see, this score occurs twice and all the other scores occur only once. Note that it is possible to have more than one mode in any set of data.

Median The median is the midpoint of a set of observations: Fifty percent of the observations lie above it, and 50 percent lie below it. To determine the median, rank the observations from lowest to highest. For an even number of scores, calculate the average of the two middle scores; as shown in table B.1, the median is 4.5 (i.e., the average of 4 and 5). For an odd number of scores, the median is the middle score. In the case of very large data sets, an alternative procedure can be used to calculate the median (see Runyon, Haber, Pittenger, & Coleman, 1996).

Mean   The mean is the statistical average, and it is based on the sum of the observations in a data set divided by the number of observations. It is symbolized $\bar{x}$ or M in written text:

[1] $$\text{Mean} = M = \bar{x} = \frac{\Sigma X}{N}$$

As shown in table B.1, the mean of the set of observations is found by summing the observations X to obtain the "sum of X," or ΣX and then dividing by the total number of observations N (here, 10). The resulting mean is 4.8.

Measures of Variability

Range   The range is the value of the largest observation in a data set minus the value of the smallest observation. As shown in table B.1, the range of the data is 8.

Sample variance   The variance indicates the degree to which observations vary about a mean. Variance is symbolized s^2 and is readily calculated using the following formula:

[2] $$s^2 = \frac{\Sigma(X - \bar{x})^2}{N - 1}$$

In this formula, $(X - \bar{x})^2$ is each individual observation, X, minus the mean or $\bar{x}$, and this obtained difference is then squared. The Σ indicates that these squared differences (or deviations) are then summed, and this total is then divided by $N - 1$. In effect, the variance is the mean of the squared deviations from a data set's mean.

Why use $N - 1$ and not just N? The former is used when the observations are from a smaller sample rather than an entire population. The latter is used if the data comprise an entire population of observations. As a sample size increases in magnitude, N and $N - 1$ will yield similar values.

There are two ways to calculate the variance of a data set. The longer way follows the steps just outlined; that is, calculate the squared deviations for $\Sigma(X - \bar{x})^2$ and then add them together:

$$(1 - 4.8)^2 + (2 - 4.8)^2 + (3 - 4.8)^2 + (3 - 4.8)^2 + (4 - 4.8)^2 + (5 - 4.8)^2$$
$$+ (6 - 4.8)^2 + (7 - 4.8)^2 + (8 - 4.8)^2 + (9 - 4.8)^2 = 63.60$$

Then, divide $\Sigma(X - \bar{x})^2$ by $N - 1$, or:

[3] $$s^2 = \frac{63.60}{9} = 7.067$$

A simpler calculation formula, one less susceptible to rounding errors and shown in table B.1, follows:

[4] $$s^2 = \frac{\Sigma X^2 - N(\bar{x})^2}{N - 1}$$

This simpler formula yields the same result, and it can be quicker to work with if a set of observations is especially large. ΣX^2 is the sum of the squared individual observations, and $(\overline{x})^2$ is the mean squared.

Sample Standard Deviation The standard deviation, the average deviation of scores from the mean, is calculated by taking the square root of the variance (see table B.1). It is symbolized s. The standard deviation represents an index of variability of a data set around the mean value. As a measure of dispersion, it is expressed in the same units of measurement found in the data's raw scores.

INFERENTIAL STATISTICS

Below are the statistical tests discussed in chapter 8. Each of these tests assumes that the researcher is pitting his or her experimental data against the null hypothesis of no difference. If the data do not conform to the null hypothesis, then it is rejected. You will need to consult the statistical tables in Appendix C to find the appropriate critical values—the minimal values needed to reach statistical significance—for each test or to make any necessary post hoc comparisons between means.

Chi-Square (χ^2) Test

The chi-square is a nonparametric test used to analyze nominal-scale data, typically frequencies. Specifically, the chi-square determines whether an observed set of frequencies ("O") is statistically different from the expected set of frequencies ("E"). Expected frequencies can be based on prior data, though in practice they tend to be based on the expected frequency due to chance.

For example, consider 100 coin tosses. If a coin is fair, the theoretical prediction is that "heads" will occur half the time, "tails" the remaining time. The expected frequency (E) is therefore 50:50; observations (O) seriously deviating from this expectation, say 65:35, would suggest a departure from chance (i.e., some causal factor is at work). The relationship between observed and expected coin tosses is shown in table B.2.

TABLE B.2

ONE VARIABLE ("GOODNESS OF FIT") CHI-SQUARE TEST FOR A 100 TRIAL COIN TOSS

	Number of Heads	Number of Tails
Observed	65	35
Expected	50	50
O − E	15	−15
$(O - E)^2$	225	225
$\dfrac{(O - E)^2}{E}$	4.5	4.5

The formula for the one variable, or "goodness of fit," chi-square test follows:

[5] $\qquad \chi^2 = \dfrac{\Sigma(O-E)^2}{E}$

It is called a goodness of fit test because its results reflect how well the observed data "fit" the expected frequencies. Using the simple calculations from table B.2 and the formula shown in [5], we find a chi-square value of

[6] $\qquad \chi^2 = 4.5 + 4.5 = 9$

Once a value is obtained, it must be compared against a critical value drawn from a table of chi-square values (see table C.1 in Appendix C). Specifically, a calculated chi-square value must be *equal to or exceed* a critical value to be significant at the .05 or .01 level. To use the table, the degrees of freedom for the test must be found (the concept underlying degrees of freedom is discussed in chapter 8). The formula for degrees of freedom for a one variable case follows:

[7] $\qquad$ df = number of categories – 1; here, 2 – 1 = 1

Using table C.1, we find that with df = 1 (see the far left column), the obtained value of 9 exceeds the critical value of 3.84, indicating that the difference is significant at the .05 level (locate the critical value in column 3). In other words, the obtained pattern of coin tosses departs from expectation so that we can assume the coin is not a fair one. Please note that the one variable chi-square test can readily deal with more than two categories (see Runyon et al., 1996, for related examples).

Effect Size for the Chi-Square Beyond identifying whether a relationship is significant, it is also important to have an index of the strength of association between the variables being examined. When using the chi-square test, effect size can be determined by the phi-coefficient, which is symbolized as ϕ. The formula to calculate ϕ follows:

[8] $\qquad \phi = \sqrt{\dfrac{\chi^2}{N}}$

Using the obtained chi-square value (see [6]) and the N of 100 from coin tossing results (see table B.2), we find

[9] $\qquad \phi = \sqrt{\dfrac{9}{100}} = .30$

The values for ϕ can range between –1.00 and + 1.00. In this case, the effect appears to be positive but not very strong.

Chi-Square $(\chi)^2$ using a contingency table Let's consider a more elaborate example, one involving two variables. Suppose you want to know if there is a relationship between Type A, or the "coronary prone personality" type, and gender. To examine this possibility, you have 30 males and 30 females complete a standardized

TABLE B.3

2 × 2 CHI-SQUARE TABLE AND ACCOMPANYING CALCULATIONS

	Personality Type		
Subject Gender	Type A	Type B	Row Totals
Male	O = 20 E = 14	O = 10 E = 16	30
Female	O = 8 E = 14	O = 22 E = 16	30
Column Totals	28	32	60

Cell 1 = 2.5714, based on $\dfrac{(O-E)^2}{E}$

Cell 2 = 2.35
Cell 3 = 2.5714
Cell 4 = 2.25

$\dfrac{\Sigma(O-E)^2}{E} = 9.6428$

measure of the Type A personality syndrome. Hypothetical data are shown in table B.3. For simplicity, we will categorize all non-Type A persons in this sample as Type Bs, individuals who demonstrate an unhurried personality profile.

The observed frequencies denoted as "O" in each of the four cells in table B.3 refer to the number of male and female participants who fall into the category of Type A or Type B. The null hypothesis in this example would be that coronary prone personality type has no relation to gender; that is, males are no more likely to be Type As than are females. The expected frequencies labeled "E" refer to the frequencies anticipated if the null hypothesis were correct (i.e., categorical equivalence). When performing a chi-square test, keep in mind that each participant can fall into one—and only one—of the available cells; that is, one cannot be both male *and* female or Type A *and* Type B.

The computational formula for the chi-square is the same as that for the one variable case shown earlier in [5]. Note that O is the observed frequency in each cell and E is the expected frequency in each cell. The difference between O and E is calculated, squared, and then divided by E. The Σ indicates that each of the following cell totals are then summed together, the grand sum of which is the test statistic.

Work through the example shown in table B.3. When doing a chi-square test, arrange the frequencies in a tabular manner similar to table B.3, and be certain to identify the row and column totals, as well as the overall N. To calculate the expected frequency for each cell, the following formula is used:

[10] $\qquad E = \dfrac{\text{row total} \times \text{column total}}{N}$

The row total refers to the row total for a particular cell, and the column total refers to the column total for that same cell. The expected frequency for cell 1 (male/Type A) would be calculated as follows:

[11] $\qquad E_1 = \dfrac{30 \times 28}{60} = 14$

The expected frequencies for the remaining three cells would be calculated in the same way (these values are already provided in table B.3). In the case of a 2×2 chi-square table, an alternative way to calculate the expected values exists. When any one expected value is known, the values for the remaining three cells can be obtained by subtraction (i.e., the known value is subtracted from the row and column totals).

Once the expected frequencies are known, the next step involves calculating the value of $(O - E)^2/E$ for each of the four cells. For cell 1, this value is

[12] $\qquad cell\,1 = \dfrac{(20 - 14)^2}{14} = \dfrac{36}{14} = 2.5714$

Each of the resulting four values is then summed (see the calculation section of table B.3 for the other 3 values). As you can see, the sum of the values at the bottom of table B.3 is 9.6428.

When a chi-square value is obtained, it can then be evaluated by comparing it with a value drawn from a table of critical values (see table C.1 in Appendix C). As always, degrees of freedom for any chi-square test must be calculated before a critical value can be determined. The degrees of freedom formula for the two variable chi-square test follows:

[13] $\qquad df = (R - 1)\,(C - 1)$

R refers to the number of rows in the table and C refers to the number of columns in the table. There are 2 rows and 2 columns in table B.3, and so this particular chi-square test has 1 degree of freedom (i.e., $[2 - 1] \times [2 - 1] = 1 \times 1 = 1$). A table with 3 rows and 2 columns would have 2 degrees of freedom, and so on.

Once the degrees of freedom are known, we turn to table C.1 and locate the critical value corresponding to 1 degree of freedom at the .05 level of significance. This value from table C.1 is 3.841. Because the calculated chi-square value of 9.6428 exceeds this critical value, the null hypothesis that there is no relationship between gender and personality can be rejected. As suggested by the data shown in table B.3, there is a relationship between gender and personality type: In this sample, males are apt to have a Type A personality whereas females are more likely to have a Type B profile.

Effect size The same formula shown earlier in [8] can be used to calculate the effect size associated with the contingency table (see table B.3). Once the values are entered into this formula, it appears as follows:

[14] $\qquad \phi = \sqrt{\dfrac{9.6428}{60}} = .40$

TABLE B.4

TABULAR DISPLAY OF A PEARSON *r* CALCULATION

Participant	X	X²	Y	Y²	XY
1	8	64	7	49	56
2	7	49	9	81	63
3	2	4	4	16	8
4	4	16	3	9	12
5	3	9	7	49	21
6	6	36	6	36	36
7	2	4	5	25	10
8	2	4	2	4	4
	$\Sigma X = 34$	$\Sigma X^2 = 186$	$\Sigma Y = 43$	$\Sigma Y^2 = 269$	$\Sigma XY = 210$

$N = 8$

$$r = \frac{N\Sigma XY - \Sigma X \Sigma Y}{\sqrt{N\Sigma X^2 - (\Sigma X)^2} \cdot \sqrt{N\Sigma Y^2 - (\Sigma Y)^2}} = \frac{8(210) - (34)(43)}{\sqrt{(8)(186) - (34)^2} \cdot \sqrt{(8)(269) - (43)^2}}$$

$$= .687$$

Thus, the association between gender and personality type in the present example appears to be moderate (i.e., $\phi = .40$). No additional significance testing is needed.

Pearson Product-Moment Correlation (*r*)

The Pearson *r* is used to describe the direction and strength of association between 2 continuous variables—X and Y—that have been measured on interval or ratio scales. Imagine that you wanted to know whether people's performance on a verbal task (X) was correlated with their performance on a mathematical task (Y). As shown in table B.4, 8 participants contributed fictitious pairs of X and Y scores (note that each X and Y pair is taken from one and only one participant). The calculations for the Pearson *r* are also shown in table B.4.
The formula for *r* follows:

$$[15] \quad r = \frac{N\Sigma XY - \Sigma X \Sigma Y}{\sqrt{N\Sigma X^2 - (\Sigma X)^2} \cdot \sqrt{N\Sigma Y^2 - (\Sigma Y)^2}}$$

Calculating *r* is not at all difficult, and the computations in table B.4 are easy to follow. Here is a description of the steps involved. The operations are carried out on the X and Y scores (see columns 1 and 3 in table B.4). The ΣX is the sum of scores for variable X, and the ΣY is the sum of scores for variable Y. ΣX^2 and ΣY^2 are the sums of the squared scores on X and Y, respectively (see columns 2 and 4 in table B.4). That is, each score in column X is squared and then these squared values are summed; the same procedure is done to the scores in the Y column. ΣXY is based on multiplying each X score in a pair by its corresponding Y score, and then summing the XY values (see column 5 in table B.4).
Please note that there is a difference between $(\Sigma X)^2$ and ΣX^2, as the parentheses around the former direct you to square the ΣX total, and the latter, as we have seen, is based on the addition of all the squared X values (the same calculations

TABLE B.5

TIPS EXPRESSED AS THE PERCENTAGE OF BILLS WITHIN THE TOUCH AND NO TOUCH GROUPS

Touch	No Touch
18.0	14.0
20.0	14.0
17.0	16.0
18.0	15.0
18.0	14.0
20.0	15.0
17.0	14.0
16.0	16.0
$N_1 = 8$	$N_2 = 8$
$\Sigma_{x_1} = 144$	$\Sigma X_2 = 118$
$\bar{x}_1 = 18.0$	$\bar{x}_2 = 14.75$
$s_1^2 = 2.0$	$s_2^2 = .7857$
$s_1 = 1.4142$	$s_2 = .8864$

$$t = \frac{18.0 - 14.75}{\sqrt{\dfrac{2.0}{8} + \dfrac{.7857}{8}}} = \frac{3.25}{\sqrt{.3482}} = \frac{3.25}{.5901} = 5.51$$

and relations hold for the Y scores). Once the sums and squared sums of X and Y are obtained, they and the N are plugged into the formula before it is solved (see the computational portion of table B.4).

To determine whether a Pearson r value is significant—that is, rejecting the null hypothesis that the population correlation coefficient is equal to 0.0—we examine a table of critical values for the r distribution. Table C.2 contains these critical values. Before selecting one, however, we must calculate the degrees of freedom for r, which is based on the formula $N - 2$. Because there are 8 pairs of scores in table B.4, the degrees of freedom are equal to 6 (i.e., $8 - 2$). As shown in table C.2, the critical value corresponding to 6 degrees of freedom at the .05 level is .707 (plus or minus depending on the observed value of r). As always, the obtained value *must equal or exceed* the critical value. Because our obtained r of .687 is less than the critical value, we cannot reject the null hypothesis. Thus, there is no significant association between the verbal and mathematical scores shown in table B.4; scoring well or poorly on one does not predict performance on the other.

THE *t*-TEST

Independent *t*-Test

A conceptual example employing the *t*-test for independent groups is shown in chapter 8, and hypothetical data illustrating the calculation of the *t*-test will be reviewed here. Crusco and Wetzel (1984) examined whether the percentage of the bill customers leave as a tip is higher when a waitress gently touched them on the hand (the so-called "Midas Touch") relative to a no touch control condition. The hypothetical results are shown at the top of table B.5. As you can see, the

---

TABLE B.6

EFFECT SIZE CALCULATION FOR THE MIDAS TOUCH EXPERIMENT

$$\text{effect size } r = \sqrt{\frac{t^2}{t^2 + df}} = \sqrt{\frac{(5.51)^2}{(5.51)^2 + 14}}$$

$$= \sqrt{\frac{30.3601}{44.3601}} = \sqrt{.6844} = .83$$

---

group receiving the subtle touch did tip more on average $(M = 18$ percent) than the control group $(M = 14.75$ percent)—but is this difference significant?

The formula for the t-test for independent groups is

[16] $$t = \frac{\overline{x}_1 - \overline{x}_2}{\sqrt{\dfrac{s_1^2}{N_1} + \dfrac{s_2^2}{N_2}}}$$

The numerator of the formula is the difference between $\overline{x}_1$, the mean of the touch group, and $\overline{x}_2$, the mean of the no touch group. The denominator is the variance of each group divided by the number of participants in each one (ideally, the groups will be equal in size). The resulting products are then added together, and the square root of the total is then calculated.

The lower half of table B.5 shows the data entered into the t-test formula. The resulting t-value is 5.51. This obtained value is then compared against a table of critical values of t, which can be found in table C.3 in Appendix C. To use the t-table, the degrees of freedom for the test must be calculated. The formula for the degrees of freedom for the independent t-test in this example is

[17] $N_1 + N_2 - 2 = 8 + 8 - 2 = 14$

The one-tailed critical value for df = 14 at the .05 level in table C.3 is 1.761. Because the obtained t-value exceeds the critical t, the null hypothesis is rejected: The touch group left significantly higher tips (based on the percentage of each bill) than did the no touch control group.

Effect Size Calculation for the Independent t-test Is the present effect a strong one? In other words, what was the magnitude of the effect of the independent variable (touch) on the dependent measure (tipping)? This *effect size* is easily calculated (see, for example, Rosenthal, 1991; Rosenthal & Rosnow, 1991; see also, Cohen, 1988), and higher values indicate that the independent variable had a stronger influence on the dependent measure.

An effect size formula for the independent groups t-test and its accompanying calculations are shown in table B.6. The necessary information, the t-value and its degrees of freedom, were taken from the previous discussion. As you can see, the effect size was .83, indicating that the touch had a relatively strong effect on people's tipping.

Estimation of the Degree of Association between the Independent Variable and the Dependent Measure for the Independent *t*-test Beyond obtaining a between-group difference and its accompanying effect size, it is also important to assess the degree of association between the independent and dependent measure. Generally speaking, the higher the degree of the relationship between the independent variable and the dependent measure, the greater the importance of the finding (Runyon et al., 1996). An index of this relationship can be calculated using omega squared, or $\hat{\omega}^2$. The formula for $\hat{\omega}^2$ is:

[18] $\qquad \hat{\omega}^2 = \dfrac{t^2 - 1}{t^2 + N_1 + N_2 - 1}$

Taking the information from the *t*-test for independent groups shown previously in table B.5, we find that $\hat{\omega}^2$ is equal to

[19] $\qquad \hat{\omega}^2 = \dfrac{(5.51)^2 - 1}{(5.51)^2 + 8 + 8 - 1} = .6473$

We then move the decimal point two places to the right (i.e., multiply the value of $\hat{\omega}^2$ by 100) and consider the resulting number a percentage. The interpretation of $\hat{\omega}^2$ is straightforward: Approximately 64.7 percent of the variance in the dependent measure is accounted for by variations in the independent variable. In most circumstances, this amount of variation would be deemed considerable; however, the judgment of what is (or is not) a meaningful effect must also be treated contextually (see Runyon et al., 1996, for further discussion of this issue). One important concluding point: $\hat{\omega}^2$ should only be calculated when a *t*-ratio is significant.

t-Test for Correlated Measures

The *t*-test for correlated measures, also known as the dependent *t*-test, examines whether an observed difference (D) between 2 conditions for the same (or matched) participants is significant or due to chance. Perhaps a researcher wanted to determine if an educational intervention resulted in a desirable attitude change toward some societal problem, such as smoking among middle school children. *Following* an effective intervention, for example, children would view cigarette smoking more negatively than *before* the intervention.

Imagine that a group of 6 middle school children had their attitudes toward smoking measured at time 1 (preintervention) and then a month later (postintervention): Do they like cigarette smoking less than they did before?

The formula for the correlated *t*-test is

[20] $\qquad t_D = \dfrac{\overline{x}_D}{\dfrac{\sigma_{\overline{D}}}{\sqrt{N-1}}}$

where $\overline{x}_D$ is the mean of the difference scores between the "before" and "after" attitudes, and σ_D is the standard deviation of the difference scores. As in the case of the Pearson *r*, note that N refers to the number of pairs and *not* the total number of observations available. The data and the accompanying calculations for the correlated measures *t*-test are shown in table B.7.

TABLE B.7

TABULAR SETUP FOR *t*-TEST FOR CORRELATED MEASURES

Participant	Attitude 1	Attitude 2	Difference(D)	$\bar{x}_D$	$x_D - \bar{x}_D$	$(x - \bar{x}_D)^2$
1	6	2	4	3	1	1
2	5	3	2	3	−1	1
3	7	2	5	3	2	4
4	6	4	2	3	−1	1
5	6	3	3	3	0	0
6	4	2	2	3	−1	1
	$\Sigma_{A_1} = 34$	$\Sigma_{A_2} = 16$	$\Sigma_D = 18$			
Mean	$\bar{x}_{A_1} = 5.67$	$\bar{x}_{A_1} = 2.67$	$\bar{x}_D = 3.0$			$\Sigma(x_D - \bar{x}_D)^2 = 8$

$$\bar{x}_D = \frac{\Sigma D}{N} = \frac{18}{6} = 3.0$$

$$\sigma_D = \sqrt{\frac{\Sigma(x_D - \bar{x}_D)^2}{N}} = \sqrt{\frac{8}{6}} = \sqrt{1.333} = 1.55$$

$$t_D = \frac{\bar{x}_D}{\dfrac{\sigma_D}{\sqrt{N-1}}} = \frac{3}{\dfrac{1.55}{\sqrt{6-1}}} = \frac{3}{\dfrac{1.55}{2.2361}} = \frac{3}{.693} = 4.33$$

$$df = N - 1 = 6 - 1 = 5$$

As shown in table B.7, the observed means are consistent with the hypothesis: The average attitude was more favorable toward smoking before ($M = 5.67$) rather than after ($M = 2.67$) the intervention. As always, a computation must be performed to be certain a difference is statistically reliable (see table B.7). To do so, begin by calculating the difference (D) between the attitudes expressed by the same people at times 1 and 2 (see column 4 in table B.7), and then determine the mean of the difference scores (see the bottom of column 4). The next step involves computing the difference between each D and the mean of D (see column 6 in table B.7). The latter difference scores are then squared and summed (see column 7 in table B.7).

The σ_D is then computed and it, along with the mean of D and N, is plugged into the correlated *t*-test formula. As always, the degrees of freedom must be calculated (as shown in table B.7, the dfs are equal to $N - 1$, or 5) before locating a critical value in table C.3 (please note that the same table is used to locate critical values for the independent as well as the correlated *t*-test). The critical value for $df = 5$ at the .05 level (two-tailed test) is 2.571, allowing us to reject the null hypothesis. As predicted, the children's opinion toward smoking became more negative *after* the intervention.

Effect Size Calculation for the Correlated *t*-Test   As was shown above in table B.6, one effect size formula for the *t*-test is effect size *r*:

[21] $$r = \sqrt{\frac{t^2}{t^2 + df}} = \sqrt{\frac{(4.33)^2}{(4.33)^2 + 5}} = .888$$

By squaring the obtained t and then entering it and the degrees of freedom in this formula, an effect size r for these data can be calculated. This effect size r is .888, pointing to a relatively strong effect.

Estimation of the Degree of Association between the Independent Variable and the Dependent Measure   You can estimate the degree of association between what is manipulated and what is measured by calculating $\hat{\omega}^2$. The $\hat{\omega}^2$ formula for the t-test is shown earlier in the discussion of the t-test for independent groups (see [18]).

ANALYSIS OF VARIANCE

As was discussed in chapter 8, researchers use the analysis of variance (ANOVA)—sometimes referred to as the F-test—when they want to demonstrate significant differences between more than two groups. To employ an ANOVA test, the data must be based on either interval or ratio scales. We will review variations of the ANOVA test for one independent ("one-way") variable, for two independent ("two-way") variables, and for a repeated-measures design for one independent variable. Different statistics books use different forms of statistical notation. If you are already familiar with the ANOVA test, you may want to use the notation you know when performing calculations. Please also note that there are other more complex ANOVA designs that are beyond the scope of this book (see, for example, Hays, 1981; Kirk, 1982).

One Independent Variable ANOVA

This ANOVA is based on two independent estimates of variance: between-group variability (i.e., presumably caused by the effect of an independent variable) and within-group variability (i.e., determined by the similarity of reactions to the independent variable within each experimental condition). The ANOVA's test statistic, the F-ratio, is calculated by dividing the numerical value of between-group variance by the value of the within-group variance. If the between-group variance is large (i.e., there are differences among the condition means) relative to low within-group variance (i.e., within a given group, behavior is more or less constant), then an F-ratio is apt to be large and a significant difference among the means is likely. Smaller between-group relative to within-group variance, however, leads to a small F-ratio and no statistically reliable differences.

Perhaps a social worker is interested in how to effectively aid educationally deprived preschool children. Nine children are randomly assigned to one of three conditions (i.e., 3 in each): an intensive preschool experience, parent-led educational activities, or a control group. At the end of 6 months, all children complete a follow-up treatment test to evaluate the effectiveness of the intervention. The data and summary statistics are shown in table B.8.

TABLE B.8

DATA AND SUMMARY STATISTICS FOR HYPOTHETICAL ONE-WAY ANOVA

Condition:					
Intensive Treatment		**Parent Treatment**		**Control**	
X_1	X_1^2	X_2	X_2^2	X_3	X_3^2
107	11,449	95	9,025	87	7,569
101	10,201	90	8,100	86	7,396
92	8,464	88	7,744	82	6,724
$\sum X_1 = 300$		$\sum X_2 = 273$		$\sum X_3 = 255$	
$\sum X_1^2 = 30,114$		$\sum X_2^2 = 24,869$		$\sum X_3^2 = 21,689$	
$\bar{x}_1 = 100$		$\bar{x}_2 = 91$		$\bar{x}_3 = 82$	
$n_1 = 3$		$n_2 = 3$		$n_3 = 3$	

$\sum X_{TOT} = 300 + 273 + 255 = 828$
$\sum X_{TOT}^2 = 30,114 + 24,689 + 21,689 = 76,672$
$N = 9$
$\bar{x}_{TOT} = 92$

To begin an ANOVA problem, the first step is to calculate what is called the Total Sum of Squares or SS_{TOT}, and then the Between-groups Sum of Squares (SS_B) and the Within-groups Sum of Squares (SS_W).

[22] $SS_{TOT} = \sum X_{TOT}^2 - \dfrac{(\sum X_{TOT})^2}{N} = 76,672 - \dfrac{(828)^2}{9} = 496$

[23] $SS_B = \sum n_i (\bar{x}_i - \bar{x}_{TOT})^2 = \sum 3(100 - 92)^2 + 3(91 - 92)^2 + 3(85 - 92)^2 = 342$

[24] $SS_W = SS_{TOT} - SS_B = 496 - 342 = 154$

The SS_B and the SS_W are then divided by their appropriate degrees of freedom in order to obtain the Between- ($\hat{s}_B^2$) and Within-group ($\hat{s}_W^2$) variance estimates:

[25] $df_B = K - 1$, where K = the number of groups, or $3 - 1 = 2$

[26] $df_W = N - k = 9 - 3 = 6$

[27] $\hat{s}_B^2 = \dfrac{SS_B}{df_B} = \dfrac{342}{2} = 171$

[28] $\hat{s}_W^2 = \dfrac{SS_W}{df_W} = \dfrac{154}{6} = 25.67$

The ($\hat{s}_B^2$) is then divided by the ($\hat{s}_W^2$) to obtain the F-ratio:

[29] $F = \dfrac{\hat{s}_B^2}{\hat{s}_W^2} = \dfrac{171}{25.67} = 6.66$

TABLE B.9

ANOVA SOURCE TABLE FOR ONE INDEPENDENT VARIABLE

Source of Variation	Sum of Squares	df	Variance Estimate	F
Between Groups	342	2	171	6.66
Within Groups	154	6	25.67	
Total	496	8		

As shown in table B.9, all of these calculations can be conveniently summarized in what is called an ANOVA source or summary table. We then turn to table C.4 in order to locate a critical value for F based on 2 df in the numerator (i.e., between-group variance) and 6 in the denominator (i.e., within-group variance). The .05 critical value corresponding to these degrees of freedom is 5.14. Because the observed F of 6.66 exceeds this critical value, the null hypothesis of no difference among the three groups is rejected. We do not know, however, which of the means differs significantly from the others—when examining more than two means, a significant, omnibus F-ratio is effectively a "hunting license." To determine where the difference or differences among the means lie, a *post hoc* test must be performed.

One of the easiest post hoc tests to use is Tukey's "honestly significant difference," or HSD, test (Jaccard, Becker, & Wood, 1984; Tukey, 1953, cited in Runyon et al., 1996). The formula for the HSD is

$$[30] \qquad \text{HSD} = q\alpha \sqrt{\frac{\hat{s}_w^2}{n}}$$

where n is equal to the number of participants in each condition and $q\alpha$ is a value taken from table C.5. The value of $q\alpha$ is located in table C.5 by using the df_w (here, 6) and the number of means (here, 3). In this instance, $q\alpha$ at the .05 level is 4.34. The value of HSD can then be readily determined:

$$[31] \qquad \text{HSD} = 4.34 \sqrt{\frac{25.67}{3}} = 12.70$$

The obtained HSD of 12.70 is then compared against the absolute value of any differences found among the means. If the absolute value of difference between any two means is greater than the HSD value, then those means are significantly different from one another. In this example, the only significant difference is between the intensive treatment group ($M = 100$) and the control group ($M = 85$); that is, the absolute difference between these means ($100 - 85$) is 15, which is greater than the HSD of 12.70.

Degree of Association between the Independent and Dependent Variables Regardless of its size or level of significance, an F-ratio only tells you whether a null hypothesis is rejected (as in this example) or accepted. To determine the degree to which an independent variable affects a dependent variable, information from the ANOVA can be used to calculate $\hat{\omega}^2$. As was previously noted with regard to the *t*-test, this indicator should only be used when an *F*-ratio is significant. The formula for $\hat{\omega}^2$ using *F* follows:

[32] $\qquad \hat{\omega}^2 = \dfrac{df_B\,(F-1)}{df_B\,(F-1)+N}$

In the current example, $\hat{\omega}^2$ would be

[33] $\qquad \hat{\omega}^2 = \dfrac{2(6.66-1)}{2(6.66-1)+9} = .5571$

In this hypothetical example, then, we can conclude that the independent variable accounted for about 55.7 percent of the variance in the scores on the dependent measure. In short, there was a fairly high degree of association between the independent variable and the dependent measure.

Calculating Effect Size for the *F*-Ratio   A straightforward index of effect size for the *F*-ratio was developed by Cohen (1988), and it is called **f**. According to Cohen, **f** indicates whether an effect is small (**f** = .10), medium (**f** = .25), or large (**f** = .40 and above) in magnitude. The formula for **f** is:

[34] $\qquad f = \sqrt{\dfrac{\eta^2}{1-\eta^2}}$

where

[35] $\qquad \eta^2 = \dfrac{SS_B}{SS_{TOT}}$

Using the data from this one-way ANOVA, we find that

[36] $\qquad \eta^2 = \dfrac{342}{496} = .6895$

so that

[37] $\qquad f = \sqrt{\dfrac{.6895}{1-.6895}} = 1.49$

An **f** of 1.49 indicates a quite large effect; however, keep in mind that the ANOVA data here are hypothetical and that I want you to get a feel for the magnitude of differences among means. Cohen (1988) suggests that effect sizes above .50 rarely occur in social or behavioral science data, so you should not despair if an effect size based on your project data is considerably smaller.

Two Independent Variable ANOVA

As was discussed in chapters 6 and 8, two-factor studies allow a researcher to gauge the effect of two independent variables on the same dependent measure. In addition, the analysis of a two-factor—called a two-way ANOVA—also assesses whether there is an interaction effect between the two variables. Finally, the two-way ANOVA represents an efficient use of research time and effort.

   The statistical logic underlying the two-way ANOVA is similar to that for the one-factor version: the relationship of between-groups variability and within-groups variability. This time, however, there are three sources of between-groups

---

TABLE B.10

HYPOTHETICAL DATA FROM THE EFFECTS OF DISCLOSING PERSONALITY AND STRESS COMMUNICATION ON RECALL STUDY

	Story Type		
	High Stress (B_1)	Low Stress (B_2)	Column Mean
Personality			
High Discloser (A_1)	5 6 5 4 6 $\bar{X}_{A_1B_1} = 5.20$ $\sum X_{A_1B_1} = 26$ $\sum X^2_{A_1B_1} = 138$	3 2 2 1 3 $\bar{X}_{A_1B_2} = 2.20$ $\sum X_{A_1B_2} = 11$ $\sum X^2_{A_1B_2} = 27$	$\bar{X}_{A_1} = 3.70$
Low Discloser (A_2)	3 3 3 2 2 $\bar{X}_{A_2B_1} = 2.60$ $\sum X_{A_2B_1} = 13$ $\sum X^2_{A_2B_1} = 35$	5 6 6 4 5 $\bar{X}_{A_2B_2} = 5.20$ $\sum X_{A_2B_2} = 26$ $\sum X^2_{A_2B_2} = 138$	$\bar{X}_{A2} = 3.90$
Row Mean	$\bar{X}_{B_1} = 3.90$	$\bar{X}_{B_2} = 3.70$	

$\sum X_{TOT} = \sum X_{A_1B_1} + \sum X_{A_1B_2} + \sum X_{A_2B_1} + \sum X_{A_2B_2} = 76$

$\sum X^2_{TOT} = \sum X^2_{A_1B_1} + \sum X^2_{A_1B_2} + \sum X^2_{A_2B_1} + \sum X^2_{A_2B_2} = 338$

Note: Table entries are hypothetical recall scores, where higher numbers indicate better recall.

---

variation—a main effect for independent variable A, one for B, and the interaction between A and B.

The hypothetical experiment described here examines the effects of personality and communication content on episode recall. Half of the participants in the experiment were identified as high in their ability to open up to others; the remaining participants were designated low disclosers. Half of the participants then listened to a highly stressful story that was rich in detail, while the rest of the participants heard a nonstressful story that was equally rich in content. All participants then performed a distraction task for 5 min—they worked on a series of maze puzzles—and then wrote down all they could remember about the story they heard.

The mean recall scores for the experiment are shown in table B.10. If you examine this table carefully, you can see the means for the two main effects and the interaction. There was no main effect for disclosure, as high and low disclosers recalled about the same level of detail (*Ms* = 3.70 vs. 3.90, respectively). There was no apparent main effect for story type, either; stressful versus nonstressful story content did not seem to matter much (*Ms* = 3.90 vs. 3.70). But take a closer look at the four cell means *inside* the table, which appear to tell a more detailed story. The interaction between variable A and B suggests that high disclosers recalled much more detail when a story was stressful than nonstressful in content. In contrast, however, low disclosers recalled more when the story was not stressful than when it was stressful (see chapter 6 for directions on how to plot an interaction).

Many of the basic calculations for the two-way ANOVA can be done ahead of time. As shown in table B.10, the row, column, and cell means must all be computed, and so must the $\sum X$ and $\sum X^2$ for each of the four cells (for your convenience, the raw data are provided). Once these preliminary calculations are accomplished, the $\sum X_{TOT}$ and the $\sum X^2_{TOT}$ can also be determined (see table B.10).

We can now work our way through each of the calculations to complete the two-way ANOVA (note the similarity between the steps here and the previous one-way ANOVA). As each step is completed, the result should be entered into an ANOVA summary table (see the bottom section of table B.11). We will begin with the SS_{TOT}, or Total Sum of the Squares:

[38] $\qquad SS_{TOT} = \sum X^2_{TOT} - \dfrac{(\sum X_{TOT})^2}{N} = 338 - \dfrac{(76)^2}{20} = 49.20$

We then calculate the SS_{BET} or the Sum of Squares Between the Groups:

[39] $\qquad SS_{BET} = \dfrac{(\sum A_i B_i)^2}{N_{A_i B_i}} - \dfrac{(\sum X)^2}{N} = \dfrac{(26)^2 + (11)^2 + (13)^2 + (26)^2}{5} - \dfrac{(76)^2}{20}$

$\qquad\qquad = 39.60$

The SS_{BET} is further broken down into the respective sums of squares for the A, B, and A x B effects. We begin with A:

[40] $\qquad SS_A = \dfrac{(\sum X_{A_1})^2 + (\sum X_{A_2})^2}{N_A} - \dfrac{(\sum X)^2}{N} = \dfrac{(26+11)^2 + (13+26)^2}{10} - \dfrac{(76)^2}{20}$

$\qquad\qquad = .20$

The next step is to calculate SS_B:

[41] $\qquad SS_B = \dfrac{(\sum X_{B_1})^2 + (\sum X_{B_2})^2}{N_B} - \dfrac{(\sum X)^2}{N} = \dfrac{(26+13)^2 + (11+26)^2}{10} - \dfrac{(76)^2}{20}$

$\qquad\qquad = .20$

We then turn to SS_{AXB}, which is easy to determine because we know SS_{BET}, SS_A, and SS_B:

[42] $\qquad SS_{A \times B} = SS_{BET} - (SS_A + SS_B) = 39.6 - .40 = 39.2$

Finally, we must compute the within-group sum of squares, or SS_W. This step, too, is a relatively easy one because we know SS_{TOT} and SS_{BET}. Note that this step—indeed, the entire first column of table B.11—serves as an opportunity to check for math errors. If the respective sum of squares calculations do not add up (i.e., $SS_{BET} + SS_W = SS_{TOT}$), you have made an error somewhere.

[43] $\qquad SS_W = SS_{TOT} - SS_{BET} = 49.2 - 39.6 = 9.60$

Degrees of Freedom Calculations The calculations for the degrees of freedom for each of the three between-groups effects—A, B, and A x B—as well as those

TABLE B.11

TWO-WAY ANOVA SOURCE TABLE WITH FORMULAS AND RESULTS

Source of Variation	Sum of Squares	df	Variance Estimate	F
Between Groups	SS_{BET}			
A Effect	SS_A	$(A-1)$	SS_{A/df_A}	$\hat{S}^2_{A}/\hat{S}^2_w$
B Effect	SS_B	$(B-1)$	SS_{B/df_B}	$\hat{S}^2_{B}/\hat{S}^2_w$
A × B Effect	$SS_{A \times B}$	$(A-1)(B-1)$	$SS_{A \times B/df_{A \times B}}$	$S^2_{A \times B}/\hat{S}^2_w$
Within Groups	SS_W	$(N-AB)$	$SS_{w/dfw}$	
Total	SS_{TOT}	$(N-1)$		
Between Groups	39.6			
A Effect	.20	1	.20	.33
B Effect	.20	1	.20	.33
A × B Effect	39.20	1	39.20	65.30
Within Groups	9.60	16	.60	
Total	49.20	19		

for the within-group calculations, are shown in the top section of table B.11 (see column 3). Note that both variable A and B have 2 levels, so A = 2 and B = 2. The overall N in the study is 20, or 5 participants per cell. The degrees of freedom corresponding to the hypothetical study are shown in the bottom half of table B.11 in column 3.

Calculating the Variance Estimates   The variance estimates for the three effects and the within-group variance estimate can be found by dividing each of the sums of squares by their appropriate degrees of freedom (see top section of table B.11, column 4, for the formulas; the results from the study are shown immediately below these formulas).

Determining the F-Ratio for the Three Effects   As shown in the last column in the top section of table B.11, each F-ratio is based on an effect's variances estimate divided by the within-group variance estimate. The three resulting F-ratios are shown in the bottom right corner of table B.11.

Determining whether an F-ratio from a two-way ANOVA reaches statistical significance is done in the same manner as that for a one-way design: Find the critical value of F corresponding to 1 (numerator) and 16 (denominator) degrees of freedom from table C.4. At the .05 level, the critical value found there is 4.49, meaning that only one F-ratio—the one for the A x B interaction—reached significance. An interpretation of this effect was noted at the start of this example, but please review the interpretive discussion provided in chapters 6 and 8.

Estimating the Degree of Association between the Independent Variables and the Dependent Measure   This time, an index of association $\hat{\omega}^2$ can be calculated for either or both of the main effects and the interaction as long as the respective effect reaches statistical significance. Use the formula for $\hat{\omega}^2$ that is provided earlier in the discussion of the one variable ANOVA (see [32]).

Calculating Effect Sizes for the Two-Way ANOVA   We can again calculate Cohen's (1988) **f**, as shown earlier. Similar to $\hat{\omega}^2$ preceding immediately, an effect size can be determined for each effect. The formula for **f** remains the same (see [34]) but you must be sure to enter the Sum of Squares (SS) for the effect of interest. Thus, the calculation of **f** for the main effect for B is

[44] $f_B = \sqrt{\dfrac{\eta^?}{1-\eta^2}}$

where

[45] $\eta^2 = \dfrac{SS_B}{SS_{TOT}} = \dfrac{.20}{49.20} = .0041$

so that

[46] $f_B = \sqrt{\dfrac{.0041}{1-.0041}} = .0642$

The **f** for the main effect of the B variable is interpreted in line with Cohen's (1988) guidelines, which are summarized earlier in the effect size discussion for the one-way ANOVA.

One Independent Variable Repeated-Measures ANOVA

Repeated-measures, also known as within-subjects designs, involve the use of the same participant in different experimental conditions. That is, a participant's own behavior is the basis for comparison before and after the introduction of an independent variable. In a real sense, each participant serves as his or her own control group. Why? Because each participant experiences each experimental condition—receives all levels of the independent variable—within a study.

Hypothetical raw and summary data from an imaginary research project are shown in table B.12. The project concerns the reduction of migraine headaches through relaxation therapy. Nine participants kept records on the number of hours they experienced migraines per week during a baseline period (weeks 1 and 2) and after relaxation training (weeks 3, 4, and 5). As can be seen by examining the week means at the bottom of table B.12, there appears to be a rather drastic reduction in incidence of headache following the relaxation training. A one-way repeated-measures ANOVA can verify whether this reduction in weeks 3, 4, and 5 is significantly different from the baseline period in weeks 1 and 2.

We begin by calculating the SS_{TOT}. To do so, every raw score must be squared to calculate the $\sum X^2_{TOT}$, which is shown at the bottom of table B.12. The $\sum X_{TOT}$, which is equal to the sum of the subject totals (see the last column in table B.12), must also be identified. Once done, SS_{TOT} is

[47] $SS_{TOT} = \sum X^2_{TOT} - \dfrac{(\sum X_{TOT})^2}{N} = 10.471 - \dfrac{(561)^2}{45} = 3477.2$

Note that the N here is equal to 45, as it refers to the number of observations and *not* the number of participants. The SS_{TOT}, as well as the subsequent calculations, are then entered into an ANOVA Summary Table (see bottom section of table B.13).

TABLE B.12

HYPOTHETICAL DATA FROM A STUDY ON MIGRAINE INCIDENCE PRE- AND POST-RELAXATION THERAPY

	Baseline		Training			
Subject	Week 1	Week 2	Week 3	Week 4	Week 5	Subject Totals
1	21	22	8	6	6	63
2	20	19	10	4	9	62
3	7	5	5	4	5	26
4	25	30	13	12	4	84
5	30	33	10	8	6	87
6	19	27	8	7	4	65
7	26	16	5	2	5	54
8	13	4	8	1	5	31
9	26	24	14	8	17	89
	$\Sigma X_1^2 = 4297$	$\Sigma X_2^2 = 4436$	$\Sigma X_3^2 = 807$	$\Sigma X_4^2 = 394$	$\Sigma X_5^2 = 537$	
Week Totals	187	180	81	52	61	561
Week Means	20.78	20.0	9.0	5.78	6.78	12.47

$\Sigma X_{TOT} = \Sigma X_1 + \Sigma X_2 + \ldots + \Sigma X_5 = 561$
$\Sigma X_{TOT}^2 = \Sigma X_1^2 + \Sigma X_2^2 + \ldots + \Sigma X_5^2 = 10{,}471$

Note: Table entries are hypothetical number of hours of migraine headache per week.

TABLE B.13

ONE-WAY REPEATED-MEASURES ANOVA SOURCE TABLE WITH FORMULAS AND RESULTS

Source of Variation	Sum of Squares	df	Variance Estimate	F
Subjects	$SS_{SUBJECTS}$	$(n-1)$		
Weeks	SS_{WEEKS}	$(w-1)$	SS_{WEEKS/df_w}	$\hat{S}^2_{WEEKS}/\hat{S}^2_{ERROR}$
Error	SS_{ERROR}	$(n-1)(w-1)$	$SS_{ERROR/df_{ERROR}}$	
Total	SS_{TOT}	$(N-1)$		
Subjects	833.6	8		
Weeks	1934.5	4	483.63	21.83
Error	709.1	32	22.16	
Total	3477.2	44		

The next step involves calculating the $SS_{SUBJECTS}$, which is

[48] $SS_{SUBJECTS} = \dfrac{\Sigma T_S^2}{w} - \dfrac{(\Sigma X_{TOT})^2}{N} =$

$$\dfrac{(63)^2 + (62)^2 + \ldots + (31)^2 + (89)^2}{5} - \dfrac{(561)^2}{45} = 833.6$$

where T_S^2 is equal to the subject totals squared and **w** is the number of times events are measured (here, weeks). The subsequent step involves computing the SS_{WEEKS} for the repeated measures variable. SS_{WEEKS} is

[49] $\quad SS_{WEEKS} = \dfrac{\sum T_w^2}{n} - \dfrac{(\sum x_{TOT})^2}{N} = \dfrac{(187)^2 + (180)^2 + (81)^2 + (52)^2 + (61)^2}{9} - \dfrac{(561)^2}{45}$

$\qquad\qquad = 1934.5$

where T_W^2 is based on the week totals squared and **n** is the number of participants in the study (here, 9).

Finally, what is called the SS_{ERROR} can be determined by subtracting the sum of the $SS_{SUBJECTS}$ and the SS_{WEEKS} from the SS_{TOT}:

[50] $\quad SS_{ERROR} = SS_{TOT} - (SS_{SUBJECTS} + SS_{WEEKS})$

$\qquad\qquad = 3477.2 - (833.6 + 1934.5) = 709.10$

Calculating the Degrees of Freedom The calculations for the degrees of freedom for the Sums of Squares are shown in column 3 of the top portion of table B.13.

Calculating the Variance Estimates Keep in mind that we are only interested in the effect corresponding to the repeated-measures variable—the average number of hours per week of reported migraine headache. Thus, we will not use the $SS_{SUBJECTS}$ further. Instead, we are only interested in the variance estimates based on the SS_{WEEKS} and the SS_{ERROR}. The corresponding formulas and results are shown in column 4 of table B.13.

Calculating the F-Ratio As shown in the top portion of column 5 of table B.13, the repeated measures F-ratio is based on the variances estimate for weeks ($\hat{s}_{WEEKS}^2$) divided by the variance estimate for error ($\hat{s}_{ERROR}^2$). The resulting omnibus F-ratio is 21.83 (see the bottom section of column 5 of table B.13).

The next step, of course, is to determine whether this value is significant by locating a critical value for comparison from table C.4. To do so, the degrees of freedom associated with the repeated measure (weeks) for the numerator and error for the denominator—here 4 and 32, respectively—are used. The critical F at the .05 level of significance corresponding to these degrees of freedom is 2.67. Thus, we know that some difference exists among the means for the baseline and relaxation training periods, but where?

Post Hoc Comparisons among Means To identify the specific differences among the 5 week averages, we again rely on Tukey's HSD test (see [30]). The value of $q\alpha$ is drawn from table C.5 by using the df_{ERROR} of 32 and the number of means, which is 5. This time, however, we discover that table C.5 does not contain an entry for 32 degrees of freedom; rather the table skips from 30 to 40. We can be statistically conservative and use the $q\alpha$ value corresponding to 40 df_{ERROR} and 5 means, which at the .05 level is 4.04.

We then draw the $\hat{s}_{ERROR}^2$ of 22.16 from table B.13 and take note of the n of 9, both of which are entered into [30]. Thus, our HSD value is

[51] $\quad HSD = 4.04\sqrt{\dfrac{22.16}{9}} = 6.34$

The HSD value of 6.34 is then compared against the absolute value of the difference between each of the means (you can create a simple 5×5 matrix of the means to keep track of the absolute differences). In this case, the two baseline means ($Ms = 20.78$ and 20) are significantly different from each of the post-training means ($Ms = 9.0, 5.78$, and 6.78).

Effect Size for F The effect size for the results of a repeated measures ANOVA can be obtained using the formula for f (see [34]). Be sure to use the SS_{WEEKS} and not $SS_{SUBJECTS}$ in the calculation, however.

Assessing the Degree of Association between the Independent Variable and the Dependent Measure As was done for the one- and two-way between-subjects ANOVAs, the degree of association between what is manipulated and measured for a repeated-measures analysis can be determined by $\hat{\omega}^2$ (see [32]).

Statistical Tables

TABLE C.1

TWO-TAILED CRITICAL RATIOS OF χ^2

Degrees of freedom df	.10	.05	.02	.01
1	2.706	3.841	5.412	6.635
2	4.605	5.991	7.824	9.210
3	6.215	7.815	9.837	11.341
4	7.779	9.488	11.668	13.277
5	9.236	11.070	13.388	15.086
6	10.645	12.592	15.033	16.812
7	12.017	14.067	16.622	18.475
8	13.362	15.507	18.168	20.090
9	14.684	16.919	19.679	21.666
10	15.987	18.307	21.161	23.209
11	17.275	19.675	22.618	24.725
12	18.549	21.026	24.054	26.217
13	19.812	22.362	25.472	27.688
14	21.064	23.685	26.873	29.141
15	22.307	24.996	28.259	30.578
16	23.542	26.296	29.633	32.000
17	24.769	27.587	30.995	33.409
18	25.989	28.869	32.346	34.805
19	27.204	30.144	33.687	36.191
20	28.412	31.410	35.020	37.566
21	29.615	32.671	36.343	38.932
22	30.813	33.924	37.659	40.289
23	32.007	35.172	38.968	41.638
24	33.196	36.415	40.270	42.980
25	34.382	37.652	41.566	44.314
26	35.563	38.885	42.856	45.642
27	36.741	40.113	44.140	46.963
28	37.916	41.337	45.419	48.278
29	39.087	42.557	46.693	49.588
30	40.256	43.773	47.962	50.892

TABLE C.2

CRITICAL VALUES OF *r* (PEARSON PRODUCT-MOMENT CORRELATION COEFFICIENT)

df	\\ Levels of significance for two-tailed test		
	.10	.05	.01
1	.988	.997	.9999
2	.900	.950	.990
3	.805	.878	.959
4	.729	.811	.917
5	.669	.754	.874
6	.622	.707	.834
7	.582	.666	.798
8	.549	.632	.765
9	.521	.602	.735
10	.497	.576	.708
11	.476	.553	.684
12	.458	.532	.661
13	.441	.514	.641
14	.426	.497	.623
15	.412	.482	.606
16	.400	.468	.590
17	.389	.456	.575
18	.378	.444	.561
19	.369	.433	.549
20	.360	.423	.537
25	.323	.381	.487
30	.296	.349	.449
35	.275	.325	.418
40	.257	.304	.393
45	.243	.288	.372
50	.231	.273	.354
60	.211	.250	.325
70	.195	.232	.303
80	.183	.217	.283
90	.173	.205	.267
100	.164	.195	.254

Source: Adapted from R. A. Fisher, *Statistical Methods for Research Workers,* 14th edition. Copyright 1973, Hafner Press.

TABLE C.3

CRITICAL VALUES OF *t*

For any given df, the table shows the values of *t* corresponding to various levels of probability. The obtained *t* is significant at a given level if it is equal to or *greater than* the value shown in the table.

Level of significance for one-tailed test

	.10	.05	.025	.01	.005	.0005

Level of significance for two-tailed test

df	.20	.10	.05	.02	.01	.001
1	3.078	6.314	12.706	31.821	63.657	636.619
2	1.886	2.920	4.303	6.965	9.925	31.598
3	1.638	2.353	3.182	4.541	5.841	12.941
4	1.533	2.132	2.776	3.747	4.604	8.610
5	1.476	2.015	2.571	3.365	4.032	6.859
6	1.440	1.943	2.447	3.143	3.707	5.959
7	1.415	1.895	2.365	2.998	3.499	5.405
8	1.397	1.860	2.306	2.896	3.355	5.041
9	1.383	1.833	2.262	2.821	3.250	4.781
10	1.372	1.812	2.228	2.764	3.169	4.587
11	1.363	1.796	2.201	2.718	3.106	4.437
12	1.356	1.782	2.179	2.681	3.055	4.318
13	1.350	1.771	2.160	2.650	3.012	4.221
14	1.345	1.761	2.145	2.624	2.977	4.140
15	1.341	1.753	2.131	2.602	2.947	4.073
16	1.337	1.746	2.120	2.583	2.921	4.015
17	1.333	1.740	2.110	2.567	2.898	3.965
18	1.330	1.734	2.101	2.552	2.878	3.922
19	1.328	1.729	2.093	2.539	2.861	3.883
20	1.325	1.725	2.086	2.528	2.845	3.850
21	1.323	1.721	2.080	2.518	2.831	3.819
22	1.321	1.717	2.074	2.508	2.819	3.792
23	1.319	1.714	2.069	2.500	2.807	3.767
24	1.318	1.711	2.064	2.492	2.797	3.745
25	1.316	1.708	2.060	2.485	2.787	3.725
26	1.315	1.706	2.056	2.479	2.779	3.707
27	1.314	1.703	2.052	2.473	2.771	3.690
28	1.313	1.701	2.048	2.467	2.763	3.674
29	1.311	1.699	2.045	2.462	2.756	3.659
30	1.310	1.697	2.042	2.457	2.750	3.646
40	1.303	1.684	2.021	2.423	2.704	3.551
60	1.296	1.671	2.000	2.390	2.660	3.460
120	1.289	1.658	1.980	2.358	2.617	3.373
∞	1.282	1.645	1.960	2.326	2.576	3.291

Source: Rand Corporation (1995). A Million Random Digits With 100,000 Normal Deviates, Glencoe, IL: The Free Press.

TABLE C.4

CRITICAL VALUES OF F

The obtained F is significant at a given level if it is equal to or *greater than* the value shown in the table. 0.05(light row) and 0.01 (dark row) points for the distribution of F.

The values shown are the right tail of the distribution obtained by dividing the larger variance estimate by the smaller variance estimate. To find the complementary left or lower tail for a given df and α-level, reverse the degrees of freedom and find the reciprocal of that value in the F-table. For example, the value cutting off the top 5% of the area for 7 and 12 df is 2.92. To find the cutoff point of the bottom 5% of the area, find the tabled value of the $\alpha = 0.05$ level for 12 and 7 df. This is found to be 3.57. The reciprocal is $1/3.57 = 0.28$. Thus 5% of the area falls *at or below an* $F = 0.28$.

Degrees of freedom for numerator

df denom	1	2	3	4	5	6	7	8	9	10	11	12	14	16	20	24	30	40	50	75	100	200	500	∞
1	161	200	216	225	230	234	237	239	241	242	243	244	245	246	248	249	250	251	252	253	253	254	254	254
	4052	4999	5403	5625	5764	5859	5928	5981	6022	6056	6082	6106	6142	6169	6208	6234	6258	6286	6302	6323	6334	6352	6361	6366
2	18.51	19.00	19.16	19.25	19.30	19.33	19.36	19.37	19.38	19.39	19.40	19.41	19.42	19.43	19.44	19.45	19.46	19.47	19.48	19.49	19.49	19.49	19.50	19.50
	98.49	99.01	99.17	99.25	99.30	99.33	99.34	99.36	99.38	99.40	99.41	99.42	99.43	99.44	99.45	99.46	99.47	99.48	99.48	99.49	99.49	99.49	99.50	99.50
3	10.13	9.55	9.28	9.12	9.01	8.94	8.88	8.84	8.81	8.78	8.76	8.74	8.71	8.69	8.66	8.64	8.62	8.60	8.58	8.57	8.56	8.54	8.54	8.53
	34.12	30.81	29.46	28.71	28.24	27.91	27.67	27.49	27.34	27.23	27.13	27.05	26.92	26.83	26.69	26.60	26.50	26.41	26.30	26.27	26.23	26.18	26.14	26.12
4	7.71	6.94	6.59	6.39	6.26	6.16	6.09	6.04	6.00	5.96	5.93	5.91	5.87	5.84	5.80	5.77	5.74	5.71	5.70	5.68	5.66	5.65	5.64	5.63
	21.20	18.00	16.69	15.98	15.52	15.21	14.98	14.80	14.66	14.54	14.45	14.37	14.24	14.15	14.02	13.93	13.83	13.74	13.69	13.61	13.57	13.52	13.48	13.46
5	6.61	5.79	5.41	5.19	5.05	4.95	4.88	4.82	4.78	4.74	4.70	4.68	4.64	4.60	4.56	4.53	4.50	4.46	4.44	4.42	4.40	4.38	4.37	4.36
	16.26	13.27	12.06	11.39	10.97	10.67	10.45	10.27	10.15	10.05	9.96	9.89	9.77	9.68	9.55	9.47	9.38	9.29	9.24	9.17	9.13	9.07	9.04	9.02
6	5.99	5.14	4.76	4.53	4.39	4.28	4.21	4.15	4.10	4.06	4.03	4.00	3.96	3.92	3.87	3.84	3.81	3.77	3.75	3.72	3.71	3.69	3.68	3.67
	13.74	10.92	9.78	9.15	8.75	8.47	8.26	8.10	7.98	7.87	7.79	7.72	7.60	7.52	7.39	7.31	7.23	7.14	7.09	7.02	6.99	6.94	6.90	6.88
7	5.59	4.74	4.35	4.12	3.97	3.87	3.79	3.73	3.68	3.63	3.60	3.57	3.52	3.49	3.44	3.41	3.38	3.34	3.32	3.29	3.28	3.25	3.24	3.23
	12.25	9.55	8.45	7.85	7.46	7.19	7.00	6.84	6.71	6.62	6.54	6.47	6.35	6.27	6.15	6.07	5.98	5.90	5.85	5.78	5.75	5.70	5.67	5.65
8	5.32	4.46	4.07	3.84	3.69	3.58	3.50	3.44	3.39	3.34	3.31	3.28	3.23	3.20	3.15	3.12	3.08	3.05	3.03	3.00	2.98	2.96	2.94	2.93
	11.26	8.65	7.59	7.01	6.63	6.37	6.19	6.03	5.91	5.82	5.74	5.67	5.56	5.48	5.36	5.28	5.20	5.11	5.06	5.00	4.96	4.91	4.88	4.86
9	5.12	4.26	3.86	3.63	3.48	3.37	3.29	3.23	3.18	3.13	3.10	3.07	3.02	2.98	2.93	2.90	2.86	2.82	2.80	2.77	2.76	2.73	2.72	2.71
	10.56	8.02	6.99	6.42	6.06	5.80	5.62	5.47	5.35	5.26	5.18	5.11	5.00	4.92	4.80	4.73	4.64	4.56	4.51	4.45	4.41	4.36	4.33	4.31
10	4.96	4.10	3.71	3.48	3.33	3.22	3.14	3.07	3.02	2.97	2.94	2.91	2.86	2.82	2.77	2.74	2.70	2.67	2.64	2.61	2.59	2.56	2.55	2.54
	10.04	7.56	6.55	5.99	5.64	5.39	5.21	5.06	4.95	4.85	4.78	4.71	4.60	4.52	4.41	4.33	4.25	4.17	4.12	4.05	4.01	3.96	3.93	3.91
11	4.84	3.98	3.59	3.36	3.20	3.09	3.01	2.95	2.90	2.86	2.82	2.79	2.74	2.70	2.65	2.61	2.57	2.53	2.50	2.47	2.45	2.42	2.41	2.40
	9.65	7.20	6.22	5.67	5.32	5.07	4.88	4.74	4.63	4.54	4.46	4.40	4.29	4.21	4.10	4.02	3.94	3.86	3.80	3.74	3.70	3.66	3.62	3.60
12	4.75	3.88	3.49	3.26	3.11	3.00	2.92	2.85	2.80	2.76	2.72	2.69	2.64	2.60	2.54	2.50	2.46	2.42	2.40	2.36	2.35	2.32	2.31	2.30
	9.33	6.93	5.95	5.41	5.06	4.82	4.65	4.50	4.39	4.30	4.22	4.16	4.05	3.98	3.86	3.78	3.70	3.61	3.56	3.49	3.46	3.41	3.38	3.36
13	4.67	3.80	3.41	3.18	3.02	2.92	2.84	2.77	2.72	2.67	2.63	2.60	2.55	2.51	2.46	2.42	2.38	2.34	2.32	2.28	2.26	2.24	2.22	2.21
	9.07	6.70	5.74	5.20	4.86	4.62	4.44	4.30	4.19	4.10	4.02	3.96	3.85	3.78	3.67	3.59	3.51	3.42	3.37	3.30	3.27	3.21	3.18	3.16
14	4.60	3.74	3.34	3.11	2.96	2.85	2.77	2.70	2.65	2.60	2.56	2.53	2.48	2.44	2.39	2.35	2.31	2.27	2.24	2.21	2.19	2.16	2.14	2.13
	8.86	6.51	5.56	5.03	4.69	4.46	4.28	4.14	4.03	3.94	3.86	3.80	3.70	3.62	3.51	3.43	3.34	3.26	3.21	3.14	3.11	3.06	3.02	3.00
15	4.54	3.68	3.29	3.06	2.90	2.79	2.70	2.64	2.59	2.55	2.51	2.48	2.43	2.39	2.33	2.29	2.25	2.21	2.18	2.15	2.12	2.10	2.08	2.07
	8.68	6.36	5.42	4.89	4.56	4.32	4.14	4.00	3.89	3.80	3.73	3.67	3.56	3.48	3.36	3.29	3.20	3.12	3.07	3.00	2.97	2.92	2.89	2.87

Degrees of freedom for denominator

TABLE C.4 (Continued)

df																								
16	4.49	3.63	3.24	3.01	2.85	2.74	2.66	2.59	2.54	2.49	2.45	2.42	2.37	2.33	2.28	2.24	2.20	2.16	2.13	2.09	2.07	2.04	2.02	2.01
	8.53	6.23	5.29	4.77	4.44	4.20	4.03	3.89	3.78	3.69	3.61	3.55	3.45	3.37	3.25	3.18	3.10	3.01	2.96	2.89	2.86	2.80	2.77	2.75
17	4.45	3.59	3.20	2.96	2.81	2.70	2.62	2.55	2.50	2.45	2.41	2.38	2.33	2.29	2.23	2.19	2.15	2.11	2.08	2.04	2.02	1.99	1.97	1.96
	8.40	6.11	5.18	4.67	4.34	4.10	3.93	3.79	3.68	3.59	3.52	3.45	3.35	3.27	3.16	3.08	3.00	2.92	2.86	2.79	2.76	2.70	2.67	2.65
18	4.41	3.55	3.16	2.93	2.77	2.66	2.58	2.51	2.46	2.41	2.37	2.34	2.29	2.25	2.19	2.15	2.11	2.07	2.04	2.00	1.98	1.95	1.93	1.92
	8.28	6.01	5.09	4.58	4.25	4.01	3.85	3.71	3.60	3.51	3.44	3.37	3.27	3.19	3.07	3.00	2.91	2.83	2.78	2.71	2.68	2.62	2.59	2.57
19	4.38	3.52	3.13	2.90	2.74	2.63	2.55	2.48	2.43	2.38	2.34	2.31	2.26	2.21	2.15	2.11	2.07	2.02	2.00	1.96	1.94	1.91	1.90	1.88
	8.18	5.93	5.01	4.50	4.17	3.94	3.77	3.63	3.52	3.43	3.36	3.30	3.19	3.12	3.00	2.92	2.84	2.76	2.70	2.63	2.60	2.54	2.51	2.49
20	4.35	3.49	3.10	2.87	2.71	2.60	2.52	2.45	2.40	2.35	2.31	2.28	2.23	2.18	2.12	2.08	2.04	1.99	1.96	1.92	1.90	1.87	1.85	1.84
	8.10	5.85	4.94	4.43	4.10	3.87	3.71	3.56	3.45	3.37	3.30	3.23	3.13	3.05	2.94	2.86	2.77	2.69	2.63	2.56	2.53	2.47	2.44	2.42
21	4.32	3.47	3.07	2.84	2.68	2.57	2.49	2.42	2.37	2.32	2.28	2.25	2.20	2.15	2.09	2.05	2.00	1.96	1.93	1.90	1.87	1.84	1.82	1.81
	8.02	5.78	4.87	4.37	4.04	3.81	3.65	3.51	3.40	3.31	3.24	3.17	3.07	2.99	2.88	2.80	2.72	2.63	2.58	2.51	2.47	2.42	2.38	2.36
22	4.30	3.44	3.05	2.82	2.66	2.55	2.47	2.40	2.35	2.30	2.26	2.23	2.18	2.13	2.07	2.03	1.98	1.93	1.91	1.87	1.84	1.81	1.80	1.78
	7.94	5.72	4.82	4.31	3.99	3.76	3.59	3.45	3.35	3.26	3.18	3.12	3.02	2.94	2.83	2.75	2.67	2.58	2.53	2.46	2.42	2.37	2.33	2.31
23	4.28	3.42	3.03	2.80	2.64	2.53	2.45	2.38	2.32	2.28	2.24	2.20	2.14	2.10	2.04	2.00	1.96	1.91	1.88	1.84	1.82	1.79	1.77	1.76
	7.88	5.66	4.76	4.26	3.94	3.71	3.54	3.41	3.30	3.21	3.14	3.07	2.97	2.89	2.78	2.70	2.62	2.53	2.48	2.41	2.37	2.32	2.28	2.26
24	4.26	3.40	3.01	2.78	2.62	2.51	2.43	2.36	2.30	2.26	2.22	2.18	2.13	2.09	2.02	1.98	1.94	1.89	1.86	1.82	1.80	1.76	1.74	1.73
	7.82	5.61	4.72	4.22	3.90	3.67	3.50	3.36	3.25	3.17	3.09	3.03	2.93	2.85	2.74	2.66	2.58	2.49	2.44	2.36	2.33	2.27	2.23	2.21
25	4.24	3.38	2.99	2.76	2.60	2.49	2.41	2.34	2.28	2.24	2.20	2.16	2.11	2.06	2.00	1.96	1.92	1.87	1.84	1.80	1.77	1.74	1.72	1.71
	7.77	5.57	4.68	4.18	3.86	3.63	3.46	3.32	3.21	3.13	3.05	2.99	2.89	2.81	2.70	2.62	2.54	2.45	2.40	2.32	2.29	2.23	2.19	2.17
26	4.22	3.37	2.98	2.74	2.59	2.47	2.39	2.32	2.27	2.22	2.18	2.15	2.10	2.05	1.99	1.95	1.90	1.85	1.82	1.78	1.76	1.72	1.70	1.69
	7.72	5.53	4.64	4.14	3.82	3.59	3.42	3.29	3.17	3.09	3.02	2.96	2.86	2.77	2.66	2.58	2.50	2.41	2.36	2.28	2.25	2.19	2.15	2.13
27	4.21	3.35	2.96	2.73	2.57	2.46	2.37	2.30	2.25	2.20	2.16	2.13	2.08	2.03	1.97	1.93	1.88	1.84	1.80	1.76	1.74	1.71	1.68	1.67
	7.68	5.49	4.60	4.11	3.79	3.56	3.39	3.26	3.14	3.06	2.98	2.93	2.83	2.74	2.63	2.55	2.47	2.38	2.33	2.25	2.21	2.16	2.12	2.10
28	4.20	3.34	2.95	2.71	2.56	2.44	2.36	2.29	2.24	2.19	2.15	2.12	2.06	2.02	1.96	1.91	1.87	1.81	1.78	1.75	1.72	1.69	1.67	1.65
	7.64	5.45	4.57	4.07	3.76	3.53	3.36	3.23	3.11	3.03	2.95	2.90	2.80	2.71	2.60	2.52	2.44	2.35	2.30	2.22	2.18	2.13	2.09	2.06
29	4.18	3.33	2.93	2.70	2.54	2.43	2.35	2.28	2.22	2.18	2.14	2.10	2.05	2.00	1.94	1.90	1.85	1.80	1.77	1.73	1.71	1.68	1.65	1.64
	7.60	5.52	4.54	4.04	3.73	3.50	3.33	3.20	3.08	3.00	2.92	2.87	2.77	2.68	2.57	2.49	2.41	2.32	2.27	2.19	2.15	2.10	2.06	2.03
30	4.17	3.32	2.92	2.69	2.53	2.42	2.34	2.27	2.21	2.16	2.12	2.09	2.04	1.99	1.93	1.89	1.84	1.79	1.76	1.72	1.69	1.66	1.64	1.62
	7.56	5.39	4.51	4.02	3.70	3.47	3.30	3.17	3.06	2.98	2.90	2.84	2.74	2.66	2.55	2.47	2.38	2.29	2.24	2.16	2.13	2.07	2.03	2.01
32	4.15	3.30	2.90	2.67	2.51	2.40	2.32	2.25	2.19	2.14	2.10	2.07	2.02	1.97	1.91	1.86	1.82	1.76	1.74	1.69	1.67	1.64	1.61	1.59
	7.50	5.34	4.46	3.97	3.66	3.42	3.25	3.12	3.01	2.94	2.86	2.80	2.70	2.62	2.51	2.42	2.34	2.25	2.20	2.12	2.08	2.02	1.98	1.96
34	4.13	3.28	2.88	2.65	2.49	2.38	2.30	2.23	2.17	2.12	2.08	2.05	2.00	1.95	1.89	1.84	1.80	1.74	1.71	1.67	1.64	1.61	1.59	1.57
	7.44	5.29	4.42	3.93	3.61	3.38	3.21	3.08	2.97	2.89	2.82	2.76	2.66	2.58	2.47	2.38	2.30	2.21	2.15	2.08	2.04	1.98	1.94	1.91

TABLE C.4 (Continued)

df																								
36	1.55 / 1.87	1.56 / 1.90	1.59 / 1.94	1.62 / 2.00	1.65 / 2.04	1.69 / 2.12	1.72 / 2.17	1.78 / 2.26	1.82 / 2.35	1.87 / 2.43	1.93 / 2.54	1.89 / 2.62	2.03 / 2.72	2.06 / 2.78	2.10 / 2.86	2.15 / 2.94	2.21 / 3.04	2.28 / 3.18	2.36 / 3.35	2.48 / 3.58	2.63 / 3.89	2.86 / 4.38	3.26 / 5.25	4.11 / 7.39
38	1.53 / 1.84	1.54 / 1.86	1.57 / 1.90	1.60 / 1.97	1.63 / 2.00	1.67 / 2.08	1.71 / 2.14	1.76 / 2.22	1.80 / 2.32	1.85 / 2.40	1.92 / 2.51	1.96 / 2.59	2.02 / 2.69	2.05 / 2.75	2.09 / 2.82	2.14 / 2.91	2.19 / 3.02	2.26 / 3.15	2.35 / 3.32	2.46 / 3.54	2.62 / 3.86	2.85 / 4.34	3.25 / 5.21	4.10 / 7.35
40	1.51 / 1.81	1.53 / 1.84	1.55 / 1.88	1.59 / 1.94	1.61 / 1.97	1.66 / 2.05	1.69 / 2.11	1.74 / 2.20	1.79 / 2.29	1.84 / 2.37	1.90 / 2.49	1.95 / 2.56	2.00 / 2.66	2.04 / 2.73	2.07 / 2.80	2.12 / 2.88	2.18 / 2.99	2.25 / 3.12	2.34 / 3.29	2.45 / 3.51	2.61 / 3.83	2.84 / 4.31	3.23 / 5.18	4.08 / 7.31
42	1.49 / 1.78	1.51 / 1.80	1.54 / 1.85	1.57 / 1.91	1.60 / 1.94	1.64 / 2.02	1.68 / 2.08	1.73 / 2.17	1.78 / 2.26	1.82 / 2.35	1.89 / 2.46	1.94 / 2.54	1.90 / 2.64	2.02 / 2.70	2.06 / 2.77	2.11 / 2.86	2.17 / 2.96	2.24 / 3.10	2.32 / 3.26	2.44 / 3.49	2.59 / 3.80	2.83 / 4.29	3.22 / 5.15	4.07 / 7.27
44	1.48 / 1.75	1.50 / 1.78	1.52 / 1.82	1.56 / 1.88	1.58 / 1.92	1.63 / 1.98	1.66 / 2.06	1.72 / 2.15	1.76 / 2.24	1.81 / 2.32	1.88 / 2.44	1.92 / 2.52	1.98 / 2.62	2.01 / 2.68	2.05 / 2.75	2.10 / 2.84	2.16 / 2.94	2.23 / 3.07	2.31 / 3.24	2.43 / 3.46	2.58 / 3.78	2.82 / 4.26	3.21 / 5.12	4.06 / 7.24
46	1.46 / 1.72	1.48 / 1.76	1.51 / 1.80	1.54 / 1.86	1.57 / 1.90	1.62 / 1.98	1.65 / 2.04	1.71 / 2.13	1.75 / 2.22	1.80 / 2.30	1.87 / 2.42	1.91 / 2.50	1.97 / 2.60	2.00 / 2.66	2.04 / 2.73	2.09 / 2.82	2.14 / 2.92	2.22 / 3.05	2.30 / 3.22	2.42 / 3.44	2.57 / 3.76	2.81 / 4.24	3.20 / 5.10	4.05 / 7.21
48	1.45 / 1.70	1.47 / 1.73	1.50 / 1.78	1.53 / 1.84	1.56 / 1.88	1.61 / 1.96	1.64 / 2.02	1.70 / 2.11	1.74 / 2.20	1.79 / 2.28	1.86 / 2.40	1.90 / 2.48	1.96 / 2.58	1.99 / 2.64	2.03 / 2.71	2.08 / 2.80	2.14 / 2.90	2.21 / 3.04	2.30 / 3.20	2.41 / 3.42	2.56 / 3.74	2.80 / 4.22	3.19 / 5.08	4.04 / 7.19
50	1.44 / 1.68	1.46 / 1.71	1.48 / 1.76	1.52 / 1.82	1.55 / 1.86	1.60 / 1.94	1.63 / 2.00	1.69 / 2.10	1.74 / 2.18	1.78 / 2.26	1.85 / 2.39	1.90 / 2.46	1.95 / 2.56	1.98 / 2.62	2.02 / 2.70	2.07 / 2.78	2.13 / 2.88	2.20 / 3.02	2.29 / 3.18	2.40 / 3.41	2.56 / 3.72	2.79 / 4.20	3.18 / 5.06	4.03 / 7.17
55	1.41 / 1.64	1.43 / 1.66	1.46 / 1.71	1.50 / 1.78	1.52 / 1.82	1.58 / 1.90	1.61 / 1.96	1.67 / 2.06	1.72 / 2.15	1.76 / 2.23	1.83 / 2.35	1.88 / 2.43	1.93 / 2.53	1.97 / 2.59	2.00 / 2.66	2.05 / 2.75	2.11 / 2.85	2.18 / 2.98	2.27 / 3.15	2.38 / 3.37	2.54 / 3.68	2.78 / 4.16	3.17 / 5.01	4.02 / 7.12
60	1.39 / 1.60	1.41 / 1.63	1.44 / 1.68	1.48 / 1.74	1.50 / 1.79	1.56 / 1.87	1.59 / 1.93	1.65 / 2.03	1.70 / 2.12	1.75 / 2.20	1.81 / 2.32	1.86 / 2.40	1.92 / 2.50	1.95 / 2.56	1.99 / 2.63	2.04 / 2.72	2.10 / 2.82	2.17 / 2.95	2.25 / 3.12	2.37 / 3.34	2.52 / 3.65	2.76 / 4.13	3.15 / 4.98	4.00 / 7.08
65	1.37 / 1.56	1.39 / 1.60	1.42 / 1.64	1.46 / 1.71	1.49 / 1.76	1.54 / 1.84	1.57 / 1.90	1.63 / 2.00	1.68 / 2.09	1.73 / 2.18	1.80 / 2.30	1.85 / 2.37	1.90 / 2.47	1.94 / 2.54	1.98 / 2.61	2.02 / 2.70	2.08 / 2.79	2.15 / 2.93	2.24 / 3.09	2.36 / 3.31	2.51 / 3.62	2.75 / 4.10	3.14 / 4.95	3.99 / 7.04
70	1.35 / 1.53	1.37 / 1.56	1.40 / 1.62	1.45 / 1.69	1.47 / 1.74	1.53 / 1.82	1.56 / 1.88	1.62 / 1.98	1.67 / 2.07	1.72 / 2.15	1.79 / 2.28	1.84 / 2.35	1.89 / 2.45	1.93 / 2.51	1.97 / 2.59	2.01 / 2.67	2.07 / 2.77	2.14 / 2.91	2.23 / 3.07	2.35 / 3.29	2.50 / 3.60	2.74 / 4.08	3.13 / 4.92	3.98 / 7.01
80	1.32 / 1.49	1.35 / 1.52	1.38 / 1.57	1.42 / 1.65	1.45 / 1.70	1.51 / 1.78	1.54 / 1.84	1.60 / 1.94	1.65 / 2.03	1.70 / 2.11	1.77 / 2.24	1.82 / 2.32	1.88 / 2.41	1.91 / 2.48	1.95 / 2.55	1.99 / 2.64	2.05 / 2.74	2.12 / 2.87	2.21 / 3.04	2.33 / 3.25	2.48 / 3.56	2.72 / 4.04	3.11 / 4.88	3.96 / 6.96
100	1.28 / 1.43	1.30 / 1.46	1.34 / 1.51	1.39 / 1.59	1.42 / 1.64	1.48 / 1.73	1.51 / 1.79	1.57 / 1.89	1.63 / 1.98	1.68 / 2.06	1.75 / 2.19	1.79 / 2.26	1.85 / 2.36	1.88 / 2.43	1.92 / 2.51	1.97 / 2.59	2.03 / 2.69	2.10 / 2.82	2.19 / 2.99	2.31 / 3.21	2.46 / 3.51	2.70 / 3.98	3.09 / 4.82	3.94 / 6.90
125	1.25 / 1.37	1.27 / 1.40	1.31 / 1.46	1.36 / 1.54	1.39 / 1.59	1.45 / 1.68	1.49 / 1.75	1.55 / 1.85	1.60 / 1.94	1.65 / 2.03	1.72 / 2.15	1.77 / 2.23	1.83 / 2.33	1.86 / 2.40	1.90 / 2.47	1.95 / 2.56	2.01 / 2.65	2.08 / 2.79	2.17 / 2.95	2.29 / 3.17	2.44 / 3.47	2.68 / 3.94	3.07 / 4.78	3.92 / 6.84
150	1.22 / 1.33	1.25 / 1.37	1.29 / 1.43	1.34 / 1.51	1.37 / 1.56	1.44 / 1.66	1.47 / 1.72	1.54 / 1.83	1.59 / 1.92	1.64 / 2.00	1.71 / 2.12	1.76 / 2.20	1.82 / 2.30	1.85 / 2.37	1.89 / 2.44	1.94 / 2.53	2.00 / 2.62	2.07 / 2.76	2.16 / 2.92	2.28 / 3.14	2.43 / 3.44	2.67 / 3.91	3.06 / 4.75	3.91 / 6.81
200	1.19 / 1.28	1.22 / 1.33	1.26 / 1.39	1.32 / 1.48	1.35 / 1.53	1.42 / 1.62	1.45 / 1.69	1.52 / 1.79	1.57 / 1.89	1.62 / 1.97	1.69 / 2.09	1.74 / 2.17	1.80 / 2.28	1.83 / 2.34	1.87 / 2.41	1.92 / 2.50	1.98 / 2.60	2.05 / 2.73	2.14 / 2.90	2.26 / 3.11	2.41 / 3.41	2.65 / 3.88	3.04 / 4.71	3.89 / 6.76
400	1.13 / 1.19	1.16 / 1.24	1.22 / 1.32	1.28 / 1.42	1.32 / 1.47	1.38 / 1.57	1.42 / 1.64	1.49 / 1.74	1.54 / 1.84	1.60 / 1.92	1.67 / 2.04	1.72 / 2.12	1.78 / 2.23	1.81 / 2.29	1.85 / 2.37	1.90 / 2.46	1.96 / 2.55	2.03 / 2.69	2.12 / 2.85	2.23 / 3.06	2.39 / 3.36	2.62 / 3.83	3.02 / 4.66	3.86 / 6.70
1000	1.08 / 1.11	1.13 / 1.19	1.19 / 1.28	1.26 / 1.38	1.30 / 1.44	1.36 / 1.54	1.41 / 1.61	1.47 / 1.71	1.53 / 1.81	1.58 / 1.89	1.65 / 2.01	1.70 / 2.09	1.76 / 2.20	1.80 / 2.26	1.84 / 2.34	1.89 / 2.43	1.95 / 2.53	2.02 / 2.66	2.10 / 2.82	2.22 / 3.04	2.38 / 3.34	2.61 / 3.80	3.00 / 4.62	3.85 / 6.66
∞	1.00 / 1.00	1.11 / 1.15	1.17 / 1.25	1.24 / 1.36	1.28 / 1.41	1.35 / 1.52	1.40 / 1.59	1.46 / 1.69	1.52 / 1.79	1.57 / 1.87	1.64 / 1.99	1.69 / 2.07	1.75 / 2.18	1.79 / 2.24	1.83 / 2.32	1.88 / 2.41	1.94 / 2.51	2.01 / 2.64	2.09 / 2.80	2.21 / 3.02	2.37 / 3.32	2.60 / 3.78	2.99 / 4.60	3.84 / 6.64

TABLE C.5

PERCENTAGE POINTS OF THE STUDENTIZED RANGE

Error df	a	\(k\) = number of means or number of steps between ordered means									
		2	3	4	5	6	7	8	9	10	11
5	.05	3.64	4.60	5.22	5.67	6.03	6.33	6.58	6.80	6.99	7.17
	.01	5.70	6.98	7.80	8.42	8.91	9.32	9.67	9.97	10.24	10.48
6	.05	3.46	4.34	4.90	5.30	5.63	5.90	6.12	6.32	6.49	6.65
	.01	5.24	6.33	7.03	7.56	7.97	8.32	8.61	8.87	9.10	9.30
7	.05	3.34	4.16	4.68	5.06	5.36	5.61	5.82	6.00	6.16	6.30
	.01	4.95	5.92	6.54	7.01	7.37	7.68	7.94	8.17	8.37	8.55
8	.05	3.26	4.04	4.53	4.89	5.17	5.40	5.60	5.77	5.92	6.05
	.01	4.75	5.64	6.20	6.62	6.96	7.24	7.47	7.68	7.86	8.03
9	.05	3.20	3.95	4.41	4.76	5.02	5.24	5.43	5.59	5.74	5.87
	.01	4.60	5.43	5.96	6.35	6.66	6.91	7.13	7.33	7.49	7.65
10	.05	3.15	3.88	4.33	4.65	4.91	5.12	5.30	5.46	5.60	5.72
	.01	4.48	5.27	5.77	6.14	6.43	6.67	6.87	7.05	7.21	7.36
11	.05	3.11	3.82	4.26	4.57	4.82	5.03	5.20	5.35	5.49	5.61
	.01	4.39	5.15	5.62	5.97	6.25	6.48	6.67	6.84	6.99	7.13
12	.05	3.08	3.77	4.20	4.51	4.75	4.95	5.12	5.27	5.39	5.51
	.01	4.32	5.05	5.50	5.84	6.10	6.32	6.51	6.67	6.81	6.94
13	.05	3.06	3.73	4.15	4.45	4.69	4.88	5.05	5.19	5.32	5.43
	.01	4.26	4.96	5.40	5.73	5.98	6.19	6.37	6.53	6.67	6.79
14	.05	3.03	3.70	4.11	4.41	4.64	4.83	4.99	5.13	5.25	5.36
	.01	4.21	4.89	5.32	5.63	5.88	6.08	6.26	6.41	6.54	6.66
15	.05	3.01	3.67	4.08	4.37	4.59	4.78	4.94	5.08	5.20	5.31
	.01	4.17	4.84	5.25	5.56	5.80	5.99	6.16	6.31	6.44	6.55
16	.05	3.00	3.65	4.05	4.33	4.56	4.74	4.90	5.03	5.15	5.26
	.01	4.13	4.79	5.19	5.49	5.72	5.92	6.08	6.22	6.35	6.46
17	.05	2.98	3.63	4.02	4.30	4.52	4.70	4.86	4.99	5.11	5.21
	.01	4.10	4.74	5.14	5.43	5.66	5.85	6.01	6.15	6.27	6.38
18	.05	2.97	3.61	4.00	4.28	4.49	4.67	4.82	4.96	5.07	5.17
	.01	4.07	4.70	5.09	5.38	5.60	5.79	5.94	6.08	6.20	6.31
19	.05	2.96	3.59	3.98	4.25	4.47	4.65	4.79	4.92	5.04	5.14
	.01	4.05	4.67	5.05	5.33	5.55	5.73	5.89	6.02	6.14	6.25
20	.05	2.95	3.58	3.96	4.23	4.45	4.62	4.77	4.90	5.01	5.11
	.01	4.02	4.64	5.02	5.29	5.51	5.69	5.84	5.97	6.09	6.19
24	.05	2.92	3.53	3.90	4.17	4.37	4.54	4.68	4.81	4.92	5.01
	.01	3.96	4.55	4.91	5.17	5.37	5.54	5.69	5.81	5.92	6.02
30	.05	2.89	3.49	3.85	4.10	4.30	4.46	4.60	4.72	4.82	4.92
	.01	3.89	4.45	4.80	5.05	5.24	5.40	5.54	5.65	5.76	5.85
40	.05	2.86	3.44	3.79	4.04	4.23	4.39	4.52	4.63	4.73	4.82
	.01	3.82	4.37	4.70	4.93	5.11	5.26	5.39	5.50	5.60	5.69
60	.05	2.83	3.40	3.74	3.98	4.16	4.31	4.44	4.55	4.65	4.73
	.01	3.76	4.28	4.59	4.82	4.99	5.13	5.25	5.36	5.45	5.53
120	.05	2.80	3.36	3.68	3.92	4.10	4.24	4.36	4.47	4.56	4.64
	.01	3.70	4.20	4.50	4.71	4.87	5.01	5.12	5.21	5.30	5.37
∞	.05	2.77	3.31	3.63	3.86	4.03	4.17	4.29	4.39	4.47	4.55
	.01	3.64	4.12	4.40	4.60	4.76	4.88	4.99	5.08	5.16	5.23

TABLE C.6

RANDOM NUMBERS TABLE

Row number										
00000	10097	32533	76520	13586	34673	54876	80959	09117	39292	74945
00001	37542	04805	64894	74296	24805	24037	20636	10402	00822	91665
00002	08422	68953	19645	09303	23209	02560	15953	34764	35080	33606
00003	99019	02529	09376	70715	38311	31165	88676	74397	04436	27659
00004	12807	99970	80157	36147	64032	36653	98951	16877	12171	76833
00005	66065	74717	34072	76850	36697	36170	65813	39885	11199	29170
00006	31060	10805	45571	82406	35303	42614	86799	07439	23403	09732
00007	85269	77602	02051	65692	68665	74818	73053	85247	18623	88579
00008	63573	32135	05325	47048	90553	57548	28468	28709	83491	25624
00009	73796	45753	03529	64778	35808	34282	60935	20344	35273	88435
00010	98520	17767	14905	68607	22109	40558	60970	93433	50500	73998
00011	11805	05431	39808	27732	50725	68248	29405	24201	52775	67851
00012	83452	99634	06288	98033	13746	70078	18475	40610	68711	77817
00013	88685	40200	86507	58401	36766	67951	90364	76493	29609	11062
00014	99594	67348	87517	64969	91826	08928	93785	61368	23478	34113
00015	65481	17674	17468	50950	58047	76974	73039	57186	40218	16544
00016	80124	35635	17727	08015	45318	22374	21115	78253	14385	53763
00017	74350	99817	77402	77214	43236	00210	45521	64237	96286	02655
00018	69916	26803	66252	29148	36936	87203	76621	13990	94400	56418
00019	09893	20505	14225	68514	46427	56788	96297	78822	54382	14598
00020	91499	14523	68479	27686	46162	83554	94750	89923	37089	20048
00021	80336	94598	26940	36858	70297	34135	53140	33340	42050	82341
00022	44104	81949	85157	47954	32979	26575	57600	40881	22222	06413
00023	12550	73742	11100	02040	12860	74697	96644	89439	28707	25815
00024	63606	49329	16505	34484	40219	52563	43651	77082	07207	31790
00025	61196	90446	26457	47774	51924	33729	65394	59593	42582	60527
00026	15474	45266	95270	79953	59367	83848	82396	10118	33211	59466
00027	94557	28573	67897	54387	54622	44431	91190	42592	92927	45973
00028	42481	16213	97344	08721	16868	48767	03071	12059	25701	46670
00029	23523	78317	73208	89837	68935	91416	26252	29663	05522	82562
00030	04493	52494	75246	33824	45862	51025	61962	79335	65337	12472
00031	00549	97654	64051	88159	96119	63896	54692	82391	23287	29529
00032	35963	15307	26898	09354	33351	35462	77974	50024	90103	39333
00033	59808	08391	45427	26842	83609	49700	13021	24892	78565	20106
00034	46058	85236	01390	92286	77281	44077	93910	83647	70617	42941
00035	32179	00597	87379	25241	05567	07007	86743	17157	85394	11838
00036	69234	61406	20117	45204	15956	60000	18743	92423	97118	96338
00037	19565	41430	01758	75379	40419	21585	66674	36806	84962	85207
00038	45155	14938	19476	07246	43667	94543	59047	90033	20826	69541
00039	94864	31994	36168	10851	34888	81553	01540	35456	05014	51176
00040	98086	24826	45240	28404	44999	08896	39094	73407	35441	31880
00041	33185	16232	41941	50949	89435	48581	88695	41994	37548	73043
00042	80951	00406	96382	70774	20151	23387	25016	25298	94624	61171
00043	79752	49140	71961	28296	69861	02591	74852	20539	00387	59579
00044	18633	32537	98145	06571	31010	24674	05455	61427	77938	91936
00045	74029	43902	77557	32270	97790	17119	52527	58021	80814	51748
00046	54178	45611	80993	37143	05335	12969	56127	19255	36040	90324
00047	11664	49883	52079	84827	59381	71539	09973	33440	88461	23356
00048	48324	77928	31249	64710	02295	36870	32307	57546	15020	09994
00049	69074	94138	87637	91976	35584	04401	10518	21615	01848	76938
00050	09188	20097	32825	39527	04220	86304	83389	87374	64278	58044
00051	90045	85497	51981	50654	94938	81997	91870	76150	68476	64659
00052	73189	50207	47677	26269	62290	64464	27124	67018	41361	82760
00053	75768	76490	20971	87749	90429	12272	95375	05871	93823	43178
00054	54016	44056	66281	31003	00682	27398	20714	53295	07706	17813
00055	08358	69910	78542	42785	13661	58873	04618	97553	31223	08420
00056	28306	03264	81333	10591	40510	07893	32604	60475	94119	01840
00057	53840	86233	81594	13628	51215	90290	28466	68795	77762	20791
00058	91757	53741	61613	62669	50263	90212	55781	76514	83483	47055
00059	89415	92694	00397	58391	12607	17646	48949	72306	94541	37408

Professional Issues for the Future: Presenting Yourself

As you plan your future, turn your knowledge of the research process—especially its planning side—to your advantage. Psychologists are prone to engage in career planning with the same enthusiasm they show in conducting empirical research (e.g., Dunn & Zaremba, 1997; Keller, 1994; Rheingold, 1994; Zanna & Darley, 1987). If you plan to attend graduate or professional school, you will need to present yourself and your skills in ways that enhance the chance of admission. If, instead, you are planning to enter the work force, then you will still want to do so in ways that increase your likelihood of being hired. The goal of the two exercises in this appendix is to help you look to the future. Although they are oriented toward students who plan graduate education in psychology, each exercise is flexible and can be altered slightly to fit more general purposes. The first exercise discusses how to write an academic resume, and the second presents a strategy for asking for letters of recommendation from psychology faculty.

Exercise D.1: Writing a Vitae

At some point during your college career, you will need to write a resume, a summary of your qualifications and experiences relevant to postgraduate opportunities. Such summaries are a useful form of self-evaluation in that they can direct people to new academic or professional goals. Resumes are also an exercise in self-appraisal, one that details past and present accomplishments in preparation for future efforts (Bostwick, 1990).

An academic resume is called a *curriculum vitae*, or vitae for short. A vitae is a brief account of a person's academic credentials. It profiles his or her education, including degrees and dates, any academic awards or professional memberships, particular course work or expertise, and professional publications and presentations. Occasionally, a short statement of purpose will indicate the desired academic, research, or professional position. Unlike the typical resume, a vitae should not include a list of hobbies or much personal information beyond your name and date of birth.

What is the structure of a typical vitae? Two key features of any vitae are organization and objectivity; information is readily accessible and understandable, reflecting reality and not puffery or hyperbole. Table D.1 illustrates the vitae of a senior psychology major. She wrote this vitae so that she would have a concise summary of her educational background to share with the faculty members who wrote letters of recommendation on her behalf (see p. 369). A copy of this vitae was also included with her applications to graduate school. Use table D.1 as a guide to writing your own vitae.

As you can see in table D.1, a few main sections stand out, including

- *Personal information.* Include your full name, current address, and phone number in this section. Some people also note their birthdate and marital status. Such information is not necessary, but be certain to omit any reference to your race, religion, or political affiliation.
- *Objective.* A short, concise summary statement tells readers what you are looking for in a graduate school or a job.
- *Education.* List your educational background chronologically, starting with the most recent degree or the one you plan to complete shortly. It is not necessary to list a high school degree once you have graduated from college.
- *Honors.* List any special awards, scholarships, fellowships, or other honors under this heading. Do not worry if you don't have any yet—many people don't—but avoid undue modesty if you have received special recognition for your work.
- *Research experience outside the classroom.* The apprenticeship model is a good one, and some students gain valuable experience volunteering their time to help with ongoing research projects. Consider asking a psychologist at your institution if he or she has a project you could work on. If you already have worked with a professor on his or her personal research, write a short description of your role and dates of service.
- *Publications and presentations.* If you have the good fortune to have published or presented a piece of research at a student conference (see chapter 9), then by all means list it in APA format beneath this heading. This section is the one that most psychologists try to increase in the course of their educations and careers. In the absence of papers or talks, you might rename this section "Relevant Course Work" and list those courses most appropriate to the graduate program or position you are after.
- *Related experience.* Any past or current employment, volunteer work, or internship experience that complements your objective should also be noted in a vitae. Graduate schools in psychology, for example, will be interested in any past positions where applicants were able to apply or acquire disciplinary knowledge. For their part, potential employers usually prefer to hire individuals with demonstrated abilities or previous job experience. Entries under this section should indicate the position title, site, dates of service, and brief descriptions of any duties performed.
- *References.* Let the person reading your vitae know that you would be willing to provide a list of professional references by using the notation "Available upon request." Who are these references? Psychologists, faculty members, and

TABLE D.1

A SAMPLE CURRICULUM VITAE

Carolyn I. Vicchiullo
Curriculum Vitae

Personal:

	Address	123 Main Street
		Boston, MA 01234
	Phone	(123) 456-7890

Objective:

To obtain admission to a graduate program in psychology.

Education:

B.A. in Psychology, Summa Cum Laude, Moravian College, May 1996

Honors:

Phi Mu Epsilon Sorority Prize, May 1996
Alumni Prize for Achievement in the Social Sciences, May 1996
Psi Chi, 1994

Research Experience:

Assisted Dr. Dana S. Dunn, Department of Psychology, Moravian College, with project development, and coding and analysis of questionnaire data on Adjustment to Living with HIV/AIDS, September 1995–June 1996.

Publications and Presentations:

Vicchiullo, C. I., & Dunn, D. S. (1996). Exploring three correlates of thought suppression: Attention, absorption, and cognitive load. *Modern Psychological Studies, 4,* 21–39.

Vicchiullo, C. I. (1995, June). *Absorption ability affects physiological response: Preliminary evidence.* Paper presented at the 10th Annual LVAIC Undergraduate Psychology Conference, Cedar Crest College, Allentown, PA.

Related Experience:

Undergraduate Clinical Internship, Psychiatric Unit, St. Thomas Hospital, Easton, PA. 8 hours weekly, September 1994–December 1994. Duties: Attended patient assessments; observed group therapy sessions; assisted with psychological testing; one-on-one patient contact.

Hot-line telephone crisis counselor: Safe Place Shelter for Women, Newtown, PA. 6 hours weekly, February 1990–May 1990. Duties: Handled incoming calls from abused women in crisis; trained to offer immediate counseling or referrals to agencies.

References: Available upon request

other people who know you, your work, character, and abilities very well. Unless the names and addresses are specifically requested by a school or employer, don't add them here, as they take up valuable space. You can provide a list later, when they are requested as part of an application or during an interview.

What about length? A student vitae will certainly be much shorter than those maintained by psychologists who have been active in the field for years. A vitae should be as long as it needs to be, but one—no more than two—pages is a sufficient length for a college student or recent graduate. Under no circumstances should it appear to be "padded" with extraneous information to increase its length (e.g., hobbies, travel experiences, photographs), nor should it have decorative fonts or frills on it. For further suggestions on resume writing more generally, see Bostwick (1990).

Exercise D.2: Obtaining Letters of Recommendation

As part of the application process, many graduate programs and employers place a great deal of emphasis on letters of recommendation from faculty members. Whom should you ask for letters of recommendation? The faculty you approach do not necessarily need to be psychologists, but they do need to know you—and your work—quite well. The best single piece of advice is to ask only those faculty members who will be able to write a strong letter on your behalf. Be direct and find out if this is a possibility because having a weak or uncomplimentary letter in an application packet is usually more damaging than no letter at all. Most professors will be honest and let you know if they are comfortable writing a strong letter for graduate school or a job recommendation. Do not try to convince any professor to change his or her mind—be gracious and ask someone else if you are refused!

There are several steps you can take to increase the chance that your letters of recommendation will be strong ones. These steps include

- *Provide each recommender with a curriculum vitae.* Anyone writing a letter of recommendation for you needs a summary of your activities, achievements, and abilities during college. The vitae described in Exercise D.1 satisfies this requirement and presents you in a professional light at the same time.
- *Provide a recent copy of your transcript.* Recommenders should know the courses you have taken during college and how well you have done in them. Be sure to note your overall grade point average (GPA), as well as the GPA in your major and minor, if applicable.
- *Provide a copy of your statement of purpose.* Most graduate programs require that applicants write an essay on why they wish to pursue a degree in psychology, their possible research interests, and so forth. This essay is an extremely important part of any graduate school application. It should be carefully crafted so that the graduate program—and your recommender—will understand your educational goals, intellectual motivation, and career aspirations. In fact, you might ask one or two of your recommenders to critique your statement of purpose before submitting it with your application.
- *Identify the basis of the professor/student relationship.* If you worked in a faculty member's lab or collaborated on a project—an excellent way to gain research experience—then you will no doubt be memorable. In general, however, most student-faculty contact is classroom based. Students often forget that faculty teach hundreds of students each year, so that keeping track of information

about any particular relationship (or worse, remembering a person's name!) is no small feat. Gently remind faculty members about your connection to them with a course list (the title, semester and year, your final grade, copies of any paper(s) you wrote, etc.). I guarantee that they will appreciate having their memories jogged a bit.

- *The recommendation form (if any) and a due date.* Be sure to complete the portions of any recommendation forms that apply to you (e.g., your full name, program title, degree being sought) before passing them on to faculty members. Keep in mind that recommendation letters take time to write. Ideally, any person writing a letter for you should have 2 or more weeks to finish it.
- *Describe the program or position you are seeking.* Recommenders can discuss relevant details about your college experience in their letters, but only if they know what to highlight. As noted previously, many schools ask applicants to write a "statement of purpose," which is a rationale for their interest in pursuing an advanced degree. Consider sharing a copy of this statement with your recommenders so they know what you hope to achieve in the future.
- *Include an already addressed and stamped envelope.* This step is a time saver and a courtesy to your recommenders.
- *Should you waive your right to see your letters of recommendation?* The Family Educational Rights and Privacy Act of 1974 gives you the choice of waiving (or not waiving) the right to see your letters of recommendation after they are submitted to the schools of your choice. Not waiving your rights means that you could later see what has been written about you; you might decide, for example, to seek other references in the future. Waiving your right of access is thought by many (including graduate schools and prospective employers) to increase the credibility of recommendations because letters writers can say what they believe in confidence. Letter writers, too, may be more honest in their assessment of your skills. Most applications will have a box for you to check and a place for your signature to verify the waiver decision. To waive or not to waive is an important choice that rests with you alone.

A SPECIAL COMMENT ON GRADUATE EDUCATION IN PSYCHOLOGY

Graduate school is a big step for anyone. It is an important decision with a relatively long time commitment, lifelong implications, and few guarantees in the short term, except the promise of hard work and its accompanying satisfactions. If you are interested in graduate training in psychology, then by all means apply—but do so for the right reasons. It is my personal belief that a large part of success in graduate school is due to three factors: organization, time management, and desire. The first two points are self-evident, and they have been examined in various ways throughout this book. The third—desire—is a personal one. If you decide to go to graduate school, please make the choice because you really want to be there. Casual observation suggests that those individuals who leave graduate school without degrees do so because they lack motivation or sincere interest, not ability. Graduate school is an opportunity, a haven for understanding—not escaping—life.

At this point, you may not be certain whether graduate school is in your future. There is plenty of time to decide and, fortunately, there are several very useful resources on educational and career issues in psychology. First, rely on local resources: Ask faculty members in psychology about their experiences with and insights on graduate education in the field. You might also seek their advice about what schools are well regarded in your area of interest. Two other useful resources are pamphlets titled *Careers in Psychology* (American Psychological Association, 1986) and *Psychology/Careers for the Twenty-First Century* (American Psychological Association, 1996). Each provides short summaries of opportunities in and outside of academic settings, profiling what psychologists actually do in their daily working lives.

A book on the admissions process in psychology graduate programs, with an emphasis on "getting in," is also available (American Psychological Association, 1993). An advantage of this book is that it includes timetables recommending what to do when in the application process. You can readily increase the chance of admission by following the practical advice in this book.

Finally, the American Psychological Association publishes a guide to *Graduate Study in Psychology* biannually. This guide summarizes over 600 diverse graduate programs, their admissions requirements, and application deadlines. With so many choices, prospective graduate students can find programs that match their interests and skills, and in locations that suit them. There is also a specialized guide to graduate programs in clinical psychology (Mayne, Norcross, & Sayette, 1994) that is well worth examining. The latter book also has "insider" information that removes much of the mystery in gaining acceptance to clinical and counseling degree programs.

REFERENCES

Abelson, R. P. (1995). *Statistics as principled argument.* Hillsdale, NJ: Erlbaum.

Abelson, R. P. (1997). On the surprising longevity of flogged horses: Why there is a case for the significance test. *Psychological Science, 8,* 12–15.

Abramson, L. Y., Seligman, M. E. P., & Teasdale, J. D. (1978). Learned helplessness in humans: Critique and reformulation. *Journal of Abnormal Psychology, 87,* 49–74.

Adams, J. L. (1974). *Conceptual blockbusting.* San Francisco: W. H. Freeman & Co.

Adler, N. E., Taylor, S. E., & Wortman, C. B. (1987). Basic field research in health psychology. In G. C. Stone, S. M. Weiss, J. D. Matarazzo, N. E. Miller, J. Rodin, C. D. Belar, M. J. Follick, & J. E. Singer (Eds.), *Health psychology: A discipline and a profession* (pp. 91–106). Chicago: University of Chicago Press.

Ainsworth, M. D. (1963). The development of infant-mother interaction among the Ganda. In B. M. Foss (Ed.), *Determinants of infant behavior* (Vol. 2). London: Methuen.

Ainsworth, M. D. S. (1967). *Infancy in Uganda: Infant care and the growth of attachment.* Baltimore, MD: The Johns Hopkins University Press.

Ainsworth, M. D. S., & Wittig, B. A. (1969). Attachment and exploratory behavior of one-year-olds in a strange situation. In B. M. Foss (Ed.), *Determinants of infant behavior* (Vol. 4, pp. 129–173). London: Methuen.

Allport, G. W. (1965). *Letters from Jenny.* New York: Harcourt, Brace & World.

American Psychological Association. (1887–present). *Psychological Abstracts.* Washington, DC: Author.

American Psychological Association. (1982). *Ethical principles in the conduct of research with human participants.* Washington, DC: Author.

American Psychological Association. (1986). *Careers in psychology.* Washington, DC: Author.

American Psychological Association. (1990). Ethical principles of psychologists. *American Psychologist, 45,* 390–395.

American Psychological Association (1992). Ethical principles of psychologists and code of conduct. *American Psychologist, 47,* 1597–1611.

American Psychological Association. (1993). *Getting in: A step-by-step guide to graduate school in psychology.* Washington, DC: Author.

American Psychological Association. (1993). *Guidelines for ethical conduct in the care and use of animals.* Washington, DC: Author.

American Psychological Association (1993). *Journals in psychology: A resource listing for authors* (4th ed.). Washington, DC: Author.

American Psychological Association. (1994). *Publication manual of the American Psychological Association* (4th ed.). Washington, DC: Author.

American Psychological Association. (1996). *Psychology/ Careers for the twenty-first century.* Washington, DC: Author.

American Psychological Association. (Rev. biannually with yearly updates). *Graduate study in psychology.* Washington, DC: Author.

Anderson, C. A. (1989). Temperature and aggression: Ubiquitous effects of heat on occurrence of human violence. *Psychological Bulletin, 106,* 74–96.

Anderson, C. A., & Anderson, D. C. (1984). Ambient temperature and violent crime: Tests of the linear and curvilinear hypotheses. *Journal of Personality and Social Psychology, 46,* 91–97.

Anderson, J. R., & Matessa, M. (1997). A production system theory of serial memory. *Psychological Review, 104,* 728–748.

Annas, G. J., & Grodin, M. A. (Eds.). (1992). *The Nazi doctors and the Nuremberg Code: Human rights and human experimentation.* New York: Oxford University Press.

Aron, A., & Aron, E. P. (1997). *Statistics for the social and behavioral sciences: A brief course.* Upper Saddle River, NJ: Prentice Hall.

Aronson, E., & Carlsmith, J. M. (1968). Experimentation in social psychology. In G. Lindzey & E. Aronson (Eds.), *The handbook of social psychology* (2nd ed., Vol. 2, pp. 1–79). Reading, MA: Addison-Wesley.

Aronson, E., & Linder, D. (1965). Gain and loss of esteem as determinants of interpersonal attractiveness. *Journal of Experimental Social Psychology, 1,* 156–171.

Aronson, E., Brewer, M., & Carlsmith, J. M. (1985). Experimentation in social psychology. In G. Lindzey & E. Aronson (Eds.), *Handbook of social psychology* (3rd ed.) (pp. 441–486). New York: Random House.

Aronson, E., Ellsworth, P. C., Carlsmith, J. M., & Gonzales, M. H. (1990). *Methods of research in social psychology* (2nd ed.). New York: McGraw-Hill.

Aronson, E., Wilson, T. D., & Brewer, M. B. (1998). Experimentation in social psychology. In D. T. Gilbert, S. T. Fiske, & G. Lindzey (Eds.), *The handbook of social psychology* (4th ed.) (Vol. 1, pp. 99–142). New York: McGraw-Hill.

Asch, S. E. (1946). Forming impressions of personality. *Journal of Abnormal and Social Psychology, 41,* 258–290.

Barker, R. G., & Wright, H. F. (1951). *One boy's day: A specimen record of behavior.* New York: Harper & Row.

Barlow, D. H., & Hersen, M. (1984). *Single case experimental designs: Strategies for studying behavior change* (2nd ed.). New York: Pergamon Press.

Barondess, J. A. (1996). Medicine against society: Lessons from the Third Reich. *JAMA, 276,* 1657–1661.

Baum, A., Gatchel, R. J., & Schaeffer, M. A. (1983). Emotional, behavioral, and physiological effects of chronic stress at Three Mile Island. *Journal of Consulting and Clinical Psychology, 51,* 565–572.

Baumrind, D. (1985). Research using intentional deception: Ethical issues revisited. *American Psychologist, 40,* 165–174.

Beals, W. B., Sebring, H. L., & Crawford, J. T. (1946–1949). Judgment of the Nuremberg Doctors Trial Tribunal. *Trials of war criminals before the Nuremberg Military Tribunals.* Washington, DC: U.S. Government Printing Office.

Belsky, J., & Rovine, M. J. (1993). Nonmaternal care in the first year of life and the security of infant-parent attachment. In R. A. Pierce & M. A. Black (Eds.), *Life-span development: A diversity reader* (pp. 17–30). Dubuque, IA: Kendall/Hunt Publishing Co.

Bem, D. J. (1987). Writing the empirical journal article. In M. P. Zanna & J. M. Darley (Eds.), *The compleat academic: A practical guide for the beginning social scientist* (pp. 171–201). New York: Random House.

Bermant, G., Kelman, H. C., & Warwick, D. P. (1978). *The ethics of social intervention.* Washington, DC: Hemisphere Publishing Corporation.

Bickman, L. (1981). Some distinctions between basic and applied approaches. In L. Bickman (Ed.), *Applied social psychology annual* (Vol. 2). Newbury Park, CA: Sage.

Blascovich, J., & Tomaka, J. (1991). Measures of self-esteem. In J. P. Robinson, P. R. Shaver, & L. S. Wrightsman (Eds.), *Measures of personality and social psychological attitudes* (pp. 115–160). San Diego: Academic Press.

Boice, R. (1990). Faculty resistance to writing-intensive courses. *Teaching of Psychology, 17,* 13–17.

Boice, R. (1996). *Procrastination and blocking: A novel, practical approach.* New York: Praeger.

Boice, R. (in press). Procrastination, busyness, and bingeing. *Behaviour Research and Therapy.*

Boice, R., & Jones, F. (1984). Why academicians don't write. *Journal of Higher Education, 55,* 567–582.

Bok, S. (1978). *Lying: Moral choice in public and private life.* New York: Pantheon.

Booth, W. C., Colomb, G. G., & Williams, J. M. (1995). *The craft of research.* Chicago, IL: University of Chicago Press.

Bostwick, B. E. (1990). *Resume writing: A comprehensive how-to-do it guide.* New York: Wiley.

Bouchard, T. J., Jr. (1972). A comparison of two group brainstorming procedures. *Journal of Applied Psychology, 56,* 418–421.

Bowd, A. B. (1990). A decade of debate on animal research in psychology: Room for consensus? *Canadian Psychology, 31,* 74–82.

Bowd, A. D., & Shapiro, K. J. (1993). The case against laboratory animal research in psychology. *Journal of Social Issues, 49 (1),* 133–142.

Bowlby, J. (1969). *Attachment and loss: Vol. 1. Attachment.* New York: Basic Books.

Boyce, J. R. (1989). Use of animals in research: Can we find a middle ground? *Journal of the American Veterinary Medical Association, 194,* 24–25.

Burns, J. M., Peltason, J. W., Cronin, T. E., & Magleby, D. B. (1994). *Government by the people.* Englewood Cliffs, NJ: Prentice Hall.

Cacioppo, J. T., & Petty, R. E. (Eds.). (1983). *Social psychophysiology: A sourcebook.* New York: Guilford Press.

Cacioppo, J. T., & Tassinary, L. G. (1990). Inferring psychological significance from physiological signals. *American Psychologist, 45,* 16–28.

Campbell, A., Converse, P., Miller, W. F., & Stokes, D. E. (1964). *The American voter: An abridgement.* New York: John Wiley & Sons.

Campbell, D. T. (1969). Reforms as experiments. *American Psychologist, 24,* 409–429.

Campbell, D. T., & Fiske, D. W. (1959). Convergent and discriminant validation by the multitrait-multimethod matrix. *Psychological Bulletin, 56,* 81–105.

Campbell, D. T., & Stanley, J. C. (1963). *Experimental and quasiexperimental designs for research.* Chicago: Rand McNally.

Canter, M. B., Bennett, B. E., Jones, S. E., & Nagy, T. F. (1994). *Ethics for psychologists: A commentary on the APA Ethics Code.* Washington, DC: American Psychological Association.

Carlsmith, J. M., & Anderson, C. A. (1979). Ambient temperature and the occurrence of collective violence: A new analysis. *Journal of Personality and Social Psychology, 37,* 337–344.

Chamove, A. S., Hosey, G. R., & Schaetzel, P. (1988). Visitors excite primates in zoos. *Zoo Biology, 7,* 359–369.

Christensen, L. (1988). Deception in psychological research: Is its use justified? *Personality and Social Psychology Bulletin, 14,* 664–675.

Churchland, P. M. (1985). *Matter and consciousness.* Cambridge, MA: MIT Press.

Churchland, P. S. (1986). *Neurophilosophy.* Cambridge, MA: MIT Press.

Cialdini, R. B. (1993). *Influence: Science and practice* (3rd ed.). New York: Harper Collins.

Coelho, A. M., Jr., & Bramblett, C. A. (1981). Interobserver agreement on a molecular ethogram of the Genus *Papio. Animal Behavior, 29,* 443–448.

Cohen, J. (1988). *Statistical power analysis for the behavioral sciences* (2nd ed.). Hillsdale, NJ: Erlbaum.

Cohen, J. (1990). Things I have learned (so far). *American Psychologist, 45,* 1304–1312.

Cohen, J. (1992). A power primer. *Psychological Bulletin, 112,* 155–159.

Cohen, J. (1994). The earth is round ($p < .05$). *American Psychologist, 49,* 997–1003.

Cohen, J. D., & Schooler, J. W. (Eds.). (1997). *Scientific approaches to the question of consciousness.* Mahwah, NJ: Erlbaum.

Cohen, J. W. (1988). *Statistical power analysis for the social and behavioral sciences* (2nd ed.). Hillsdale, NJ: Earlbaum.

Cohen, S., Tyrell, D. A., & Smith, A. P. (1993). Negative life events, perceived stress, negative affect, and susceptibility to the common cold. *Journal of Personality and Social Psychology, 64,* 131–140.

Converse, J. M., & Presser, S. (1986). *Survey questions: Handcrafting the standardized questionnaire.* Newbury Park, CA: Sage.

Cook, T. D., & Campbell, D. T. (1979). *Quasi-experimentation: Design & analysis issues for field settings.* Boston: Houghton Mifflin Company.

Cooper, H. M., & Hedges, L. V. (Eds.). (1994). *The handbook of research synthesis.* New York: Russell Sage.

Cooper, L., & Shepard, R. N. (1973). Chronometric studies of the rotation of mental images. In W. G. Chase (Ed.), *Visual information processing* (pp. 75–162). New York: Academic Press.

Coren, S., & Girgus, J. S. (1978). *Seeing is deceiving: The psychology of visual illusions.* Hillsdale, NJ: Erlbaum.

Cozby, P. C. (1997). *Methods in behavioral research* (6th ed.). Mountain View, CA: Mayfield.

Craik, F. I. M., & Lockhart, R. S. (1972). Levels of processing: A framework for memory research. *Journal of Verbal Learning and Verbal Behavior, 11,* 671–684.

Creswell, J. W. (1994). *Research design: Qualitative and quantitative approaches.* Thousand Oaks, CA: Sage.

Crusco, A. H., & Wetzel, C. G. (1984). The Midas touch: The effects of interpersonal touch on restaurant tipping. *Personality and Social Psychology Bulletin, 10,* 512–517.

Darley, J. M., & Latane, B. (1968). Bystander intervention in emergencies: Diffusion of responsibility. *Journal of Personality and Social Psychology, 8,* 377–383.

Dawes, R. M. (1988). *Rational choice in an uncertain world.* San Diego, CA: Harcourt Brace Jovanovich.

Dawes, R. M. (1991, June). *Discovering "human nature" versus discovering how people cope with the task of getting through college: An extension of Sear's argument.* Paper presented at the Third Annual Convention of the American Psychological Society, Washington, DC.

Dembo, T. (1964). Sensitivity of one person to another. *Rehabilitation Literature, 25,* 231–235.

Devane, J. R. (1993). The method of reproduction and Mueller-Lyer changes. *Perceptual and Motor Skills, 76,* 43–46.

Diener, E., & Crandall, R. (1978). *Ethics in social and behavioral research.* Chicago: University of Chicago Press.

Dillon, K. M. (1988). Statisticophobia. In M. Ware & C. L. Brewer (Eds.), *Handbook for teaching statistics and research methods* (pp. 3). Hillsdale, NJ: Erlbaum.

Dunn, D. S. (1994). Amputee golfers cope by finding a silver lining. *Amputee Golfer Magazine,* 15–16.

Dunn, D. S. (1994). Lessons learned from an interdisciplinary writing course: Implications for student writing in psychology. *Teaching of Psychology, 21,* 223–227.

Dunn, D. S. (1996). Collaborative writing in a statistics and research methods course. *Teaching of Psychology, 23,* 38–40.

Dunn, D. S. (1996). Well being following amputation: Salutary effects of positive meaning, optimism, and control. *Rehabilitation Psychology, 41,* 283–300.

Dunn, D. S. (1997). Identifying imagoes: A personality exercise on myth, self, and identity. *Teaching of Psychology, 24,* 193–195.

Dunn, D. S., & Toedter, L. J. (1991). The collaborative honors project in psychology: Enhancing student and faculty development. *Teaching of Psychology, 18,* 178–180.

Dunn, D. S., & Wilson, T. D. (1990). When the stakes are high: A limit to the illusion of control effect. *Social Cognition, 8,* 305–323.

Dunn, D. S.., & Zaremba, S. B. (1997). Thriving at liberal arts colleges: The more compleat academic. *Teaching of Psychology, 24,* 8–14.

Eagly, A. H. (1978). Sex differences in influenceability. *Psychological Bulletin, 85,* 86–116.

Eagly, A. H., & Chaiken, S. (1993). *The psychology of attitudes.* Fort Worth, TX: Harcourt Brace Jovanovich.

Elbow, P. (1993). Ranking, evaluating, and liking: Sorting out three forms of judgment. *College English, 55,* 187–206.

Elbow, P., & Belanoff, P. (1989). *Sharing and responding.* New York: Random House.

Elbow, P., & Belanoff, P. (1995). *A community of writers: A workshop course in writing* (2nd ed.). New York: McGraw-Hill.

Ericsson, K. A., & Simon, H. A. (1980). Verbal reports as data. *Psychological Review, 87,* 215–251.

Ericsson, K. A., & Simon, H. A. (1993). *Protocol analysis: Verbal reports as data* (Rev. ed.). Cambridge, MA: MIT Press.

Ericsson, K. A., Chase, W. G., & Faloon, S. (1980). Acquisition of memory skill. *Science, 208,* 1181–1182.

Eysenck, H. J. (1976). *Sex and personality.* Austin: University of Texas Press.

Eysenck, H. J., Arnold, W., & Meili, R. (1979). *Encyclopedia of Psychology.* New York: The Seabury Press.

Feather, N. T., & Volkmer, R. E. (1988). Preference for situations involving effort, time pressure, and feedback in relation to Type A behavior, locus of control, and test anxiety. *Journal of Personality and Social Psychology, 55,* 266–271.

Feeney, D. (1987). Human rights and animal welfare. *American Psychologist, 42,* 593–599.

Festinger, L. (1954). A theory of social comparison processes. *Human Relations, 7,* 117–140.

Festinger, L. (1957). *A theory of cognitive dissonance.* Stanford, CA: Stanford University Press.

Festinger, L., Riecken, H. W., & Schachter, S. (1956). *When prophecy fails.* Minneapolis: University of Minnesota Press.

Feynman, R. P. (1988). *What do you care what other people think? Further adventures of a curious character.* New York: W. W. Norton and Company.

Fillenbaum, S. (1966). Prior deception and subsequent experimental performance: The "faithful" subject. *Journal of Personality and Social Psychology, 4,* 532–537.

Fine, M. A., & Kurdek, L. A. (1993). Reflections on determining authorship credit and authorship order on faculty-student collaborations. *American Psychologist, 48,* 1141–1147.

Fisher, C. B., & Fyrberg, D. (1994). Participant partners: College students weight the costs and benefits of deceptive research. *American Psychologist, 49,* 417–427.

Fisher, J. D., Rytting, M., & Heslin, R. (1976). Hands touching hands: Affective and evaluative effects of an interpersonal touch. *Sociometry, 39,* 416–421.

Flower, L. (1993). *Problem-solving strategies for writing* (4th ed.). Fort Worth, TX: Harcourt Brace Jovanovich.

Fong, G. T., Krantz, D. H., & Nisbett, R. E. (1986). The effects of statistical training on thinking about everyday problems. *Cognitive Psychology, 18,* 253–292.

Frances, S. J. (1979). Sex differences in non-verbal behavior. *Sex Roles, 5,* 519–535.

Freedman, J. L., & Fraser, S. C. (1966). Compliance without pressure: The foot-in-the-door technique. *Journal of Personality and Social Psychology, 4,* 195–202.

Freud, S. (1952). *On dreams.* New York: W. W. Norton & Co. (Originally published in 1901).

Freud, S. (1961). *Civilization and its discontents.* New York: Norton. (Original work published 1930).

Freud, S. (1965). *The interpretation of dreams.* New York: Avon. (Original work published 1900).

Gallup, G. G., & Suarez, S. D. (1980). On the use of animals in psychological research. *Psychological Record, 30,* 211–218.

Gallup, G. G., & Suarez, S. D. (1985). Alternatives to the use of animals in psychological research. *American Psychologist, 40,* 1104–1111.

Garner, W. R., Hake, H. W., & Eriksen, C. W. (1956). Operationism and the concept of perception. *Psychological Review, 63,* 149–159.

Gay, P. (1988). *Freud: A life for our time.* New York: Norton.

Gay, P. (Ed.). (1989). *The Freud reader.* New York: Norton.

Gibbs, J. (1988). Gastrointestinal peptides and the limitation of meal size. In B. J. Blinder, B. F. Chaitin, & R. Goldstein (Eds.), *The eating disorders* (pp. 57–62). Baypoint, CA: PMA Publishing.

Glass, G. V., McGaw, B., & Smith, M. L. (1981). *Meta-analysis in social research.* Beverly Hills, CA: Sage.

Glass, G. V. (1976). Primary, secondary, and meta-analysis of research. *Educational Researcher, 5*, 3–8.

Gleitman, H. (1991). *Psychology* (3rd ed.). New York: Norton.

Goldstein, G. S. (1993). Using a group workshop to encourage collaborative learning in an undergraduate counseling course. *Teaching of Psychology, 20*, 108–110.

Goleman, D. (1984, December 18). Social anxiety: New focus leads to insights and therapy. *The New York Times*, pp. C1, C14.

Gottesman, I. I., & Wolfgram, D. L. (1991). *Schizophrenia genesis: The origins of madness*. New York: Freeman.

Grady, K. E., & Strudler Wallston, B. (1988). *Research in health care settings*. Newbury Park, CA: Sage.

Greenberg, R. P., Bornstein, R. F., Greenberg, M. D., & Fisher, S. (1992). A meta-analysis of antidepressant outcome under "blinder" conditions. *Journal of Consulting and Clinical Psychology, 60*, 664–669.

Griffitt, W. (1970). Environmental effects on interpersonal affective behavior: Ambient effective temperature and attraction. *Journal of Personality and Social Psychology, 15*, 240–244.

Griffitt, W., & Veitch, R. (1971). Hot and crowded: Influences of population density and temperature on interpersonal affective behavior. *Journal of Personality and Social Psychology, 17*, 92–98.

Gronbeck, B. E., McKerrow, R. E., Ehninger, D., & Monroe, A. H. (1997). *Principles and types of speech communication* (13th ed.). New York: Longman.

Guthrie, R. V. (1998). *Even the rat was white: A historical view of psychology* (2nd ed.). Boston: Allyn and Bacon.

Hacker, D. (1991). *The Bedford Handbook for writers* (3rd ed.). Boston: St. Martin's Press.

Hahner, J. C., Sokoloff, M. A., & Salisch, S. L. (1993). *Speaking clearly: Improving voice and diction* (4th ed.). New York: McGraw-Hill.

Hall, R. V., Lund, D., & Jackson, D. (1968). Effects of teacher attention on study behavior. *Journal of Applied Behavior Analysis, 1*, 1–12.

Hamill, R., Wilson, T. D., & Nisbett, R. E. (1980). Insensitivity to sample bias: Generalizing from atypical cases. *Journal of Personality and Social Psychology, 39*, 578–589.

Haney, C., Banks, C., & Zimbardo, P. (1973). Interpersonal dynamics in a simulated prison. *International Journal of Criminology and Penology, 1*, 69–97.

Harris, R. J. (1997). Significance tests have their place. *Psychological Science, 8*, 8–11.

Hayes, N. (1996). What makes a psychology graduate distinctive? *European Psychologist, 1*, 130–134.

Hayes, J. R. (1981). *The complete problem solver*. Philadelphia, PA: Franklin Institute.

Hayes, N. (1997, July). The distinctive skills of a psychology graduate. *APA Monitor*, p. 33.

Hays, W. C. (1981). *Statistics*. New York: Holt, Rhinehart & Winston.

Hedrick, T. E., Bickman, L., & Rog, D. J. (1993). *Applied research design: A practical guide*. Newbury Park, CA: Sage.

Hersen, M., & Barlow, D. H. (1984). *Single-case experimental designs: Strategies for studying behavior change*. New York: Pergamon Press.

Highlen, P. S., & Finley, H. C. (1996). Doing qualitative analysis. In F. T. L. Leong & J. A. Austin (Eds.), *The psychology research handbook: A guide for graduate students and research assistants* (pp. 177–192). Thousand Oaks, CA: Sage.

Hill, C. E. (Ed.). (1994). Special section: Qualitative research in counseling process and outcome. *Journal of Counseling Psychology, 41*, 427–512.

Hills, P. J. (1983). The scholarly communication process. *Annual Review of Information Science and Technology, 18*, 99–125.

Hiroto, D. S., & Seligman, M. E. P. (1975). Generality of learned helplessness in man. *Journal of Personality and Social Psychology, 31*, 311–327.

Hochschild, A. R. (1990). *The second shift*. New York: Avon.

Hochschild, A. R. (1997). *The time bind: When work becomes home and home becomes work*. New York: Metropolitan Books.

Holsti, O. R. (1969). *Content analysis for the social sciences*. Reading, MA: Addison-Wesley.

Hornik, J. (1992). Tactile stimulation and consumer response. *Journal of Consumer Research, 19*, 449–458.

Hull, D. L. (1984). Historical entities and historical narratives. In C. Hookway (Ed.), *Minds, machines, and programs* (pp. 17–42). New York: Cambridge University Press.

Hult, C. A. (1996). *Research and writing in the social sciences*. Boston: Allyn and Bacon.

Hume, D. (1777/1962). *David Hume on human nature and the understanding* (Anthony Flew, Ed.). New York: Collier Books.

Humphreys, L. (1975). *Tearoom trade: Impersonal sex in public places* (2nd ed.). Chicago: Aldine.

Isen, A. M., & Levin, P. F. (1972). Effect of feeling good on helping: Cookies and kindness. *Journal of Personality and Social Psychology, 21*, 384–388.

Jaccard, J., Becker, M. A., & Wood, G. (1984). Pairwise multiple comparison procedures: A review. *Psychological Bulletin, 96*, 589–596.

James, W. (1950). *The principles of psychology*. New York: Dover. (Original work published 1890).

Janoff-Bulman, R. (1992). *Shattered assumptions: Towards a new psychology of trauma*. New York: Free Press.

Johnson, D. (1990). Animal rights and human lives: Time for scientists to right the balance. *Psychological Science, 1*, 213–214.

Judd, C. M., & Kenny, D. A. (1981). *Estimating the effects of social interventions.* Cambridge: Cambridge University Press.

Judd, C. M., Smith, E. R., & Kidder, L. H. (1991). *Research methods in social relations* (6th ed.). Ft. Worth, TX: Holt, Rhinehart & Winston.

Kagan, J. (1994). *Galen's prophecy: Temperament in human nature.* New York: Basic Books.

Kant, I. (1909). *Kant's critique of reason and other works on the theory of ethics* (T. K. Abbott, Trans.). London: Longmans, Green and Co. (Original work published 1785).

Katz, J. (1996). The Nuremberg Code and the Nuremberg Trial. *JAMA, 276,* 1662–1666.

Kazdin, A. E. (1976). Statistical techniques for single-case experimental designs. In M. Hersen & D. H. Barlow (Eds.), *Single case experimental designs: Strategies for studying behavior change* (pp. 265–316). Oxford, England: Pergamon Press.

Kazdin, A. E., & Tuma, A. H. (Eds.). (1982). *Single-case research designs.* San Francisco, CA: Jossey-Bass.

Keil, R. (1996, September 17). Welfare study debunks myths about recipients. *The Morning Call,* p. A3.

Keith-Spiegel, P., & Koocher, G. P. (1985). *Ethics in psychology: Professional standards and cases.* New York: Random House.

Keller, P. A. (Ed.). (1994). *Academic paths: Career decisions and experiences of psychologists.* Hillsdale, NJ: Lawrence Erlbaum Associates, Inc.

Kelman, H. C. (1967). Human use of human subjects: The problem of deception in social psychological experiments. *Psychological Bulletin, 27,* 1–11.

Kelman, H. C. (1968). *A time to speak: On human values and social research.* San Francisco: Jossey-Bass.

Kimmel, A. J. (1988). *Ethics and values in applied social research.* Beverly Hills, CA: Sage.

Kimmel, A. J. (1991). Predictable biases in the ethical decision making of American psychologists. *American Psychologist, 46,* 786–788.

Kimmel, A. J. (Ed.). (1981). *Ethics of human subject research.* San Francisco: Jossey-Bass.

Kirk, R. E. (1995). *Experimental design: Procedures for the behavioral sciences* (3rd ed.). Pacific Grove, CA: Brooks/Cole.

Kirk, R. E. (1982). *Experimental designs: Procedures for the behavioral sciences* (2nd ed.). Monterey, CA: Brooks/Cole.

Korn, J. H. (1997). *Illusions of reality: A history of deception in social psychology.* Albany, NY: State University of New York Press.

Kosslyn, S. M. (1983). *Ghosts in the mind's machine.* New York: Norton.

Kraemer, H. C., & Thiemann, S. (1987). *How many subjects? Statistical power analysis in research.* Newbury Park, CA: Sage.

Kratochwill, T. R., & Levin J. R. (Eds.). (1992). *Single-case research design and analysis: New directions for psychology and education.* Hillsdale, NJ: Erlbaum.

Kuhn, T. S. (1970). *The structure of scientific revolutions* (Rev. ed.). Chicago: University of Chicago Press.

Langer, E. J. (1975). The illusion of control. *Journal of Personality and Social Psychology, 32,* 311–328.

Langer, E. J., & Rodin, J. (1976). The effects of choice and enhanced personal responsibility for the aged: A field experiment in an institutional setting. *Journal of Personality and Social Psychology, 34,* 191–198.

Lassiter, G. D., & Stone, J. I. (1984). Affective consequences of variation in behavior perception: When liking is in the level of analysis. *Personality and Social Psychology Bulletin, 10,* 253–259.

Lassiter, G. D., Koenig, L. J., & Apple, K. J. (1996). Mood and behavior perception: Dysphoria can increase and decrease effortful processing of information. *Personality and Social Psychology Bulletin, 22,* 794–810.

Leahey, T. H. (1990, August). *Waiting for Newton.* Paper presented at the annual meeting of the American Psychological Association, Boston.

Leahey, T. H. (1992). *A history of psychology: Main currents in psychological thought* (3rd ed.). Englewood Cliffs, NJ: Prentice Hall.

Leahey, T. H. (1997). *A history of psychology: Main currents in psychological thought* (4th ed.). Englewood Cliffs, NJ: Prentice Hall.

Lee, F., Hallahan, M., & Herzog, T. (1996). Explaining real-life events: How culture and domain shape attributions. *Personality and Social Psychology Bulletin, 22,* 732–741.

Lehman, D. R., & Nisbett, R. E. (1990). A longitudinal study of the effects of undergraduate training on reasoning. *Developmental Psychology, 26,* 952–960.

Levine, J. R. (1990). Using a peer tutor to improve writing in a psychology course: One instructor's experience. *Teaching of Psychology, 17,* 57–58.

Lewin, K. (1943). Psychology and the process of group living. *The Journal of Social Psychology, SPSSI Bulletin, 17,* 113–131.

Library of Congress (1995). *Library of Congress subject headings.* Washington, DC: Author.

Likert, R. (1932). A technique for the measurement of attitudes. *Archives of Psychology, 19,* 44–53.

Lincoln, Y. S., & Guba, E. G. (1985). *Naturalistic inquiry.* Newbury Park, CA: Sage.

Loftus, G. R. (1993). Editorial comment. *Memory & Cognition, 21,* 1–3.

Loftus, G. R. (1996). Psychology will be a much better science when we change the way we analyze data. *Current Directions in Psychological Science, 5,* 161–171.

Lucas, S. E. (1995). *The art of public speaking* (5th ed.). New York: McGraw-Hill.

Luria, A. R. (1968). *The mind of mnemonist.* New York: Basic Books.

MacKenzie, T. A., & Aguinis, H. (1996). The World Wide Web: A new resource for psychology students, faculty, and professionals. *Eye on Psi Chi, 1,* 21–23.

Maggio, R. (1991). *The bias-free word finder: A dictionary of nondiscriminatory language.* Boston: Beacon Press.

Maimon, E. P., Nodine, B. F., & O'Connor, F. W. (1989). *Thinking, reasoning, and writing.* New York: Longman.

Malcolm, J. (1982). *Psychoanalysis: The impossible profession.* New York: Vintage.

Malcolm, J. (1984). *In the Freud Archives.* New York: Knopf.

Marrow, A. J. (1969). *The practical theorist: The life and work of Kurt Lewin.* New York: Teachers College Press.

Martin, D. W. (1996). *Doing psychology experiments* (4th ed.). Pacific Grove, CA: Brooks/Cole.

Martin, G., & Pear, J. (1996). *Behavior modification: What it is and how to do it* (5th ed.). Upper Saddle River, NJ: Prentice Hall.

Masson, J. M. (1985). *The assault on truth: Freud's suppression of the seduction theory.* New York: Penguin.

Matlin, M. W. (1993). *The psychology of women* (2nd ed.). Fort Worth, TX: Harcourt Brace Jovanovich.

Mayne, T., Norcross, J. T., & Sayette, M. (1994). *Insider's guide to graduate programs in clinical psychology.* New York: Guilford.

McAdams, D. P. (1985). The "imago": A key narrative component of identity. In P. Shaver (Ed.), *Review of personality and social psychology* (Vol. 6, pp. 115–141). Beverly Hills, CA: Sage.

McAdams, D. P. (1993). *The stories we live by: Personal myths and the making of the self.* New York: Morrow.

McGuire, W. J. (1967). Some impending reorientations in social psychology. *Journal of Experimental Social Psychology, 3,* 124–139.

McGuire, W. J. (1997). Creative hypothesis generating in psychology: Some useful heuristics. In J. T. Spence, J. M. Darley, & D. J. Foss (Eds.), *Annual Review of Psychology* (Vol. 48, pp. 1–30). Palo Alto, CA: Annual Reviews, Inc.

McKenna, R. J. (1995). *The undergraduate researcher's handbook: Creative experimentation in social psychology.* Boston: Allyn and Bacon.

Milgram, S. (1963). Behavioral study of obedience. *Journal of Abnormal Psychology, 67,* 371–378.

Milgram, S. (1974). *Obedience to authority.* New York: Harper Torchbooks.

Miller, G. A. (1956). The magical number seven, plus or minus two: Some limits on our capacity for processing information. *Psychological Review, 63,* 81–97.

Miller, G. A. (1969). Psychology as a means of promoting human welfare. *American Psychologist, 24,* 1063–1075.

Miller, N. E. (1985). The value of behavioral research on animals. *American Psychologist, 40,* 423–440.

Moffatt, M. (1989). *Coming of age in New Jersey: College and American culture.* New Brunswick, NJ: Rutgers University Press.

Mook, D. G. (1983). In defense of external invalidity. *American Psychologist, 38,* 379–387.

Murphy, C. (1990, June). New findings: Hold on to your hat. *The Atlantic,* pp. 22–23.

Neisser, U. (1976). *Cognition and reality: Principles and implications of cognitive psychology.* San Francisco: W. H. Freeman and Company.

Neufeld, R. W. J. (1975). Effect of cognitive appraisal on d' and response bias to experimental stress. *Journal of Personality and Social Psychology, 31,* 735–743.

Newton, I. (1675/1676). Newton to Hooke, 5 February 1675/6. In H. W. Turnbull (Ed.), *The correspondence of Isaac Newton* (Vol. 1, p. 416). Cambridge: Cambridge University Press.

Nie, N. H., Verba, S., & Petrocik, J. R. (1979). *The changing American voter.* Cambridge, MA: Harvard.

Nisbett, R. E., & Ross, L. (1980). *Human inference; Strategies and shortcomings of social judgment.* Englewood Cliffs, NJ: Prentice Hall.

Nisbett, R. E., & Wilson, T. D. (1977). Telling more than we can know: Verbal reports on mental processes. *Psychological Review, 84,* 231–259.

Nisbett, R. E., Fong, G. T., Lehman, D. R., & Cheng, P. W. (1987). Teaching reasoning. *Science, 238,* 625–631.

Nisbett, R. E., Krantz, D. H., Jepson, C., & Kunda, Z. (1983). The use of statistical heuristics in everyday inductive reasoning. *Psychological Review, 90,* 339–363.

Nowlis, V. (1965). Research with the Mood Adjective Checklist. In S. S. Tompkins & C. E. Izard (Eds.), *Affect, cognition, and personality* (pp. 352–389). New York: Springer.

Nuland, S. B. (1993). *How we die.* New York: Vintage.

Oppenheim, A. N. (1966). *Questionnaire design and attitude measurement.* New York: Basic Books.

Orne, M. T. (1962). On the social psychology of the psychological experiment: With particular reference to demand characteristics and their implications. *American Psychologist, 17,* 776–783.

Osborn, A. (1984). *Your creative power.* New York: Charles Scribner's Sons.

Overmier, J. B., & Seligman, M. E. P. (1967). Effects of inescapable shock upon subsequent escape and avoidance learning. *Journal of Comparative and Physiological Psychology, 63,* 23–33.

Paivio, A. (1971). *Imagery and verbal processes.* New York: Holt, Rhinehart, & Winston.

Paivio, A. (1986). *Mental representations: A dual coding approach.* New York: Oxford University Press.

Pennebaker, J. W. (1982). *The psychology of physical symptoms.* New York: Springer-Verlag.

Pennebaker, J. W. (1989). Confession, inhibition, and disease. In L. Berkowitz (Ed.), *Advances in experimental so-*

cial psychology (Vol. 22, pp. 211–244). New York: Academic Press.

Pennebaker, J. W. (1990a). *Opening up: The healing power of confiding in others.* New York: Morrow.

Pennebaker, J. W. (1990b). Self-expressive writing: Implications for health, education, and welfare. In P. Belanoff, P. Elbow, & S. I. Fontaine (Eds.), *Nothing begins with n: New investigations of freewriting* (pp. 157–170). Carbondale and Edwardsville, IL: Southern Illinois University Press.

Pennebaker, J. W. (1997). *Opening up: The healing power of expressing emotions.* New York: The Guilford Press.

Pennebaker, J. W., Barger, S. D., & Tiebout, J. (1989). Disclosure of traumas and health among holocaust survivors. *Psychosomatic Medicine, 51,* 577–589.

Peterson, C. (1988). Explanatory style as a risk factor for illness. *Cognitive Therapy and Research, 12,* 119–132.

Peterson, C. (1996). Writing rough drafts. In F. T. L. Leong & J. T. Austin (Eds.), *The psychology research handbook: A guide for graduate students and research assistants* (pp. 282–290). Thousand Oaks, CA: Sage Publications.

Peterson, C., & Barrett, L. C. (1987). Explanatory style and academic performance among university freshmen. *Journal of Personality and Social Psychology, 53,* 603–607.

Peterson, C., & Bossio, L. M. (1989). Learned helplessness. In R. C. Curtis (Ed.), *Self-defeating behaviors* (pp. 235–257). New York: Plenum.

Peterson, C., & Bossio, L. M. (1991). *Health and optimism: New research on the relationship between positive thinking and physical well-being.* New York: Free Press.

Peterson, C., & Seligman, M. E. P. (1984). Causal explanations as a risk factor for depression: Theory and evidence. *Psychological Review, 91,* 347–374.

Peterson, C., Seligman, M. E. P., & Vaillant, G. E. (1988). Pessimistic explanatory style is a risk factor for physical illness: A thirty-five-year longitudinal study. *Journal of Personality and Social Psychology, 55,* 23–27.

Pi-Sunyer, X., Kissileff, H. R., Thornton, J., & Smith, G. P. (1982). C-terminal octapeptide of cholecystokinin decreases food intake in obese men. *Physiology & Behavior, 29,* 627–630.

Platt, J. R. (1964). Strong inference. *Science, 146,* 347–353.

Plous, S. (1991). An attitude survey of animal rights activists. *Psychological Science, 2,* 194–196.

Plous, S. (Ed.). (1993). The role of animals in human society [Special issue]. *Journal of Social Issues, 49 (1),* 1–167.

Popper, K. R. (1959). *The logic of scientific discovery.* New York: Basic Books.

PsycINFO [Bibliographic Database] (1887–present). Washington, DC: American Psychological Association [Publisher].

PsycLIT [Bibliographic CD-ROM Database] (1887–present). Washington, DC: American Psychological Association [Publisher].

Putnam, H. (1982). Reductionism and the nature of psychology. *Cognition, 2,* 131–146.

Raphael, M. (1997, June 5). Stressed? Rushed? Guess what! Book says there's more free time. *The Morning Call,* pp. A1, A13.

Rheingold, H. L. (1994). *The psychologist's guide to an academic career.* Washington, DC: American Psychological Association.

Robinson, J., & Godbey, G. (1997). *Time for life: The surprising ways Americans use their time.* State College, PA: Pennsylvania State University Press.

Robinson, J. P., Athanasiou, R., & Head, K. B. (1969). *Measures of occupational attitudes and occupational characteristics.* Ann Arbor, MI: Institute for Social Research.

Robinson, J. P., Rusk, J. G., & Head, K. B. (1968). *Measures of political attitudes.* Ann Arbor, MI: Institute for Social Research.

Robinson, J. P., Shaver, P. R., & Wrightsman, L. S. (1991). *Measures of personality and social psychological attitudes* (Vol. 1). San Diego, CA: Academic Press.

Robinson, P. W., & Foster, D. F. (1979). *Experimental psychology: A small-N approach.* New York: Harper & Row.

Rodin, J., & Langer, E. J. (1977). Long-term effects of a control-relevant intervention with the institutionalized aged. *Journal of Personality and Social Psychology, 35,* 897–902.

Rosenberg, A. (1980). *Sociobiology and the preemption of social science.* Baltimore: Johns Hopkins University Press.

Rosenberg, M. (1965). *Society and the adolescent self-image.* Princeton, NJ: Princeton University Press.

Rosenthal, R. (1991). *Meta-analytic procedures for social research* (Rev. ed.). Newbury Park, CA: Sage.

Rosenthal, R. (1994). Science and ethics in conducting, analyzing, and reporting psychological research *Psychological Science, 5,* 127–134.

Rosenthal, R., & Fode, K. L. (1963). The effect of experimenter bias on the performance of the albino rat. *Behavioral Science, 8,* 183–189.

Rosenthal, R., & Jacobson, L. (1968). *Psychodynamics in the classroom.* New York: Holt.

Rosenthal, R., & Rosnow, R. L. (1991). *Essentials of behavioral research* (2nd ed.). New York: McGraw-Hill.

Rosenthal, R., & Rubin, D. B. (1978). Interpersonal expectancy effects: The first 345 studies. *Behavioral and Brain Sciences, 3,* 377–386.

Rosenzweig, S. E. G. (1970). Boring and the Zeitgeist: Eruditone gesta beavit. *Journal of Psychology, 75,* 59–71.

Rosnow, R. L., & Rosenthal, R. (1989). Statistical procedures and the justification of knowledge in psychological science. *American Psychologist, 44,* 1276–1284.

Rosnow, R. L., & Rosenthal, R. (1996). *Beginning behavioral research* (2nd ed). Englewood Cliffs, NJ: Prentice Hall.

Rosnow, R. L., & Rosenthal, R. (1997). *People studying people: Artifacts and ethics in behavioral research.* New York: W. H. Freeman and Company.

Rosnow, R. L., & Rosnow, M. (1995). *Writing papers in psychology* (3rd ed.). Pacific Grove, CA: Brooks/Cole.

Ross, L., & Nisbett, R. E. (1991). *The person and the situation: Perspectives of social psychology.,* New York: Mc-Graw-Hill.

Ross, M., & Sicoly, F. (1979). Egocentric biases in availability and attribution. *Journal of Personality and Social Psychology, 37,* 322–336.

Runyon, R. P., Haber, A., Pittenger, D. J., & Coleman, K. A. (1996). *Fundamentals of behavioral statistics* (8th ed.). New York: McGraw-Hill.

Sacks, O. (1985). *The man who mistook his wife for a hat and other clinical tales.* New York: Summit Books.

Salkind, N. J. (1997). *Exploring research* (3rd ed.). Upper Saddle River, NJ: Prentice Hall.

Sasson, R., & Nelson, T. M. (1969). The human experimental subject in context. *Canadian Psychologist, 10,* 409–437.

Sax, L. J., Astin, A. W., Arredondo, M., & Korn, W. S. (1996). *The American college teacher: National norms for the 1995-96 HERI faculty survey.* Los Angeles: Higher Education Research Institute.

Scarr, S. (1997). Rules of evidence: A larger context for the statistical debate. *Psychological Science, 8,* 16–17.

Schaeffer, J. (1997). *Music and emotion.* Unpublished honors thesis, Departments of Psychology and Music, Moravian College, Bethelehm, PA.

Schlenker, B. R., & Weigold, M. F. (1992). Interpersonal processes involving impression regulation and management. *Annual Review of Psychology, 43,* 133–168.

Schor, J. B. (1991). *The overworked American: The unexpected decline of leisure.* New York: Basic Books.

Schuler, H. (1982). *Ethical problems in psychological research* (M. S. Woodruff & R. A. Wicklund, Trans.). New York: Academic Press.

Schulz, R. (1976). Effects of control and predictability on the psychological well-being of the institutionalized aged. *Journal of Personality and Social Psychology, 33,* 563–573.

Schulz, R., & Hanusa, B. H. (1978). Long-term effects of control and predictability-enhancing interventions: Findings and ethical issues. *Journal of Personality and Social Psychology, 36,* 1202–1212.

Schumacher, E. F. (1973). *Small is beautiful: Economics as if people mattered.* New York: Harper & Row.

Schuman, H., & Presser, S. (1996). *Questions and answers in attitude surveys: Experiments on question form, wording, & context.* Thousand Oaks, CA: Sage Publications.

Schuman, H., & Scott, J. (1987). Problems in the use of survey questions to measure public opinion. *Science, 236,* 957–959.

Schuman, H., Presser, S., & Ludwig, J. (1981). Context effects on survey responses to questions about abortion. *Public Opinion Quarterly, 45,* 216–233.

Schwarz, N., Groves, R. M., & Schuman, H. (1998). Survey methods. In D. T. Gilbert, S. T. Fiske, & G. Lindzey (Eds.), *The handbook of social psychology* (4th ed.). (Vol. 1, pp. 143–179). New York: McGraw-Hill.

Searle, J. R. (1990). Consciousness, explanatory inversion, and cognitive science. *Behavioral and Brain Sciences, 13,* 585–642.

Sears, D. O. (1986). College sophomores in the laboratory: Influences of a narrow data base on social psychology's view of human nature. *Journal of Personality and Social Psychology, 51,* 515–539.

Sechrest, L. (1971). Situational sampling and contrived situations in assessment of behavior. *Pakistan Journal of Psychology, 4,* 3–19.

Seligman, M. E. P. (1975). *Helplessness: On depression, development, and death.* San Francisco: Freeman.

Seligman, M. E. P. (1990). *Learned optimism.* New York: Knopf.

Seligman, M. E. P. (1995a). *The optimistic child.* Boston: Houghton Mifflin.

Seligman, M. E. P. (1995b). *What you can change—and what you can't: The complete guide to successful self-improvement.* New York: Fawcett.

Shepard, R. N., & Cooper, L. (1982). *Mental images and their transformations.* Cambridge, MA: MIT Press.

Shepard, R. N., & Cooper, L. A. (1983). *Mental images and their transformations.* Cambridge, MA: MIT Press.

Shepard, R. N., & Metzler, J. (1971). Mental rotation of three-dimensional objects. *Science, 171,* 701–703.

Shrout, P. E. (1997). Should significance tests be banned? Introduction to a special section exploring the pros and cons. *Psychological Science, 8,* 1–2.

Sidman, M. (1960). *Tactics of scientific research.* New York: Basic Books.

Sieber, J. E. (Ed.). (1982a). *The ethics of social research: Surveys and experiments.* New York: Springer-Verlag.

Sieber, J. E. (Ed.). (1982b). *The ethics of social research: Fieldwork, regulation, and publication.* New York: Springer-Verlag.

Siegel, S. & Castellan, N. J. (1988). *Nonparametric statistics for the behavioral sciences* (2nd ed.). New York: McGraw-Hill.

Skinner, B. F. (1948). 'Superstition' in the pigeon. *Journal of Experimental Psychology, 38,* 168–172.

Skinner, B. F. (1953). *Science and human behavior.* New York: Macmillan.

Skinner, B. F. (1956). A case study in scientific method. *American Psychologist, 11,* 221–233.

Skinner, B. F. (1981). How to discover what to say—a talk to students. *The Behavior Analyst, 4*, 1–7.

Smart, R. (1966). Subject selection bias in psychological research. *Canadian Psychologist, 7*, 115–121.

Smyth, T. R. (1996). *Writing in psychology: A student guide* (2nd ed). New York: John Wiley & Sons.

Sociological Abstracts, Inc. (1952–present). *Sociological Abstracts.* San Diego, CA: Author.

Sperling, G. (1960). The information available in brief visual presentations. *Psychological Monographs, 74* (11, Whole No. 498).

Sperling, S. (1988). *Animal liberators: Research & morality.* Berkeley: University of California.

Spradley, J. P. (1980). *Participant observation.* New York: Holt, Rhinehart & Winston.

Sternberg, R. J. (1993). *The psychologist's companion: A guide to scientific writing for students and researchers* (3rd ed.). Cambridge: Cambridge University Press.

Sternberg, R. J. (1997, September). What do students still most need to learn about research in psychology? *APS Observer*, p. 14, 19.

Sternberg, S. (1967). Two operations in character recognition: Some evidence from reaction-time measurements. *Perception and Psychophysics, 2*, 45–53.

Stroop, J. R. (1935). Studies of interference on serial verbal reactions. *Journal of Experimental Psychology, 18*, 643–662.

Sudman, S., & Bradburn, N. M. (1982). *Asking questions: A practical guide to questionnaire design.* San Francisco: Jossey-Bass.

Swacker, M. (1975). The sex of the speaker as a sociolinguistic variable. In B. Thorne & N. Henley (Eds.), *Language and sex: Differences and dominance* (pp. 76–83). Rowley, MA: Newbury House.

Tannen, D. (1990). *You just don't understand: Men and women in conversation.* New York: Morrow.

Taylor, S. E., & Lobel, M. (1989). Social comparison activity under threat: Downward evaluation and upward contacts. *Psychological Review, 96*, 569–575.

Taylor, S. E., & Martin, J. M. (1987). The present-minded professor: Controlling one's career. In M. P. Zanna & J. M. Darley (Eds.), *The compleat academic: A practical guide for the beginning social scientist* (pp. 23–60). New York: Random House.

Thoreau, H. D. (1983). *Walden and civil disobedience.* New York: Penguin Books.

Tobias, S. (1978). *Overcoming math anxiety.* New York: Norton.

Toedter, L. J. (1996). *What makes a good reference for a literature review paper?* Unpublished course materials, Moravian College, Bethlehem, PA.

Tourangeau, R., & Rasinski, K. A. (1988). Cognitive processes underlying context effects in attitude measurement. *Psychological Bulletin, 103*, 299–314.

Tourangeau, R., Rasinski, K. A., Bradburn, N., & D'Andrade, R. (1989). Carryover effects in attitude surveys. *Public Opinion Quarterly, 53*, 495–524.

Traue, H. C., & Pennebaker, J. W. (Eds.). (1993). *Emotion inhibition and health.* Gottingen: Hogrefe & Huber.

Tufte, E. R. (1983). *The visual display of quantitative information.* Cheshire, CT. Graphics Press.

Tufte, E. R. (1990). *Envisioning information.* Cheshire, CT: Graphics Press.

Tufte, E. R. (1997). *Visual explanations: Images and quantities, evidence and narrative.* Cheshire, CT: Graphics Press.

Tukey, J. W. (1977). *Exploratory data analysis.* Reading, MA: Addison-Wesley.

Vadum, A. C., & Rankin, N. O. (1997). *Psychological research: Methods for discovery and validation.* New York: McGraw-Hill.

Vaillant, G. E. (1995a). *Adaptation to life.* Cambridge, MA: Harvard.

Vaillant, G. E. (1995b). *The wisdom of the ego.* Cambridge, MA: Harvard.

VanderStoep, S. W., & Shaughnessy, J. J. (1997). Taking a course in research methods improves reasoning about real-life events. *Teaching of Psychology, 24*, 122–124.

Vicchiullo, C. I. (1994). *The effect of proximity on college academic achievement, attendance, and attitudes in the classroom.* Unpublished course paper, Moravian College, Bethlehem, PA.

Viney, L. L. (1983). The assessment of psychological states through content analysis of verbal communications. *Psychological Bulletin, 94*, 542–563.

Wade, N. (1997, September 9). First gene for social behavior identified in Whiskery mice. *The New York Times*, p. C4.

Walker, A., Jr. (Ed.). (1997). *Thesaurus of psychological index terms* (8th ed.). Washington, DC: American Psychological Association.

Wallas, G. (1926). *The art of thought.* New York: Harcourt, Brace and Company.

Wallgreen, A., Wallgreen, B., Persson, R., Jorner, U., & Haaland, J. A. (1996). *Graphing statistics and data: Creating better charts.* Newbury Park, CA: Sage.

Watson, R. I. (1967). Psychology: A prescriptive science. *American Psychologist, 22*, 435–443.

Webb, E. J., Campbell, D. T., Schwartz, R. D., Sechrest, L., & Grove, J. B. (1981). *Nonreactive measures in the social sciences* (2nd ed). Boston MA: Houghton Mifflin.

Weber, S. J., & Cook, T. D. (1972). Subject effects in laboratory research: An examination of subject roles, demand characteristics, and valid inference. *Psychological Bulletin, 77*, 273–295.

Wegner, D. M. (1989). *White bears and other unwanted thoughts: Suppression, obsession, and the psychology of mental control.* New York: Guilford.

Weick, K. E. (1968). Systematic observational methods. In G. Lindzey & E. Aronson (Eds.), *The handbook of social psychology* (Vol. 2, pp. 357–451). Reading, MA: Addison-Wesley.

Whishaw, I. Q., & Mittleman, G. (1986). Visits to starts, routes, and places by rats (Rattus norvegicus) in swimming pool navigation tasks. *Journal of Comparative Psychology, 100,* 422–431.

Whitman, W. (1921). *Leaves of grass.* New York: Modern Library. (Original work published 1891).

Wicker, A. W. (1969). Attitudes versus actions: The relationship of verbal and overt behavioral responses to attitude objects. *Journal of Social Issues, 25,* 41–78.

Williams, B. T., & Brydon-Miller, M. (1997). *Concept to completion: Writing well in the social sciences.* Fort Worth, TX: Harcourt Brace.

Wilson Co., H. W. (1974–present). *Social Sciences Index.* Bronx, NY: Author.

Wilson, T. D. (1985). Strangers to ourselves. The origins and accuracy of beliefs about one's own mental states. In J. H. Harvey & G. Wewary (Eds.), *Attribution in contemporary psychology* (pp. 9–36). New York: Academic Press.

Wilson, T. D. (1994). The proper protocol: Validity and the completeness of verbal reports. *Psychological Science, 5,* 249–252.

Wilson, T. D., & Linville, P. W. (1982). Improving the academic performance of freshmen: Attribution therapy revisited. *Journal of Personality and Social Psychology, 42,* 367–376.

Wilson, T. D., & Linville, P. W. (1985). Improving the performance of college freshmen with attributional techniques. *Journal of Personality and Social Psychology, 49,* 287–293.

Winer, B. J., Brown, D. R., & Michels, K. M. (1991). *Statistical principles in experimental design* (3rd ed.). New York: McGraw-Hill.

Wolfe, A. (1997). The moral meaning of work. *The American Prospect, 34* (September–October), 82–90.

Wright, B. A. (1991). Labeling: The need for greater person-environment individuation. In C. R. Snyder & D. R. Forsyth (Eds.), *Handbook of social and clinical psychology: The health perspective* (pp. 469–487). New York: Pergamon.

Wright, D. B. (1997). *Understanding statistics: An introduction for the social sciences.* London: Sage Publications.

Wundt, W. M. (1904). *Principles of physiological psychology* (E. B. Titchener, Trans.). New York: Macmillan. (Original work published 1873).

Zanna, M. P. (Ed.). (1992). *Advances in experimental social psychology* (Vol. 25). San Diego, CA: Academic.

Zanna, M. P., & Darley, J. M. (Eds.). (1987). *The compleat academic: A practical guide for the beginning social scientist.* New York: Random House.

Zaremba, S. B., & Toedter, L. J. (1991). Educating college students at the new zoo. *American Association of Zoological Parks and Aquariums Regional Conference Proceedings,* 585–591.

Zullow, H. M., & Seligman, M. E. P. (1990). Pessimistic rumination predicts defeat of presidential candidates, 1900 to 1944. *Psychological Inquiry, 1,* 52–61.

INDEX